Machine Learning with R

Second Edition

Expert techniques for predictive modeling to solve
all your data analysis problems

Brett Lantz

[PACKT] open source *
PUBLISHING   community experience distilled

BIRMINGHAM - MUMBAI

Machine Learning with R
Second Edition

First published: October 2013

Second edition: July 2015

Production reference: 2120619

Published by Packt Publishing Ltd.
Livery Place
35 Livery Street
Birmingham B3 2PB, UK.

ISBN 978-1-78439-390-8

www.packtpub.com

Credits

Author
Brett Lantz

Reviewers
Vijayakumar Nattamai Jawaharlal
Kent S. Johnson
Mzabalazo Z. Ngwenya
Anuj Saxena

Commissioning Editor
Ashwin Nair

Acquisition Editor
James Jones

Content Development Editor
Natasha D'Souza

Technical Editor
Rahul C. Shah

Copy Editors
Akshata Lobo
Swati Priya

Project Coordinator
Vijay Kushlani

Proofreader
Safis Editing

Indexer
Monica Ajmera Mehta

Production Coordinator
Arvindkumar Gupta

Cover Work
Arvindkumar Gupta

About the Author

Brett Lantz has spent more than 10 years using innovative data methods to understand human behavior. A trained sociologist, he was first enchanted by machine learning while studying a large database of teenagers' social networking website profiles. Since then, Brett has worked on interdisciplinary studies of cellular telephone calls, medical billing data, and philanthropic activity, among others. When not spending time with family, following college sports, or being entertained by his dachshunds, he maintains `http://dataspelunking.com/`, a website dedicated to sharing knowledge about the search for insight in data.

This book could not have been written without the support of my friends and family. In particular, my wife, Jessica, deserves many thanks for her endless patience and encouragement. My son, Will, who was born in the midst of the first edition and supplied much-needed diversions while writing this edition, will be a big brother shortly after this book is published. In spite of cautionary tales about correlation and causation, it seems that every time I expand my written library, my family likewise expands! I dedicate this book to my children in the hope that one day they will be inspired to tackle big challenges and follow their curiosity wherever it may lead.

I am also indebted to many others who supported this book indirectly. My interactions with educators, peers, and collaborators at the University of Michigan, the University of Notre Dame, and the University of Central Florida seeded many of the ideas I attempted to express in the text; any lack of clarity in their expression is purely mine. Additionally, without the work of the broader community of researchers who shared their expertise in publications, lectures, and source code, this book might not have existed at all. Finally, I appreciate the efforts of the R team and all those who have contributed to R packages, whose work has helped bring machine learning to the masses. I sincerely hope that my work is likewise a valuable piece in this mosaic.

About the Reviewers

Vijayakumar Nattamai Jawaharlal is a software engineer with an experience of 2 decades in the IT industry. His background lies in machine learning, big data technologies, business intelligence, and data warehouse.

He develops scalable solutions for many distributed platforms, and is very passionate about scalable distributed machine learning.

Kent S. Johnson is a software developer who loves data analysis, statistics, and machine learning. He currently develops software to analyze tissue samples related to cancer research. According to him, a day spent with R and ggplot2 is a good day. For more information about him, visit `http://kentsjohnson.com`.

I'd like to thank, Gile, for always loving me.

Mzabalazo Z. Ngwenya holds a postgraduate degree in mathematical statistics from the University of Cape Town. He has worked extensively in the field of statistical consulting, and currently works as a biometrician at a research and development entity in South Africa. His areas of interest are primarily centered around statistical computing, and he has over 10 years of experience with R for data analysis and statistical research. Previously, he was involved in reviewing *Learning RStudio for R Statistical Computing, R Statistical Application Development by Example Beginner's Guide, R Graph Essentials, R Object-oriented Programming, Mastering Scientific Computing with R*, and *Machine Learning with R*, all by Packt Publishing.

Anuj Saxena is a data scientist at IGATE Corporation. He has an MS in analytics from the University of San Francisco and an MSc in Statistics from the NMIMS University in India. He is passionate about data science and likes using open source languages such as R and Python as primary tools for data science projects. In his spare time, he participates in predictive analytics competitions on kaggle.com. For more information about him, visit http://www.anuj-saxena.com.

I'd like to thank my father, Dr. Sharad Kumar, who inspired me at an early age to learn math and statistics and my mother, Mrs. Ranjana Saxena, who has been a backbone throughout my educational life.

I'd also like to thank my wonderful professors at the University of San Francisco and the NMIMS University who triggered my interest in this field and taught me the power of data and how it can be used to tell a wonderful story.

www.PacktPub.com

Support files, eBooks, discount offers, and more

For support files and downloads related to your book, please visit www.PacktPub.com.

Did you know that Packt offers eBook versions of every book published, with PDF and ePub files available? You can upgrade to the eBook version at www.PacktPub.com and as a print book customer, you are entitled to a discount on the eBook copy. Get in touch with us at service@packtpub.com for more details.

At www.PacktPub.com, you can also read a collection of free technical articles, sign up for a range of free newsletters and receive exclusive discounts and offers on Packt books and eBooks.

https://www2.packtpub.com/books/subscription/packtlib

Do you need instant solutions to your IT questions? PacktLib is Packt's online digital book library. Here, you can search, access, and read Packt's entire library of books.

Why subscribe?

- Fully searchable across every book published by Packt
- Copy and paste, print, and bookmark content
- On demand and accessible via a web browser

Free access for Packt account holders

If you have an account with Packt at www.PacktPub.com, you can use this to access PacktLib today and view 9 entirely free books. Simply use your login credentials for immediate access.

Table of Contents

Preface

Machine learning, at its core, is concerned with the algorithms that transform information into actionable intelligence. This fact makes machine learning well-suited to the present-day era of big data. Without machine learning, it would be nearly impossible to keep up with the massive stream of information.

Given the growing prominence of R—a cross-platform, zero-cost statistical programming environment—there has never been a better time to start using machine learning. R offers a powerful but easy-to-learn set of tools that can assist you with finding data insights.

By combining hands-on case studies with the essential theory that you need to understand how things work under the hood, this book provides all the knowledge that you will need to start applying machine learning to your own projects.

What this book covers

Chapter 1, Introducing Machine Learning, presents the terminology and concepts that define and distinguish machine learners, as well as a method for matching a learning task with the appropriate algorithm.

Chapter 2, Managing and Understanding Data, provides an opportunity to get your hands dirty working with data in R. Essential data structures and procedures used for loading, exploring, and understanding data are discussed.

Chapter 3, Lazy Learning – Classification Using Nearest Neighbors, teaches you how to understand and apply a simple yet powerful machine learning algorithm to your first real-world task—identifying malignant samples of cancer.

Chapter 4, Probabilistic Learning – Classification Using Naive Bayes, reveals the essential concepts of probability that are used in the cutting-edge spam filtering systems. You'll learn the basics of text mining in the process of building your own spam filter.

Chapter 5, Divide and Conquer – Classification Using Decision Trees and Rules, explores a couple of learning algorithms whose predictions are not only accurate, but also easily explained. We'll apply these methods to tasks where transparency is important.

Chapter 6, Forecasting Numeric Data – Regression Methods, introduces machine learning algorithms used for making numeric predictions. As these techniques are heavily embedded in the field of statistics, you will also learn the essential metrics needed to make sense of numeric relationships.

Chapter 7, Black Box Methods – Neural Networks and Support Vector Machines, covers two complex but powerful machine learning algorithms. Though the math may appear intimidating, we will work through examples that illustrate their inner workings in simple terms.

Chapter 8, Finding Patterns – Market Basket Analysis Using Association Rules, exposes the algorithm used in the recommendation systems employed by many retailers. If you've ever wondered how retailers seem to know your purchasing habits better than you know yourself, this chapter will reveal their secrets.

Chapter 9, Finding Groups of Data – Clustering with k-means, is devoted to a procedure that locates clusters of related items. We'll utilize this algorithm to identify profiles within an online community.

Chapter 10, Evaluating Model Performance, provides information on measuring the success of a machine learning project and obtaining a reliable estimate of the learner's performance on future data.

Chapter 11, Improving Model Performance, reveals the methods employed by the teams at the top of machine learning competition leaderboards. If you have a competitive streak, or simply want to get the most out of your data, you'll need to add these techniques to your repertoire.

Chapter 12, Specialized Machine Learning Topics, explores the frontiers of machine learning. From working with big data to making R work faster, the topics covered will help you push the boundaries of what is possible with R.

What you need for this book

The examples in this book were written for and tested with R version 3.2.0 on Microsoft Windows and Mac OS X, though they are likely to work with any recent version of R.

Who this book is for

This book is intended for anybody hoping to use data for action. Perhaps you already know a bit about machine learning, but have never used R; or perhaps you know a little about R, but are new to machine learning. In any case, this book will get you up and running quickly. It would be helpful to have a bit of familiarity with basic math and programming concepts, but no prior experience is required. All you need is curiosity.

Conventions

In this book, you will find a number of text styles that distinguish between different kinds of information. Here are some examples of these styles and an explanation of their meaning.

Code words in text, database table names, folder names, filenames, file extensions, pathnames, dummy URLs, user input, and Twitter handles are shown as follows: "The most direct way to install a package is via the `install.packages()` function."

A block of code is set as follows:

```
subject_name,temperature,flu_status,gender,blood_type
John Doe,        98.1,      FALSE,     MALE,      O
Jane Doe,        98.6,      FALSE,     FEMALE,    AB
Steve Graves,    101.4,     TRUE,      MALE,      A
```

Any command-line input or output is written as follows:

```
> summary(wbcd_z$area_mean)
   Min. 1st Qu.  Median    Mean 3rd Qu.     Max.
-1.4530 -0.6666 -0.2949  0.0000  0.3632   5.2460
```

New terms and **important words** are shown in bold. Words that you see on the screen, for example, in menus or dialog boxes, appear in the text like this: "The **Task Views** link on the left side of the CRAN page provides a curated list of packages."

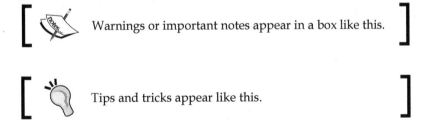

[Warnings or important notes appear in a box like this.   ]

[Tips and tricks appear like this.   ]

Reader feedback

Feedback from our readers is always welcome. Let us know what you think about this book—what you liked or disliked. Reader feedback is important for us as it helps us develop titles that you will really get the most out of.

To send us general feedback, simply e-mail feedback@packtpub.com, and mention the book's title in the subject of your message.

If there is a topic that you have expertise in and you are interested in either writing or contributing to a book, see our author guide at www.packtpub.com/authors.

Customer support

Now that you are the proud owner of a Packt book, we have a number of things to help you to get the most from your purchase.

Downloading the example code

You can download the example code files from your account at http://www.packtpub.com for all the Packt Publishing books you have purchased. If you purchased this book elsewhere, you can visit http://www.packtpub.com/support and register to have the files e-mailed directly to you.

New to the second edition of this book, the example code is also available via GitHub at https://github.com/dataspelunking/MLwR/. Check here for the most up-to-date R code, as well as issue tracking and a public wiki. Please join the community!

Downloading the color images of this book

We also provide you with a PDF file that has color images of the screenshots/diagrams used in this book. The color images will help you better understand the changes in the output. You can download this file from http://www.packtpub.com/sites/default/files/downloads/Machine_Learning_With_R_Second_Edition_ColoredImages.pdf.

Errata

Although we have taken every care to ensure the accuracy of our content, mistakes do happen. If you find a mistake in one of our books—maybe a mistake in the text or the code—we would be grateful if you could report this to us. By doing so, you can save other readers from frustration and help us improve subsequent versions of this book. If you find any errata, please report them by visiting `http://www.packtpub.com/submit-errata`, selecting your book, clicking on the **Errata Submission Form** link, and entering the details of your errata. Once your errata are verified, your submission will be accepted and the errata will be uploaded to our website or added to any list of existing errata under the Errata section of that title.

To view the previously submitted errata, go to `https://www.packtpub.com/books/content/support` and enter the name of the book in the search field. The required information will appear under the **Errata** section.

Piracy

Piracy of copyrighted material on the Internet is an ongoing problem across all media. At Packt, we take the protection of our copyright and licenses very seriously. If you come across any illegal copies of our works in any form on the Internet, please provide us with the location address or website name immediately so that we can pursue a remedy.

Please contact us at `copyright@packtpub.com` with a link to the suspected pirated material.

We appreciate your help in protecting our authors and our ability to bring you valuable content.

Questions

If you have a problem with any aspect of this book, you can contact us at `questions@packtpub.com`, and we will do our best to address the problem.

Introducing Machine Learning

If science fiction stories are to be believed, the invention of artificial intelligence inevitably leads to apocalyptic wars between machines and their makers. In the early stages, computers are taught to play simple games of tic-tac-toe and chess. Later, machines are given control of traffic lights and communications, followed by military drones and missiles. The machines' evolution takes an ominous turn once the computers become sentient and learn how to teach themselves. Having no more need for human programmers, humankind is then "deleted."

Thankfully, at the time of this writing, machines still require user input.

Though your impressions of machine learning may be colored by these mass media depictions, today's algorithms are too application-specific to pose any danger of becoming self-aware. The goal of today's machine learning is not to create an artificial brain, but rather to assist us in making sense of the world's massive data stores.

Putting popular misconceptions aside, by the end of this chapter, you will gain a more nuanced understanding of machine learning. You also will be introduced to the fundamental concepts that define and differentiate the most commonly used machine learning approaches.

You will learn:

- The origins and practical applications of machine learning
- How computers turn data into knowledge and action
- How to match a machine learning algorithm to your data

The field of machine learning provides a set of algorithms that transform data into actionable knowledge. Keep reading to see how easy it is to use R to start applying machine learning to real-world problems.

The origins of machine learning

Since birth, we are inundated with data. Our body's sensors — the eyes, ears, nose, tongue, and nerves — are continually assailed with raw data that our brain translates into sights, sounds, smells, tastes, and textures. Using language, we are able to share these experiences with others.

From the advent of written language, human observations have been recorded. Hunters monitored the movement of animal herds, early astronomers recorded the alignment of planets and stars, and cities recorded tax payments, births, and deaths. Today, such observations, and many more, are increasingly automated and recorded systematically in the ever-growing computerized databases.

The invention of electronic sensors has additionally contributed to an explosion in the volume and richness of recorded data. Specialized sensors see, hear, smell, taste, and feel. These sensors process the data far differently than a human being would. Unlike a human's limited and subjective attention, an electronic sensor never takes a break and never lets its judgment skew its perception.

Although sensors are not clouded by subjectivity, they do not necessarily report a single, definitive depiction of reality. Some have an inherent measurement error, due to hardware limitations. Others are limited by their scope. A black and white photograph provides a different depiction of its subject than one shot in color. Similarly, a microscope provides a far different depiction of reality than a telescope.

Between databases and sensors, many aspects of our lives are recorded. Governments, businesses, and individuals are recording and reporting information, from the monumental to the mundane. Weather sensors record temperature and pressure data, surveillance cameras watch sidewalks and subway tunnels, and all manner of electronic behaviors are monitored: transactions, communications, friendships, and many others.

This deluge of data has led some to state that we have entered an era of **Big Data**, but this may be a bit of a misnomer. Human beings have always been surrounded by large amounts of data. What makes the current era unique is that we have vast amounts of *recorded* data, much of which can be directly accessed by computers. Larger and more interesting data sets are increasingly accessible at the tips of our fingers, only a web search away. This wealth of information has the potential to inform action, given a systematic way of making sense from it all.

The field of study interested in the development of computer algorithms to transform data into intelligent action is known as **machine learning**. This field originated in an environment where available data, statistical methods, and computing power rapidly and simultaneously evolved. Growth in data necessitated additional computing power, which in turn spurred the development of **statistical methods** to analyze large datasets. This created a cycle of advancement, allowing even larger and more interesting data to be collected.

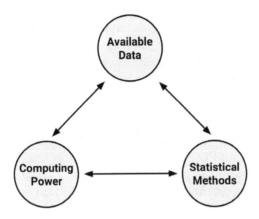

A closely related sibling of machine learning, **data mining**, is concerned with the generation of novel insights from large databases. As the implies, data mining involves a systematic hunt for nuggets of actionable intelligence. Although there is some disagreement over how widely machine learning and data mining overlap, a potential point of distinction is that machine learning focuses on teaching computers how to use data to solve a problem, while data mining focuses on teaching computers to identify patterns that humans then use to solve a problem.

Virtually all data mining involves the use of machine learning, but not all machine learning involves data mining. For example, you might apply machine learning to data mine automobile traffic data for patterns related to accident rates; on the other hand, if the computer is learning how to drive the car itself, this is purely machine learning without data mining.

 The phrase "data mining" is also sometimes used as a pejorative to describe the deceptive practice of cherry-picking data to support a theory.

Uses and abuses of machine learning

Most people have heard of the chess-playing computer **Deep Blue**—the first to win a game against a world champion—or **Watson**, the computer that defeated two human opponents on the television trivia game show Jeopardy. Based on these stunning accomplishments, some have speculated that computer intelligence will replace humans in many information technology occupations, just as machines replaced humans in the fields, and robots replaced humans on the assembly line.

The truth is that even as machines reach such impressive milestones, they are still relatively limited in their ability to thoroughly understand a problem. They are pure intellectual horsepower without direction. A computer may be more capable than a human of finding subtle patterns in large databases, but it still needs a human to motivate the analysis and turn the result into meaningful action.

Machines are not good at asking questions, or even knowing what questions to ask. They are much better at answering them, provided the question is stated in a way the computer can comprehend. Present-day machine learning algorithms partner with people much like a bloodhound partners with its trainer; the dog's sense of smell may be many times stronger than its master's, but without being carefully directed, the hound may end up chasing its tail.

To better understand the real-world applications of machine learning, we'll now consider some cases where it has been used successfully, some places where it still has room for improvement, and some situations where it may do more harm than good.

Machine learning successes

Machine learning is most successful when it augments rather than replaces the specialized knowledge of a subject-matter expert. It works with medical doctors at the forefront of the fight to eradicate cancer, assists engineers and programmers with our efforts to create smarter homes and automobiles, and helps social scientists build knowledge of how societies function. Toward these ends, it is employed in countless businesses, scientific laboratories, hospitals, and governmental organizations. Any organization that generates or aggregates data likely employs at least one machine learning algorithm to help make sense of it.

Though it is impossible to list every use case of machine learning, a survey of recent success stories includes several prominent applications:

- Identification of unwanted spam messages in e-mail
- Segmentation of customer behavior for targeted advertising
- Forecasts of weather behavior and long-term climate changes
- Reduction of fraudulent credit card transactions
- Actuarial estimates of financial damage of storms and natural disasters
- Prediction of popular election outcomes
- Development of algorithms for auto-piloting drones and self-driving cars
- Optimization of energy use in homes and office buildings
- Projection of areas where criminal activity is most likely
- Discovery of genetic sequences linked to diseases

By the end of this book, you will understand the basic machine learning algorithms that are employed to teach computers to perform these tasks. For now, it suffices to say that no matter what the context is, the machine learning process is the same. Regardless of the task, an algorithm takes data and identifies patterns that form the basis for further action.

The limits of machine learning

Although machine learning is used widely and has tremendous potential, it is important to understand its limits. Machine learning, at this time, is not in any way a substitute for a human brain. It has very little flexibility to extrapolate outside of the strict parameters it learned and knows no common sense. With this in mind, one should be extremely careful to recognize exactly what the algorithm has learned before setting it loose in the real-world settings.

Without a lifetime of past experiences to build upon, computers are also limited in their ability to make simple common sense inferences about logical next steps. Take, for instance, the banner advertisements seen on many web sites. These may be served, based on the patterns learned by data mining the browsing history of millions of users. According to this data, someone who views the websites selling shoes should see advertisements for shoes, and those viewing websites for mattresses should see advertisements for mattresses. The problem is that this becomes a never-ending cycle in which additional shoe or mattress advertisements are served rather than advertisements for shoelaces and shoe polish, or bed sheets and blankets.

Many are familiar with the deficiencies of machine learning's ability to understand or translate language or to recognize speech and handwriting. Perhaps the earliest example of this type of failure is in a 1994 episode of the television show, *The Simpsons*, which showed a parody of the Apple Newton tablet. For its time, the Newton was known for its state-of-the-art handwriting recognition. Unfortunately for Apple, it would occasionally fail to great effect. The television episode illustrated this through a sequence in which a bully's note to **Beat up Martin** was misinterpreted by the Newton as **Eat up Martha**, as depicted in the following screenshots:

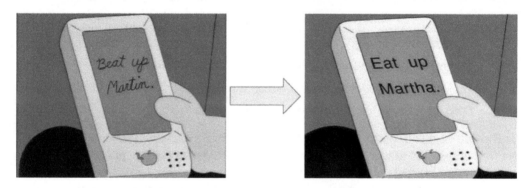

Screenshots from "Lisa on Ice" The Simpsons, 20th Century Fox (1994)

Machines' ability to understand language has improved enough since 1994, such that Google, Apple, and Microsoft are all confident enough to offer virtual concierge services operated via voice recognition. Still, even these services routinely struggle to answer relatively simple questions. Even more, online translation services sometimes misinterpret sentences that a toddler would readily understand. The predictive text feature on many devices has also led to a number of humorous *autocorrect fail* sites that illustrate the computer's ability to understand basic language but completely misunderstand context.

Some of these mistakes are to be expected, for sure. Language is complicated with multiple layers of text and subtext and even human beings, sometimes, understand the context incorrectly. This said, these types of failures in machines illustrate the important fact that machine learning is only as good as the data it learns from. If the context is not directly implicit in the input data, then just like a human, the computer will have to make its best guess.

Machine learning ethics

At its core, machine learning is simply a tool that assists us in making sense of the world's complex data. Like any tool, it can be used for good or evil. Machine learning may lead to problems when it is applied so broadly or callously that humans are treated as lab rats, automata, or mindless consumers. A process that may seem harmless may lead to unintended consequences when automated by an emotionless computer. For this reason, those using machine learning or data mining would be remiss not to consider the ethical implications of the art.

Due to the relative youth of machine learning as a discipline and the speed at which it is progressing, the associated legal issues and social norms are often quite uncertain and constantly in flux. Caution should be exercised while obtaining or analyzing data in order to avoid breaking laws, violating terms of service or data use agreements, and abusing the trust or violating the privacy of customers or the public.

 The informal corporate motto of Google, an organization that collects perhaps more data on individuals than any other, is "don't be evil." While this seems clear enough, it may not be sufficient. A better approach may be to follow the *Hippocratic Oath*, a medical principle that states "above all, do no harm."

Retailers routinely use machine learning for advertising, targeted promotions, inventory management, or the layout of the items in the store. Many have even equipped checkout lanes with devices that print coupons for promotions based on the customer's buying history. In exchange for a bit of personal data, the customer receives discounts on the specific products he or she wants to buy. At first, this appears relatively harmless. But consider what happens when this practice is taken a little bit further.

One possibly apocryphal tale concerns a large retailer in the U.S. that employed machine learning to identify expectant mothers for coupon mailings. The retailer hoped that if these mothers-to-be received substantial discounts, they would become loyal customers, who would later purchase profitable items like diapers, baby formula, and toys.

Equipped with machine learning methods, the retailer identified items in the customer purchase history that could be used to predict with a high degree of certainty, not only whether a woman was pregnant, but also the approximate timing for when the baby was due.

After the retailer used this data for a promotional mailing, an angry man contacted the chain and demanded to know why his teenage daughter received coupons for maternity items. He was furious that the retailer seemed to be encouraging teenage pregnancy! As the story goes, when the retail chain's manager called to offer an apology, it was the father that ultimately apologized because, after confronting his daughter, he discovered that she was indeed pregnant!

Whether completely true or not, the lesson learned from the preceding tale is that common sense should be applied before blindly applying the results of a machine learning analysis. This is particularly true in cases where sensitive information such as health data is concerned. With a bit more care, the retailer could have foreseen this scenario, and used greater discretion while choosing how to reveal the pattern its machine learning analysis had discovered.

Certain jurisdictions may prevent you from using racial, ethnic, religious, or other protected class data for business reasons. Keep in mind that excluding this data from your analysis may not be enough, because machine learning algorithms might inadvertently learn this information independently. For instance, if a certain segment of people generally live in a certain region, buy a certain product, or otherwise behave in a way that uniquely identifies them as a group, some machine learning algorithms can infer the protected information from these other factors. In such cases, you may need to fully "de-identify" these people by excluding any *potentially* identifying data in addition to the protected information.

Apart from the legal consequences, using data inappropriately may hurt the bottom line. Customers may feel uncomfortable or become spooked if the aspects of their lives they consider private are made public. In recent years, several high-profile web applications have experienced a mass exodus of users who felt exploited when the applications' terms of service agreements changed, and their data was used for purposes beyond what the users had originally agreed upon. The fact that privacy expectations differ by context, age cohort, and locale adds complexity in deciding the appropriate use of personal data. It would be wise to consider the cultural implications of your work before you begin your project.

[The fact that you *can* use data for a particular end does not always mean that you *should*.]

How machines learn

A formal definition of machine learning proposed by computer scientist Tom M. Mitchell states that a machine learns whenever it is able to utilize its an experience such that its performance improves on similar experiences in the future. Although this definition is intuitive, it completely ignores the process of exactly how experience can be translated into future action—and of course learning is always easier said than done!

While human brains are naturally capable of learning from birth, the conditions necessary for computers to learn must be made explicit. For this reason, although it is not strictly necessary to understand the theoretical basis of learning, this foundation helps understand, distinguish, and implement machine learning algorithms.

 As you compare machine learning to human learning, you may discover yourself examining your own mind in a different light.

Regardless of whether the learner is a human or machine, the basic learning process is similar. It can be divided into four interrelated components:

- **Data storage** utilizes observation, memory, and recall to provide a factual basis for further reasoning.
- **Abstraction** involves the translation of stored data into broader representations and concepts.
- **Generalization** uses abstracted data to create knowledge and inferences that drive action in new contexts.
- **Evaluation** provides a feedback mechanism to measure the utility of learned knowledge and inform potential improvements.

The following figure illustrates the steps in the learning process:

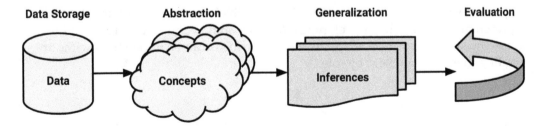

Keep in mind that although the learning process has been conceptualized as four distinct components, they are merely organized this way for illustrative purposes. In reality, the entire learning process is inextricably linked. In human beings, the process occurs subconsciously. We recollect, deduce, induct, and intuit with the confines of our mind's eye, and because this process is hidden, any differences from person to person are attributed to a vague notion of subjectivity. In contrast, with computers these processes are explicit, and because the entire process is transparent, the learned knowledge can be examined, transferred, and utilized for future action.

Data storage

All learning must begin with data. Humans and computers alike utilize **data storage** as a foundation for more advanced reasoning. In a human being, this consists of a brain that uses electrochemical signals in a network of biological cells to store and process observations for short- and long-term future recall. Computers have similar capabilities of short- and long-term recall using hard disk drives, flash memory, and random access memory (RAM) in combination with a central processing unit (CPU).

It may seem obvious to say so, but the ability to store and retrieve data alone is not sufficient for learning. Without a higher level of understanding, knowledge is limited exclusively to recall, meaning exclusively what is seen before and nothing else. The data is merely ones and zeros on a disk. They are stored memories with no broader meaning.

To better understand the nuances of this idea, it may help to think about the last time you studied for a difficult test, perhaps for a university final exam or a career certification. Did you wish for an eidetic (photographic) memory? If so, you may be disappointed to learn that perfect recall is unlikely to be of much assistance. Even if you could memorize material perfectly, your rote learning is of no use, unless you know in advance the exact questions and answers that will appear in the exam. Otherwise, you would be stuck in an attempt to memorize answers to every question that could conceivably be asked. Obviously, this is an unsustainable strategy.

Instead, a better approach is to spend time selectively, memorizing a small set of representative ideas while developing strategies on how the ideas relate and how to use the stored information. In this way, large ideas can be understood without needing to memorize them by rote.

Abstraction

This work of assigning meaning to stored data occurs during the **abstraction** process, in which raw data comes to have a more abstract meaning. This type of connection, say between an object and its representation, is exemplified by the famous René Magritte painting *The Treachery of Images*:

Source: http://collections.lacma.org/node/239578

The painting depicts a tobacco pipe with the caption *Ceci n'est pas une pipe* ("this is not a pipe"). The point Magritte was illustrating is that a representation of a pipe is not truly a pipe. Yet, in spite of the fact that the pipe is not real, anybody viewing the painting easily recognizes it as a pipe. This suggests that the observer's mind is able to connect the *picture* of a pipe to the *idea* of a pipe, to a memory of a *physical* pipe that could be held in the hand. Abstracted connections like these are the basis of **knowledge representation**, the formation of logical structures that assist in turning raw sensory information into a meaningful insight.

During a machine's process of knowledge representation, the computer summarizes stored raw data using a **model**, an explicit description of the patterns within the data. Just like Magritte's pipe, the model representation takes on a life beyond the raw data. It represents an idea greater than the sum of its parts.

There are many different types of models. You may be already familiar with some. Examples include:

- Mathematical equations
- Relational diagrams such as trees and graphs
- Logical if/else rules
- Groupings of data known as clusters

The choice of model is typically not left up to the machine. Instead, the learning task and data on hand inform model selection. Later in this chapter, we will discuss methods to choose the type of model in more detail.

The process of fitting a model to a dataset is known as **training**. When the model has been trained, the data is transformed into an abstract form that summarizes the original information.

 You might wonder why this step is called training rather than learning. First, note that the process of learning does not end with data abstraction; the learner must still generalize and evaluate its training. Second, the word training better connotes the fact that the human teacher trains the machine student to understand the data in a specific way.

It is important to note that a learned model does not itself provide new data, yet it does result in new knowledge. How can this be? The answer is that imposing an assumed structure on the underlying data gives insight into the unseen by supposing a concept about how data elements are related. Take for instance the discovery of gravity. By fitting equations to observational data, Sir Isaac Newton inferred the concept of gravity. But the force we now know as gravity was always present. It simply wasn't recognized until Newton recognized it as an abstract concept that relates some data to others — specifically, by becoming the g term in a model that explains observations of falling objects.

| Observations | → | Data | → | Model |

Distance	Time
4.9m	1s
19.6m	2s
44.1m	3s
78.5m	4s

$$g = 9.8m/s^2$$

Most models may not result in the development of theories that shake up scientific thought for centuries. Still, your model might result in the discovery of previously unseen relationships among data. A model trained on genomic data might find several genes that, when combined, are responsible for the onset of diabetes; banks might discover a seemingly innocuous type of transaction that systematically appears prior to fraudulent activity; and psychologists might identify a combination of personality characteristics indicating a new disorder. These underlying patterns were always present, but by simply presenting information in a different format, a new idea is conceptualized.

Generalization

The learning process is not complete until the learner is able to use its abstracted knowledge for future action. However, among the countless underlying patterns that might be identified during the abstraction process and the myriad ways to model these patterns, some will be more useful than others. Unless the production of abstractions is limited, the learner will be unable to proceed. It would be stuck where it started — with a large pool of information, but no actionable insight.

The term **generalization** describes the process of turning abstracted knowledge into a form that can be utilized for future action, on tasks that are similar, but not identical, to those it has seen before. Generalization is a somewhat vague process that is a bit difficult to describe. Traditionally, it has been imagined as a search through the entire set of models (that is, theories or inferences) that could be abstracted during training. In other words, if you can imagine a hypothetical set containing every possible theory that could be established from the data, generalization involves the reduction of this set into a manageable number of important findings.

In generalization, the learner is tasked with limiting the patterns it discovers to only those that will be most relevant to its future tasks. Generally, it is not feasible to reduce the number of patterns by examining them one-by-one and ranking them by future utility. Instead, machine learning algorithms generally employ shortcuts that reduce the search space more quickly. Toward this end, the algorithm will employ **heuristics**, which are educated guesses about where to find the most useful inferences.

> Because heuristics utilize approximations and other rules of thumb, they do not guarantee to find the single best model. However, without taking these shortcuts, finding useful information in a large dataset would be infeasible.

Heuristics are routinely used by human beings to quickly generalize experience to new scenarios. If you have ever utilized your gut instinct to make a snap decision prior to fully evaluating your circumstances, you were intuitively using mental heuristics.

The incredible human ability to make quick decisions often relies not on computer-like logic, but rather on heuristics guided by emotions. Sometimes, this can result in illogical conclusions. For example, more people express fear of airline travel versus automobile travel, despite automobiles being statistically more dangerous. This can be explained by the availability heuristic, which is the tendency of people to estimate the likelihood of an event by how easily its examples can be recalled. Accidents involving air travel are highly publicized. Being traumatic events, they are likely to be recalled very easily, whereas car accidents barely warrant a mention in the newspaper.

The folly of misapplied heuristics is not limited to human beings. The heuristics employed by machine learning algorithms also sometimes result in erroneous conclusions. The algorithm is said to have a **bias** if the conclusions are systematically erroneous, or wrong in a predictable manner.

For example, suppose that a machine learning algorithm learned to identify faces by finding two dark circles representing eyes, positioned above a straight line indicating a mouth. The algorithm might then have trouble with, or be *biased against*, faces that do not conform to its model. Faces with glasses, turned at an angle, looking sideways, or with various skin tones might not be detected by the algorithm. Similarly, it could be *biased toward* faces with certain skin tones, face shapes, or other characteristics that do not conform to its understanding of the world.

In modern usage, the word bias has come to carry quite negative connotations. Various forms of media frequently claim to be free from bias, and claim to report the facts objectively, untainted by emotion. Still, consider for a moment the possibility that a little bias might be useful. Without a bit of arbitrariness, might it be a bit difficult to decide among several competing choices, each with distinct strengths and weaknesses? Indeed, some recent studies in the field of psychology have suggested that individuals born with damage to portions of the brain responsible for emotion are ineffectual in decision making, and might spend hours debating simple decisions such as what color shirt to wear or where to eat lunch. Paradoxically, bias is what blinds us from some information while also allowing us to utilize other information for action. It is how machine learning algorithms choose among the countless ways to understand a set of data.

Evaluation

Bias is a necessary evil associated with the abstraction and generalization processes inherent in any learning task. In order to drive action in the face of limitless possibility, each learner must be biased in a particular way. Consequently, each learner has its weaknesses and there is no single learning algorithm to rule them all. Therefore, the final step in the generalization process is to **evaluate** or measure the learner's success in spite of its biases and use this information to inform additional training if needed.

Once you've had success with one machine learning technique, you might be tempted to apply it to everything. It is important to resist this temptation because no machine learning approach is the best for every circumstance. This fact is described by the *No Free Lunch* theorem, introduced by David Wolpert in 1996. For more information, visit: http://www.no-free-lunch.org.

Generally, evaluation occurs after a model has been trained on an initial training dataset. Then, the model is evaluated on a new test dataset in order to judge how well its characterization of the training data generalizes to new, unseen data. It's worth noting that it is exceedingly rare for a model to perfectly generalize to every unforeseen case.

In parts, models fail to perfectly generalize due to the problem of **noise**, a term that describes unexplained or unexplainable variations in data. Noisy data is caused by seemingly random events, such as:

- Measurement error due to imprecise sensors that sometimes add or subtract a bit from the readings
- Issues with human subjects, such as survey respondents reporting random answers to survey questions, in order to finish more quickly
- Data quality problems, including missing, null, truncated, incorrectly coded, or corrupted values
- Phenomena that are so complex or so little understood that they impact the data in ways that appear to be unsystematic

Trying to model noise is the basis of a problem called **overfitting**. Because most noisy data is unexplainable by definition, attempting to explain the noise will result in erroneous conclusions that do not generalize well to new cases. Efforts to explain the noise will also typically result in more complex models that will miss the true pattern that the learner tries to identify. A model that seems to perform well during training, but does poorly during evaluation, is said to be overfitted to the training dataset, as it does not generalize well to the test dataset.

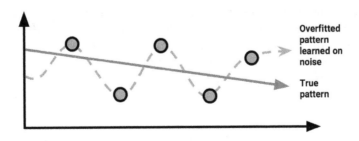

Solutions to the problem of overfitting are specific to particular machine learning approaches. For now, the important point is to be aware of the issue. How well the models are able to handle noisy data is an important source of distinction among them.

Machine learning in practice

So far, we've focused on how machine learning works in theory. To apply the learning process to real-world tasks, we'll use a five-step process. Regardless of the task at hand, any machine learning algorithm can be deployed by following these steps:

1. **Data collection**: The data collection step involves gathering the learning material an algorithm will use to generate actionable knowledge. In most cases, the data will need to be combined into a single source like a text file, spreadsheet, or database.

2. **Data exploration and preparation**: The quality of any machine learning project is based largely on the quality of its input data. Thus, it is important to learn more about the data and its nuances during a practice called data exploration. Additional work is required to prepare the data for the learning process. This involves fixing or cleaning so-called "messy" data, eliminating unnecessary data, and recoding the data to conform to the learner's expected inputs.

3. **Model training**: By the time the data has been prepared for analysis, you are likely to have a sense of what you are capable of learning from the data. The specific machine learning task chosen will inform the selection of an appropriate algorithm, and the algorithm will represent the data in the form of a model.

4. **Model evaluation**: Because each machine learning model results in a biased solution to the learning problem, it is important to evaluate how well the algorithm learns from its experience. Depending on the type of model used, you might be able to evaluate the accuracy of the model using a test dataset or you may need to develop measures of performance specific to the intended application.

5. **Model improvement**: If better performance is needed, it becomes necessary to utilize more advanced strategies to augment the performance of the model. Sometimes, it may be necessary to switch to a different type of model altogether. You may need to supplement your data with additional data or perform additional preparatory work as in step two of this process.

After these steps are completed, if the model appears to be performing well, it can be deployed for its intended task. As the case may be, you might utilize your model to provide score data for predictions (possibly in real time), for projections of financial data, to generate useful insight for marketing or research, or to automate tasks such as mail delivery or flying aircraft. The successes and failures of the deployed model might even provide additional data to train your next generation learner.

Types of input data

The practice of machine learning involves matching the characteristics of input data to the biases of the available approaches. Thus, before applying machine learning to real-world problems, it is important to understand the terminology that distinguishes among input datasets.

The phrase **unit of observation** is used to describe the smallest entity with measured properties of interest for a study. Commonly, the unit of observation is in the form of persons, objects or things, transactions, time points, geographic regions, or measurements. Sometimes, units of observation are combined to form units such as person-years, which denote cases where the same person is tracked over multiple years; each person-year comprises of a person's data for one year.

 The unit of observation is related, but not identical, to the **unit of analysis**, which is the smallest unit from which the inference is made. Although it is often the case, the observed and analyzed units are not always the same. For example, data observed from people might be used to analyze trends across countries.

Datasets that store the units of observation and their properties can be imagined as collections of data consisting of:

- **Examples**: Instances of the unit of observation for which properties have been recorded
- **Features**: Recorded properties or attributes of examples that may be useful for learning

It is easiest to understand features and examples through real-world cases. To build a learning algorithm to identify spam e-mail, the unit of observation could be e-mail messages, the examples would be specific messages, and the features might consist of the words used in the messages. For a cancer detection algorithm, the unit of observation could be patients, the examples might include a random sample of cancer patients, and the features may be the genomic markers from biopsied cells as well as the characteristics of patient such as weight, height, or blood pressure.

While examples and features do not have to be collected in any specific form, they are commonly gathered in **matrix format**, which means that each example has exactly the same features.

The following spreadsheet shows a dataset in matrix format. In matrix data, each row in the spreadsheet is an example and each column is a feature. Here, the rows indicate examples of automobiles, while the columns record various each automobile's features, such as price, mileage, color, and transmission type. Matrix format data is by far the most common form used in machine learning. Though, as you will see in the later chapters, other forms are used occasionally in specialized cases:

features

year	model	price	mileage	color	transmission
2011	SEL	21992	7413	Yellow	AUTO
2011	SEL	20995	10926	Gray	AUTO
2011	SEL	19995	7351	Silver	AUTO
2011	SEL	17809	11613	Gray	AUTO
2012	SE	17500	8367	White	MANUAL
2010	SEL	17495	25125	Silver	AUTO
2011	SEL	17000	27393	Blue	AUTO
2010	SEL	16995	21026	Silver	AUTO
2011	SES	16995	32655	Silver	AUTO

examples

Features also come in various forms. If a feature represents a characteristic measured in numbers, it is unsurprisingly called **numeric**. Alternatively, if a feature is an attribute that consists of a set of categories, the feature is called **categorical** or **nominal**. A special case of categorical variables is called **ordinal**, which designates a nominal variable with categories falling in an ordered list. Some examples of ordinal variables include clothing sizes such as small, medium, and large; or a measurement of customer satisfaction on a scale from "not at all happy" to "very happy." It is important to consider what the features represent, as the type and number of features in your dataset will assist in determining an appropriate machine learning algorithm for your task.

Types of machine learning algorithms

Machine learning algorithms are divided into categories according to their purpose. Understanding the categories of learning algorithms is an essential first step towards using data to drive the desired action.

A **predictive model** is used for tasks that involve, as the name implies, the prediction of one value using other values in the dataset. The learning algorithm attempts to discover and model the relationship between the **target** feature (the feature being predicted) and the other features. Despite the common use of the word "prediction" to imply forecasting, predictive models need not necessarily foresee events in the future. For instance, a predictive model could be used to predict past events, such as the date of a baby's conception using the mother's present-day hormone levels. Predictive models can also be used in real time to control traffic lights during rush hours.

Because predictive models are given clear instruction on what they need to learn and how they are intended to learn it, the process of training a predictive model is known as **supervised learning**. The supervision does not refer to human involvement, but rather to the fact that the target values provide a way for the learner to know how well it has learned the desired task. Stated more formally, given a set of data, a supervised learning algorithm attempts to optimize a function (the model) to find the combination of feature values that result in the target output.

The often used supervised machine learning task of predicting which category an example belongs to is known as **classification**. It is easy to think of potential uses for a classifier. For instance, you could predict whether:

- An e-mail message is spam
- A person has cancer
- A football team will win or lose
- An applicant will default on a loan

In classification, the target feature to be predicted is a categorical feature known as the **class**, and is divided into categories called **levels**. A class can have two or more levels, and the levels may or may not be ordinal. Because classification is so widely used in machine learning, there are many types of classification algorithms, with strengths and weaknesses suited for different types of input data. We will see examples of these later in this chapter and throughout this book.

Supervised learners can also be used to predict numeric data such as income, laboratory values, test scores, or counts of items. To predict such numeric values, a common form of **numeric prediction** fits linear regression models to the input data. Although regression models are not the only type of numeric models, they are, by far, the most widely used. Regression methods are widely used for forecasting, as they quantify in exact terms the association between inputs and the target, including both, the magnitude and uncertainty of the relationship.

Since it is easy to convert numbers into categories (for example, ages 13 to 19 are teenagers) and categories into numbers (for example, assign 1 to all males, 0 to all females), the boundary between classification models and numeric prediction models is not necessarily firm.

A **descriptive model** is used for tasks that would benefit from the insight gained from summarizing data in new and interesting ways. As opposed to predictive models that predict a target of interest, in a descriptive model, no single feature is more important than any other. In fact, because there is no target to learn, the process of training a descriptive model is called **unsupervised learning**. Although it can be more difficult to think of applications for descriptive models — after all, what good is a learner that isn't learning anything in particular — they are used quite regularly for data mining.

For example, the descriptive modeling task called **pattern discovery** is used to identify useful associations within data. Pattern discovery is often used for **market basket analysis** on retailers' transactional purchase data. Here, the goal is to identify items that are frequently purchased together, such that the learned information can be used to refine marketing tactics. For instance, if a retailer learns that swimming trunks are commonly purchased at the same time as sunglasses, the retailer might reposition the items more closely in the store or run a promotion to "up-sell" customers on associated items.

Originally used only in retail contexts, pattern discovery is now starting to be used in quite innovative ways. For instance, it can be used to detect patterns of fraudulent behavior, screen for genetic defects, or identify hot spots for criminal activity.

The descriptive modeling task of dividing a dataset into homogeneous groups is called **clustering**. This is sometimes used for **segmentation analysis** that identifies groups of individuals with similar behavior or demographic information, so that advertising campaigns could be tailored for particular audiences. Although the machine is capable of identifying the clusters, human intervention is required to interpret them. For example, given five different clusters of shoppers at a grocery store, the marketing team will need to understand the differences among the groups in order to create a promotion that best suits each group.

Lastly, a class of machine learning algorithms known as **meta-learners** is not tied to a specific learning task, but is rather focused on learning how to learn more effectively. A meta-learning algorithm uses the result of some learnings to inform additional learning. This can be beneficial for very challenging problems or when a predictive algorithm's performance needs to be as accurate as possible.

Matching input data to algorithms

The following table lists the general types of machine learning algorithms covered in this book. Although this covers only a fraction of the entire set of machine learning algorithms, learning these methods will provide a sufficient foundation to make sense of any other method you may encounter in the future.

Model	Learning task	Chapter
Supervised Learning Algorithms		
Nearest Neighbor	Classification	3
Naive Bayes	Classification	4
Decision Trees	Classification	5
Classification Rule Learners	Classification	5
Linear Regression	Numeric prediction	6
Regression Trees	Numeric prediction	6
Model Trees	Numeric prediction	6
Neural Networks	Dual use	7
Support Vector Machines	Dual use	7
Unsupervised Learning Algorithms		
Association Rules	Pattern detection	8
k-means clustering	Clustering	9
Meta-Learning Algorithms		
Bagging	Dual use	11
Boosting	Dual use	11
Random Forests	Dual use	11

To begin applying machine learning to a real-world project, you will need to determine which of the four learning tasks your project represents: classification, numeric prediction, pattern detection, or clustering. The task will drive the choice of algorithm. For instance, if you are undertaking pattern detection, you are likely to employ association rules. Similarly, a clustering problem will likely utilize the k-means algorithm, and numeric prediction will utilize regression analysis or regression trees.

For classification, more thought is needed to match a learning problem to an appropriate classifier. In these cases, it is helpful to consider various distinctions among algorithms — distinctions that will only be apparent by studying each of the classifiers in depth. For instance, within classification problems, decision trees result in models that are readily understood, while the models of neural networks are notoriously difficult to interpret. If you were designing a credit-scoring model, this could be an important distinction because law often requires that the applicant must be notified about the reasons he or she was rejected for the loan. Even if the neural network is better at predicting loan defaults, if its predictions cannot be explained, then it is useless for this application.

To assist with the algorithm selection, in every chapter, the key strengths and weaknesses of each learning algorithm are listed. Although you will sometimes find that these characteristics exclude certain models from consideration, in many cases, the choice of algorithm is arbitrary. When this is true, feel free to use whichever algorithm you are most comfortable with. Other times, when predictive accuracy is primary, you may need to test several algorithms and choose the one that fits the best, or use a meta-learning algorithm that combines several different learners to utilize the strengths of each.

Machine learning with R

Many of the algorithms needed for machine learning with R are not included as part of the base installation. Instead, the algorithms needed for machine learning are available via a large community of experts who have shared their work freely. These must be installed on top of base R manually. Thanks to R's status as free open source software, there is no additional charge for this functionality.

A collection of R functions that can be shared among users is called a **package**. Free packages exist for each of the machine learning algorithms covered in this book. In fact, this book only covers a small portion of all of R's machine learning packages.

If you are interested in the breadth of R packages, you can view a list at **Comprehensive R Archive Network (CRAN)**, a collection of web and FTP sites located around the world to provide the most up-to-date versions of R software and packages. If you obtained the R software via download, it was most likely from CRAN at http://cran.r-project.org/index.html.

> If you do not already have R, the CRAN website also provides installation instructions and information on where to find help if you have trouble.

The **Packages** link on the left side of the page will take you to a page where you can browse packages in an alphabetical order or sorted by the publication date. At the time of writing this, a total 6,779 packages were available — a jump of over 60% in the time since the first edition was written, and this trend shows no sign of slowing!

The **Task Views** link on the left side of the CRAN page provides a curated list of packages as per the subject area. The task view for machine learning, which lists the packages covered in this book (and many more), is available at http://cran.r-project.org/web/views/MachineLearning.html.

Installing R packages

Despite the vast set of available R add-ons, the package format makes installation and use a virtually effortless process. To demonstrate the use of packages, we will install and load the RWeka package, which was developed by Kurt Hornik, Christian Buchta, and Achim Zeileis (see *Open-Source Machine Learning: R Meets Weka* in Computational Statistics 24: 225-232 for more information). The RWeka package provides a collection of functions that give R access to the machine learning algorithms in the Java-based Weka software package by Ian H. Witten and Eibe Frank. More information on Weka is available at http://www.cs.waikato.ac.nz/~ml/weka/

> To use the RWeka package, you will need to have Java installed (many computers come with Java preinstalled). Java is a set of programming tools available for free, which allow for the use of cross-platform applications such as Weka. For more information, and to download Java on your system, you can visit http://java.com.

The most direct way to install a package is via the `install.packages()` function. To install the RWeka package, at the R command prompt, simply type:

```
> install.packages("RWeka")
```

R will then connect to CRAN and download the package in the correct format for your OS. Some packages such as RWeka require additional packages to be installed before they can be used (these are called dependencies). By default, the installer will automatically download and install any dependencies.

> The first time you install a package, R may ask you to choose a CRAN mirror. If this happens, choose the mirror residing at a location close to you. This will generally provide the fastest download speed.

The default installation options are appropriate for most systems. However, in some cases, you may want to install a package to another location. For example, if you do not have root or administrator privileges on your system, you may need to specify an alternative installation path. This can be accomplished using the `lib` option, as follows:

```
> install.packages("RWeka", lib="/path/to/library")
```

The installation function also provides additional options for installation from a local file, installation from source, or using experimental versions. You can read about these options in the help file, by using the following command:

```
> ?install.packages
```

More generally, the question mark operator can be used to obtain help on any R function. Simply type ? before the name of the function.

Loading and unloading R packages

In order to conserve memory, R does not load every installed package by default. Instead, packages are loaded by users as they are needed, using the `library()` function.

> The name of this function leads some people to incorrectly use the terms library and package interchangeably. However, to be precise, a library refers to the location where packages are installed and never to a package itself.

To load the `RWeka` package we installed previously, you can type the following:

```
> library(RWeka)
```

Aside from `RWeka`, there are several other R packages that will be used in the later chapters. Installation instructions will be provided as additional packages are used.

To unload an R package, use the `detach()` function. For example, to unload the `RWeka` package shown previously use the following command:

```
> detach("package:RWeka", unload = TRUE)
```

This will free up any resources used by the package.

Summary

Machine learning originated at the intersection of statistics, database science, and computer science. It is a powerful tool, capable of finding actionable insight in large quantities of data. Still, caution must be used in order to avoid common abuses of machine learning in the real world.

Conceptually, learning involves the abstraction of data into a structured representation, and the generalization of this structure into action that can be evaluated for utility. In practical terms, a machine learner uses data containing examples and features of the concept to be learned, and summarizes this data in the form of a model, which is then used for predictive or descriptive purposes. These purposes can be grouped into tasks, including classification, numeric prediction, pattern detection, and clustering. Among the many options, machine learning algorithms are chosen on the basis of the input data and the learning task.

R provides support for machine learning in the form of community-authored packages. These powerful tools are free to download, but need to be installed before they can be used. Each chapter in this book will introduce such packages as they are needed.

In the next chapter, we will further introduce the basic R commands that are used to manage and prepare data for machine learning. Though you might be tempted to skip this step and jump directly into thick of things, a common rule of thumb suggests that 80 percent or more of the time spent on typical machine learning projects is devoted to this step. As a result, investing in this early work will pay dividends later on.

2
Managing and Understanding Data

A key early component of any machine learning project involves managing and understanding data. Although this may not be as gratifying as building and deploying models—the stages in which you begin to see the fruits of your labor—it is unwise to ignore this important preparatory work.

Any learning algorithm is only as good as its input data, and in many cases, the input data is complex, messy, and spread across multiple sources and formats. Because of this complexity, often the largest portion of effort invested in machine learning projects is spent on data preparation and exploration.

This chapter approaches these topics in three ways. The first section discusses the basic data structures R uses to store data. You will become very familiar with these structures as you create and manipulate datasets. The second section is practical, as it covers several functions that are useful to get data in and out of R. In the third section, methods for understanding data are illustrated while exploring a real-world dataset.

By the end of this chapter, you will understand:

- How to use R's basic data structures to store and extract data
- Simple functions to get data into R from common source formats
- Typical methods to understand and visualize complex data

Since the way R thinks about data will define the way you work with data, it is helpful to know R's data structures before jumping directly into data preparation. However, if you are already familiar with R programming, feel free to skip ahead to the section on data preprocessing.

R data structures

There are numerous types of data structures across programming languages, each with strengths and weaknesses suited to particular tasks. Since R is a programming language used widely for statistical data analysis, the data structures it utilizes were designed with this type of work in mind.

The R data structures used most frequently in machine learning are vectors, factors, lists, arrays and matrices, and data frames. Each is tailored to a specific data management task, which makes it important to understand how they will interact in your R project. In the sections that follow, we will review their similarities and differences.

Vectors

The fundamental R data structure is the **vector**, which stores an ordered set of values called **elements**. A vector can contain any number of elements, but all of the elements must be of the same **type** of values. For instance, a vector cannot contain both numbers and text. To determine the type of vector v, use the `typeof(v)` command.

Several vector types are commonly used in machine learning: `integer` (numbers without decimals), `double` (numbers with decimals), `character` (text data), and `logical` (`TRUE` or `FALSE` values). There are also two special values: `NULL`, which is used to indicate the absence of any value, and `NA`, which indicates a missing value.

> Some R functions will report both `integer` and `double` vectors as `numeric`, while others will distinguish between the two. As a result, although all `double` vectors are `numeric`, not all `numeric` vectors are `double` type.

It is tedious to enter large amounts of data manually, but small vectors can be created by using the `c()` combine function. The vector can also be given a name using the `<-` arrow operator, which is R's way of assigning values, much like the `=` assignment operator is used in many other programming languages.

For example, let's construct several vectors to store the diagnostic data of three medical patients. We'll create a `character` vector named `subject_name` to store the three patient names, a `double` vector named `temperature` to store each patient's body temperature, and a logical vector named `flu_status` to store each patient's diagnosis (TRUE if he or she has influenza, FALSE otherwise). Let's have a look at the following code to create these three vectors:

```
> subject_name <- c("John Doe", "Jane Doe", "Steve Graves")
> temperature <- c(98.1, 98.6, 101.4)
> flu_status <- c(FALSE, FALSE, TRUE)
```

Because R vectors are inherently ordered, the records can be accessed by counting the item's number in the set, beginning at one, and surrounding this number with square brackets (that is, `[` and `]`) after the name of the vector. For instance, to obtain the body temperature for patient Jane Doe (the second element in the `temperature` vector) simply type:

```
> temperature[2]
[1] 98.6
```

R offers a variety of convenient methods to extract data from vectors. A range of values can be obtained using the (`:`) colon operator. For instance, to obtain the body temperature of Jane Doe and Steve Graves, type:

```
> temperature[2:3]
[1] 98.6 101.4
```

Items can be excluded by specifying a negative item number. To exclude Jane Doe's `temperature` data, type:

```
> temperature[-2]
[1]  98.1 101.4
```

Finally, it is also sometimes useful to specify a logical vector indicating whether each item should be included. For example, to include the first two `temperature` readings but exclude the third, type:

```
> temperature[c(TRUE, TRUE, FALSE)]
[1] 98.1 98.6
```

As you will see shortly, the vector provides the foundation for many other R data structures. Therefore, the knowledge of the various vector operations is crucial to work with data in R.

Factors

If you recall from *Chapter 1, Introducing Machine Learning*, features that represent a characteristic with categories of values are known as **nominal**. Although it is possible to use a character vector to store nominal data, R provides a data structure specifically for this purpose. A **factor** is a special case of vector that is solely used to represent categorical or ordinal variables. In the medical dataset we are building, we might use a factor to represent gender, because it uses two categories: MALE and FEMALE.

Why not use character vectors? An advantage of factors is that the category labels are stored only once. For instance, rather than storing MALE, MALE, FEMALE, the computer can store 1, 1, 2, which reduces the size of memory needed to store the same information. Additionally, many machine learning algorithms treat nominal and numeric data differently. Coding as factors is often needed to inform an R function to treat categorical data appropriately.

A factor should not be used for character vectors that are not truly categorical. If a vector stores mostly unique values like names or identification strings, keep it as a character vector.

To create a factor from a character vector, simply apply the factor() function. For example:

```
> gender <- factor(c("MALE", "FEMALE", "MALE"))
> gender
[1] MALE    FEMALE MALE
Levels: FEMALE MALE
```

Notice that when the gender data for John Doe and Jane Doe were displayed, R printed additional information about the gender factor. The levels variable comprise the set of possible categories factor could take, in this case: MALE or FEMALE.

When we create factors, we can add additional levels that may not appear in the data. Suppose we add another factor for the blood type, as shown in the following example:

```
> blood <- factor(c("O", "AB", "A"),
                        levels = c("A", "B", "AB", "O"))
> blood[1:2]
[1] O  AB
Levels: A B AB O
```

Notice that when we defined the `blood` factor for the three patients, we specified an additional vector of four possible blood types using the `levels` parameter. As a result, even though our data included only types `O`, `AB`, and `A`, all the four types are stored with the `blood` factor as indicated by the output. Storing the additional level allows for the possibility of adding data with the other blood types in the future. It also ensures that if we were to create a table of blood types, we would know that the `B` type exists, despite it not being recorded in our data.

The factor data structure also allows us to include information about the order of a nominal variable's categories, which provides a convenient way to store ordinal data. For example, suppose we have data on the severity of a patient's `symptoms` coded in an increasing level of severity from mild, to moderate, to severe. We indicate the presence of ordinal data by providing the factor's `levels` in the desired order, listed in ascending order from lowest to highest, and setting the `ordered` parameter to `TRUE`, as shown:

```
> symptoms <- factor(c("SEVERE", "MILD", "MODERATE"),
                        levels = c("MILD", "MODERATE", "SEVERE"),
                        ordered = TRUE)
```

The resulting `symptoms` factor now includes information about the order we requested. Unlike our prior factors, the levels value of this factor are separated by < symbols, to indicate the presence of a sequential order from mild to severe:

```
> symptoms
[1] SEVERE    MILD       MODERATE
Levels: MILD < MODERATE < SEVERE
```

A helpful feature of the ordered factors is that logical tests work as you expect. For instance, we can test whether each patient's symptoms are greater than moderate:

```
> symptoms > "MODERATE"
[1]   TRUE FALSE FALSE
```

Machine learning algorithms capable of modeling ordinal data will expect the ordered factors, so be sure to code your data accordingly.

Lists

A **list** is a data structure, much like a vector, in that it is used for storing an ordered set of elements. However, where a vector requires all its elements to be the same type, a list allows different types of elements to be collected. Due to this flexibility, lists are often used to store various types of input and output data and sets of configuration parameters for machine learning models.

To illustrate lists, consider the medical patient dataset we have been constructing with the data for three patients stored in six vectors. If we want to display all the data on John Doe (subject 1), we would need to enter five R commands:

```
> subject_name[1]
[1] "John Doe"
> temperature[1]
[1] 98.1
> flu_status[1]
[1] FALSE
> gender[1]
[1] MALE
Levels: FEMALE MALE
> blood[1]
[1] O
Levels: A B AB O
> symptoms[1]
[1] SEVERE
Levels: MILD < MODERATE < SEVERE
```

This seems like a lot of work to display one patient's medical data. The list structure allows us to group all of the patient's data into one object that we can use repeatedly.

Similar to creating a vector with `c()`, a list is created using the `list()` function, as shown in the following example. One notable difference is that when a list is constructed, each component in the sequence is almost always given a name. The names are not technically required, but allow the list's values to be accessed later on by name rather than by numbered position. To create a list with named components for all of the first patient's data, type the following:

```
> subject1 <- list(fullname = subject_name[1],
                   temperature = temperature[1],
                   flu_status = flu_status[1],
                   gender = gender[1],
                   blood = blood[1],
                   symptoms = symptoms[1])
```

This patient's data is now collected in the `subject1` list:

```
> subject1
$fullname
[1] "John Doe"

$temperature
[1] 98.1

$flu_status
[1] FALSE

$gender
[1] MALE
Levels: FEMALE MALE

$blood
[1] O
Levels: A B AB O

$symptoms
[1] SEVERE
Levels: MILD < MODERATE < SEVERE
```

Note that the values are labeled with the names we specified in the preceding command. However, a list can still be accessed using methods similar to a vector. To access the `temperature` value, use the following command:

```
> subject1[2]
$temperature
[1] 98.1
```

The result of using vector-style operators on a list object is another list object, which is a subset of the original list. For example, the preceding code returned a list with a single `temperature` component. To return a single list item in its native data type, use double brackets (`[[` and `]]`) when attempting to select the list component. For example, the following returns a numeric vector of length one:

```
> subject1[[2]]
[1] 98.1
```

For clarity, it is often easier to access list components directly, by appending a `$` and the value's name to the name of the list component, as follows:

```
> subject1$temperature
[1] 98.1
```

Like the double bracket notation, this returns the list component in its native data type (in this case, a numeric vector of length one).

 Accessing the value by name also ensures that the correct item is retrieved, even if the order of the list's elements is changed later on.

It is possible to obtain several items in a list by specifying a vector of names. The following returns a subset of the `subject1` list, which contains only the `temperature` and `flu_status` components:

```
> subject1[c("temperature", "flu_status")]
$temperature
[1] 98.1

$flu_status
[1] FALSE
```

Entire datasets could be constructed using lists and lists of lists. For example, you might consider creating a `subject2` and `subject3` list, and combining these into a single list object named `pt_data`. However, constructing a dataset in this way is common enough that R provides a specialized data structure specifically for this task.

Data frames

By far, the most important R data structure utilized in machine learning is the **data frame**, a structure analogous to a spreadsheet or database, since it has both rows and columns of data. In R terms, a data frame can be understood as a list of vectors or factors, each having exactly the same number of values. Because the data frame is literally a list of vector type objects, it combines aspects of both vectors and lists.

Let's create a data frame for our patient dataset. Using the patient data vectors we created previously, the `data.frame()` function combines them into a data frame:

```
> pt_data <- data.frame(subject_name, temperature, flu_status,
      gender, blood, symptoms, stringsAsFactors = FALSE)
```

You might notice something new in the preceding code. We included an additional parameter: `stringsAsFactors = FALSE`. If we do not specify this option, R will automatically convert every character vector to a factor.

This feature is occasionally useful, but also sometimes unwarranted. Here, for example, the `subject_name` field is definitely not categorical data, as names are not categories of values. Therefore, setting the `stringsAsFactors` option to `FALSE` allows us to convert character vectors to factors only where it makes sense for the project.

When we display the `pt_data` data frame, we see that the structure is quite different from the data structures we worked with previously:

```
> pt_data
  subject_name temperature flu_status gender blood symptoms
1     John Doe        98.1      FALSE   MALE     O   SEVERE
2     Jane Doe        98.6      FALSE FEMALE    AB     MILD
3 Steve Graves       101.4       TRUE   MALE     A MODERATE
```

Compared to the one-dimensional vectors, factors, and lists, a data frame has two dimensions and is displayed in matrix format. This particular data frame has one column for each vector of patient data and one row for each patient. In machine learning terms, the data frame's columns are the features or attributes and the rows are the examples.

To extract entire columns (vectors) of data, we can take advantage of the fact that a data frame is simply a list of vectors. Similar to lists, the most direct way to extract a single element is by referring to it by name. For example, to obtain the `subject_name` vector, type:

```
> pt_data$subject_name
[1] "John Doe"     "Jane Doe"     "Steve Graves"
```

Also similar to lists, a vector of names can be used to extract several columns from a data frame:

```
> pt_data[c("temperature", "flu_status")]
  temperature flu_status
1        98.1      FALSE
2        98.6      FALSE
3       101.4       TRUE
```

When we access the data frame in this way, the result is a data frame containing all the rows of data for all the requested columns. Alternatively, the `pt_data[2:3]` command will also extract the `temperature` and `flu_status` columns. However, requesting the columns by name results in a clear and easy-to-maintain R code that will not break if the data frame is restructured in the future.

To extract values in the data frame, methods like those for accessing values in vectors are used. However, there is an important exception. Because the data frame is two-dimensional, both the desired rows and columns to be extracted must be specified. Rows are specified first, followed by a comma and then the columns in a format like this: `[rows, columns]`. As with vectors, rows and columns are counted beginning at one.

For instance, to extract the value in the first row and second column of the patient data frame (the `temperature` value for John Doe), use the following command:

```
> pt_data[1, 2]
[1] 98.1
```

If you like more than a single row or column of data, specify vectors for the rows and columns desired. The following command will pull data from the first and third rows and the second and fourth columns:

```
> pt_data[c(1, 3), c(2, 4)]
  temperature gender
1        98.1   MALE
3       101.4   MALE
```

To extract all the rows or columns, simply leave the row or column portion blank. For example, to extract all the rows of the first column:

```
> pt_data[, 1]
[1] "John Doe"      "Jane Doe"      "Steve Graves"
```

To extract all the columns of the first row, use the following command:

```
> pt_data[1, ]
  subject_name temperature flu_status gender blood symptoms
1     John Doe        98.1      FALSE   MALE     O   SEVERE
```

To extract everything, use the following command:

```
> pt_data[ , ]
  subject_name temperature flu_status gender blood symptoms
1     John Doe        98.1      FALSE   MALE     O   SEVERE
2     Jane Doe        98.6      FALSE FEMALE    AB     MILD
3 Steve Graves       101.4       TRUE   MALE     A MODERATE
```

Other methods to access values in lists and vectors can also be used to retrieve data frame rows and columns. For example, columns can be accessed by name rather than position, and negative signs can be used to exclude rows or columns of data. Therefore, the following command:

```
> pt_data[c(1, 3), c("temperature", "gender")]
```

Is equivalent to:

```
> pt_data[-2, c(-1, -3, -5, -6)]
```

To become more familiar with data frames, try practicing similar operations with the patient dataset, or even better, use data from one of your own projects. These types of operations are crucial for much of the work we will do in the upcoming chapters.

Matrixes and arrays

In addition to data frames, R provides other structures that store values in a tabular form. A **matrix** is a data structure that represents a two-dimensional table with rows and columns of data. Like vectors, R matrixes can contain any one type of data, although they are most often used for mathematical operations and, therefore, typically store only numeric data.

To create a matrix, simply supply a vector of data to the matrix() function along with a parameter specifying the number of rows (nrow) or number of columns (ncol). For example, to create a 2 x 2 matrix storing the numbers one through four, we can use the nrow parameter to request the data to be divided into two rows:

```
> m <- matrix(c(1, 2, 3, 4), nrow = 2)
> m
     [,1] [,2]
[1,]   1    3
[2,]   2    4
```

This is equivalent to the matrix produced using ncol = 2:

```
> m <- matrix(c(1, 2, 3, 4), ncol = 2)
> m
     [,1] [,2]
[1,]   1    3
[2,]   2    4
```

You will notice that R loaded the first column of the matrix first before loading the second column. This is called **column-major order**, and is R's default method for loading matrices.

To override this default setting and load a matrix by rows, set the parameter byrow = TRUE when creating the matrix.

To illustrate this further, let's see what happens if we add more values to the matrix.

With six values, requesting two rows creates a matrix with three columns:

```
> m <- matrix(c(1, 2, 3, 4, 5, 6), nrow = 2)
> m
     [,1] [,2] [,3]
[1,]   1    3    5
[2,]   2    4    6
```

Requesting two columns creates a matrix with three rows:

```
> m <- matrix(c(1, 2, 3, 4, 5, 6), ncol = 2)
> m
     [,1] [,2]
[1,]   1    4
```

```
[2,]    2    5
[3,]    3    6
```

As with data frames, values in matrixes can be extracted using `[row, column]` notation. For instance, `m[1, 1]` will return the value 1 and `m[3, 2]` will extract 6 from the `m` matrix. Additionally, entire rows or columns can be requested:

```
> m[1, ]
[1] 1 4
> m[, 1]
[1] 1 2 3
```

Closely related to the matrix structure is the **array**, which is a multidimensional table of data. Where a matrix has rows and columns of values, an array has rows, columns, and any number of additional layers of values. Although we will be occasionally using matrixes in the upcoming chapters, the use of arrays is outside the scope of this book.

Managing data with R

One of the challenges faced while working with massive datasets involves gathering, preparing, and otherwise managing data from a variety of sources. Although we will cover data preparation, data cleaning, and data management in depth by working on real-world machine learning tasks in the later chapters, this section will highlight the basic functionality to get data into and out of R.

Saving, loading, and removing R data structures

When you have spent a lot of time getting a data frame into the desired form, you shouldn't need to recreate your work each time you restart your R session. To save a data structure to a file that can be reloaded later or transferred to another system, use the `save()` function. The `save()` function writes one or more R data structures to the location specified by the `file` parameter. R data files have an `.RData` extension.

Suppose you have three objects named `x`, `y`, and `z` that you would like to save in a permanent file. Regardless of whether they are vectors, factors, lists, or data frames, we could save them to a file named `mydata.RData` using the following command:

```
> save(x, y, z, file = "mydata.RData")
```

The `load()` command can recreate any data structures that have been saved to an `.RData` file. To load the `mydata.RData` file we saved in the preceding code, simply type:

```
> load("mydata.RData")
```

This will recreate the x, y, and z data structures.

> Be careful of what you are loading! All data structures stored in the file you are importing with the `load()` command will be added to your workspace, even if they overwrite something else you are working on.

If you need to wrap up your R session in a hurry, the `save.image()` command will write your entire session to a file simply called `.RData`. By default, R will look for this file the next time you start R, and your session will be recreated just as you had left it.

After working on an R session for sometime, you may have accumulated a number of data structures. The `ls()` listing function returns a vector of all the data structures currently in the memory. For example, if you've been following along with the code in this chapter, the `ls()` function returns the following:

```
> ls()
[1] "blood"        "flu_status"  "gender"       "m"
[5] "pt_data"      "subject_name" "subject1"     "symptoms"
[9] "temperature"
```

R will automatically remove these from its memory upon quitting the session, but for large data structures, you may want to free up the memory sooner. The `rm()` remove function can be used for this purpose. For example, to eliminate the m and `subject1` objects, simply type:

```
> rm(m, subject1)
```

The `rm()` function can also be supplied with a character vector of the object names to be removed. This works with the `ls()` function to clear the entire R session:

```
> rm(list=ls())
```

Be very careful while executing the preceding command, as you will not be prompted before your objects are removed!

Importing and saving data from CSV files

It is very common for public datasets to be stored in text files. Text files can be read on virtually any computer or operating system, which makes the format nearly universal. They can also be exported and imported to and from programs such as Microsoft Excel, providing a quick and easy way to work with spreadsheet data.

A **tabular** (as in "table") data file is structured in the matrix form, such that each line of text reflects one example, and each example has the same number of features. The feature values on each line are separated by a predefined symbol, known as a **delimiter**. Often, the first line of a tabular data file lists the names of the columns of data. This is called a **header** line.

Perhaps the most common tabular text file format is the **CSV** (**Comma-Separated Values**) file, which as the name suggests, uses the comma as a delimiter. The CSV files can be imported to and exported from many common applications. A CSV file representing the medical dataset constructed previously could be stored as:

```
subject_name,temperature,flu_status,gender,blood_type
John Doe,98.1,FALSE,MALE,O
Jane Doe,98.6,FALSE,FEMALE,AB
Steve Graves,101.4,TRUE,MALE,A
```

Given a patient data file named `pt_data.csv` located in the R working directory, the `read.csv()` function can be used as follows to load the file into R:

```
> pt_data <- read.csv("pt_data.csv", stringsAsFactors = FALSE)
```

This will read the CSV file into a data frame titled `pt_data`. Just as we did previously while constructing a data frame, we need to use the `stringsAsFactors = FALSE` parameter to prevent R from converting all text variables into factors. This step is better left to you, not R, to perform.

> If your dataset resides outside the R working directory, the full path to the CSV file (for example, `/path/to/mydata.csv`) can be used when calling the `read.csv()` function.

By default, R assumes that the CSV file includes a header line listing the names of the features in the dataset. If a CSV file does not have a header, specify the option `header = FALSE`, as shown in the following command, and R will assign default feature names in the `V1` and `V2` forms and so on:

```
> mydata <- read.csv("mydata.csv", stringsAsFactors = FALSE,
                      header = FALSE)
```

The `read.csv()` function is a special case of the `read.table()` function, which can read tabular data in many different forms, including other delimited formats such as **Tab-Separated Values (TSV)**. For more detailed information on the `read.table()` family of functions, refer to the R help page using the `?read.table` command.

To save a data frame to a CSV file, use the `write.csv()` function. If your data frame is named `pt_data`, simply enter:

```
> write.csv(pt_data, file = "pt_data.csv", row.names = FALSE)
```

This will write a CSV file with the name `pt_data.csv` to the R working folder. The `row.names` parameter overrides R's default setting, which is to output row names in the CSV file. Unless row names have been added to a data frame, this output is unnecessary and will simply inflate the size of the resulting file.

Exploring and understanding data

After collecting data and loading it into R's data structures, the next step in the machine learning process involves examining the data in detail. It is during this step that you will begin to explore the data's features and examples, and realize the peculiarities that make your data unique. The better you understand your data, the better you will be able to match a machine learning model to your learning problem.

The best way to learn the process of data exploration is with an example. In this section, we will explore the `usedcars.csv` dataset, which contains actual data about used cars recently advertised for sale on a popular U.S. website.

The `usedcars.csv` dataset is available for download on the Packt Publishing support page for this book. If you are following along with the examples, be sure that this file has been downloaded and saved to your R working directory.

Since the dataset is stored in the CSV form, we can use the `read.csv()` function to load the data into an R data frame:

```
> usedcars <- read.csv("usedcars.csv", stringsAsFactors = FALSE)
```

Given the `usedcars` data frame, we will now assume the role of a data scientist who has the task of understanding the used car data. Although data exploration is a fluid process, the steps can be imagined as a sort of investigation in which questions about the data are answered. The exact questions may vary across projects, but the types of questions are always similar. You should be able to adapt the basic steps of this investigation to any dataset you like, whether large or small.

Exploring the structure of data

One of the first questions to ask in an investigation of a new dataset should be about how the dataset is organized. If you are fortunate, your source will provide a **data dictionary**, which is a document that describes the dataset's features. In our case, the used car data does not come with this documentation, so we'll need to create one on our own.

The `str()` function provides a method to display the structure of R data structures such as data frames, vectors, or lists. It can be used to create the basic outline for our data dictionary:

```
> str(usedcars)
'data.frame':   150 obs. of 6 variables:
 $ year        : int   2011 2011 2011 2011 ...
 $ model       : chr   "SEL" "SEL" "SEL" "SEL" ...
 $ price       : int   21992 20995 19995 17809 ...
 $ mileage     : int   7413 10926 7351 11613 ...
 $ color       : chr   "Yellow" "Gray" "Silver" "Gray" ...
 $ transmission: chr   "AUTO" "AUTO" "AUTO" "AUTO" ...
```

Using such a simple command, we learn a wealth of information about the dataset. The statement `150 obs` informs us that the data includes 150 **observations**, which is just another way of saying that the dataset contains 150 records or examples. The number of observations is often simply abbreviated as *n*. Since we know that the data describes used cars, we can now presume that we have examples of *n = 150* automobiles for sale.

The `6 variables` statement refers to the six features that were recorded in the data. These features are listed by name on separate lines. Looking at the line for the feature called `color`, we can note some additional details:

```
 $ color       : chr   "Yellow" "Gray" "Silver" "Gray" ...
```

After the variable's name, the `chr` label tells us that the feature is character type. In this dataset, three of the variables are character while three are noted as `int`, which indicates `integer` type. Although the `usedcars` dataset includes only `character` and `integer` variables, you are also likely to encounter `num` or `numeric` type while using noninteger data. Any factors would be listed as `factor` type. Following each variable's type, R presents a sequence of the first few feature values. The values `"Yellow" "Gray" "Silver" "Gray"` are the first four values of the `color` feature.

Applying a bit of the subject-area knowledge to the feature names and values allows us to make some assumptions about what the variables represent. The year variable could refer to the year the vehicle was manufactured or it could specify the year the advertisement was posted. We will have to investigate this feature more in detail later, since the four example values (2011 2011 2011 2011) could be used to argue for either possibility. The model, price, mileage, color, and transmission variables most likely refer to the characteristics of the car for sale.

Although our data seems to have been given meaningful variable names, this is not always the case. Sometimes datasets have features with nonsensical names or codes like V1. In these cases it may be necessary to do additional sleuthing to determine what a feature actually represents. Still, even with helpful feature names, it is always prudent to be skeptical about the labels you have been provided with. Let's investigate further.

Exploring numeric variables

To investigate the numeric variables in the used car data, we will employ a common set of measurements to describe values known as **summary statistics**. The summary() function displays several common summary statistics. Let's take a look at a single feature, year:

```
> summary(usedcars$year)
   Min.  1st Qu.  Median    Mean  3rd Qu.    Max.
   2000     2008    2009    2009     2010    2012
```

Even if you aren't already familiar with summary statistics, you may be able to guess some of them from the heading before the summary() output. Ignoring the meaning of the values for now, the fact that we see numbers such as 2000, 2008, and 2009 could lead us to believe that the year variable indicates the year of manufacture rather than the year the advertisement was posted, since we know the vehicles were recently listed for sale.

We can also use the summary() function to obtain summary statistics for several numeric variables at the same time:

```
> summary(usedcars[c("price", "mileage")])
     price              mileage
 Min.   : 3800    Min.   :   4867
 1st Qu.:10995    1st Qu.:  27200
 Median :13592    Median :  36385
 Mean   :12962    Mean   :  44261
 3rd Qu.:14904    3rd Qu.:  55125
 Max.   :21992    Max.   : 151479
```

The six summary statistics that the `summary()` function provides are simple, yet powerful tools to investigate data. They can be divided into two types: measures of center and measures of spread.

Measuring the central tendency – mean and median

Measures of **central tendency** are a class of statistics used to identify a value that falls in the middle of a set of data. You most likely are already familiar with one common measure of center: the average. In common use, when something is deemed average, it falls somewhere between the extreme ends of the scale. An average student might have marks falling in the middle of his or her classmates; an average weight is neither unusually light nor heavy. An average item is typical and not too unlike the others in the group. You might think of it as an exemplar by which all the others are judged.

In statistics, the average is also known as the **mean**, which is a measurement defined as the sum of all values divided by the number of values. For example, to calculate the mean income in a group of three people with incomes of $36,000, $44,000, and $56,000, use the following command:

```
> (36000 + 44000 + 56000) / 3
[1] 45333.33
```

R also provides a `mean()` function, which calculates the mean for a vector of numbers:

```
> mean(c(36000, 44000, 56000))
[1] 45333.33
```

The mean income of this group of people is about $45,333. Conceptually, this can be imagined as the income each person would have, if the total amount of income were divided equally across every person.

Recall that the preceding `summary()` output listed mean values for the `price` and `mileage` variables. The means suggest that the typical used car in this dataset was listed at a price of $12,962 and had an odometer reading of 44,261. What does this tell us about our data? Since the average price is relatively low, we might expect that the dataset contains economy class cars. Of course, the data can also include late-model luxury cars with high mileage, but the relatively low mean mileage statistic doesn't provide evidence to support this hypothesis. On the other hand, it doesn't provide evidence to ignore the possibility either. We'll need to keep this in mind as we examine the data further.

Although the mean is by far the most commonly cited statistic to measure the center of a dataset, it is not always the most appropriate one. Another commonly used measure of central tendency is the **median**, which is the value that occurs halfway through an ordered list of values. As with the mean, R provides a `median()` function, which we can apply to our salary data, as shown in the following example:

```
> median(c(36000, 44000, 56000))
[1] 44000
```

Because the middle value is `44000`, the median income is $44,000.

 If a dataset has an even number of values, there is no middle value. In this case, the median is commonly calculated as the average of the two values at the center of the ordered list. For example, the median of the values 1, 2, 3, and 4 is 2.5.

At the first glance, it seems like the median and mean are very similar measures. Certainly, the mean value of $45,333 and the median value of $44,000 are not very different. Why have two measures of central tendency? The reason is due to the fact that the mean and median are affected differently by the values falling at the far ends of the range. In particular, the mean is highly sensitive to **outliers**, or values that are atypically high or low in relation to the majority of data. Because the mean is sensitive to outliers, it is more likely to be shifted higher or lower by a small number of extreme values.

Recall again the reported median values in the `summary()` output for the used car dataset. Although the mean and median price are fairly similar (differing by approximately five percent), there is a much larger difference between the mean and median for mileage. For mileage, the mean of 44,261 is approximately 20 percent more than the median of 36,385. Since the mean is more sensitive to extreme values than the median, the fact that the mean is much higher than the median might lead us to suspect that there are some used cars in the dataset with extremely high mileage values. To investigate this further, we'll need to add additional summary statistics to our analysis.

Measuring spread – quartiles and the five-number summary

Measuring the mean and median provides one way to quickly summarize the values, but these measures of center tell us little about whether or not there is diversity in the measurements. To measure the diversity, we need to employ another type of summary statistics that is concerned with the **spread** of data, or how tightly or loosely the values are spaced. Knowing about the spread provides a sense of the data's highs and lows and whether most values are like or unlike the mean and median.

The **five-number summary** is a set of five statistics that roughly depict the spread of a feature's values. All five of the statistics are included in the output of the summary() function. Written in order, they are:

1. Minimum (Min.)
2. First quartile, or Q1 (1st Qu.)
3. Median, or Q2 (Median)
4. Third quartile, or Q3 (3rd Qu.)
5. Maximum (Max.)

As you would expect, minimum and maximum are the most extreme feature values, indicating the smallest and largest values, respectively. R provides the min() and max() functions to calculate these values on a vector of data.

The span between the minimum and maximum value is known as the **range**. In R, the range() function returns both the minimum and maximum value. Combining range() with the diff() difference function allows you to examine the range of data with a single line of code:

```
> range(usedcars$price)
[1]  3800 21992
> diff(range(usedcars$price))
[1] 18192
```

The first and third quartiles—Q1 and Q3—refer to the value below or above which one quarter of the values are found. Along with the (Q2) median, the **quartiles** divide a dataset into four portions, each with the same number of values.

Quartiles are a special case of a type of statistics called **quantiles**, which are numbers that divide data into equally sized quantities. In addition to quartiles, commonly used quantiles include **tertiles** (three parts), **quintiles** (five parts), **deciles** (10 parts), and **percentiles** (100 parts).

Percentiles are often used to describe the ranking of a value; for instance, a student whose test score was ranked at the 99th percentile performed better than, or equal to, 99 percent of the other test takers.

The middle 50 percent of data between the first and third quartiles is of particular interest because it in itself is a simple measure of spread. The difference between Q1 and Q3 is known as the **Interquartile Range (IQR)**, and it can be calculated with the IQR() function:

```
> IQR(usedcars$price)
[1] 3909.5
```

We could have also calculated this value by hand from the summary() output for the usedcars$price variable by computing *14904 – 10995 = 3909*. The small difference between our calculation and the IQR() output is due to the fact that R automatically rounds the summary() output.

The quantile() function provides a robust tool to identify quantiles for a set of values. By default, the quantile() function returns the five-number summary. Applying the function to the used car data results in the same statistics as done earlier:

```
> quantile(usedcars$price)
      0%     25%     50%     75%    100%
  3800.0 10995.0 13591.5 14904.5 21992.0
```

While computing quantiles, there are many methods to handle ties among values and datasets with no middle value. The quantile() function allows you to specify among nine different algorithms by specifying the type parameter. If your project requires a precisely defined quantile, it is important to read the function documentation using the ?quantile command.

If we specify an additional probs parameter using a vector denoting cut points, we can obtain arbitrary quantiles, such as the 1st and 99th percentiles:

```
> quantile(usedcars$price, probs = c(0.01, 0.99))
      1%      99%
 5428.69 20505.00
```

The `seq()` function is used to generate vectors of evenly-spaced values. This makes it easy to obtain other slices of data, such as the quintiles (five groups), as shown in the following command:

```
> quantile(usedcars$price, seq(from = 0, to = 1, by = 0.20))
    0%      20%      40%      60%      80%     100%
 3800.0  10759.4  12993.8  13992.0  14999.0  21992.0
```

Equipped with an understanding of the five-number summary, we can re-examine the used car `summary()` output. On the `price` variable, the minimum was $3,800 and the maximum was $21,992. Interestingly, the difference between the minimum and Q1 is about $7,000, as is the difference between Q3 and the maximum; yet, the difference from Q1 to the median to Q3 is roughly $2,000. This suggests that the lower and upper 25 percent of values are more widely dispersed than the middle 50 percent of values, which seem to be more tightly grouped around the center. We see a similar trend with the `mileage` variable, which is not unsurprising. As you will learn later in this chapter, this pattern of spread is common enough that it has been called a "normal" distribution of data.

The spread of the `mileage` variable also exhibits another interesting property: the difference between Q3 and the maximum value is far greater than that between the minimum value and Q1. In other words, the larger values are far more spread out than the smaller values.

This finding explains why the mean value is much greater than the median. Because the mean is sensitive to extreme values, it is pulled higher, while the median stays relatively in the same place. This is an important property, which becomes more apparent when the data is presented visually.

Visualizing numeric variables – boxplots

Visualizing numeric variables can be helpful in diagnosing data problems. A common visualization of the five-number summary is **boxplot**, also known as a **box-and-whiskers** plot. The boxplot displays the center and spread of a numeric variable in a format that allows you to quickly obtain a sense of the range and skew of a variable or compare it to other variables.

Let's take a look at a boxplot for the used car price and mileage data. To obtain a boxplot for a variable, we will use the `boxplot()` function. We will also specify a pair of extra parameters, `main` and `ylab`, to add a title to the figure and label the *y* axis (the vertical axis), respectively. The commands to create the `price` and `mileage` boxplots are:

```
> boxplot(usedcars$price, main="Boxplot of Used Car Prices",
                    ylab="Price ($)")
> boxplot(usedcars$mileage, main="Boxplot of Used Car Mileage",
                    ylab="Odometer (mi.)")
```

R will produce figures as follows:

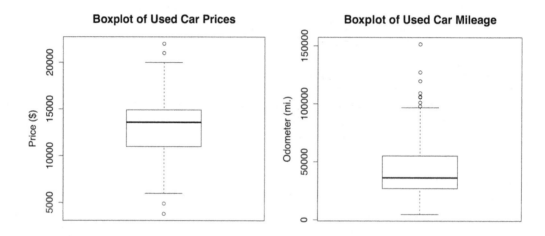

The box-and-whiskers plot depicts the five-number summary values using the horizontal lines and dots. The horizontal lines forming the box in the middle of each figure represent Q1, Q2 (the median), and Q3 while reading the plot from the bottom to the top. The median is denoted by the dark line, which lines up with $13,592 on the vertical axis for `price` and 36,385 mi. on the vertical axis for `mileage`.

In simple boxplots such as those in the preceding diagram, the width of the box-and-whiskers plot is arbitrary and does not illustrate any characteristic of the data. For more sophisticated analyses, it is possible to use the shape and size of the boxes to facilitate comparisons of the data across several groups. To learn more about such features, begin by examining the `notch` and `varwidth` options in the R `boxplot()` documentation by typing the `?boxplot` command.

The minimum and maximum values can be illustrated using the whiskers that extend below and above the box; however, a widely used convention only allows the whiskers to extend to a minimum or maximum of 1.5 times the IQR below Q1 or above Q3. Any values that fall beyond this threshold are considered outliers and are denoted as circles or dots. For example, recall that the IQR for the price variable was 3,909 with a Q1 of 10,995 and a Q3 of 14,904. An outlier is therefore any value that is less than *10995 - 1.5 * 3909= 5131.5* or greater than *14904 + 1.5 * 3909 = 20767.5*.

The plot shows two such outliers on both the high and low ends. On the mileage boxplot, there are no outliers on the low end and thus, the bottom whisker extends to the minimum value, 4,867. On the high end, we see several outliers beyond the 100,000 mile mark. These outliers are responsible for our earlier finding, which noted that the mean value was much greater than the median.

Visualizing numeric variables – histograms

A **histogram** is another way to graphically depict the spread of a numeric variable. It is similar to a boxplot in a way that it divides the variable's values into a predefined number of portions or **bins** that act as containers for values. Their similarities end there, however. On one hand, a boxplot requires that each of the four portions of data must contain the same number of values, and widens or narrows the bins as needed. On the other hand, a histogram uses any number of bins of an identical width, but allows the bins to contain different number of values.

We can create a histogram for the used car price and mileage data using the hist() function. As we did with the boxplot, we will specify a title for the figure using the main parameter, and label the *x* axis with the xlab parameter. The commands to create the histograms are:

```
> hist(usedcars$price, main = "Histogram of Used Car Prices",
              xlab = "Price ($)")
> hist(usedcars$mileage, main = "Histogram of Used Car Mileage",
              xlab = "Odometer (mi.)")
```

This produces the following diagram:

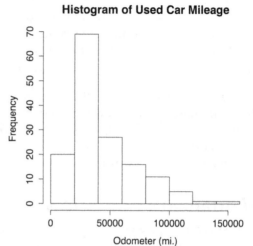

The histogram is composed of a series of bars with heights indicating the count, or **frequency** of values falling within each of the equal width bins partitioning the values. The vertical lines that separate the bars, as labeled on the horizontal axis, indicate the start and end points of the range of values for the bin.

You may have noticed that the preceding histograms have a different number of bins. This is because the hist() function attempts to identify a reasonable number of bins for the variable's range. If you'd like to override this default, use the breaks parameter. Supplying an integer like breaks = 10 would create exactly 10 bins of equal width; supplying a vector like c(5000, 10000, 15000, 20000) would create bins that break at the specified values.

On the price histogram, each of the 10 bars spans an interval of $2,000, beginning at $2,000 and ending at $22,000. The tallest bar at the center of the figure covers the $12,000 to $14,000 range and has a frequency of 50. Since we know that our data includes 150 cars, we know that one-third of all the cars are priced from $12,000 to $14,000. Nearly 90 cars—more than half—are priced from $12,000 to $16,000.

The mileage histogram includes eight bars indicating bins of 20,000 miles each, beginning at 0 and ending at 160,000 miles. Unlike the price histogram, the tallest bar is not at the center of the data, but on the left-hand side of the diagram. The 70 cars contained in this bin have odometer readings from 20,000 to 40,000 miles.

You might also notice that the shape of the two histograms is somewhat different. It seems that the used car prices tend to be evenly divided on both sides of the middle, while the car mileages stretch further to the right. This characteristic is known as **skew**, or more specifically right skew, because the values on the high end (right side) are far more spread out than the values on the low end (left side). As shown in the following diagram, histograms of skewed data look stretched on one of the sides:

Right Skew   No Skew   Left Skew

The ability to quickly diagnose such patterns in our data is one of the strengths of the histogram as a data exploration tool. This will become even more important as we start examining other patterns of spread in numeric data.

Understanding numeric data – uniform and normal distributions

Histograms, boxplots, and statistics describing the center and spread provide ways to examine the distribution of a variable's values. A variable's **distribution** describes how likely a value is to fall within various ranges.

If all the values are equally likely to occur—say, for instance, in a dataset recording the values rolled on a fair six-sided die—the distribution is said to be **uniform**. A uniform distribution is easy to detect with a histogram, because the bars are approximately the same height. When visualized with a histogram, it may look something like the following diagram:

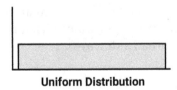

Uniform Distribution

It's important to note that not all random events are uniform. For instance, rolling a weighted six-sided trick die would result in some numbers coming up more often than others. While each roll of the die results in a randomly selected number, they are not equally likely.

Take, for instance, the used car data. This is clearly not uniform, since some values are seemingly far more likely to occur than others. In fact, on the price histogram, it seems that values grow less likely to occur as they are further away from both sides of the center bar, resulting in a bell-shaped distribution of data. This characteristic is so common in real-world data that it is the hallmark of the so-called **normal distribution**. The stereotypical bell-shaped curve of normal distribution is shown in the following diagram:

Normal Distribution

Although there are numerous types of non-normal distributions, many real-world phenomena generate data that can be described by the normal distribution. Therefore, the normal distribution's properties have been studied in great detail.

Measuring spread – variance and standard deviation

Distributions allow us to characterize a large number of values using a smaller number of parameters. The normal distribution, which describes many types of real-world data, can be defined with just two: center and spread. The center of normal distribution is defined by its mean value, which we have used earlier. The spread is measured by a statistic called the **standard deviation**.

In order to calculate the standard deviation, we must first obtain the **variance**, which is defined as the average of the squared differences between each value and the mean value. In mathematical notation, the variance of a set of n values of x is defined by the following formula. The Greek letter *mu* (similar in appearance to an *m* or *u*) denotes the mean of the values, and the variance itself is denoted by the Greek letter *sigma* squared (similar to a *b* turned sideways):

$$\text{Var}(X) = \sigma^2 = \frac{1}{n}\sum_{i=1}^{n}(x_i - \mu)^2$$

The standard deviation is the square root of the variance, and is denoted by *sigma*, as shown in the following formula:

$$\text{StdDev}(X) = \sigma = \sqrt{\frac{1}{n}\sum_{i=1}^{n}(x_i - \mu)^2}$$

The `var()` and `sd()` functions can be used to obtain the variance and standard deviation in R. For example, computing the variance and standard deviation on our `price` and `mileage` variables, we find:

```
> var(usedcars$price)
[1] 9749892
> sd(usedcars$price)
[1] 3122.482
> var(usedcars$mileage)
[1] 728033954
> sd(usedcars$mileage)
[1] 26982.1
```

While interpreting the variance, larger numbers indicate that the data are spread more widely around the mean. The standard deviation indicates, on average, how much each value differs from the mean.

If you compute these statistics by hand using the formulas in the preceding diagrams, you will obtain a slightly different result than the built-in R functions. This is because the preceding formulae use the population variance (which divides by *n*), while R uses the sample variance (which divides by *n* - 1). Except for very small datasets, the distinction is minor.

The standard deviation can be used to quickly estimate how extreme a given value is under the assumption that it came from a normal distribution. The **68-95-99.7 rule** states that 68 percent of the values in a normal distribution fall within one standard deviation of the mean, while 95 percent and 99.7 percent of the values fall within two and three standard deviations, respectively. This is illustrated in the following diagram:

Applying this information to the used car data, we know that since the mean and standard deviation of `price` were $12,962 and $3,122, respectively, assuming that the prices are normally distributed, approximately 68 percent of cars in our data were advertised at prices between $12,962 - $3,122 = $9,840 and $12,962 + $3,122 = $16,804.

Although, strictly speaking, the 68-95-99.7 rule only applies to normal distributions, the basic principle applies to any data; values more than three standard deviations away from the mean are exceedingly rare events.

Exploring categorical variables

If you recall, the used car dataset had three categorical variables: `model`, `color`, and `transmission`. Because we used the `stringsAsFactors = FALSE` parameter while loading the data, R has left them as the `character` (`chr`) type vectors rather than automatically converting them into `factor` type. Additionally, we might consider treating the year variable as categorical; although it has been loaded as a `numeric` (`int`) type vector, each year is a category that could apply to multiple cars.

In contrast to `numeric` data, categorical data is typically examined using tables rather than summary statistics. A table that presents a single categorical variable is known as a **one-way table**. The `table()` function can be used to generate one-way tables for our used car data:

```
> table(usedcars$year)

2000 2001 2002 2003 2004 2005 2006 2007 2008 2009 2010 2011 2012
   3    1    1    1    3    2    6   11   14   42   49   16    1
> table(usedcars$model)

 SE SEL SES
 78  23  49
> table(usedcars$color)

 Black   Blue   Gold   Gray  Green    Red Silver  White Yellow
    35     17      1     16      5     25     32     16      3
```

The `table()` output lists the categories of the nominal variable and a count of the number of values falling into this category. Since we know that there are 150 used cars in the dataset, we can determine that roughly one-third of all the cars were manufactured in the year `2010`, given that *49/150 = 0.327*.

R can also perform the calculation of table proportions directly, by using the `prop.table()` command on a table produced by the `table()` function:

```
> model_table <- table(usedcars$model)
> prop.table(model_table)

        SE       SEL       SES
0.5200000 0.1533333 0.3266667
```

The results of `prop.table()` can be combined with other R functions to transform the output. Suppose that we would like to display the results in percentages with a single decimal place. We can do this by multiplying the proportions by 100, then using the `round()` function while specifying `digits = 1`, as shown in the following example:

```
> color_pct <- table(usedcars$color)
> color_pct <- prop.table(color_table) * 100
> round(color_pct, digits = 1)
Black   Blue   Gold   Gray  Green    Red Silver  White Yellow
 23.3   11.3    0.7   10.7    3.3   16.7   21.3   10.7    2.0
```

Although this includes the same information as the default `prop.table()` output, this is easier to read. The results show that black is the most common color, since nearly a quarter (23.3 percent) of all the advertised cars are `Black`. `Silver` is a close second with 21.3 percent and `Red` is third with 16.7 percent.

Measuring the central tendency – the mode

In statistics terms, the **mode** of a feature is the value occurring most often. Like the mean and median, the mode is another measure of central tendency. It is often used for categorical data, since the mean and median are not defined for nominal variables.

For example, in the used car data, the mode of the `year` variable is 2010, while the modes for the `model` and `color` variables are `SE` and `Black`, respectively. A variable may have more than one mode; a variable with a single mode is **unimodal**, while a variable with two modes is **bimodal**. Data having multiple modes is more generally called **multimodal**.

 Although you might suspect that you could use the `mode()` function, R uses this to obtain the type of variable (as in `numeric`, `list`, and so on) rather than the statistical mode. Instead, to find the statistical mode, simply look at the table output of the category with the greatest number of values.

The mode or modes are used in a qualitative sense to gain an understanding of important values. Yet, it would be dangerous to place too much emphasis on the mode, since the most common value is not necessarily a majority. For instance, although `Black` was the most common value for the `color` variable, black cars were only about a quarter of all advertised cars.

It is best to think about modes in relation to the other categories. Is there one category that dominates all the others or are there several? From here, we may ask what the most common values tell us about the variable being measured. If black and silver are commonly used car colors, we might assume that the data are for luxury cars, which tend to be sold in more conservative colors. These colors could also indicate economy cars, which are sold with fewer color options. We will keep this question in mind as we continue to examine this data.

Thinking about modes as common values allows us to apply the concept of statistical mode to the numeric data. Strictly speaking, it would be unlikely to have a mode for a continuous variable, since no two values are likely to repeat. Yet, if we think about modes as the highest bars on a histogram, we can discuss the modes of variables such as `price` and `mileage`. It can be helpful to consider mode while exploring the numeric data, particularly to examine whether or not the data is multimodal.

Unimodal Distribution

Bimodal Distribution

Exploring relationships between variables

So far, we have examined variables one at a time, calculating only **univariate** statistics. During our investigation, we raised questions that we were unable to answer at that time:

- Does the `price` data imply that we are examining only economy-class cars or are there also luxury cars with high mileage?
- Do relationships between the `model` and `color` data provide insight into the types of cars we are examining?

These type of questions can be addressed by looking at **bivariate** relationships, which consider the relationship between two variables. Relationships of more than two variables are called **multivariate** relationships. Let's begin with the bivariate case.

Visualizing relationships – scatterplots

A **scatterplot** is a diagram that visualizes a bivariate relationship. It is a two-dimensional figure in which dots are drawn on a coordinate plane using the values of one feature to provide the horizontal x coordinates and the values of another feature to provide the vertical y coordinates. Patterns in the placement of dots reveal the underlying associations between the two features.

To answer our question about the relationship between `price` and `mileage`, we will examine a scatterplot. We'll use the `plot()` function along with the `main`, `xlab` and `ylab` parameters used previously to label the diagram.

To use plot (), we need to specify x and y vectors containing the values used to position the dots on the figure. Although the conclusions would be the same regardless of the variable used to supply the x and y coordinates, convention dictates that the y variable is the one that is presumed to depend on the other (and is therefore known as the dependent variable). Since a seller cannot modify the odometer reading, mileage is unlikely to be dependent on the car's price. Instead, our hypothesis is that the price depends on the odometer mileage. Therefore, we will use price as the y, or dependent, variable.

The full command to create our scatterplot is:

```
> plot(x = usedcars$mileage, y = usedcars$price,
         main = "Scatterplot of Price vs. Mileage",
         xlab = "Used Car Odometer (mi.)",
         ylab = "Used Car Price ($)")
```

This results in the following scatterplot:

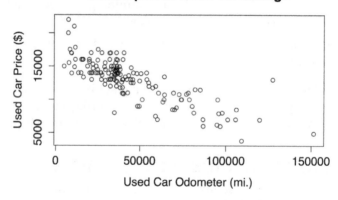

Using the scatterplot, we notice a clear relationship between the price of a used car and the odometer reading. To read the plot, examine how values of the y axis variable change as the values on the x axis increase. In this case, car prices tend to be lower as the mileage increases. If you have ever sold or shopped for a used car, this is not a profound insight.

Perhaps a more interesting finding is the fact that there are very few cars that have both high price and high mileage, aside from a lone outlier at about 125,000 miles and $14,000. The absence of more points like this provides evidence to support a conclusion that our data is unlikely to include any high mileage luxury cars. All of the most expensive cars in the data, particularly those above $17,500, seem to have extraordinarily low mileage, implying that we could be looking at a brand new type of car retailing for about $20,000.

The relationship we've found between car prices and mileage is known as a negative association, because it forms a pattern of dots in a line sloping downward. A positive association would appear to form a line sloping upward. A flat line, or a seemingly random scattering of dots, is evidence that the two variables are not associated at all. The strength of a linear association between two variables is measured by a statistic known as **correlation**. Correlations are discussed in detail in *Chapter 6, Forecasting Numeric Data – Regression Methods*, which covers the methods for modeling linear relationships.

Keep in mind that not all associations form straight lines. Sometimes the dots form a *U* shape, or a *V* shape; sometimes the pattern seems to be weaker or stronger for increasing values of the x or y variable. Such patterns imply that the relationship between the two variables is not linear.

Examining relationships – two-way cross-tabulations

To examine a relationship between two nominal variables, a **two-way cross-tabulation** is used (also known as a **crosstab** or **contingency table**). A cross-tabulation is similar to a scatterplot in that it allows you to examine how the values of one variable vary by the values of another. The format is a table in which the rows are the levels of one variable, while the columns are the levels of another. Counts in each of the table's cells indicate the number of values falling into the particular row and column combination.

To answer our earlier question about whether there is a relationship between car `model` and `color`, we will examine a crosstab. There are several functions to produce two-way tables in R, including `table()`, which we used for one-way tables. The `CrossTable()` option in the `gmodels` package by Gregory R. Warnes is perhaps the most user-friendly function, as it presents the row, column, and margin percentages in a single table, saving us the trouble of combining this data ourselves. To install the `gmodels` package, type:

```
> install.packages("gmodels")
```

After the package installs, type `library(gmodels)` to load the package. You will need to do this during each R session in which you plan on using the `CrossTable()` function.

Before proceeding with our analysis, let's simplify our project by reducing the number of levels in the `color` variable. This variable has nine levels, but we don't really need this much detail. What we are really interested in is whether or not the car's color is conservative. Toward this end, we'll divide the nine colors into two groups: the first group will include the conservative colors `Black`, `Gray`, `Silver`, and `White`; and the second group will include `Blue`, `Gold`, `Green`, `Red`, and `Yellow`. We will create a binary indicator variable (often called a **dummy variable**), indicating whether or not the car's color is conservative by our definition. Its value will be 1 if true, 0 otherwise:

```
> usedcars$conservative <-
        usedcars$color %in% c("Black", "Gray", "Silver", "White")
```

You may have noticed a new command here: the `%in%` operator returns `TRUE` or `FALSE` for each value in the vector on the left-hand side of the operator depending on whether the value is found in the vector on the right-hand side. In simple terms, you can translate this line as "Is the used car color in the set of `Black`, `Gray`, `Silver`, and `White`?"

Examining the `table()` output for our newly created variable, we see that about two-thirds of the cars have conservative colors, while one-third do not have conservative colors:

```
> table(usedcars$conservative)

FALSE   TRUE
   51     99
```

Now, let's look at a cross-tabulation to see how the proportion of conservatively colored cars varies by the model. Since we're assuming that the model of the car dictates the choice of color, we'll treat the conservative color indicator as the dependent (y) variable. The `CrossTable()` command is therefore:

```
> CrossTable(x = usedcars$model, y = usedcars$conservative)
```

The preceding command results in the following table:

```
     Cell Contents
|-----------------------|
|                     N |
|   Chi-square contribution |
|           N / Row Total |
|           N / Col Total |
|         N / Table Total |
|-----------------------|


Total Observations in Table:   150


               | usedcars$conservative
usedcars$model |     FALSE |      TRUE | Row Total |
---------------|-----------|-----------|-----------|
            SE |        27 |        51 |        78 |
               |     0.009 |     0.004 |           |
               |     0.346 |     0.654 |     0.520 |
               |     0.529 |     0.515 |           |
               |     0.180 |     0.340 |           |
---------------|-----------|-----------|-----------|
           SEL |         7 |        16 |        23 |
               |     0.086 |     0.044 |           |
               |     0.304 |     0.696 |     0.153 |
               |     0.137 |     0.162 |           |
               |     0.047 |     0.107 |           |
---------------|-----------|-----------|-----------|
           SES |        17 |        32 |        49 |
               |     0.007 |     0.004 |           |
               |     0.347 |     0.653 |     0.327 |
               |     0.333 |     0.323 |           |
               |     0.113 |     0.213 |           |
---------------|-----------|-----------|-----------|
  Column Total |        51 |        99 |       150 |
               |     0.340 |     0.660 |           |
---------------|-----------|-----------|-----------|
```

There is a wealth of data in the CrossTable() output. The legend at the top (labeled Cell Contents) indicates how to interpret each value. The rows in the table indicate the three models of used cars: SE, SEL, and SES (plus an additional row for the total across all models). The columns indicate whether or not the car's color is conservative (plus a column totaling across both types of color). The first value in each cell indicates the number of cars with that combination of model and color. The proportions indicate that the cell's proportion is relative to the chi-square statistic, row's total, column's total, and table's total.

What we are most interested in is the row proportion for conservative cars for each model. The row proportions tell us that 0.654 (65 percent) of SE cars are colored conservatively in comparison to 0.696 (70 percent) of SEL cars and 0.653 (65 percent) of SES. These differences are relatively small, suggesting that there are no substantial differences in the types of colors chosen by the model of the car.

The chi-square values refer to the cell's contribution in the **Pearson's Chi-squared test for independence** between two variables. This test measures how likely it is that the difference in the cell counts in the table is due to chance alone. If the probability is very low, it provides strong evidence that the two variables are associated.

You can obtain the chi-squared test results by adding an additional parameter specifying chisq = TRUE while calling the CrossTable() function. In this case, the probability is about 93 percent, suggesting that it is very likely that the variations in cell count are due to chance alone and not due to a true association between the model and the color.

Summary

In this chapter, we learned about the basics of managing data in R. We started by taking an in-depth look at the structures used for storing various types of data. The foundational R data structure is the vector, which is extended and combined into more complex data types such as lists and data frames. The data frame is an R data structure that corresponds to the notion of a dataset, having both features and examples. R provides functions for reading and writing data frames to spreadsheet-like tabular data files.

We then explored a real-world dataset containing data on used car prices. We examined numeric variables using common summary statistics of center and spread, and visualized relationships between prices and odometer readings with a scatterplot. We examined nominal variables using tables. In examining the used car data, we followed an exploratory process that can be used to understand any dataset. These skills will be required for the other projects throughout this book.

Now that we have spent some time understanding the basics of data management with R, you are ready to begin using machine learning to solve real-world problems. In the next chapter, we will tackle our first classification task using nearest neighbor methods.

Lazy Learning – Classification Using Nearest Neighbors

3

An interesting new type of dining experience has been appearing in cities around the world. Patrons are served in a completely darkened restaurant by waiters who move carefully around memorized routes using only their sense of touch and sound. The allure of these establishments is the belief that depriving oneself of visual sensory input will enhance the sense of taste and smell, and foods will be experienced in new ways. Each bite provides a sense of wonder while discovering the flavors the chef has prepared.

Can you imagine how a diner experiences the unseen food? Upon first bite, the senses are overwhelmed. What are the dominant flavors? Does the food taste savory or sweet? Does it taste similar to something eaten previously? Personally, I imagine this process of discovery in terms of a slightly modified adage: if it smells like a duck and tastes like a duck, then you are probably eating duck.

This illustrates an idea that can be used for machine learning—as does another maxim involving poultry: "birds of a feather flock together." Stated differently, things that are alike are likely to have properties that are alike. Machine learning uses this principle to classify data by placing it in the same category as similar or "nearest" neighbors. This chapter is devoted to the classifiers that use this approach. You will learn:

- The key concepts that define **nearest neighbor** classifiers, and why they are considered "lazy" learners

- Methods to measure the similarity of two examples using distance

- To apply a popular nearest neighbor classifier called k-NN

If all these talks about food is making you hungry, feel free to grab a snack. Our first task will be to understand the k-NN approach by putting it to use by settling a long-running culinary debate.

Understanding nearest neighbor classification

In a single sentence, **nearest neighbor** classifiers are defined by their characteristic of classifying unlabeled examples by assigning them the class of similar labeled examples. Despite the simplicity of this idea, nearest neighbor methods are extremely powerful. They have been used successfully for:

- Computer vision applications, including optical character recognition and facial recognition in both still images and video

- Predicting whether a person will enjoy a movie or music recommendation

- Identifying patterns in genetic data, perhaps to use them in detecting specific proteins or diseases

In general, nearest neighbor classifiers are well-suited for classification tasks, where relationships among the features and the target classes are numerous, complicated, or extremely difficult to understand, yet the items of similar class type tend to be fairly homogeneous. Another way of putting it would be to say that if a concept is difficult to define, but you know it when you see it, then nearest neighbors might be appropriate. On the other hand, if the data is noisy and thus no clear distinction exists among the groups, the nearest neighbor algorithms may struggle to identify the class boundaries.

The k-NN algorithm

The nearest neighbors approach to classification is exemplified by the **k-nearest neighbors algorithm (k-NN)**. Although this is perhaps one of the simplest machine learning algorithms, it is still used widely.

The strengths and weaknesses of this algorithm are as follows:

Strengths	Weaknesses
• Simple and effective • Makes no assumptions about the underlying data distribution • Fast training phase	• Does not produce a model, limiting the ability to understand how the features are related to the class • Requires selection of an appropriate k • Slow classification phase • Nominal features and missing data require additional processing

The k-NN algorithm gets its name from the fact that it uses information about an example's k-nearest neighbors to classify unlabeled examples. The letter k is a variable term implying that any number of nearest neighbors could be used. After choosing k, the algorithm requires a training dataset made up of examples that have been classified into several categories, as labeled by a nominal variable. Then, for each unlabeled record in the test dataset, k-NN identifies k records in the training data that are the "nearest" in similarity. The unlabeled test instance is assigned the class of the majority of the k nearest neighbors.

To illustrate this process, let's revisit the blind tasting experience described in the introduction. Suppose that prior to eating the mystery meal we had created a dataset in which we recorded our impressions of a number of ingredients we tasted previously. To keep things simple, we rated only two features of each ingredient. The first is a measure from 1 to 10 of how crunchy the ingredient is and the second is a 1 to 10 score of how sweet the ingredient tastes. We then labeled each ingredient as one of the three types of food: fruits, vegetables, or proteins. The first few rows of such a dataset might be structured as follows:

Ingredient	Sweetness	Crunchiness	Food type
apple	10	9	fruit
bacon	1	4	protein
banana	10	1	fruit
carrot	7	10	vegetable
celery	3	10	vegetable
cheese	1	1	protein

The k-NN algorithm treats the features as coordinates in a multidimensional feature space. As our dataset includes only two features, the feature space is two-dimensional. We can plot two-dimensional data on a scatter plot, with the x dimension indicating the ingredient's sweetness and the y dimension, the crunchiness. After adding a few more ingredients to the taste dataset, the scatter plot might look similar to this:

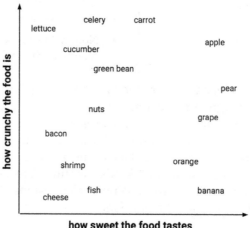

Did you notice the pattern? Similar types of food tend to be grouped closely together. As illustrated in the next diagram, vegetables tend to be crunchy but not sweet, fruits tend to be sweet and either crunchy or not crunchy, while proteins tend to be neither crunchy nor sweet:

Suppose that after constructing this dataset, we decide to use it to settle the age-old question: is tomato a fruit or vegetable? We can use the nearest neighbor approach to determine which class is a better fit, as shown in the following diagram:

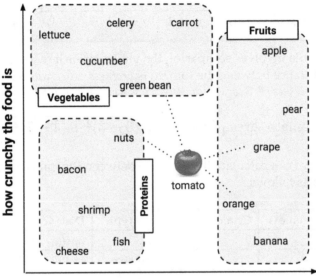

Measuring similarity with distance

Locating the tomato's nearest neighbors requires a **distance function**, or a formula that measures the similarity between the two instances.

There are many different ways to calculate distance. Traditionally, the k-NN algorithm uses **Euclidean distance**, which is the distance one would measure if it were possible to use a ruler to connect two points, illustrated in the previous figure by the dotted lines connecting the tomato to its neighbors.

 Euclidean distance is measured "as the crow flies," implying the shortest direct route. Another common distance measure is Manhattan distance, which is based on the paths a pedestrian would take by walking city blocks. If you are interested in learning more about other distance measures, you can read the documentation for R's distance function (a useful tool in its own right), using the `?dist` command.

Euclidean distance is specified by the following formula, where p and q are the examples to be compared, each having n features. The term p_1 refers to the value of the first feature of example p, while q_1 refers to the value of the first feature of example q:

$$dist(p, q) = \sqrt{(p_1 - q_1)^2 + (p_2 - q_2)^2 + \dots + (p_n - q_n)^2}$$

The distance formula involves comparing the values of each feature. For example, to calculate the distance between the tomato (*sweetness* = 6, *crunchiness* = 4), and the green bean (*sweetness* = 3, *crunchiness* = 7), we can use the formula as follows:

$$dist(\text{tomato, green bean}) = \sqrt{(6 - 3)^2 + (4 - 7)^2} = 4.2$$

In a similar vein, we can calculate the distance between the tomato and several of its closest neighbors as follows:

Ingredient	Sweetness	Crunchiness	Food type	Distance to the tomato
grape	8	5	fruit	sqrt((6 - 8)^2 + (4 - 5)^2) = 2.2
green bean	3	7	vegetable	sqrt((6 - 3)^2 + (4 - 7)^2) = 4.2
nuts	3	6	protein	sqrt((6 - 3)^2 + (4 - 6)^2) = 3.6
orange	7	3	fruit	sqrt((6 - 7)^2 + (4 - 3)^2) = 1.4

To classify the tomato as a vegetable, protein, or fruit, we'll begin by assigning the tomato, the food type of its single nearest neighbor. This is called 1-NN classification because $k = 1$. The orange is the nearest neighbor to the tomato, with a distance of 1.4. As orange is a fruit, the 1-NN algorithm would classify tomato as a fruit.

If we use the k-NN algorithm with $k = 3$ instead, it performs a vote among the three nearest neighbors: orange, grape, and nuts. Since the majority class among these neighbors is fruit (two of the three votes), the tomato again is classified as a fruit.

Choosing an appropriate k

The decision of how many neighbors to use for k-NN determines how well the model will generalize to future data. The balance between overfitting and underfitting the training data is a problem known as **bias-variance tradeoff**. Choosing a large k reduces the impact or variance caused by noisy data, but can bias the learner so that it runs the risk of ignoring small, but important patterns.

Suppose we took the extreme stance of setting a very large *k*, as large as the total number of observations in the training data. With every training instance represented in the final vote, the most common class always has a majority of the voters. The model would consequently always predict the majority class, regardless of the nearest neighbors.

On the opposite extreme, using a single nearest neighbor allows the noisy data or outliers to unduly influence the classification of examples. For example, suppose some of the training examples were accidentally mislabeled. Any unlabeled example that happens to be nearest to the incorrectly labeled neighbor will be predicted to have the incorrect class, even if nine other nearest neighbors would have voted differently.

Obviously, the best *k* value is somewhere between these two extremes.

The following figure illustrates, more generally, how the decision boundary (depicted by a dashed line) is affected by larger or smaller *k* values. Smaller values allow more complex decision boundaries that more carefully fit the training data. The problem is that we do not know whether the straight boundary or the curved boundary better represents the true underlying concept to be learned.

Larger k

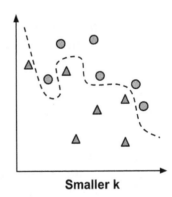
Smaller k

In practice, choosing *k* depends on the difficulty of the concept to be learned, and the number of records in the training data. One common practice is to begin with *k* equal to the square root of the number of training examples. In the food classifier we developed previously, we might set *k* = 4 because there were 15 example ingredients in the training data and the square root of 15 is 3.87.

However, such rules may not always result in the single best *k*. An alternative approach is to test several *k* values on a variety of test datasets and choose the one that delivers the best classification performance. That said, unless the data is very noisy, a large training dataset can make the choice of *k* less important. This is because even subtle concepts will have a sufficiently large pool of examples to vote as nearest neighbors.

A less common, but interesting solution to this problem is to choose a larger *k*, but apply a **weighted voting** process in which the vote of the closer neighbors is considered more authoritative than the vote of the far away neighbors. Many k-NN implementations offer this option.

Preparing data for use with k-NN

Features are typically transformed to a standard range prior to applying the k-NN algorithm. The rationale for this step is that the distance formula is highly dependent on how features are measured. In particular, if certain features have a much larger range of values than the others, the distance measurements will be strongly dominated by the features with larger ranges. This wasn't a problem for food tasting example as both sweetness and crunchiness were measured on a scale from 1 to 10.

However, suppose we added an additional feature to the dataset for a food's spiciness, which was measured using the Scoville scale. If you are not familiar with this metric, it is a standardized measure of spice heat, ranging from zero (not at all spicy) to over a million (for the hottest chili peppers). Since the difference between spicy and non-spicy foods can be over a million, while the difference between sweet and non-sweet or crunchy and non-crunchy foods is at most 10, the difference in scale allows the spice level to impact the distance function much more than the other two factors. Without adjusting our data, we might find that our distance measures only differentiate foods by their spiciness; the impact of crunchiness and sweetness would be dwarfed by the contribution of spiciness.

The solution is to rescale the features by shrinking or expanding their range such that each one contributes relatively equally to the distance formula. For example, if sweetness and crunchiness are both measured on a scale from 1 to 10, we would also like spiciness to be measured on a scale from 1 to 10. There are several common ways to accomplish such scaling.

The traditional method of rescaling features for k-NN is **min-max normalization**. This process transforms a feature such that all of its values fall in a range between 0 and 1. The formula for normalizing a feature is as follows:

$$X_{new} = \frac{X - \min(X)}{\max(X) - \min(X)}$$

Essentially, the formula subtracts the minimum of feature X from each value and divides by the range of X.

Normalized feature values can be interpreted as indicating how far, from 0 percent to 100 percent, the original value fell along the range between the original minimum and maximum.

Another common transformation is called **z-score standardization**. The following formula subtracts the mean value of feature X, and divides the outcome by the standard deviation of X:

$$X_{new} = \frac{X - \mu}{\sigma} = \frac{X - \text{Mean}(X)}{\text{StdDev}(X)}$$

This formula, which is based on the properties of the normal distribution covered in *Chapter 2, Managing and Understanding Data*, rescales each of the feature's values in terms of how many standard deviations they fall above or below the mean value. The resulting value is called a **z-score**. The z-scores fall in an unbound range of negative and positive numbers. Unlike the normalized values, they have no predefined minimum and maximum.

The same rescaling method used on the k-NN training dataset must also be applied to the examples the algorithm will later classify. This can lead to a tricky situation for min-max normalization, as the minimum or maximum of future cases might be outside the range of values observed in the training data. If you know the plausible minimum or maximum value ahead of time, you can use these constants rather than the observed values. Alternatively, you can use z-score standardization under the assumption that the future examples will have similar mean and standard deviation as the training examples.

The Euclidean distance formula is not defined for nominal data. Therefore, to calculate the distance between nominal features, we need to convert them into a numeric format. A typical solution utilizes **dummy coding**, where a value of *1* indicates one category, and *0*, the other. For instance, dummy coding for a gender variable could be constructed as:

$$\text{male} = \begin{cases} 1 & \text{if } x = \text{male} \\ 0 & \text{otherwise} \end{cases}$$

Notice how the dummy coding of the two-category (binary) gender variable results in a single new feature named male. There is no need to construct a separate feature for female; since the two sexes are mutually exclusive, knowing one or the other is enough.

This is true more generally as well. An *n*-category nominal feature can be dummy coded by creating the binary indicator variables for (*n* - 1) levels of the feature. For example, the dummy coding for a three-category temperature variable (for example, hot, medium, or cold) could be set up as *(3 - 1) = 2* features, as shown here:

$$hot = \begin{cases} 1 & \text{if } x = \text{hot} \\ 0 & \text{otherwise} \end{cases}$$

$$medium = \begin{cases} 1 & \text{if } x = \text{medium} \\ 0 & \text{otherwise} \end{cases}$$

Knowing that hot and medium are both *0* is enough to know that the temperature is cold. We, therefore, do not need a third feature for the cold category.

A convenient aspect of dummy coding is that the distance between dummy coded features is always one or zero, and thus, the values fall on the same scale as min-max normalized numeric data. No additional transformation is necessary.

If a nominal feature is ordinal (one could make such an argument for temperature), an alternative to dummy coding is to number the categories and apply normalization. For instance, cold, warm, and hot could be numbered as 1, 2, and 3, which normalizes to 0, 0.5, and 1. A caveat to this approach is that it should only be used if the steps between the categories are equivalent. For instance, although income categories for poor, middle class, and wealthy are ordered, the difference between the poor and middle class may be different than the difference between the middle class and wealthy. Since the steps between groups are not equal, dummy coding is a safer approach.

Why is the k-NN algorithm lazy?

Classification algorithms based on the nearest neighbor methods are considered **lazy learning** algorithms because, technically speaking, no abstraction occurs. The abstraction and generalization processes are skipped altogether, and this undermines the definition of learning, proposed in *Chapter 1, Introducing Machine Learning*.

Under the strict definition of learning, a lazy learner is not really learning anything. Instead, it merely stores the training data verbatim. This allows the training phase, which is not actually training anything, to occur very rapidly. Of course, the downside is that the process of making predictions tends to be relatively slow in comparison to training. Due to the heavy reliance on the training instances rather than an abstracted model, lazy learning is also known as **instance-based learning** or **rote learning**.

As instance-based learners do not build a model, the method is said to be in a class of **non-parametric** learning methods — no parameters are learned about the data. Without generating theories about the underlying data, non-parametric methods limit our ability to understand how the classifier is using the data. On the other hand, this allows the learner to find natural patterns rather than trying to fit the data into a preconceived and potentially biased functional form.

Although k-NN classifiers may be considered lazy, they are still quite powerful. As you will soon see, the simple principles of nearest neighbor learning can be used to automate the process of screening for cancer.

Example – diagnosing breast cancer with the k-NN algorithm

Routine breast cancer screening allows the disease to be diagnosed and treated prior to it causing noticeable symptoms. The process of early detection involves examining the breast tissue for abnormal lumps or masses. If a lump is found, a fine-needle aspiration biopsy is performed, which uses a hollow needle to extract a small sample of cells from the mass. A clinician then examines the cells under a microscope to determine whether the mass is likely to be malignant or benign.

If machine learning could automate the identification of cancerous cells, it would provide considerable benefit to the health system. Automated processes are likely to improve the efficiency of the detection process, allowing physicians to spend less time diagnosing and more time treating the disease. An automated screening system might also provide greater detection accuracy by removing the inherently subjective human component from the process.

We will investigate the utility of machine learning for detecting cancer by applying the k-NN algorithm to measurements of biopsied cells from women with abnormal breast masses.

Step 1 – collecting data

We will utilize the Wisconsin Breast Cancer Diagnostic dataset from the UCI Machine Learning Repository at `http://archive.ics.uci.edu/ml`. This data was donated by researchers of the University of Wisconsin and includes the measurements from digitized images of fine-needle aspirate of a breast mass. The values represent the characteristics of the cell nuclei present in the digital image.

 To read more about this dataset, refer to: Mangasarian OL, Street WN, Wolberg WH. Breast cancer diagnosis and prognosis via linear programming. *Operations Research*. 1995; 43:570-577.

The breast cancer data includes 569 examples of cancer biopsies, each with 32 features. One feature is an identification number, another is the cancer diagnosis, and 30 are numeric-valued laboratory measurements. The diagnosis is coded as "M" to indicate malignant or "B" to indicate benign.

The other 30 numeric measurements comprise the mean, standard error, and worst (that is, largest) value for 10 different characteristics of the digitized cell nuclei. These include:

- Radius
- Texture
- Perimeter
- Area
- Smoothness
- Compactness
- Concavity
- Concave points
- Symmetry
- Fractal dimension

Based on these names, all the features seem to relate to the shape and size of the cell nuclei. Unless you are an oncologist, you are unlikely to know how each relates to benign or malignant masses. These patterns will be revealed as we continue in the machine learning process.

Step 2 – exploring and preparing the data

Let's explore the data and see whether we can shine some light on the relationships. In doing so, we will prepare the data for use with the k-NN learning method.

> If you plan on following along, download the `wisc_bc_data.csv` file from the Packt website and save it to your R working directory. The dataset was modified very slightly from its original form for this book. In particular, a header line was added and the rows of data were randomly ordered.

We'll begin by importing the CSV data file, as we have done in previous chapters, saving the Wisconsin breast cancer data to the `wbcd` data frame:

```
> wbcd <- read.csv("wisc_bc_data.csv", stringsAsFactors = FALSE)
```

Using the `str(wbcd)` command, we can confirm that the data is structured with 569 examples and 32 features as we expected. The first several lines of output are as follows:

```
'data.frame':   569 obs. of  32 variables:
 $ id              : int  87139402 8910251 905520 ...
 $ diagnosis       : chr  "B" "B" "B" "B" ...
 $ radius_mean     : num  12.3 10.6 11 11.3 15.2 ...
 $ texture_mean    : num  12.4 18.9 16.8 13.4 13.2 ...
 $ perimeter_mean  : num  78.8 69.3 70.9 73 97.7 ...
 $ area_mean       : num  464 346 373 385 712 ...
```

The first variable is an integer variable named `id`. As this is simply a unique identifier (ID) for each patient in the data, it does not provide useful information, and we will need to exclude it from the model.

> Regardless of the machine learning method, ID variables should always be excluded. Neglecting to do so can lead to erroneous findings because the ID can be used to uniquely "predict" each example. Therefore, a model that includes an identifier will suffer from overfitting, and is unlikely to generalize well to other data.

Let's drop the `id` feature altogether. As it is located in the first column, we can exclude it by making a copy of the `wbcd` data frame without column 1:

```
> wbcd <- wbcd[-1]
```

The next variable, `diagnosis`, is of particular interest as it is the outcome we hope to predict. This feature indicates whether the example is from a benign or malignant mass. The `table()` output indicates that 357 masses are benign while 212 are malignant:

```
> table(wbcd$diagnosis)

  B   M
357 212
```

Many R machine learning classifiers require that the target feature is coded as a factor, so we will need to recode the `diagnosis` variable. We will also take this opportunity to give the `"B"` and `"M"` values more informative labels using the `labels` parameter:

```
> wbcd$diagnosis<- factor(wbcd$diagnosis, levels = c("B", "M"),
      labels = c("Benign", "Malignant"))
```

Now, when we look at the `prop.table()` output, we notice that the values have been labeled `Benign` and `Malignant` with 62.7 percent and 37.3 percent of the masses, respectively:

```
> round(prop.table(table(wbcd$diagnosis)) * 100, digits = 1)

   Benign Malignant
     62.7      37.3
```

The remaining 30 features are all numeric, and as expected, they consist of three different measurements of ten characteristics. For illustrative purposes, we will only take a closer look at three of these features:

```
> summary(wbcd[c("radius_mean", "area_mean", "smoothness_mean")])
  radius_mean        area_mean      smoothness_mean
 Min.   : 6.981   Min.   : 143.5   Min.   :0.05263
 1st Qu.:11.700   1st Qu.: 420.3   1st Qu.:0.08637
 Median :13.370   Median : 551.1   Median :0.09587
 Mean   :14.127   Mean   : 654.9   Mean   :0.09636
 3rd Qu.:15.780   3rd Qu.: 782.7   3rd Qu.:0.10530
 Max.   :28.110   Max.   :2501.0   Max.   :0.16340
```

Looking at the features side-by-side, do you notice anything problematic about the values? Recall that the distance calculation for k-NN is heavily dependent upon the measurement scale of the input features. Since smoothness ranges from 0.05 to 0.16 and area ranges from 143.5 to 2501.0, the impact of area is going to be much larger than the smoothness in the distance calculation. This could potentially cause problems for our classifier, so let's apply normalization to rescale the features to a standard range of values.

Transformation – normalizing numeric data

To normalize these features, we need to create a normalize() function in R. This function takes a vector x of numeric values, and for each value in x, subtracts the minimum value in x and divides by the range of values in x. Finally, the resulting vector is returned. The code for this function is as follows:

```
> normalize <- function(x) {
        return ((x - min(x)) / (max(x) - min(x)))
}
```

After executing the preceding code, the normalize() function is available for use in R. Let's test the function on a couple of vectors:

```
> normalize(c(1, 2, 3, 4, 5))
[1] 0.00 0.25 0.50 0.75 1.00
> normalize(c(10, 20, 30, 40, 50))
[1] 0.00 0.25 0.50 0.75 1.00
```

The function appears to be working correctly. Despite the fact that the values in the second vector are 10 times larger than the first vector, after normalization, they both appear exactly the same.

We can now apply the normalize() function to the numeric features in our data frame. Rather than normalizing each of the 30 numeric variables individually, we will use one of R's functions to automate the process.

The lapply() function takes a list and applies a specified function to each list element. As a data frame is a list of equal-length vectors, we can use lapply() to apply normalize() to each feature in the data frame. The final step is to convert the list returned by lapply() to a data frame, using the as.data.frame() function. The full process looks like this:

```
> wbcd_n <- as.data.frame(lapply(wbcd[2:31], normalize))
```

In plain English, this command applies the `normalize()` function to columns 2 through 31 in the `wbcd` data frame, converts the resulting list to a data frame, and assigns it the name `wbcd_n`. The `_n` suffix is used here as a reminder that the values in `wbcd` have been normalized.

To confirm that the transformation was applied correctly, let's look at one variable's summary statistics:

```
> summary(wbcd_n$area_mean)
Min. 1st Qu.Median    Mean 3rd Qu.    Max.
0.0000  0.1174  0.1729  0.2169  0.2711  1.0000
```

As expected, the `area_mean` variable, which originally ranged from 143.5 to 2501.0, now ranges from 0 to 1.

Data preparation – creating training and test datasets

Although all the 569 biopsies are labeled with a benign or malignant status, it is not very interesting to predict what we already know. Additionally, any performance measures we obtain during the training may be misleading as we do not know the extent to which cases have been overfitted or how well the learner will generalize to unseen cases. A more interesting question is how well our learner performs on a dataset of unlabeled data. If we had access to a laboratory, we could apply our learner to the measurements taken from the next 100 masses of unknown cancer status, and see how well the machine learner's predictions compare to the diagnoses obtained using conventional methods.

In the absence of such data, we can simulate this scenario by dividing our data into two portions: a training dataset that will be used to build the k-NN model and a test dataset that will be used to estimate the predictive accuracy of the model. We will use the first 469 records for the training dataset and the remaining 100 to simulate new patients.

Using the data extraction methods given in *Chapter 2, Managing and Understanding Data*, we will split the `wbcd_n` data frame into `wbcd_train` and `wbcd_test`:

```
> wbcd_train <- wbcd_n[1:469, ]
> wbcd_test <- wbcd_n[470:569, ]
```

If the preceding commands are confusing, remember that data is extracted from data frames using the [row, column] syntax. A blank value for the row or column value indicates that all the rows or columns should be included. Hence, the first line of code takes rows 1 to 469 and all columns, and the second line takes 100 rows from 470 to 569 and all columns.

> When constructing training and test datasets, it is important that each dataset is a representative subset of the full set of data. The wbcd records were already randomly ordered, so we could simply extract 100 consecutive records to create a test dataset. This would not be appropriate if the data was ordered chronologically or in groups of similar values. In these cases, random sampling methods would be needed. Random sampling will be discussed in *Chapter 5, Divide and Conquer – Classification Using Decision Trees and Rules*.

When we constructed our normalized training and test datasets, we excluded the target variable, diagnosis. For training the k-NN model, we will need to store these class labels in factor vectors, split between the training and test datasets:

```
> wbcd_train_labels <- wbcd[1:469, 1]
> wbcd_test_labels <- wbcd[470:569, 1]
```

This code takes the diagnosis factor in the first column of the wbcd data frame, and creates the vectors wbcd_train_labels and wbcd_test_labels. We will use these in the next steps of training and evaluating our classifier.

Step 3 – training a model on the data

Equipped with our training data and labels vector, we are now ready to classify our unknown records. For the k-NN algorithm, the training phase actually involves no model building; the process of training a lazy learner like k-NN simply involves storing the input data in a structured format.

To classify our test instances, we will use a k-NN implementation from the class package, which provides a set of basic R functions for classification. If this package is not already installed on your system, you can install it by typing:

```
> install.packages("class")
```

To load the package during any session in which you wish to use the functions, simply enter the library(class) command.

The knn() function in the class package provides a standard, classic implementation of the k-NN algorithm. For each instance in the test data, the function will identify the k-Nearest Neighbors, using Euclidean distance, where *k* is a user-specified number. The test instance is classified by taking a "vote" among the k-Nearest Neighbors—specifically, this involves assigning the class of the majority of the *k* neighbors. A tie vote is broken at random.

> There are several other k-NN functions in other R packages, which provide more sophisticated or more efficient implementations. If you run into limits with knn(), search for k-NN at the **Comprehensive R Archive Network (CRAN)**.

Training and classification using the knn() function is performed in a single function call, using four parameters, as shown in the following table:

kNN classification syntax
using the knn() function in the class package
Building the classifier and making predictions: `p <- knn(train, test, class, k)` •   **train** is a data frame containing numeric training data •   **test** is a data frame containing numeric test data •   **class** is a factor vector with the class for each row in the training data •   **k** is an integer indicating the number of nearest neighbors The function returns a factor vector of predicted classes for each row in the test data frame.

Example:
 	
`wbcd_pred <- knn(train = wbcd_train, test = wbcd_test,`
`                 cl = wbcd_train_labels, k = 3)`

We now have nearly everything that we need to apply the k-NN algorithm to this data. We've split our data into training and test datasets, each with exactly the same numeric features. The labels for the training data are stored in a separate factor vector. The only remaining parameter is k, which specifies the number of neighbors to include in the vote.

As our training data includes 469 instances, we might try k = 21, an odd number roughly equal to the square root of 469. With a two-category outcome, using an odd number eliminates the chance of ending with a tie vote.

Now we can use the `knn()` function to classify the `test` data:

```
> wbcd_test_pred <- knn(train = wbcd_train, test = wbcd_test,
                        cl = wbcd_train_labels, k = 21)
```

The `knn()` function returns a factor vector of predicted labels for each of the examples in the `test` dataset, which we have assigned to `wbcd_test_pred`.

Step 4 – evaluating model performance

The next step of the process is to evaluate how well the predicted classes in the `wbcd_test_pred` vector match up with the known values in the `wbcd_test_labels` vector. To do this, we can use the `CrossTable()` function in the `gmodels` package, which was introduced in *Chapter 2, Managing and Understanding Data*. If you haven't done so already, please install this package, using the `install.packages("gmodels")` command.

After loading the package with the `library(gmodels)` command, we can create a cross tabulation indicating the agreement between the two vectors. Specifying `prop.chisq = FALSE` will remove the unnecessary chi-square values from the output:

```
> CrossTable(x = wbcd_test_labels, y = wbcd_test_pred,
             prop.chisq=FALSE)
```

The resulting table looks like this:

```
                 | wbcd_test_pred
wbcd_test_labels |    Benign | Malignant | Row Total |
-----------------|-----------|-----------|-----------|
          Benign |        61 |         0 |        61 |
                 |     1.000 |     0.000 |     0.610 |
                 |     0.968 |     0.000 |           |
                 |     0.610 |     0.000 |           |
-----------------|-----------|-----------|-----------|
       Malignant |         2 |        37 |        39 |
                 |     0.051 |     0.949 |     0.390 |
                 |     0.032 |     1.000 |           |
                 |     0.020 |     0.370 |           |
-----------------|-----------|-----------|-----------|
    Column Total |        63 |        37 |       100 |
                 |     0.630 |     0.370 |           |
-----------------|-----------|-----------|-----------|
```

The cell percentages in the table indicate the proportion of values that fall into four categories. The top-left cell indicates the **true negative** results. These 61 of 100 values are cases where the mass was benign and the k-NN algorithm correctly identified it as such. The bottom-right cell indicates the **true positive** results, where the classifier and the clinically determined label agree that the mass is malignant. A total of 37 of 100 predictions were true positives.

The cells falling on the other diagonal contain counts of examples where the k-NN approach disagreed with the true label. The two examples in the lower-left cell are **false negative** results; in this case, the predicted value was benign, but the tumor was actually malignant. Errors in this direction could be extremely costly as they might lead a patient to believe that she is cancer-free, but in reality, the disease may continue to spread. The top-right cell would contain the **false positive** results, if there were any. These values occur when the model classifies a mass as malignant, but in reality, it was benign. Although such errors are less dangerous than a false negative result, they should also be avoided as they could lead to additional financial burden on the health care system or additional stress for the patient as additional tests or treatment may have to be provided.

If we desired, we could totally eliminate false negatives by classifying every mass as malignant. Obviously, this is not a realistic strategy. Still, it illustrates the fact that prediction involves striking a balance between the false positive rate and the false negative rate. In *Chapter 10, Evaluating Model Performance*, you will learn more sophisticated methods for measuring predictive accuracy that can be used to identify places where the error rate can be optimized depending on the costs of each type of error.

A total of 2 out of 100, or 2 percent of masses were incorrectly classified by the k-NN approach. While 98 percent accuracy seems impressive for a few lines of R code, we might try another iteration of the model to see whether we can improve the performance and reduce the number of values that have been incorrectly classified, particularly because the errors were dangerous false negatives.

Step 5 – improving model performance

We will attempt two simple variations on our previous classifier. First, we will employ an alternative method for rescaling our numeric features. Second, we will try several different values for *k*.

Transformation – z-score standardization

Although normalization is traditionally used for k-NN classification, it may not always be the most appropriate way to rescale features. Since the z-score standardized values have no predefined minimum and maximum, extreme values are not compressed towards the center. One might suspect that with a malignant tumor, we might see some very extreme outliers as the tumors grow uncontrollably. It might, therefore, be reasonable to allow the outliers to be weighted more heavily in the distance calculation. Let's see whether z-score standardization can improve our predictive accuracy.

To standardize a vector, we can use the R's built-in `scale()` function, which, by default, rescales values using the z-score standardization. The `scale()` function offers the additional benefit that it can be applied directly to a data frame, so we can avoid the use of the `lapply()` function. To create a z-score standardized version of the wbcd data, we can use the following command:

```
> wbcd_z <- as.data.frame(scale(wbcd[-1]))
```

This command rescales all the features, with the exception of `diagnosis` and stores the result as the `wbcd_z` data frame. The `_z` suffix is a reminder that the values were z-score transformed.

To confirm that the transformation was applied correctly, we can look at the summary statistics:

```
> summary(wbcd_z$area_mean)
   Min. 1st Qu.  Median    Mean 3rd Qu.    Max.
-1.4530 -0.6666 -0.2949  0.0000  0.3632  5.2460
```

The mean of a z-score standardized variable should always be zero, and the range should be fairly compact. A z-score greater than 3 or less than -3 indicates an extremely rare value. With this in mind, the transformation seems to have worked.

As we had done earlier, we need to divide the data into training and test sets, and then classify the test instances using the `knn()` function. We'll then compare the predicted labels to the actual labels using `CrossTable()`:

```
> wbcd_train <- wbcd_z[1:469, ]
> wbcd_test <- wbcd_z[470:569, ]
> wbcd_train_labels <- wbcd[1:469, 1]
> wbcd_test_labels <- wbcd[470:569, 1]
```

```
> wbcd_test_pred <- knn(train = wbcd_train, test = wbcd_test,
                    cl = wbcd_train_labels, k = 21)
> CrossTable(x = wbcd_test_labels, y = wbcd_test_pred,
                    prop.chisq = FALSE)
```

Unfortunately, in the following table, the results of our new transformation show a slight decline in accuracy. The instances where we had correctly classified 98 percent of examples previously, we classified only 95 percent correctly this time. Making matters worse, we did no better at classifying the dangerous false negatives:

```
                 | wbcd_test_pred
wbcd_test_labels |    Benign | Malignant | Row Total |
-----------------|-----------|-----------|-----------|
          Benign |        61 |         0 |        61 |
                 |     1.000 |     0.000 |     0.610 |
                 |     0.924 |     0.000 |           |
                 |     0.610 |     0.000 |           |
-----------------|-----------|-----------|-----------|
       Malignant |         5 |        34 |        39 |
                 |     0.128 |     0.872 |     0.390 |
                 |     0.076 |     1.000 |           |
                 |     0.050 |     0.340 |           |
-----------------|-----------|-----------|-----------|
    Column Total |        66 |        34 |       100 |
                 |     0.660 |     0.340 |           |
-----------------|-----------|-----------|-----------|
```

Testing alternative values of k

We may be able do even better by examining performance across various *k* values. Using the normalized training and test datasets, the same 100 records were classified using several different *k* values. The number of false negatives and false positives are shown for each iteration:

k value	False negatives	False positives	Percent classified incorrectly
1	1	3	4 percent
5	2	0	2 percent
11	3	0	3 percent
15	3	0	3 percent
21	2	0	2 percent
27	4	0	4 percent

Although the classifier was never perfect, the 1-NN approach was able to avoid some of the false negatives at the expense of adding false positives. It is important to keep in mind, however, that it would be unwise to tailor our approach too closely to our test data; after all, a different set of 100 patient records is likely to be somewhat different from those used to measure our performance.

 If you need to be certain that a learner will generalize to future data, you might create several sets of 100 patients at random and repeatedly retest the result. The methods to carefully evaluate the performance of machine learning models will be discussed further in *Chapter 10, Evaluating Model Performance*.

Summary

In this chapter, we learned about classification using k-NN. Unlike many classification algorithms, k-NN does not do any learning. It simply stores the training data verbatim. Unlabeled test examples are then matched to the most similar records in the training set using a distance function, and the unlabeled example is assigned the label of its neighbors.

In spite of the fact that k-NN is a very simple algorithm, it is capable of tackling extremely complex tasks, such as the identification of cancerous masses. In a few simple lines of R code, we were able to correctly identify whether a mass was malignant or benign 98 percent of the time.

In the next chapter, we will examine a classification method that uses probability to estimate the likelihood that an observation falls into certain categories. It will be interesting to compare how this approach differs from k-NN. Later on, in *Chapter 9, Finding Groups of Data – Clustering with k-means*, we will learn about a close relative to k-NN, which uses distance measures for a completely different learning task.

4
Probabilistic Learning – Classification Using Naive Bayes

When a meteorologist provides a weather forecast, precipitation is typically described with terms such as "70 percent chance of rain." Such forecasts are known as probability of precipitation reports. Have you ever considered how they are calculated? It is a puzzling question, because in reality, either it will rain or not.

Weather estimates are based on probabilistic methods or those concerned with describing uncertainty. They use data on past events to extrapolate future events. In the case of weather, the chance of rain describes the proportion of prior days to similar measurable atmospheric conditions in which precipitation occurred. A 70 percent chance of rain implies that in 7 out of the 10 past cases with similar conditions, precipitation occurred somewhere in the area.

This chapter covers the Naive Bayes algorithm, which uses probabilities in much the same way as a weather forecast. While studying this method, you will learn:

- Basic principles of probability
- The specialized methods and data structures needed to analyze text data with R
- How to employ Naive Bayes to build an SMS junk message filter

If you've taken a statistics class before, some of the material in this chapter may be a review. Even so, it may be helpful to refresh your knowledge on probability, as these principles are the basis of how Naive Bayes got such a strange name.

Understanding Naive Bayes

The basic statistical ideas necessary to understand the Naive Bayes algorithm have existed for centuries. The technique descended from the work of the 18th century mathematician Thomas Bayes, who developed foundational principles to describe the probability of events, and how probabilities should be revised in the light of additional information. These principles formed the foundation for what are now known as **Bayesian methods**.

We will cover these methods in greater detail later on. But, for now, it suffices to say that a probability is a number between 0 and 1 (that is, between 0 percent and 100 percent), which captures the chance that an event will occur in the light of the available evidence. The lower the probability, the less likely the event is to occur. A probability of 0 indicates that the event will definitely not occur, while a probability of 1 indicates that the event will occur with 100 percent certainty.

Classifiers based on Bayesian methods utilize training data to calculate an observed probability of each outcome based on the evidence provided by feature values. When the classifier is later applied to unlabeled data, it uses the observed probabilities to predict the most likely class for the new features. It's a simple idea, but it results in a method that often has results on par with more sophisticated algorithms. In fact, Bayesian classifiers have been used for:

- Text classification, such as junk e-mail (spam) filtering
- Intrusion or anomaly detection in computer networks
- Diagnosing medical conditions given a set of observed symptoms

Typically, Bayesian classifiers are best applied to problems in which the information from numerous attributes should be considered simultaneously in order to estimate the overall probability of an outcome. While many machine learning algorithms ignore features that have weak effects, Bayesian methods utilize all the available evidence to subtly change the predictions. If large number of features have relatively minor effects, taken together, their combined impact could be quite large.

Basic concepts of Bayesian methods

Before jumping into the Naive Bayes algorithm, it's worth spending some time defining the concepts that are used across Bayesian methods. Summarized in a single sentence, Bayesian probability theory is rooted in the idea that the estimated likelihood of an **event**, or a potential outcome, should be based on the evidence at hand across multiple **trials**, or opportunities for the event to occur.

The following table illustrates events and trials for several real-world outcomes:

Event	Trial
Heads result	Coin flip
Rainy weather	A single day
Message is spam	Incoming e-mail message
Candidate becomes president	Presidential election
Win the lottery	Lottery ticket

Bayesian methods provide insights into how the probability of these events can be estimated from the observed data. To see how, we'll need to formalize our understanding of probability.

Understanding probability

The probability of an event is estimated from the observed data by dividing the number of trials in which the event occurred by the total number of trials. For instance, if it rained 3 out of 10 days with similar conditions as today, the probability of rain today can be estimated as $3 / 10 = 0.30$ or 30 percent. Similarly, if 10 out of 50 prior email messages were spam, then the probability of any incoming message being spam can be estimated as $10 / 50 = 0.20$ or 20 percent.

To denote these probabilities, we use notation in the form $P(A)$, which signifies the probability of event A. For example, $P(rain) = 0.30$ and $P(spam) = 0.20$.

The probability of all the possible outcomes of a trial must always sum to 1, because a trial always results in some outcome happening. Thus, if the trial has two outcomes that cannot occur simultaneously, such as rainy versus sunny or spam versus ham (nonspam), then knowing the probability of either outcome reveals the probability of the other. For example, given the value $P(spam) = 0.20$, we can calculate $P(ham)$ $= 1 - 0.20 = 0.80$. This concludes that spam and ham are **mutually exclusive and exhaustive** events, which implies that they cannot occur at the same time and are the only possible outcomes.

Because an event cannot simultaneously happen and not happen, an event is always mutually exclusive and exhaustive with its **complement**, or the event comprising of the outcomes in which the event of interest does not happen. The complement of event A is typically denoted A^c or A'. Additionally, the shorthand notation $P(\neg A)$ can used to denote the probability of event A not occurring, as in $P(\neg spam) = 0.80$. This notation is equivalent to $P(A^c)$.

To illustrate events and their complements, it is often helpful to imagine a two-dimensional space that is partitioned into probabilities for each event. In the following diagram, the rectangle represents the possible outcomes for an e-mail message. The circle represents the 20 percent probability that the message is spam. The remaining 80 percent represents the complement $P(\neg spam)$ or the messages that are not spam:

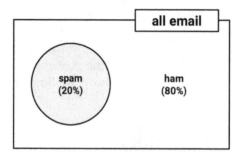

Understanding joint probability

Often, we are interested in monitoring several nonmutually exclusive events for the same trial. If certain events occur with the event of interest, we may be able to use them to make predictions. Consider, for instance, a second event based on the outcome that an e-mail message contains the word Viagra. In most cases, this word is likely to appear only in a spam message; its presence in an incoming e-mail is therefore a very strong piece of evidence that the message is spam. The preceding diagram, updated for this second event, might appear as shown in the following diagram:

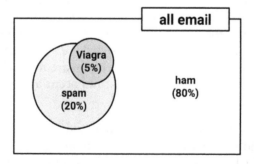

Notice in the diagram that the Viagra circle does not completely fill the spam circle, nor is it completely contained by the spam circle. This implies that not all spam messages contain the word Viagra and not every e-mail with the word Viagra is spam.

To zoom in for a closer look at the overlap between the spam and Viagra circles, we'll employ a visualization known as a **Venn diagram**. First used in the late 19th century by John Venn, the diagram uses circles to illustrate the overlap between sets of items. In most Venn diagrams, the size of the circles and the degree of the overlap is not meaningful. Instead, it is used as a reminder to allocate probability to all possible combinations of events:

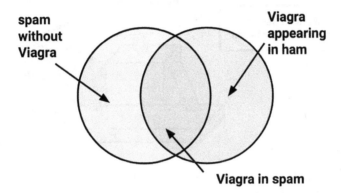

We know that 20 percent of all messages were spam (the left circle) and 5 percent of all messages contained the word Viagra (the right circle). We would like to quantify the degree of overlap between these two proportions. In other words, we hope to estimate the probability that both *P(spam)* and *P(Viagra)* occur, which can be written as *P(spam ∩ Viagra)*. The upside down 'U' symbol signifies the **intersection** of the two events; the notation $A \cap B$ refers to the event in which both A and B occur.

Calculating *P(spam ∩ Viagra)* depends on the **joint probability** of the two events or how the probability of one event is related to the probability of the other. If the two events are totally unrelated, they are called **independent events**. This is not to say that independent events cannot occur at the same time; event independence simply implies that knowing the outcome of one event does not provide any information about the outcome of the other. For instance, the outcome of a heads result on a coin flip is independent from whether the weather is rainy or sunny on any given day.

If all events were independent, it would be impossible to predict one event by observing another. In other words, **dependent events** are the basis of predictive modeling. Just as the presence of clouds is predictive of a rainy day, the appearance of the word Viagra is predictive of a spam e-mail.

Calculating the probability of dependent events is a bit more complex than for independent events. If *P(spam)* and *P(Viagra)* were independent, we could easily calculate *P(spam ∩ Viagra)*, the probability of both events happening at the same time. Because 20 percent of all the messages are spam, and 5 percent of all the e-mails contain the word Viagra, we could assume that 1 percent of all messages are spam with the term Viagra. This is because *0.05 * 0.20 = 0.01*. More generally, for independent events *A* and *B*, the probability of both happening can be expressed as *P(A ∩ B) = P(A) * P(B)*.

This said, we know that *P(spam)* and *P(Viagra)* are likely to be highly dependent, which means that this calculation is incorrect. To obtain a reasonable estimate, we need to use a more careful formulation of the relationship between these two events, which is based on advanced Bayesian methods.

Computing conditional probability with Bayes' theorem

The relationships between dependent events can be described using **Bayes' theorem**, as shown in the following formula. This formulation provides a way of thinking about how to revise an estimate of the probability of one event in light of the evidence provided by another event:

$$P(A|B) = \frac{P(A \cap B)}{P(B)}$$

The notation $P(A \mid B)$ is read as the probability of event A, given that event B occurred. This is known as **conditional probability**, since the probability of A is dependent (that is, conditional) on what happened with event B. Bayes' theorem tells us that our estimate of $P(A \mid B)$ should be based on $P(A \cap B)$, a measure of how often A and B are observed to occur together, and $P(B)$, a measure of how often B is observed to occur in general.

Bayes' theorem states that the best estimate of $P(A \mid B)$ is the proportion of trials in which A occurred with B out of all the trials in which B occurred. In plain language, this tells us that if we know event B occurred, the probability of event A is higher the more often that A and B occur together each time B is observed. In a way, this adjusts $P(A \cap B)$ for the probability of B occurring; if B is extremely rare, $P(B)$ and $P(A \cap B)$ will always be small; however, if A and B almost always happen together, $P(A \mid B)$ will be high regardless of the probability of B.

By definition, $P(A \cap B) = P(A \mid B) * P(B)$, a fact that can be easily derived by applying a bit of algebra to the previous formula. Rearranging this formula once more with the knowledge that $P(A \cap B) = P(B \cap A)$ results in the conclusion that $P(A \cap B) = P(B \mid A) * P(A)$, which we can then use in the following formulation of Bayes' theorem:

$$P(A|B) = \frac{P(A \cap B)}{P(B)} = \frac{P(B|A)P(A)}{P(B)}$$

In fact, this is the traditional way in which Bayes' theorem has been specified, for reasons that will become clear as we apply it to machine learning. First, to better understand how Bayes' theorem works in practice, let's revisit our hypothetical spam filter.

Without knowledge of an incoming message's content, the best estimate of its spam status would be $P(spam)$, the probability that any prior message was spam, which we calculated previously to be 20 percent. This estimate is known as the **prior probability**.

Suppose that you obtained additional evidence by looking more carefully at the set of previously received messages to examine the frequency that the term Viagra appeared. The probability that the word Viagra was used in previous spam messages, or $P(Viagra \mid spam)$, is called the **likelihood**. The probability that Viagra appeared in any message at all, or $P(Viagra)$, is known as the **marginal likelihood**.

By applying Bayes' theorem to this evidence, we can compute a **posterior probability** that measures how likely the message is to be spam. If the posterior probability is greater than 50 percent, the message is more likely to be spam than ham and it should perhaps be filtered. The following formula shows how Bayes' theorem is applied to the evidence provided by the previous e-mail messages:

$$P(\text{spam}|\text{Viagra}) = \frac{P(\text{Viagra}|\text{spam})P(\text{spam})}{P(\text{Viagra})}$$

likelihood

prior probability

posterior probability

marginal likelihood

To calculate these components of Bayes' theorem, it helps to construct a **frequency table** (shown on the left in the following diagram) that records the number of times Viagra appeared in spam and ham messages. Just like a two-way cross-tabulation, one dimension of the table indicates levels of the class variable (spam or ham), while the other dimension indicates levels for features (Viagra: yes or no). The cells then indicate the number of instances having the particular combination of class value and feature value. The frequency table can then be used to construct a **likelihood table**, as shown on right in the following diagram. The rows of the likelihood table indicate the conditional probabilities for Viagra (yes/no), given that an e-mail was either spam or ham:

Frequency	Viagra Yes	No	Total
spam	4	16	20
ham	1	79	80
Total	5	95	100

Likelihood	Viagra Yes	No	Total
spam	4 / 20	16 / 20	20
ham	1 / 80	79 / 80	80
Total	5 / 100	95 / 100	100

The likelihood table reveals that *P(Viagra=Yes | spam)* = 4/20 = 0.20, indicating that the probability is 20 percent that a message contains the term Viagra, given that the message is spam. Additionally, since *P(A ∩ B) = P(B | A) * P(A)*, we can calculate *P(spam ∩ Viagra)* as *P(Viagra | spam) * P(spam)* = (4/20) * (20/100) = 0.04. The same result can be found in the frequency table, which notes that 4 out of the 100 messages were spam with the term Viagra. Either way, this is four times greater than the previous estimate of 0.01 we calculated as *P(A ∩ B) = P(A) * P(B)* under the false assumption of independence. This, of course, illustrates the importance of Bayes' theorem while calculating joint probability.

To compute the posterior probability, *P(spam | Viagra)*, we simply take
P(Viagra | spam) * *P(spam)* / *P(Viagra)* or *(4/20)* * *(20/100)* / *(5/100)* = *0.80*. Therefore,
the probability is 80 percent that a message is spam, given that it contains the word
Viagra. In light of this result, any message containing this term should probably
be filtered.

This is very much how commercial spam filters work, although they consider a
much larger number of words simultaneously while computing the frequency and
likelihood tables. In the next section, we'll see how this concept is put to use when
additional features are involved.

The Naive Bayes algorithm

The **Naive Bayes** algorithm describes a simple method to apply Bayes' theorem to
classification problems. Although it is not the only machine learning method that
utilizes Bayesian methods, it is the most common one. This is particularly true for
text classification, where it has become the de facto standard. The strengths and
weaknesses of this algorithm are as follows:

Strengths	Weaknesses
<ul><li>Simple, fast, and very effective</li><li>Does well with noisy and missing data</li><li>Requires relatively few examples for training, but also works well with very large numbers of examples</li><li>Easy to obtain the estimated probability for a prediction</li></ul>	<ul><li>Relies on an often-faulty assumption of equally important and independent features</li><li>Not ideal for datasets with many numeric features</li><li>Estimated probabilities are less reliable than the predicted classes</li></ul>

The Naive Bayes algorithm is named as such because it makes some "naive"
assumptions about the data. In particular, Naive Bayes assumes that all of the
features in the dataset are equally important and independent. These assumptions
are rarely true in most real-world applications.

For example, if you were attempting to identify spam by monitoring e-mail
messages, it is almost certainly true that some features will be more important
than others. For example, the e-mail sender may be a more important indicator of
spam than the message text. Additionally, the words in the message body are not
independent from one another, since the appearance of some words is a very good
indication that other words are also likely to appear. A message with the word
Viagra will probably also contain the words prescription or drugs.

However, in most cases when these assumptions are violated, Naive Bayes still performs fairly well. This is true even in extreme circumstances where strong dependencies are found among the features. Due to the algorithm's versatility and accuracy across many types of conditions, Naive Bayes is often a strong first candidate for classification learning tasks.

The exact reason why Naive Bayes works well in spite of its faulty assumptions has been the subject of much speculation. One explanation is that it is not important to obtain a precise estimate of probability, so long as the predictions are accurate. For instance, if a spam filter correctly identifies spam, does it matter whether it was 51 percent or 99 percent confident in its prediction? For one discussion of this topic, refer to: Domingos P, Pazzani M. On the optimality of the simple Bayesian classifier under zero-one loss. *Machine Learning*. 1997; 29:103-130.

Classification with Naive Bayes

Let's extend our spam filter by adding a few additional terms to be monitored in addition to the term Viagra: Money, Groceries, and Unsubscribe. The Naive Bayes learner is trained by constructing a likelihood table for the appearance of these four words (labeled W_1, W_2, W_3, and W_4), as shown in the following diagram for 100 e-mails:

Likelihood	Viagra (W_1)		Money (W_2)		Groceries (W_3)		Unsubscribe (W_4)		Total
	Yes	No	Yes	No	Yes	No	Yes	No	
spam	4 / 20	16 / 20	10 / 20	10 / 20	0 / 20	20 / 20	12 / 20	8 / 20	20
ham	1 / 80	79 / 80	14 / 80	66 / 80	8 / 80	71 / 80	23 / 80	57 / 80	80
Total	5 / 100	95 / 100	24 / 100	76 / 100	8 / 100	91 / 100	35 / 100	65 / 100	100

As new messages are received, we need to calculate the posterior probability to determine whether they are more likely to be spam or ham, given the likelihood of the words found in the message text. For example, suppose that a message contains the terms Viagra and Unsubscribe, but does not contain either Money or Groceries.

Using Bayes' theorem, we can define the problem as shown in the following formula. It captures the probability that a message is spam, given that *Viagra = Yes, Money = No, Groceries = No*, and *Unsubscribe = Yes*:

$$P(\text{spam}|W_1 \cap \neg W_2 \cap \neg W_3 \cap W_4) = \frac{P(W_1 \cap \neg W_2 \cap \neg W_3 \cap W_4|\text{spam})P(\text{spam})}{P(W_1 \cap \neg W_2 \cap \neg W_3 \cap W_4)}$$

For a number of reasons, this formula is computationally difficult to solve. As additional features are added, tremendous amounts of memory are needed to store probabilities for all of the possible intersecting events; imagine the complexity of a Venn diagram for the events for four words, let alone for hundreds or more.

The work becomes much easier if we can exploit the fact that Naive Bayes assumes independence among events. Specifically, it assumes **class-conditional independence**, which means that events are independent so long as they are conditioned on the same class value. Assuming conditional independence allows us to simplify the formula using the probability rule for independent events, which states that $P(A \cap B) = P(A) * P(B)$. Because the denominator does not depend on the class (spam or ham), it is treated as a constant value and can be ignored for the time being. This means that the conditional probability of spam can be expressed as:

$$P(\text{spam}|W_1 \cap \neg W_2 \cap \neg W_3 \cap W_4) \propto P(W_1|\text{spam})P(\neg W_2|\text{spam})P(\neg W_3|\text{spam})P(W_4|\text{spam})P(\text{spam})$$

And the probability that the message is ham can be expressed as:

$$P(\text{ham}|W_1 \cap \neg W_2 \cap \neg W_3 \cap W_4) \propto P(W_1|\text{ham})P(\neg W_2|\text{ham})P(\neg W_3|\text{ham})P(W_4|\text{ham})P(\text{ham})$$

Note that the equals symbol has been replaced by the proportional-to symbol (similar to a sideways, open-ended '8') to indicate the fact that the denominator has been omitted.

Using the values in the likelihood table, we can start filling numbers in these equations. The overall likelihood of spam is then:

$$(4/20) * (10/20) * (20/20) * (12/20) * (20/100) = 0.012$$

While the likelihood of ham is:

$$(1/80) * (66/80) * (71/80) * (23/80) * (80/100) = 0.002$$

Because *0.012/0.002 = 6*, we can say that this message is six times more likely to be spam than ham. However, to convert these numbers into probabilities, we need to perform one last step to reintroduce the denominator that had been excluded. Essentially, we must rescale the likelihood of each outcome by dividing it by the total likelihood across all possible outcomes.

In this way, the probability of spam is equal to the likelihood that the message is spam divided by the likelihood that the message is either spam or ham:

$$0.012/(0.012 + 0.002) = 0.857$$

Similarly, the probability of ham is equal to the likelihood that the message is ham divided by the likelihood that the message is either spam or ham:

$$0.002/(0.012 + 0.002) = 0.143$$

Given the pattern of words found in this message, we expect that the message is spam with 85.7 percent probability and ham with 14.3 percent probability. Because these are mutually exclusive and exhaustive events, the probabilities sum to 1.

The Naive Bayes classification algorithm we used in the preceding example can be summarized by the following formula. The probability of level L for class C, given the evidence provided by features F_1 through F_n, is equal to the product of the probabilities of each piece of evidence conditioned on the class level, the prior probability of the class level, and a scaling factor $1/Z$, which converts the likelihood values into probabilities:

$$P(C_L|F_1, ..., F_n) = \frac{1}{Z}p(C_L) \prod_{i=1}^{n} p(F_i|C_L)$$

Although this equation seems intimidating, as the prior example illustrated, the series of steps is fairly straightforward. Begin by building a frequency table, use this to build a likelihood table, and multiply the conditional probabilities according to the Naive Bayes' rule. Finally, divide by the total likelihood to transform each class likelihood into a probability. After attempting this calculation a few times by hand, it will become second nature.

The Laplace estimator

Before we employ Naive Bayes in more complex problems, there are some nuances to consider. Suppose that we received another message, this time containing all four terms: Viagra, Groceries, Money, and Unsubscribe. Using the Naive Bayes algorithm as before, we can compute the likelihood of spam as:

$$(4/20) * (10/20) * (0/20) * (12/20) * (20/100) = 0$$

The likelihood of ham is:

$$(1/80) * (14/80) * (8/80) * (23/80) * (80/100) = 0.00005$$

Therefore, the probability of spam is:

$$0/(0 + 0.00005) = 0$$

The probability of ham is:

$$0.00005/(0 + 0.\ 0.00005) = 1$$

These results suggest that the message is spam with 0 percent probability and ham with 100 percent probability. Does this prediction make sense? Probably not. The message contains several words usually associated with spam, including Viagra, which is rarely used in legitimate messages. It is therefore very likely that the message has been incorrectly classified.

This problem might arise if an event never occurs for one or more levels of the class. For instance, the term Groceries had never previously appeared in a spam message. Consequently, *P(spam | groceries) = 0%*.

Because probabilities in the Naive Bayes formula are multiplied in a chain, this 0 percent value causes the posterior probability of spam to be zero, giving the word Groceries the ability to effectively nullify and overrule all of the other evidence. Even if the e-mail was otherwise overwhelmingly expected to be spam, the absence of the word Groceries in spam will always veto the other evidence and result in the probability of spam being zero.

A solution to this problem involves using something called the **Laplace estimator,** which is named after the French mathematician Pierre-Simon Laplace. The Laplace estimator essentially adds a small number to each of the counts in the frequency table, which ensures that each feature has a nonzero probability of occurring with each class. Typically, the Laplace estimator is set to 1, which ensures that each class-feature combination is found in the data at least once.

The Laplace estimator can be set to any value and does not necessarily even have to be the same for each of the features. If you were a devoted Bayesian, you could use a Laplace estimator to reflect a presumed prior probability of how the feature relates to the class. In practice, given a large enough training dataset, this step is unnecessary and the value of 1 is almost always used.

Let's see how this affects our prediction for this message. Using a Laplace value of 1, we add one to each numerator in the likelihood function. The total number of 1 values must also be added to each conditional probability denominator. The likelihood of spam is therefore:

$$(5/24) * (11/24) * (1/24) * (13/24) * (20/100) = 0.0004$$

The likelihood of ham is:

$$(2/84) * (15/84) * (9/84) * (24/84) * (80/100) = 0.0001$$

This means that the probability of spam is 80 percent, and the probability of ham is 20 percent, which is a more plausible result than the one obtained when the term Groceries alone determined the result.

Using numeric features with Naive Bayes

Because Naive Bayes uses frequency tables to learn the data, each feature must be categorical in order to create the combinations of class and feature values comprising of the matrix. Since numeric features do not have categories of values, the preceding algorithm does not work directly with numeric data. There are, however, ways that this can be addressed.

One easy and effective solution is to **discretize** numeric features, which simply means that the numbers are put into categories known as **bins**. For this reason, discretization is also sometimes called **binning**. This method is ideal when there are large amounts of training data, a common condition while working with Naive Bayes.

There are several different ways to discretize a numeric feature. Perhaps the most common is to explore the data for natural categories or **cut points** in the distribution of data. For example, suppose that you added a feature to the spam dataset that recorded the time of night or day the e-mail was sent, from 0 to 24 hours past midnight.

Depicted using a histogram, the time data might look something like the following diagram. In the early hours of the morning, the message frequency is low. The activity picks up during business hours and tapers off in the evening. This seems to create four natural bins of activity, as partitioned by the dashed lines indicating places where the numeric data are divided into levels of a new nominal feature, which could then be used with Naive Bayes:

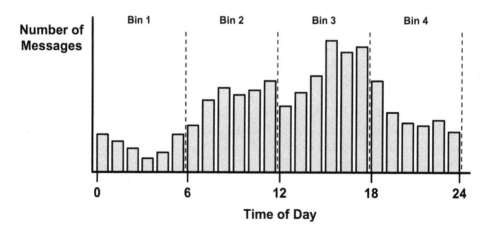

Keep in mind that the choice of four bins was somewhat arbitrary based on the natural distribution of data and a hunch about how the proportion of spam might change throughout the day. We might expect that spammers operate in the late hours of the night or they may operate during the day, when people are likely to check their e-mail. This said, to capture these trends, we could have just as easily used three bins or twelve.

 If there are no obvious cut points, one option will be to discretize the feature using quantiles. You could divide the data into three bins with tertiles, four bins with quartiles, or five bins with quintiles.

One thing to keep in mind is that discretizing a numeric feature always results in a reduction of information as the feature's original granularity is reduced to a smaller number of categories. It is important to strike a balance here. Too few bins can result in important trends being obscured. Too many bins can result in small counts in the Naive Bayes frequency table, which can increase the algorithm's sensitivity to noisy data.

Example – filtering mobile phone spam with the Naive Bayes algorithm

As the worldwide use of mobile phones has grown, a new avenue for electronic junk mail has opened for disreputable marketers. These advertisers utilize Short Message Service (SMS) text messages to target potential consumers with unwanted advertising known as SMS spam. This type of spam is particularly troublesome because, unlike e-mail spam, many cellular phone users pay a fee per SMS received. Developing a classification algorithm that could filter SMS spam would provide a useful tool for cellular phone providers.

Since Naive Bayes has been used successfully for e-mail spam filtering, it seems likely that it could also be applied to SMS spam. However, relative to e-mail spam, SMS spam poses additional challenges for automated filters. SMS messages are often limited to 160 characters, reducing the amount of text that can be used to identify whether a message is junk. The limit, combined with small mobile phone keyboards, has led many to adopt a form of SMS shorthand lingo, which further blurs the line between legitimate messages and spam. Let's see how a simple Naive Bayes classifier handles these challenges.

Step 1 – collecting data

To develop the Naive Bayes classifier, we will use data adapted from the SMS Spam Collection at `http://www.dt.fee.unicamp.br/~tiago/smsspamcollection/`.

 To read more about how the SMS Spam Collection was developed, refer to: Gómez JM, Almeida TA, Yamakami A. On the validity of a new SMS spam collection. *Proceedings of the 11th IEEE International Conference on Machine Learning and Applications*. 2012.

This dataset includes the text of SMS messages along with a label indicating whether the message is unwanted. Junk messages are labeled spam, while legitimate messages are labeled ham. Some examples of spam and ham are shown in the following table:

Sample SMS ham	Sample SMS spam
• Better. Made up for Friday and stuffed myself like a pig yesterday. Now I feel bleh. But, at least, its not writhing pain kind of bleh.	• Congratulations ur awarded 500 of CD vouchers or 125 gift guaranteed & Free entry 2 100 wkly draw txt MUSIC to 87066.
• If he started searching, he will get job in few days. He has great potential and talent.	• December only! Had your mobile 11mths+? You are entitled to update to the latest colour camera mobile for Free! Call The Mobile Update Co FREE on 08002986906.
• I got another job! The one at the hospital, doing data analysis or something, starts on Monday! Not sure when my thesis will finish.	• Valentines Day Special! Win over £1000 in our quiz and take your partner on the trip of a lifetime! Send GO to 83600 now. 150 p/msg rcvd.

Looking at the preceding messages, did you notice any distinguishing characteristics of spam? One notable characteristic is that two of the three spam messages use the word "free," yet the word does not appear in any of the ham messages. On the other hand, two of the ham messages cite specific days of the week, as compared to zero in spam messages.

Our Naive Bayes classifier will take advantage of such patterns in the word frequency to determine whether the SMS messages seem to better fit the profile of spam or ham. While it's not inconceivable that the word "free" would appear outside of a spam SMS, a legitimate message is likely to provide additional words explaining the context. For instance, a ham message might state "are you free on Sunday?" Whereas, a spam message might use the phrase "free ringtones." The classifier will compute the probability of spam and ham, given the evidence provided by all the words in the message.

Step 2 – exploring and preparing the data

The first step towards constructing our classifier involves processing the raw data for analysis. Text data are challenging to prepare, because it is necessary to transform the words and sentences into a form that a computer can understand. We will transform our data into a representation known as **bag-of-words**, which ignores word order and simply provides a variable indicating whether the word appears at all.

> The data used here has been modified slightly from the original in order to make it easier to work with in R. If you plan on following along with the example, download the sms_spam.csv file from the Packt website and save it in your R working directory.

We'll begin by importing the CSV data and saving it in a data frame:

```
> sms_raw <- read.csv("sms_spam.csv", stringsAsFactors = FALSE)
```

Using the str() function, we see that the sms_raw data frame includes 5,559 total SMS messages with two features: type and text. The SMS type has been coded as either ham or spam. The text element stores the full raw SMS text.

```
> str(sms_raw)
'data.frame':   5559 obs. of  2 variables:
 $ type: chr   "ham" "ham" "ham" "spam" ...
 $ text: chr   "Hope you are having a good week. Just checking in"
"K..give back my thanks." "Am also doing in cbe only. But have to
pay." "complimentary 4 STAR Ibiza Holiday or £10,000 cash needs
your URGENT collection. 09066364349 NOW from Landline not to lose
out"| __truncated__ ...
```

The type element is currently a character vector. Since this is a categorical variable, it would be better to convert it into a factor, as shown in the following code:

```
> sms_raw$type <- factor(sms_raw$type)
```

Examining this with the `str()` and `table()` functions, we see that `type` has now been appropriately recoded as a factor. Additionally, we see that 747 (about 13 percent) of SMS messages in our data were labeled as spam, while the others were labeled as ham:

```
> str(sms_raw$type)
 Factor w/ 2 levels "ham","spam": 1 1 1 2 2 1 1 1 2 1 ...
> table(sms_raw$type)

 ham spam
4812  747
```

For now, we will leave the message text alone. As you will learn in the next section, processing the raw SMS messages will require the use of a new set of powerful tools designed specifically to process text data.

Data preparation – cleaning and standardizing text data

SMS messages are strings of text composed of words, spaces, numbers, and punctuation. Handling this type of complex data takes a lot of thought and effort. One needs to consider how to remove numbers and punctuation; handle uninteresting words such as *and*, *but*, and *or*; and how to break apart sentences into individual words. Thankfully, this functionality has been provided by the members of the R community in a text mining package titled `tm`.

> The `tm` package was originally created by Ingo Feinerer as a dissertation project at the Vienna University of Economics and Business. To learn more, see: Feinerer I, Hornik K, Meyer D. Text Mining Infrastructure in R. *Journal of Statistical Software*. 2008; 25:1-54.

The `tm` package can be installed via the `install.packages("tm")` command and loaded with the `library(tm)` command. Even if you already have it installed, it may be worth re-running the install process to ensure that your version is up-to-date, as the `tm` package is still being actively developed. This occasionally results in changes to its functionality.

> This chapter was written and tested using tm version 0.6-2, which was current as of July 2015. If you see differences in the output or if the code does not work, you may be using a different version. The Packt Publishing support page for this book will post solutions for future `tm` packages if significant changes are noted.

The first step in processing text data involves creating a **corpus**, which is a collection of text documents. The documents can be short or long, from individual news articles, pages in a book or on the web, or entire books. In our case, the corpus will be a collection of SMS messages.

In order to create a corpus, we'll use the VCorpus() function in the tm package, which refers to a volatile corpus—volatile as it is stored in memory as opposed to being stored on disk (the PCorpus() function can be used to access a permanent corpus stored in a database). This function requires us to specify the source of documents for the corpus, which could be from a computer's filesystem, a database, the Web, or elsewhere. Since we already loaded the SMS message text into R, we'll use the VectorSource() reader function to create a source object from the existing sms_raw$text vector, which can then be supplied to VCorpus() as follows:

```
> sms_corpus <- VCorpus(VectorSource(sms_raw$text))
```

The resulting corpus object is saved with the name sms_corpus.

 By specifying an optional readerControl parameter, the VCorpus() function offers functionality to import text from sources such as PDFs and Microsoft Word files. To learn more, examine the *Data Import* section in the tm package vignette using the vignette("tm") command.

By printing the corpus, we see that it contains documents for each of the 5,559 SMS messages in the training data:

```
> print(sms_corpus)
<<VCorpus>>
Metadata:  corpus specific: 0, document level (indexed): 0
Content:  documents: 5559
```

Because the tm corpus is essentially a complex list, we can use list operations to select documents in the corpus. To receive a summary of specific messages, we can use the inspect() function with list operators. For example, the following command will view a summary of the first and second SMS messages in the corpus:

```
> inspect(sms_corpus[1:2])
<<VCorpus>>
Metadata:  corpus specific: 0, document level (indexed): 0
Content:  documents: 2
```

```
[[1]]
<<PlainTextDocument>>
Metadata:   7
Content:   chars: 49


[[2]]
<<PlainTextDocument>>
Metadata:   7
Content:   chars: 23
```

To view the actual message text, the `as.character()` function must be applied to the desired messages. To view one message, use the `as.character()` function on a single list element, noting that the double-bracket notation is required:

```
> as.character(sms_corpus[[1]])
[1] "Hope you are having a good week. Just checking in"
```

To view multiple documents, we'll need to use `as.character()` on several items in the sms_corpus object. To do so, we'll use the `lapply()` function, which is a part of a family of R functions that applies a procedure to each element of an R data structure. These functions, which include `apply()` and `sapply()` among others, are one of the key idioms of the R language. Experienced R coders use these much like the way `for` or `while` loops are used in other programming languages, as they result in more readable (and sometimes more efficient) code. The `lapply()` command to apply `as.character()` to a subset of corpus elements is as follows:

```
> lapply(sms_corpus[1:2], as.character)
$`1`
[1] "Hope you are having a good week. Just checking in"


$`2`
[1] "K..give back my thanks."
```

As noted earlier, the corpus contains the raw text of 5,559 text messages. In order to perform our analysis, we need to divide these messages into individual words. But first, we need to clean the text, in order to standardize the words, by removing punctuation and other characters that clutter the result. For example, we would like the strings *Hello!*, *HELLO*, and *hello* to be counted as instances of the same word.

The `tm_map()` function provides a method to apply a transformation (also known as mapping) to a tm corpus. We will use this function to clean up our corpus using a series of transformations and save the result in a new object called `corpus_clean`.

Our first order of business will be to standardize the messages to use only lowercase characters. To this end, R provides a `tolower()` function that returns a lowercase version of text strings. In order to apply this function to the corpus, we need to use the `tm` wrapper function `content_transformer()` to treat `tolower()` as a transformation function that can be used to access the corpus. The full command is as follows:

```
> sms_corpus_clean <- tm_map(sms_corpus,
    content_transformer(tolower))
```

To check whether the command worked as advertised, let's inspect the first message in the original corpus and compare it to the same in the transformed corpus:

```
> as.character(sms_corpus[[1]])
[1] "Hope you are having a good week. Just checking in"
> as.character(sms_corpus_clean[[1]])
[1] "hope you are having a good week. just checking in"
```

As expected, uppercase letters have been replaced by lowercase versions of the same.

> The `content_transformer()` function can be used to apply more sophisticated text processing and cleanup processes, such as `grep` pattern matching and replacement. Simply write a custom function and wrap it before applying via `tm_map()` as done earlier.

Let's continue our cleanup by removing numbers from the SMS messages. Although some numbers may provide useful information, the majority would likely be unique to individual senders and thus will not provide useful patterns across all messages. With this in mind, we'll strip all the numbers from the corpus as follows:

```
> sms_corpus_clean <- tm_map(sms_corpus_clean, removeNumbers)
```

> Note that the preceding code did not use the `content_transformer()` function. This is because `removeNumbers()` is built into `tm` along with several other mapping functions that do not need to be wrapped. To see the other built-in transformations, simply type `getTransformations()`.

Our next task is to remove filler words such as *to, and, but,* and *or* from our SMS messages. These terms are known as **stop words** and are typically removed prior to text mining. This is due to the fact that although they appear very frequently, they do not provide much useful information for machine learning.

Rather than define a list of stop words ourselves, we'll use the `stopwords()` function provided by the `tm` package. This function allows us to access various sets of stop words, across several languages. By default, common English language stop words are used. To see the default list, type `stopwords()` at the command line. To see the other languages and options available, type `?stopwords` for the documentation page.

> Even within a single language, there is no single definitive list of stop words. For example, the default English list in `tm` includes about 174 words while another option includes 571 words. You can even specify your own list of stop words if you prefer. Regardless of the list you choose, keep in mind the goal of this transformation, which is to eliminate all useless data while keeping as much useful information as possible.

The stop words alone are not a useful transformation. What we need is a way to remove any words that appear in the stop words list. The solution lies in the `removeWords()` function, which is a transformation included with the `tm` package. As we have done before, we'll use the `tm_map()` function to apply this mapping to the data, providing the `stopwords()` function as a parameter to indicate exactly the words we would like to remove. The full command is as follows:

```
> sms_corpus_clean <- tm_map(sms_corpus_clean,
    removeWords, stopwords())
```

Since `stopwords()` simply returns a vector of stop words, had we chosen so, we could have replaced it with our own vector of words to be removed. In this way, we could expand or reduce the list of stop words to our liking or remove a completely different set of words entirely.

Continuing with our cleanup process, we can also eliminate any punctuation from the text messages using the built-in `removePunctuation()` transformation:

```
> sms_corpus_clean <- tm_map(sms_corpus_clean, removePunctuation)
```

The `removePunctuation()` transformation strips punctuation characters from the text blindly, which can lead to unintended consequences. For example, consider what happens when it is applied as follows:

```
> removePunctuation("hello...world")
[1] "helloworld"
```

As shown, the lack of blank space after the ellipses has caused the words *hello* and *world* to be joined as a single word. While this is not a substantial problem for our analysis, it is worth noting for the future.

To work around the default behavior of `removePunctuation()`, simply create a custom function that replaces rather than removes punctuation characters:

```
> replacePunctuation <- function(x) {
    gsub("[[:punct:]]+", " ", x)
}
```

Essentially, this uses R's `gsub()` function to substitute any punctuation characters in x with a blank space. The `replacePunctuation()` function can then be used with `tm_map()` as with other transformations.

Another common standardization for text data involves reducing words to their root form in a process called **stemming**. The stemming process takes words like *learned*, *learning*, and *learns*, and strips the suffix in order to transform them into the base form, *learn*. This allows machine learning algorithms to treat the related terms as a single concept rather than attempting to learn a pattern for each variant.

The `tm` package provides stemming functionality via integration with the `SnowballC` package. At the time of this writing, `SnowballC` was not installed by default with `tm`. Do so with `install.packages("SnowballC")` if it is not installed already.

The `SnowballC` package is maintained by Milan Bouchet-Valat and provides an R interface to the C-based `libstemmer` library, which is based on M.F. Porter's "Snowball" word stemming algorithm, a widely used open source stemming method. For more detail, see `http://snowball.tartarus.org`.

The `SnowballC` package provides a `wordStem()` function, which for a character vector, returns the same vector of terms in its root form. For example, the function correctly stems the variants of the word *learn*, as described previously:

```
> library(SnowballC)
> wordStem(c("learn", "learned", "learning", "learns"))
[1] "learn"    "learn"    "learn"    "learn"
```

In order to apply the `wordStem()` function to an entire corpus of text documents, the `tm` package includes a `stemDocument()` transformation. We apply this to our corpus with the `tm_map()` function exactly as done earlier:

```
> sms_corpus_clean <- tm_map(sms_corpus_clean, stemDocument)
```

If you receive an error message while applying the stemDocument() transformation, please confirm that you have the SnowballC package installed. If after installing the package you still encounter the message that all scheduled cores encountered errors, you can also try forcing the tm_map() command to a single core, by adding an additional parameter to specify mc.cores=1.

After removing numbers, stop words, and punctuation as well as performing stemming, the text messages are left with the blank spaces that previously separated the now-missing pieces. The final step in our text cleanup process is to remove additional whitespace, using the built-in stripWhitespace() transformation:

```
> sms_corpus_clean <- tm_map(sms_corpus_clean, stripWhitespace)
```

The following table shows the first three messages in the SMS corpus before and after the cleaning process. The messages have been limited to the most interesting words, and punctuation and capitalization have been removed:

SMS messages before cleaning	SMS messages after cleaning
> as.character(sms_corpus[1:3]) [[1]] Hope you are having a good week. Just checking in [[2]] K..give back my thanks. [[3]] Am also doing in cbe only. But have to pay.	> as.character(sms_corpus_clean[1:3]) [[1]] hope good week just check [[2]] kgive back thank [[3]] also cbe pay

Data preparation – splitting text documents into words

Now that the data are processed to our liking, the final step is to split the messages into individual components through a process called **tokenization**. A token is a single element of a text string; in this case, the tokens are words.

As you might assume, the tm package provides functionality to tokenize the SMS message corpus. The DocumentTermMatrix() function will take a corpus and create a data structure called a **Document Term Matrix (DTM)** in which rows indicate documents (SMS messages) and columns indicate terms (words).

The tm package also provides a data structure for a **Term Document Matrix (TDM)**, which is simply a transposed DTM in which the rows are terms and the columns are documents. Why the need for both? Sometimes, it is more convenient to work with one or the other. For example, if the number of documents is small, while the word list is large, it may make sense to use a TDM because it is generally easier to display many rows than to display many columns. This said, the two are often interchangeable.

Each cell in the matrix stores a number indicating a count of the times the word represented by the column appears in the document represented by the row. The following illustration depicts only a small portion of the DTM for the SMS corpus, as the complete matrix has 5,559 rows and over 7,000 columns:

message #	balloon	balls	bam	bambling	band
1	0	0	0	0	0
2	0	0	0	0	0
3	0	0	0	0	0
4	0	0	0	0	0
5	0	0	0	0	0

The fact that each cell in the table is zero implies that none of the words listed on the top of the columns appear in any of the first five messages in the corpus. This highlights the reason why this data structure is called a **sparse matrix**; the vast majority of the cells in the matrix are filled with zeros. Stated in real-world terms, although each message must contain at least one word, the probability of any one word appearing in a given message is small.

Creating a DTM sparse matrix, given a tm corpus, involves a single command:

```
> sms_dtm <- DocumentTermMatrix(sms_corpus_clean)
```

This will create an sms_dtm object that contains the tokenized corpus using the default settings, which apply minimal processing. The default settings are appropriate because we have already prepared the corpus manually.

On the other hand, if we hadn't performed the preprocessing, we could do so here by providing a list of control parameter options to override the defaults. For example, to create a DTM directly from the raw, unprocessed SMS corpus, we can use the following command:

```
> sms_dtm2 <- DocumentTermMatrix(sms_corpus, control = list(
    tolower = TRUE,
```

```
    removeNumbers = TRUE,

    stopwords = TRUE,

    removePunctuation = TRUE,

    stemming = TRUE

))
```

This applies the same preprocessing steps to the SMS corpus in the same order as done earlier. However, comparing sms_dtm to sms_dtm2, we see a slight difference in the number of terms in the matrix:

```
> sms_dtm

<<DocumentTermMatrix (documents: 5559, terms: 6518)>>

Non-/sparse entries: 42113/36191449

Sparsity            : 100%

Maximal term length: 40

Weighting           : term frequency (tf)


> sms_dtm2

<<DocumentTermMatrix (documents: 5559, terms: 6909)>>

Non-/sparse entries: 43192/38363939

Sparsity            : 100%

Maximal term length: 40

Weighting           : term frequency (tf)
```

The reason for this discrepancy has to do with a minor difference in the ordering of the preprocessing steps. The DocumentTermMatrix() function applies its cleanup functions to the text strings only after they have been split apart into words. Thus, it uses a slightly different stop words removal function. Consequently, some words split differently than when they are cleaned before tokenization.

To force the two prior document term matrices to be identical, we can override the default stop words function with our own that uses the original replacement function. Simply replace stopwords = TRUE with the following:

```
stopwords = function(x) { removeWords(x, stopwords()) }
```

The differences between these two cases illustrate an important principle of cleaning text data: the order of operations matters. With this in mind, it is very important to think through how early steps in the process are going to affect later ones. The order presented here will work in many cases, but when the process is tailored more carefully to specific datasets and use cases, it may require rethinking. For example, if there are certain terms you hope to exclude from the matrix, consider whether you should search for them before or after stemming. Also, consider how the removal of punctuation—and whether the punctuation is eliminated or replaced by blank space—affects these steps.

Data preparation – creating training and test datasets

With our data prepared for analysis, we now need to split the data into training and test datasets, so that once our spam classifier is built, it can be evaluated on data it has not previously seen. But even though we need to keep the classifier blinded as to the contents of the test dataset, it is important that the split occurs after the data have been cleaned and processed; we need exactly the same preparation steps to occur on both the training and test datasets.

We'll divide the data into two portions: 75 percent for training and 25 percent for testing. Since the SMS messages are sorted in a random order, we can simply take the first 4,169 for training and leave the remaining 1,390 for testing. Thankfully, the DTM object acts very much like a data frame and can be split using the standard [row, col] operations. As our DTM stores SMS messages as rows and words as columns, we must request a specific range of rows and all columns for each:

```
> sms_dtm_train <- sms_dtm[1:4169, ]
> sms_dtm_test  <- sms_dtm[4170:5559, ]
```

For convenience later on, it is also helpful to save a pair of vectors with labels for each of the rows in the training and testing matrices. These labels are not stored in the DTM, so we would need to pull them from the original sms_raw data frame:

```
> sms_train_labels <- sms_raw[1:4169, ]$type
> sms_test_labels  <- sms_raw[4170:5559, ]$type
```

To confirm that the subsets are representative of the complete set of SMS data, let's compare the proportion of spam in the training and test data frames:

```
> prop.table(table(sms_train_labels))
      ham       spam
0.8647158 0.1352842
> prop.table(table(sms_test_labels))
      ham       spam
0.8683453 0.1316547
```

Both the training data and test data contain about 13 percent spam. This suggests that the spam messages were divided evenly between the two datasets.

Visualizing text data – word clouds

A **word cloud** is a way to visually depict the frequency at which words appear in text data. The cloud is composed of words scattered somewhat randomly around the figure. Words appearing more often in the text are shown in a larger font, while less common terms are shown in smaller fonts. This type of figures grew in popularity recently, since it provides a way to observe trending topics on social media websites.

The wordcloud package provides a simple R function to create this type of diagrams. We'll use it to visualize the types of words in SMS messages, as comparing the clouds for spam and ham will help us gauge whether our Naive Bayes spam filter is likely to be successful. If you haven't already done so, install and load the package by typing install.packages("wordcloud") and library(wordcloud) at the R command line.

> The wordcloud package was written by Ian Fellows. For more information on this package, visit his blog at http://blog.fellstat.com/?cat=11.

A word cloud can be created directly from a tm corpus object using the syntax:

```
> wordcloud(sms_corpus_clean, min.freq = 50, random.order = FALSE)
```

This will create a word cloud from our prepared SMS corpus. Since we specified random.order = FALSE, the cloud will be arranged in a nonrandom order with higher frequency words placed closer to the center. If we do not specify random.order, the cloud would be arranged randomly by default. The min.freq parameter specifies the number of times a word must appear in the corpus before it will be displayed in the cloud. Since a frequency of 50 is about 1 percent of the corpus, this means that a word must be found in at least 1 percent of the SMS messages to be included in the cloud.

You might get a warning message noting that R was unable to fit all of the words in the figure. If so, try increasing `min.freq` to reduce the number of words in the cloud. It might also help to use the `scale` parameter to reduce the font size.

The resulting word cloud should appear similar to the following figure:

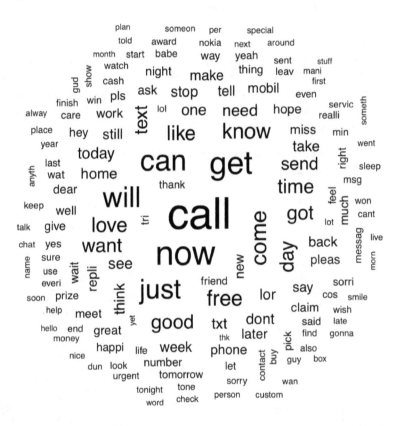

A perhaps more interesting visualization involves comparing the clouds for SMS spam and ham. Since we did not construct separate corpora for spam and ham, this is an appropriate time to note a very helpful feature of the `wordcloud()` function. Given a vector of raw text strings, it will automatically apply common text preparation processes before displaying the cloud.

Let's use R's `subset()` function to take a subset of the `sms_raw` data by the SMS type. First, we'll create a subset where the message `type` is `spam`:

```
> spam <- subset(sms_raw, type == "spam")
```

Next, we'll do the same thing for the `ham` subset:

```
> ham <- subset(sms_raw, type == "ham")
```

> Be careful to note the double equals sign. Like many programming languages, R uses == to test equality. If you accidently use a single equals sign, you'll end up with a subset much larger than you expected!

We now have two data frames, `spam` and `ham`, each with a `text` feature containing the raw text strings for SMSes. Creating word clouds is as simple as before. This time, we'll use the `max.words` parameter to look at the 40 most common words in each of the two sets. The scale parameter allows us to adjust the maximum and minimum font size for words in the cloud. Feel free to adjust these parameters as you see fit. This is illustrated in the following commands:

```
> wordcloud(spam$text, max.words = 40, scale = c(3, 0.5))
> wordcloud(ham$text, max.words = 40, scale = c(3, 0.5))
```

The resulting word clouds are shown in the following diagram:

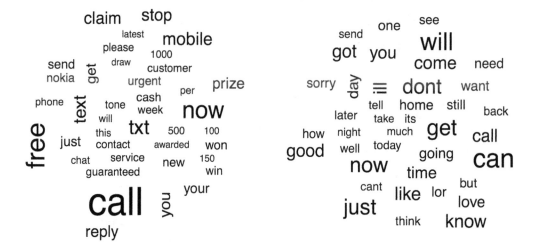

Do you have a hunch about which one is the spam cloud and which represents ham?

> Because of the randomization process, each word cloud may look slightly different. Running the `wordcloud()` function several times allows you to choose the cloud that is the most visually appealing for presentation purposes.

As you probably guessed, the spam cloud is on the left. Spam messages include words such as *urgent*, *free*, *mobile*, *claim*, and *stop*; these terms do not appear in the ham cloud at all. Instead, ham messages use words such as *can*, *sorry*, *need*, and *time*. These stark differences suggest that our Naive Bayes model will have some strong key words to differentiate between the classes.

Data preparation – creating indicator features for frequent words

The final step in the data preparation process is to transform the sparse matrix into a data structure that can be used to train a Naive Bayes classifier. Currently, the sparse matrix includes over 6,500 features; this is a feature for every word that appears in at least one SMS message. It's unlikely that all of these are useful for classification. To reduce the number of features, we will eliminate any word that appear in less than five SMS messages, or in less than about 0.1 percent of the records in the training data.

Finding frequent words requires use of the `findFreqTerms()` function in the `tm` package. This function takes a DTM and returns a character vector containing the words that appear for at least the specified number of times. For instance, the following command will display the words appearing at least five times in the `sms_dtm_train` matrix:

```
> findFreqTerms(sms_dtm_train, 5)
```

The result of the function is a character vector, so let's save our frequent words for later on:

```
> sms_freq_words <- findFreqTerms(sms_dtm_train, 5)
```

A peek into the contents of the vector shows us that there are 1,136 terms appearing in at least five SMS messages:

```
> str(sms_freq_words)
 chr [1:1136] "abiola" "abl" "abt" "accept" "access" "account"
"across" "act" "activ" ...
```

We now need to filter our DTM to include only the terms appearing in a specified vector. As done earlier, we'll use the data frame style `[row, col]` operations to request specific portions of the DTM, noting that the columns are named after the words the DTM contains. We can take advantage of this to limit the DTM to specific words. Since we want all the rows, but only the columns representing the words in the `sms_freq_words` vector, our commands are:

```
> sms_dtm_freq_train<- sms_dtm_train[ , sms_freq_words]
> sms_dtm_freq_test <- sms_dtm_test[ , sms_freq_words]
```

The training and test datasets now include 1,136 features, which correspond to words appearing in at least five messages.

The Naive Bayes classifier is typically trained on data with categorical features. This poses a problem, since the cells in the sparse matrix are numeric and measure the number of times a word appears in a message. We need to change this to a categorical variable that simply indicates yes or no depending on whether the word appears at all.

The following defines a `convert_counts()` function to convert counts to `Yes`/`No` strings:

```
> convert_counts <- function(x) {
    x <- ifelse(x > 0, "Yes", "No")
  }
```

By now, some of the pieces of the preceding function should look familiar. The first line defines the function. The `ifelse(x > 0, "Yes", "No")` statement transforms the values in x, so that if the value is greater than 0, then it will be replaced by `"Yes"`, otherwise it will be replaced by a `"No"` string. Lastly, the newly transformed x vector is returned.

We now need to apply `convert_counts()` to each of the columns in our sparse matrix. You may be able to guess the R function to do exactly this. The function is simply called `apply()` and is used much like `lapply()` was used previously.

The `apply()` function allows a function to be used on each of the rows or columns in a matrix. It uses a `MARGIN` parameter to specify either rows or columns. Here, we'll use `MARGIN = 2`, since we're interested in the columns (`MARGIN = 1` is used for rows). The commands to convert the training and test matrices are as follows:

```
> sms_train <- apply(sms_dtm_freq_train, MARGIN = 2,
                                        convert_counts)
> sms_test <- apply(sms_dtm_freq_test, MARGIN = 2,
                                        convert_counts)
```

The result will be two character type matrixes, each with cells indicating `"Yes"` or `"No"` for whether the word represented by the column appears at any point in the message represented by the row.

Step 3 – training a model on the data

Now that we have transformed the raw SMS messages into a format that can be represented by a statistical model, it is time to apply the Naive Bayes algorithm. The algorithm will use the presence or absence of words to estimate the probability that a given SMS message is spam.

The Naive Bayes implementation we will employ is in the `e1071` package. This package was developed in the statistics department of the Vienna University of Technology (TU Wien), and includes a variety of functions for machine learning. If you have not done so already, be sure to install and load the package using the `install.packages("e1071")` and `library(e1071)` commands before continuing.

 Many machine learning approaches are implemented in more than one R package, and Naive Bayes is no exception. One other option is `NaiveBayes()` in the `klaR` package, which is nearly identical to the one in the `e1071` package. Feel free to use whichever option you prefer.

Unlike the k-NN algorithm we used for classification in the previous chapter, a Naive Bayes learner is trained and used for classification in separate stages. Still, as shown in the following table, these steps are is fairly straightforward:

Naive Bayes classification syntax

using the `naiveBayes()` function in the `e1071` package

Building the classifier:

```
m <- naiveBayes(train, class, laplace = 0)
```

- `train` is a data frame or matrix containing training data
- `class` is a factor vector with the class for each row in the training data
- `laplace` is a number to control the Laplace estimator (by default, 0)

The function will return a naive Bayes model object that can be used to make predictions.

Making predictions:

```
p <- predict(m, test, type = "class")
```

- `m` is a model trained by the `naiveBayes()` function
- `test` is a data frame or matrix containing test data with the same features as the training data used to build the classifier
- `type` is either `"class"` or `"raw"` and specifies whether the predictions should be the most likely class value or the raw predicted probabilities

The function will return a vector of predicted class values or raw predicted probabilities depending upon the value of the `type` parameter.

Example:

```
sms_classifier <- naiveBayes(sms_train, sms_type)
sms_predictions <- predict(sms_classifier, sms_test)
```

To build our model on the `sms_train` matrix, we'll use the following command:

```
> sms_classifier <- naiveBayes(sms_train, sms_train_labels)
```

The `sms_classifier` object now contains a `naiveBayes` classifier object that can be used to make predictions.

Step 4 – evaluating model performance

To evaluate the SMS classifier, we need to test its predictions on unseen messages in the test data. Recall that the unseen message features are stored in a matrix named `sms_test`, while the class labels (spam or ham) are stored in a vector named `sms_test_labels`. The classifier that we trained has been named `sms_classifier`. We will use this classifier to generate predictions and then compare the predicted values to the true values.

The `predict()` function is used to make the predictions. We will store these in a vector named `sms_test_pred`. We will simply supply the function with the names of our classifier and test dataset, as shown:

```
> sms_test_pred <- predict(sms_classifier, sms_test)
```

To compare the predictions to the true values, we'll use the `CrossTable()` function in the `gmodels` package, which we used previously. This time, we'll add some additional parameters to eliminate unnecessary cell proportions and use the `dnn` parameter (dimension names) to relabel the rows and columns, as shown in the following code:

```
> library(gmodels)
> CrossTable(sms_test_pred, sms_test_labels,
    prop.chisq = FALSE, prop.t = FALSE,
    dnn = c('predicted', 'actual'))
```

This produces the following table:

```
               Total Observations in Table:  1390

                   | actual
         predicted |       ham |      spam | Row Total |
-------------------|-----------|-----------|-----------|
               ham |      1201 |        30 |      1231 |
                   |     0.995 |     0.164 |           |
-------------------|-----------|-----------|-----------|
              spam |         6 |       153 |       159 |
                   |     0.005 |     0.836 |           |
-------------------|-----------|-----------|-----------|
      Column Total |      1207 |       183 |      1390 |
                   |     0.868 |     0.132 |           |
-------------------|-----------|-----------|-----------|
```

Looking at the table, we can see that a total of only *6 + 30 = 36* of the 1,390 SMS messages were incorrectly classified (2.6 percent). Among the errors were 6 out of 1,207 ham messages that were misidentified as spam, and 30 of the 183 spam messages were incorrectly labeled as ham. Considering the little effort we put into the project, this level of performance seems quite impressive. This case study exemplifies the reason why Naive Bayes is the standard for text classification; directly out of the box, it performs surprisingly well.

On the other hand, the six legitimate messages that were incorrectly classified as spam could cause significant problems for the deployment of our filtering algorithm, because the filter could cause a person to miss an important text message. We should investigate to see whether we can slightly tweak the model to achieve better performance.

Step 5 – improving model performance

You may have noticed that we didn't set a value for the Laplace estimator while training our model. This allows words that appeared in zero spam or zero ham messages to have an indisputable say in the classification process. Just because the word "ringtone" only appeared in the spam messages in the training data, it does not mean that every message with this word should be classified as spam.

We'll build a Naive Bayes model as done earlier, but this time set `laplace = 1`:

```
> sms_classifier2 <- naiveBayes(sms_train, sms_train_labels,
    laplace = 1)
```

Next, we'll make predictions:

```
> sms_test_pred2 <- predict(sms_classifier2, sms_test)
```

Finally, we'll compare the predicted classes to the actual classifications using a cross tabulation:

```
> CrossTable(sms_test_pred2, sms_test_labels,
    prop.chisq = FALSE, prop.t = FALSE, prop.r = FALSE,
    dnn = c('predicted', 'actual'))
```

This results in the following table:

```
Total Observations in Table:  1390

              | actual
   predicted  |       ham |      spam | Row Total |
--------------|-----------|-----------|-----------|
          ham |      1202 |        28 |      1230 |
              |     0.996 |     0.153 |           |
--------------|-----------|-----------|-----------|
         spam |         5 |       155 |       160 |
              |     0.004 |     0.847 |           |
--------------|-----------|-----------|-----------|
 Column Total |      1207 |       183 |      1390 |
              |     0.868 |     0.132 |           |
--------------|-----------|-----------|-----------|
```

Adding the Laplace estimator reduced the number of false positives (ham messages erroneously classified as spam) from six to five and the number of false negatives from 30 to 28. Although this seems like a small change, it's substantial considering that the model's accuracy was already quite impressive. We'd need to be careful before tweaking the model too much in order to maintain the balance between being overly aggressive and overly passive while filtering spam. Users would prefer that a small number of spam messages slip through the filter than an alternative in which ham messages are filtered too aggressively.

Summary

In this chapter, we learned about classification using Naive Bayes. This algorithm constructs tables of probabilities that are used to estimate the likelihood that new examples belong to various classes. The probabilities are calculated using a formula known as Bayes' theorem, which specifies how dependent events are related. Although Bayes' theorem can be computationally expensive, a simplified version that makes so-called "naive" assumptions about the independence of features is capable of handling extremely large datasets.

The Naive Bayes classifier is often used for text classification. To illustrate its effectiveness, we employed Naive Bayes on a classification task involving spam SMS messages. Preparing the text data for analysis required the use of specialized R packages for text processing and visualization. Ultimately, the model was able to classify over 97 percent of all the SMS messages correctly as spam or ham.

In the next chapter, we will examine two more machine learning methods. Each performs classification by partitioning data into groups of similar values.

5
Divide and Conquer – Classification Using Decision Trees and Rules

While deciding between several job offers with various levels of pay and benefits, many people begin by making lists of pros and cons, and eliminate options based on simple rules. For instance, "if I have to commute for more than an hour, I will be unhappy." Or, "if I make less than $50k, I won't be able to support my family." In this way, the complex and difficult decision of predicting one's future happiness can be reduced to a series of simple decisions.

This chapter covers decision trees and rule learners—two machine learning methods that also make complex decisions from sets of simple choices. These methods then present their knowledge in the form of logical structures that can be understood with no statistical knowledge. This aspect makes these models particularly useful for business strategy and process improvement.

By the end of this chapter, you will learn:

- How trees and rules "greedily" partition data into interesting segments
- The most common decision tree and classification rule learners, including the C5.0, 1R, and RIPPER algorithms
- How to use these algorithms to perform real-world classification tasks, such as identifying risky bank loans and poisonous mushrooms

We will begin by examining decision trees, followed by a look at classification rules. Then, we will summarize what we've learned by previewing later chapters, which discuss methods that use trees and rules as a foundation for more advanced machine learning techniques.

Understanding decision trees

Decision tree learners are powerful classifiers, which utilize a **tree structure** to model the relationships among the features and the potential outcomes. As illustrated in the following figure, this structure earned its name due to the fact that it mirrors how a literal tree begins at a wide trunk, which if followed upward, splits into narrower and narrower branches. In much the same way, a decision tree classifier uses a structure of branching decisions, which channel examples into a final predicted class value.

To better understand how this works in practice, let's consider the following tree, which predicts whether a job offer should be accepted. A job offer to be considered begins at the **root node**, where it is then passed through **decision nodes** that require choices to be made based on the attributes of the job. These choices split the data across **branches** that indicate potential outcomes of a decision, depicted here as yes or no outcomes, though in some cases there may be more than two possibilities.
In the case a final decision can be made, the tree is terminated by **leaf nodes** (also known as **terminal nodes**) that denote the action to be taken as the result of the series of decisions. In the case of a predictive model, the leaf nodes provide the expected result given the series of events in the tree.

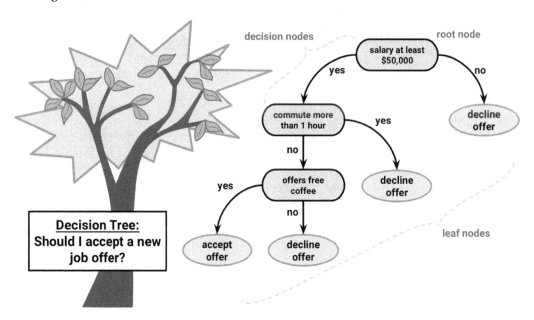

A great benefit of decision tree algorithms is that the flowchart-like tree structure is not necessarily exclusively for the learner's internal use. After the model is created, many decision tree algorithms output the resulting structure in a human-readable format. This provides tremendous insight into how and why the model works or doesn't work well for a particular task. This also makes decision trees particularly appropriate for applications in which the classification mechanism needs to be transparent for legal reasons, or in case the results need to be shared with others in order to inform future business practices. With this in mind, some potential uses include:

- Credit scoring models in which the criteria that causes an applicant to be rejected need to be clearly documented and free from bias

- Marketing studies of customer behavior such as satisfaction or churn, which will be shared with management or advertising agencies

- Diagnosis of medical conditions based on laboratory measurements, symptoms, or the rate of disease progression

Although the previous applications illustrate the value of trees in informing decision processes, this is not to suggest that their utility ends here. In fact, decision trees are perhaps the single most widely used machine learning technique, and can be applied to model almost any type of data—often with excellent out-of-the-box applications.

This said, in spite of their wide applicability, it is worth noting some scenarios where trees may not be an ideal fit. One such case might be a task where the data has a large number of nominal features with many levels or it has a large number of numeric features. These cases may result in a very large number of decisions and an overly complex tree. They may also contribute to the tendency of decision trees to overfit data, though as we will soon see, even this weakness can be overcome by adjusting some simple parameters.

Divide and conquer

Decision trees are built using a heuristic called **recursive partitioning**. This approach is also commonly known as **divide and conquer** because it splits the data into subsets, which are then split repeatedly into even smaller subsets, and so on and so forth until the process stops when the algorithm determines the data within the subsets are sufficiently homogenous, or another stopping criterion has been met.

To see how splitting a dataset can create a decision tree, imagine a bare root node that will grow into a mature tree. At first, the root node represents the entire dataset, since no splitting has transpired. Next, the decision tree algorithm must choose a feature to split upon; ideally, it chooses the feature most predictive of the target class. The examples are then partitioned into groups according to the distinct values of this feature, and the first set of tree branches are formed.

Working down each branch, the algorithm continues to divide and conquer the data, choosing the best candidate feature each time to create another decision node, until a stopping criterion is reached. Divide and conquer might stop at a node in a case that:

- All (or nearly all) of the examples at the node have the same class
- There are no remaining features to distinguish among the examples
- The tree has grown to a predefined size limit

To illustrate the tree building process, let's consider a simple example. Imagine that you work for a Hollywood studio, where your role is to decide whether the studio should move forward with producing the screenplays pitched by promising new authors. After returning from a vacation, your desk is piled high with proposals. Without the time to read each proposal cover-to-cover, you decide to develop a decision tree algorithm to predict whether a potential movie would fall into one of three categories: **Critical Success**, **Mainstream Hit**, or **Box Office Bust**.

To build the decision tree, you turn to the studio archives to examine the factors leading to the success and failure of the company's 30 most recent releases. You quickly notice a relationship between the film's estimated shooting budget, the number of A-list celebrities lined up for starring roles, and the level of success. Excited about this finding, you produce a scatterplot to illustrate the pattern:

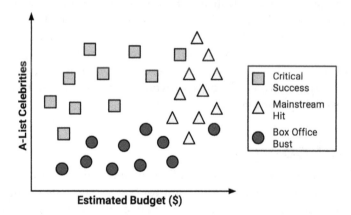

Using the divide and conquer strategy, we can build a simple decision tree from this data. First, to create the tree's root node, we split the feature indicating the number of celebrities, partitioning the movies into groups with and without a significant number of A-list stars:

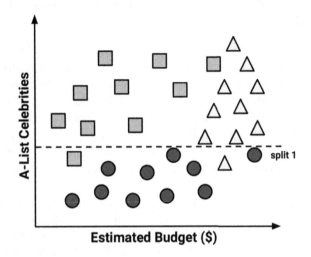

Next, among the group of movies with a larger number of celebrities, we can make another split between movies with and without a high budget:

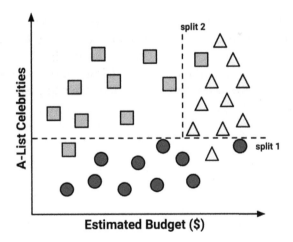

At this point, we have partitioned the data into three groups. The group at the top-left corner of the diagram is composed entirely of critically acclaimed films. This group is distinguished by a high number of celebrities and a relatively low budget. At the top-right corner, majority of movies are box office hits with high budgets and a large number of celebrities. The final group, which has little star power but budgets ranging from small to large, contains the flops.

If we wanted, we could continue to divide and conquer the data by splitting it based on the increasingly specific ranges of budget and celebrity count, until each of the currently misclassified values resides in its own tiny partition, and is correctly classified. However, it is not advisable to overfit a decision tree in this way. Though there is nothing to stop us from splitting the data indefinitely, overly specific decisions do not always generalize more broadly. We'll avoid the problem of overfitting by stopping the algorithm here, since more than 80 percent of the examples in each group are from a single class. This forms the basis of our stopping criterion.

You might have noticed that diagonal lines might have split the data even more cleanly. This is one limitation of the decision tree's knowledge representation, which uses **axis-parallel splits**. The fact that each split considers one feature at a time prevents the decision tree from forming more complex decision boundaries. For example, a diagonal line could be created by a decision that asks, "is the number of celebrities is greater than the estimated budget?" If so, then "it will be a critical success."

Our model for predicting the future success of movies can be represented in a simple tree, as shown in the following diagram. To evaluate a script, follow the branches through each decision until the script's success or failure has been predicted. In no time, you will be able to identify the most promising options among the backlog of scripts and get back to more important work, such as writing an Academy Awards acceptance speech.

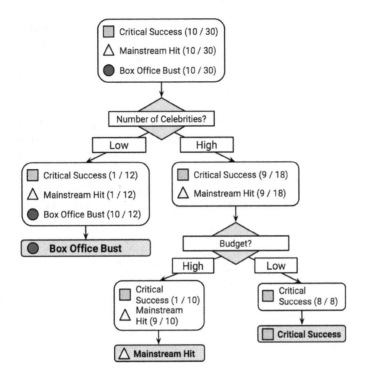

Since real-world data contains more than two features, decision trees quickly become far more complex than this, with many more nodes, branches, and leaves. In the next section, you will learn about a popular algorithm to build decision tree models automatically.

The C5.0 decision tree algorithm

There are numerous implementations of decision trees, but one of the most well-known implementations is the **C5.0 algorithm**. This algorithm was developed by computer scientist J. Ross Quinlan as an improved version of his prior algorithm, **C4.5**, which itself is an improvement over his **Iterative Dichotomiser 3 (ID3)** algorithm. Although Quinlan markets C5.0 to commercial clients (see http://www. rulequest.com/ for details), the source code for a single-threaded version of the algorithm was made publically available, and it has therefore been incorporated into programs such as R.

To further confuse matters, a popular Java-based open source alternative to C4.5, titled **J48**, is included in R's RWeka package. Because the differences among C5.0, C4.5, and J48 are minor, the principles in this chapter will apply to any of these three methods, and the algorithms should be considered synonymous.

The C5.0 algorithm has become the industry standard to produce decision trees, because it does well for most types of problems directly out of the box. Compared to other advanced machine learning models, such as those described in *Chapter 7, Black Box Methods – Neural Networks and Support Vector Machines*, the decision trees built by C5.0 generally perform nearly as well, but are much easier to understand and deploy. Additionally, as shown in the following table, the algorithm's weaknesses are relatively minor and can be largely avoided:

Strengths	Weaknesses
• An all-purpose classifier that does well on most problems • Highly automatic learning process, which can handle numeric or nominal features, as well as missing data • Excludes unimportant features • Can be used on both small and large datasets • Results in a model that can be interpreted without a mathematical background (for relatively small trees) • More efficient than other complex models	• Decision tree models are often biased toward splits on features having a large number of levels • It is easy to overfit or underfit the model • Can have trouble modeling some relationships due to reliance on axis-parallel splits • Small changes in the training data can result in large changes to decision logic • Large trees can be difficult to interpret and the decisions they make may seem counterintuitive

To keep things simple, our earlier decision tree example ignored the mathematics involved in how a machine would employ a divide and conquer strategy. Let's explore this in more detail to examine how this heuristic works in practice.

Choosing the best split

The first challenge that a decision tree will face is to identify which feature to split upon. In the previous example, we looked for a way to split the data such that the resulting partitions contained examples primarily of a single class. The degree to which a subset of examples contains only a single class is known as **purity**, and any subset composed of only a single class is called **pure**.

There are various measurements of purity that can be used to identify the best decision tree splitting candidate. C5.0 uses **entropy**, a concept borrowed from information theory that quantifies the randomness, or disorder, within a set of class values. Sets with high entropy are very diverse and provide little information about other items that may also belong in the set, as there is no apparent commonality. The decision tree hopes to find splits that reduce entropy, ultimately increasing homogeneity within the groups.

Typically, entropy is measured in **bits**. If there are only two possible classes, entropy values can range from 0 to 1. For n classes, entropy ranges from 0 to $log_2(n)$. In each case, the minimum value indicates that the sample is completely homogenous, while the maximum value indicates that the data are as diverse as possible, and no group has even a small plurality.

In the mathematical notion, entropy is specified as follows:

$$\text{Entropy}(S) = \sum_{i=1}^{c} -p_i \ log_2(p_i)$$

In this formula, for a given segment of data *(S)*, the term *c* refers to the number of class levels and p_i refers to the proportion of values falling into class level *i*. For example, suppose we have a partition of data with two classes: red (60 percent) and white (40 percent). We can calculate the entropy as follows:

```
> -0.60 * log2(0.60) - 0.40 * log2(0.40)
[1] 0.9709506
```

We can examine the entropy for all the possible two-class arrangements. If we know that the proportion of examples in one class is *x*, then the proportion in the other class is *(1 – x)*. Using the curve() function, we can then plot the entropy for all the possible values of *x*:

```
> curve(-x * log2(x) - (1 - x) * log2(1 - x),
        col = "red", xlab = "x", ylab = "Entropy", lwd = 4)
```

This results in the following figure:

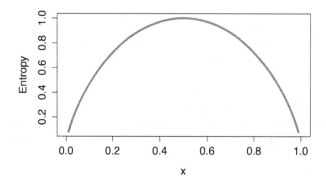

As illustrated by the peak in entropy at $x = 0.50$, a 50-50 split results in maximum entropy. As one class increasingly dominates the other, the entropy reduces to zero.

To use entropy to determine the optimal feature to split upon, the algorithm calculates the change in homogeneity that would result from a split on each possible feature, which is a measure known as **information gain**. The information gain for a feature F is calculated as the difference between the entropy in the segment before the split (S_1) and the partitions resulting from the split (S_2):

$$\text{InfoGain}(F) = \text{Entropy}(S_1) - \text{Entropy}(S_2)$$

One complication is that after a split, the data is divided into more than one partition. Therefore, the function to calculate $Entropy(S_2)$ needs to consider the total entropy across all of the partitions. It does this by weighing each partition's entropy by the proportion of records falling into the partition. This can be stated in a formula as:

$$\text{Entropy}(S) = \sum_{i=1}^{n} w_i \, \text{Entropy}(P_i)$$

In simple terms, the total entropy resulting from a split is the sum of the entropy of each of the n partitions weighted by the proportion of examples falling in the partition (w_i).

The higher the information gain, the better a feature is at creating homogeneous groups after a split on this feature. If the information gain is zero, there is no reduction in entropy for splitting on this feature. On the other hand, the maximum information gain is equal to the entropy prior to the split. This would imply that the entropy after the split is zero, which means that the split results in completely homogeneous groups.

The previous formulae assume nominal features, but decision trees use information gain for splitting on numeric features as well. To do so, a common practice is to test various splits that divide the values into groups greater than or less than a numeric threshold. This reduces the numeric feature into a two-level categorical feature that allows information gain to be calculated as usual. The numeric cut point yielding the largest information gain is chosen for the split.

> Though it is used by C5.0, information gain is not the only splitting criterion that can be used to build decision trees. Other commonly used criteria are **Gini index**, **Chi-Squared statistic**, and **gain ratio**. For a review of these (and many more) criteria, refer to Mingers J. *An Empirical Comparison of Selection Measures for Decision-Tree Induction.* Machine Learning. 1989; 3:319-342.

Pruning the decision tree

A decision tree can continue to grow indefinitely, choosing splitting features and dividing the data into smaller and smaller partitions until each example is perfectly classified or the algorithm runs out of features to split on. However, if the tree grows overly large, many of the decisions it makes will be overly specific and the model will be overfitted to the training data. The process of **pruning** a decision tree involves reducing its size such that it generalizes better to unseen data.

One solution to this problem is to stop the tree from growing once it reaches a certain number of decisions or when the decision nodes contain only a small number of examples. This is called **early stopping** or **pre-pruning** the decision tree. As the tree avoids doing needless work, this is an appealing strategy. However, one downside to this approach is that there is no way to know whether the tree will miss subtle, but important patterns that it would have learned had it grown to a larger size.

An alternative, called **post-pruning**, involves growing a tree that is intentionally too large and pruning leaf nodes to reduce the size of the tree to a more appropriate level. This is often a more effective approach than pre-pruning, because it is quite difficult to determine the optimal depth of a decision tree without growing it first. Pruning the tree later on allows the algorithm to be certain that all the important data structures were discovered.

> The implementation details of pruning operations are very technical and beyond the scope of this book. For a comparison of some of the available methods, see Esposito F, Malerba D, Semeraro G. *A Comparative Analysis of Methods for Pruning Decision Trees.* IEEE Transactions on Pattern Analysis and Machine Intelligence. 1997;19: 476-491.

One of the benefits of the C5.0 algorithm is that it is opinionated about pruning – it takes care of many decisions automatically using fairly reasonable defaults. Its overall strategy is to post-prune the tree. It first grows a large tree that overfits the training data. Later, the nodes and branches that have little effect on the classification errors are removed. In some cases, entire branches are moved further up the tree or replaced by simpler decisions. These processes of grafting branches are known as **subtree raising** and **subtree replacement**, respectively.

Balancing overfitting and underfitting a decision tree is a bit of an art, but if model accuracy is vital, it may be worth investing some time with various pruning options to see if it improves the performance on test data. As you will soon see, one of the strengths of the C5.0 algorithm is that it is very easy to adjust the training options.

Example – identifying risky bank loans using C5.0 decision trees

The global financial crisis of 2007-2008 highlighted the importance of transparency and rigor in banking practices. As the availability of credit was limited, banks tightened their lending systems and turned to machine learning to more accurately identify risky loans.

Decision trees are widely used in the banking industry due to their high accuracy and ability to formulate a statistical model in plain language. Since government organizations in many countries carefully monitor lending practices, executives must be able to explain why one applicant was rejected for a loan while the others were approved. This information is also useful for customers hoping to determine why their credit rating is unsatisfactory.

It is likely that automated credit scoring models are employed to instantly approve credit applications on the telephone and web. In this section, we will develop a simple credit approval model using C5.0 decision trees. We will also see how the results of the model can be tuned to minimize errors that result in a financial loss for the institution.

Step 1 – collecting data

The idea behind our credit model is to identify factors that are predictive of higher risk of default. Therefore, we need to obtain data on a large number of past bank loans and whether the loan went into default, as well as information on the applicant.

Data with these characteristics is available in a dataset donated to the UCI Machine Learning Data Repository (http://archive.ics.uci.edu/ml) by Hans Hofmann of the University of Hamburg. The dataset contains information on loans obtained from a credit agency in Germany.

> The dataset presented in this chapter has been modified slightly from the original in order to eliminate some preprocessing steps. To follow along with the examples, download the credit.csv file from Packt Publishing's website and save it to your R working directory.

The credit dataset includes 1,000 examples on loans, plus a set of numeric and nominal features indicating the characteristics of the loan and the loan applicant. A class variable indicates whether the loan went into default. Let's see whether we can determine any patterns that predict this outcome.

Step 2 – exploring and preparing the data

As we did previously, we will import data using the read.csv() function. We will ignore the stringsAsFactors option and, therefore, use the default value of TRUE, as the majority of the features in the data are nominal:

```
> credit <- read.csv("credit.csv")
```

The first several lines of output from the str() function are as follows:

```
> str(credit)
'data.frame':1000 obs. of  17 variables:
 $ checking_balance : Factor w/ 4 levels "< 0 DM","> 200 DM",..
 $ months_loan_duration: int  6 48 12 ...
 $ credit_history      : Factor w/ 5 levels "critical","good",..
 $ purpose             : Factor w/ 6 levels "business","car",..
 $ amount              : int  1169 5951 2096 ...
```

We see the expected 1,000 observations and 17 features, which are a combination of factor and integer data types.

Let's take a look at the table() output for a couple of loan features that seem likely to predict a default. The applicant's checking and savings account balance are recorded as categorical variables:

```
> table(credit$checking_balance)
    < 0 DM    > 200 DM 1 - 200 DM     unknown
```

```
     274           63          269          394
> table(credit$savings_balance)

   < 100 DM > 1000 DM  100 - 500 DM 500 - 1000 DM    unknown
        603          48          103           63        183
```

The checking and savings account balance may prove to be important predictors of loan default status. Note that since the loan data was obtained from Germany, the currency is recorded in Deutsche Marks (DM).

Some of the loan's features are numeric, such as its duration and the amount of credit requested:

```
> summary(credit$months_loan_duration)
   Min. 1st Qu.  Median    Mean 3rd Qu.    Max.
    4.0    12.0    18.0    20.9    24.0    72.0
> summary(credit$amount)
   Min. 1st Qu.  Median    Mean 3rd Qu.    Max.
    250    1366    2320    3271    3972   18420
```

The loan amounts ranged from 250 DM to 18,420 DM across terms of 4 to 72 months with a median duration of 18 months and an amount of 2,320 DM.

The `default` vector indicates whether the loan applicant was unable to meet the agreed payment terms and went into default. A total of 30 percent of the loans in this dataset went into default:

```
> table(credit$default)
 no yes
700 300
```

A high rate of default is undesirable for a bank, because it means that the bank is unlikely to fully recover its investment. If we are successful, our model will identify applicants that are at high risk to default, allowing the bank to refuse credit requests.

Data preparation – creating random training and test datasets

As we have done in the previous chapters, we will split our data into two portions: a training dataset to build the decision tree and a test dataset to evaluate the performance of the model on new data. We will use 90 percent of the data for training and 10 percent for testing, which will provide us with 100 records to simulate new applicants.

As prior chapters used data that had been sorted in a random order, we simply divided the dataset into two portions, by taking the first 90 percent of records for training, and the remaining 10 percent for testing. In contrast, the credit dataset is not randomly ordered, making the prior approach unwise. Suppose that the bank had sorted the data by the loan amount, with the largest loans at the end of the file. If we used the first 90 percent for training and the remaining 10 percent for testing, we would be training a model on only the small loans and testing the model on the big loans. Obviously, this could be problematic.

We'll solve this problem by using a **random sample** of the credit data for training. A random sample is simply a process that selects a subset of records at random. In R, the `sample()` function is used to perform random sampling. However, before putting it in action, a common practice is to set a **seed** value, which causes the randomization process to follow a sequence that can be replicated later on if desired. It may seem that this defeats the purpose of generating random numbers, but there is a good reason for doing it this way. Providing a seed value via the `set.seed()` function ensures that if the analysis is repeated in the future, an identical result is obtained.

> You may wonder how a so-called random process can be seeded to produce an identical result. This is due to the fact that computers use a mathematical function called a **pseudorandom number generator** to create random number sequences that appear to act very random, but are actually quite predictable given knowledge of the previous values in the sequence. In practice, modern pseudorandom number sequences are virtually indistinguishable from true random sequences, but have the benefit that computers can generate them quickly and easily.

The following commands use the `sample()` function to select 900 values at random out of the sequence of integers from 1 to 1000. Note that the `set.seed()` function uses the arbitrary value `123`. Omitting this seed will cause your training and testing split to differ from those shown in the remainder of this chapter:

```
> set.seed(123)
> train_sample <- sample(1000, 900)
```

As expected, the resulting `train_sample` object is a vector of 900 random integers:

```
> str(train_sample)
 int [1:900] 288 788 409 881 937 46 525 887 548 453 ...
```

By using this vector to select rows from the credit data, we can split it into the 90 percent training and 10 percent test datasets we desired. Recall that the dash operator used in the selection of the test records tells R to select records that are not in the specified rows; in other words, the test data includes only the rows that are not in the training sample.

```
> credit_train <- credit[train_sample, ]
> credit_test  <- credit[-train_sample, ]
```

If all went well, we should have about 30 percent of defaulted loans in each of the datasets:

```
> prop.table(table(credit_train$default))

       no       yes
0.7033333 0.2966667


> prop.table(table(credit_test$default))

  no  yes
0.67 0.33
```

This appears to be a fairly even split, so we can now build our decision tree.

 If your results do not match exactly, ensure that you ran the command `set.seed(123)` immediately prior to creating the `train_sample` vector.

Step 3 – training a model on the data

We will use the C5.0 algorithm in the `C50` package to train our decision tree model. If you have not done so already, install the package with `install.packages("C50")` and load it to your R session, using `library(C50)`.

The following syntax box lists some of the most commonly used commands to build decision trees. Compared to the machine learning approaches we used previously, the C5.0 algorithm offers many more ways to tailor the model to a particular learning problem, but more options are available. Once the `C50` package has been loaded, the `?C5.0Control` command displays the help page for more details on how to finely-tune the algorithm.

C5.0 decision tree syntax
using the C5.0() function in the C50 package

Building the classifier:

```
m <- C5.0(train, class, trials = 1, costs = NULL)
```

- train is a data frame containing training data
- class is a factor vector with the class for each row in the training data
- trials is an optional number to control the number of boosting iterations (set to 1 by default)
- costs is an optional matrix specifying costs associated with various types of errors

The function will return a C5.0 model object that can be used to make predictions.

Making predictions:

```
p <- predict(m, test, type = "class")
```

- m is a model trained by the C5.0() function
- test is a data frame containing test data with the same features as the training data used to build the classifier.
- type is either "class" or "prob" and specifies whether the predictions should be the most probable class value or the raw predicted probabilities

The function will return a vector of predicted class values or raw predicted probabilities depending upon the value of the type parameter.

Example:

```
credit_model <- C5.0(credit_train, loan_default)
credit_prediction <- predict(credit_model,
  credit_test)
```

For the first iteration of our credit approval model, we'll use the default C5.0 configuration, as shown in the following code. The 17th column in credit_train is the default class variable, so we need to exclude it from the training data frame, but supply it as the target factor vector for classification:

```
> credit_model <- C5.0(credit_train[-17], credit_train$default)
```

The credit_model object now contains a C5.0 decision tree. We can see some basic data about the tree by typing its name:

```
> credit_model
```

```
Call:
C5.0.default(x = credit_train[-17], y = credit_train$default)

Classification Tree
Number of samples: 900
```

```
Number of predictors: 16
```

```
Tree size: 57
```

```
Non-standard options: attempt to group attributes
```

The preceding text shows some simple facts about the tree, including the function call that generated it, the number of features (labeled `predictors`), and examples (labeled `samples`) used to grow the tree. Also listed is the tree size of 57, which indicates that the tree is 57 decisions deep – quite a bit larger than the example trees we've considered so far!

To see the tree's decisions, we can call the `summary()` function on the model:

```
> summary(credit_model)
```

This results in the following output:

```
C5.0 [Release 2.07 GPL Edition]
-------------------------------

Class specified by attribute `outcome'

Read 900 cases (17 attributes) from undefined.data

Decision tree:

checking_balance in {> 200 DM,unknown}: no (412/50)
checking_balance in {< 0 DM,1 - 200 DM}:
:...credit_history in {perfect,very good}: yes (59/18)
    credit_history in {critical,good,poor}:
    :...months_loan_duration <= 22:
        :...credit_history = critical: no (72/14)
        :   credit_history = poor:
        :   :...dependents > 1: no (5)
        :   :   dependents <= 1:
        :   :   :...years_at_residence <= 3: yes (4/1)
        :   :       years_at_residence > 3: no (5/1)
```

The preceding output shows some of the first branches in the decision tree. The first three lines could be represented in plain language as:

1. If the checking account balance is unknown or greater than 200 DM, then classify as "not likely to default."

2. Otherwise, if the checking account balance is less than zero DM or between one and 200 DM.

3. And the credit history is perfect or very good, then classify as "likely to default."

The numbers in parentheses indicate the number of examples meeting the criteria for that decision, and the number incorrectly classified by the decision. For instance, on the first line, `412/50` indicates that of the 412 examples reaching the decision, 50 were incorrectly classified as not likely to default. In other words, 50 applicants actually defaulted, in spite of the model's prediction to the contrary.

> Sometimes a tree results in decisions that make little logical sense. For example, why would an applicant whose credit history is very good be likely to default, while those whose checking balance is unknown are not likely to default? Contradictory rules like this occur sometimes. They might reflect a real pattern in the data, or they may be a statistical anomaly. In either case, it is important to investigate such strange decisions to see whether the tree's logic makes sense for business use.

After the tree, the `summary(credit_model)` output displays a confusion matrix, which is a cross-tabulation that indicates the model's incorrectly classified records in the training data:

```
Evaluation on training data (900 cases):


    Decision Tree

    ----------------

  Size      Errors
    56   133(14.8%)    <<


   (a)    (b)    <-classified as

   ----   ----
   598     35    (a): class no
    98    169    (b): class yes
```

The Errors output notes that the model correctly classified all but 133 of the 900 training instances for an error rate of 14.8 percent. A total of 35 actual no values were incorrectly classified as yes (false positives), while 98 yes values were misclassified as no (false negatives).

Decision trees are known for having a tendency to overfit the model to the training data. For this reason, the error rate reported on training data may be overly optimistic, and it is especially important to evaluate decision trees on a test dataset.

Step 4 – evaluating model performance

To apply our decision tree to the test dataset, we use the `predict()` function, as shown in the following line of code:

```
> credit_pred <- predict(credit_model, credit_test)
```

This creates a vector of predicted class values, which we can compare to the actual class values using the `CrossTable()` function in the `gmodels` package. Setting the `prop.c` and `prop.r` parameters to `FALSE` removes the column and row percentages from the table. The remaining percentage (`prop.t`) indicates the proportion of records in the cell out of the total number of records:

```
> library(gmodels)
> CrossTable(credit_test$default, credit_pred,
           prop.chisq = FALSE, prop.c = FALSE, prop.r = FALSE,
           dnn = c('actual default', 'predicted default'))
```

This results in the following table:

```
                |   predicted default
actual default  |        no |       yes | Row Total |
----------------|-----------|-----------|-----------|
            no  |        59 |         8 |        67 |
                |     0.590 |     0.080 |           |
----------------|-----------|-----------|-----------|
           yes  |        19 |        14 |        33 |
                |     0.190 |     0.140 |           |
----------------|-----------|-----------|-----------|
   Column Total |        78 |        22 |       100 |
----------------|-----------|-----------|-----------|
```

Out of the 100 test loan application records, our model correctly predicted that 59 did not default and 14 did default, resulting in an accuracy of 73 percent and an error rate of 27 percent. This is somewhat worse than its performance on the training data, but not unexpected, given that a model's performance is often worse on unseen data. Also note that the model only correctly predicted 14 of the 33 actual loan defaults in the test data, or 42 percent. Unfortunately, this type of error is a potentially very costly mistake, as the bank loses money on each default. Let's see if we can improve the result with a bit more effort.

Step 5 – improving model performance

Our model's error rate is likely to be too high to deploy it in a real-time credit scoring application. In fact, if the model had predicted "no default" for every test case, it would have been correct 67 percent of the time—a result not much worse than our model's, but requiring much less effort! Predicting loan defaults from 900 examples seems to be a challenging problem.

Making matters even worse, our model performed especially poorly at identifying applicants who do default on their loans. Luckily, there are a couple of simple ways to adjust the C5.0 algorithm that may help to improve the performance of the model, both overall and for the more costly type of mistakes.

Boosting the accuracy of decision trees

One way the C5.0 algorithm improved upon the C4.5 algorithm was through the addition of **adaptive boosting**. This is a process in which many decision trees are built and the trees vote on the best class for each example.

 The idea of boosting is based largely upon the research by Rob Schapire and Yoav Freund. For more information, try searching the web for their publications or their recent textbook *Boosting: Foundations and Algorithms*. The MIT Press (2012).

As boosting can be applied more generally to any machine learning algorithm, it is covered in detail later in this book in *Chapter 11, Improving Model Performance*. For now, it suffices to say that boosting is rooted in the notion that by combining a number of weak performing learners, you can create a team that is much stronger than any of the learners alone. Each of the models has a unique set of strengths and weaknesses and they may be better or worse in solving certain problems. Using a combination of several learners with complementary strengths and weaknesses can therefore dramatically improve the accuracy of a classifier.

The c5.0() function makes it easy to add boosting to our C5.0 decision tree. We simply need to add an additional trials parameter indicating the number of separate decision trees to use in the boosted team. The trials parameter sets an upper limit; the algorithm will stop adding trees if it recognizes that additional trials do not seem to be improving the accuracy. We'll start with 10 trials, a number that has become the de facto standard, as research suggests that this reduces error rates on test data by about 25 percent:

```
> credit_boost10 <- C5.0(credit_train[-17], credit_train$default,
                         trials = 10)
```

While examining the resulting model, we can see that some additional lines have been added, indicating the changes:

```
> credit_boost10
Number of boosting iterations: 10
Average tree size: 47.5
```

Across the 10 iterations, our tree size shrunk. If you would like, you can see all 10 trees by typing `summary(credit_boost10)` at the command prompt. It also lists the model's performance on the training data:

```
> summary(credit_boost10)


    (a)     (b)     <-classified as

    ----    ----

    629     4       (a): class no
    30      237     (b): class yes
```

The classifier made 34 mistakes on 900 training examples for an error rate of 3.8 percent. This is quite an improvement over the 13.9 percent training error rate we noted before adding boosting! However, it remains to be seen whether we see a similar improvement on the test data. Let's take a look:

```
> credit_boost_pred10 <- predict(credit_boost10, credit_test)
> CrossTable(credit_test$default, credit_boost_pred10,
             prop.chisq = FALSE, prop.c = FALSE, prop.r = FALSE,
             dnn = c('actual default', 'predicted default'))
```

The resulting table is as follows:

actual default	predicted default		
	no	yes	Row Total
no	62	5	67
	0.620	0.050	
yes	13	20	33
	0.130	0.200	
Column Total	75	25	100

Here, we reduced the total error rate from 27 percent prior to boosting down to 18 percent in the boosted model. It does not seem like a large gain, but it is in fact larger than the 25 percent reduction we expected. On the other hand, the model is still not doing well at predicting defaults, predicting only *20/33 = 61%* correctly. The lack of an even greater improvement may be a function of our relatively small training dataset, or it may just be a very difficult problem to solve.

This said, if boosting can be added this easily, why not apply it by default to every decision tree? The reason is twofold. First, if building a decision tree once takes a great deal of computation time, building many trees may be computationally impractical. Secondly, if the training data is very noisy, then boosting might not result in an improvement at all. Still, if greater accuracy is needed, it's worth giving it a try.

Making mistakes more costlier than others

Giving a loan out to an applicant who is likely to default can be an expensive mistake. One solution to reduce the number of false negatives may be to reject a larger number of borderline applicants, under the assumption that the interest the bank would earn from a risky loan is far outweighed by the massive loss it would incur if the money is not paid back at all.

The C5.0 algorithm allows us to assign a penalty to different types of errors, in order to discourage a tree from making more costly mistakes. The penalties are designated in a **cost matrix**, which specifies how much costlier each error is, relative to any other prediction.

To begin constructing the cost matrix, we need to start by specifying the dimensions. Since the predicted and actual values can both take two values, yes or no, we need to describe a 2 x 2 matrix, using a list of two vectors, each with two values. At the same time, we'll also name the matrix dimensions to avoid confusion later on:

```
> matrix_dimensions <- list(c("no", "yes"), c("no", "yes"))
> names(matrix_dimensions) <- c("predicted", "actual")
```

Examining the new object shows that our dimensions have been set up correctly:

```
> matrix_dimensions
$predicted
[1] "no"  "yes"

$actual
[1] "no"  "yes"
```

Next, we need to assign the penalty for the various types of errors by supplying four values to fill the matrix. Since R fills a matrix by filling columns one by one from top to bottom, we need to supply the values in a specific order:

- Predicted no, actual no
- Predicted yes, actual no
- Predicted no, actual yes
- Predicted yes, actual yes

Suppose we believe that a loan default costs the bank four times as much as a missed opportunity. Our penalty values could then be defined as:

```
> error_cost <- matrix(c(0, 1, 4, 0), nrow = 2,
    dimnames = matrix_dimensions)
```

This creates the following matrix:

```
> error_cost
          actual
predicted no yes
      no   0   4
      yes  1   0
```

As defined by this matrix, there is no cost assigned when the algorithm classifies a no or yes correctly, but a false negative has a cost of 4 versus a false positive's cost of 1. To see how this impacts classification, let's apply it to our decision tree using the costs parameter of the C5.0() function. We'll otherwise use the same steps as we did earlier:

```
> credit_cost <- C5.0(credit_train[-17], credit_train$default,
                        costs = error_cost)
> credit_cost_pred <- predict(credit_cost, credit_test)
> CrossTable(credit_test$default, credit_cost_pred,
             prop.chisq = FALSE, prop.c = FALSE, prop.r = FALSE,
             dnn = c('actual default', 'predicted default'))
```

This produces the following confusion matrix:

```
                | predicted default
actual default |     no  |      yes | Row Total |
---------------|---------|----------|-----------|
            no |     37  |      30  |       67  |
               |  0.370  |   0.300  |           |
---------------|---------|----------|-----------|
           yes |      7  |      26  |       33  |
               |  0.070  |   0.260  |           |
---------------|---------|----------|-----------|
  Column Total |     44  |      56  |      100  |
---------------|---------|----------|-----------|
```

Compared to our boosted model, this version makes more mistakes overall: 37 percent error here versus 18 percent in the boosted case. However, the types of mistakes are very different. Where the previous models incorrectly classified only 42 and 61 percent of defaults correctly, in this model, 79 percent of the actual defaults were predicted to be non-defaults. This trade resulting in a reduction of false negatives at the expense of increasing false positives may be acceptable if our cost estimates were accurate.

Understanding classification rules

Classification rules represent knowledge in the form of logical if-else statements that assign a class to unlabeled examples. They are specified in terms of an **antecedent** and a **consequent**; these form a hypothesis stating that "if this happens, then that happens." A simple rule might state, "if the hard drive is making a clicking sound, then it is about to fail." The antecedent comprises certain combinations of feature values, while the consequent specifies the class value to assign when the rule's conditions are met.

Rule learners are often used in a manner similar to decision tree learners. Like decision trees, they can be used for applications that generate knowledge for future action, such as:

- Identifying conditions that lead to a hardware failure in mechanical devices
- Describing the key characteristics of groups of people for customer segmentation
- Finding conditions that precede large drops or increases in the prices of shares on the stock market

On the other hand, rule learners offer some distinct advantages over trees for some tasks. Unlike a tree, which must be applied from top-to-bottom through a series of decisions, rules are propositions that can be read much like a statement of fact. Additionally, for reasons that will be discussed later, the results of a rule learner can be more simple, direct, and easier to understand than a decision tree built on the same data.

 As you will see later in this chapter, rules can be generated using decision trees. So, why bother with a separate group of rule learning algorithms? The reason is that decision trees bring a particular set of biases to the task that a rule learner avoids by identifying the rules directly.

Rule learners are generally applied to problems where the features are primarily or entirely nominal. They do well at identifying rare events, even if the rare event occurs only for a very specific interaction among feature values.

Separate and conquer

Classification rule learning algorithms utilize a heuristic known as **separate and conquer**. The process involves identifying a rule that covers a subset of examples in the training data, and then separating this partition from the remaining data. As the rules are added, additional subsets of the data are separated until the entire dataset has been covered and no more examples remain.

One way to imagine the rule learning process is to think about drilling down into the data by creating increasingly specific rules to identify class values. Suppose you were tasked with creating rules to identify whether or not an animal is a mammal. You could depict the set of all animals as a large space, as shown in the following diagram:

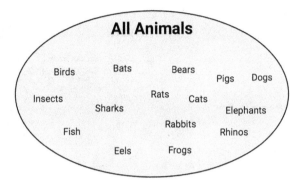

A rule learner begins by using the available features to find homogeneous groups. For example, using a feature that indicates whether the species travels via land, sea, or air, the first rule might suggest that any land-based animals are mammals:

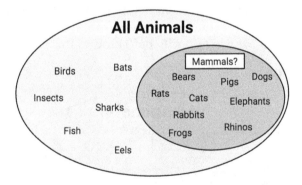

Do you notice any problems with this rule? If you're an animal lover, you might have realized that frogs are amphibians, not mammals. Therefore, our rule needs to be a bit more specific. Let's drill down further by suggesting that mammals must walk on land and have a tail:

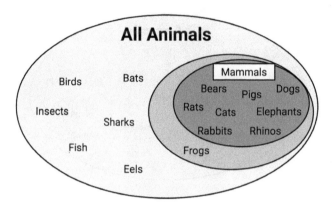

An additional rule can be defined to separate out the bats, the only remaining mammal. Thus, this subset can be separated from the other data.

An additional rule can be defined to separate out the bats, the only remaining mammal. A potential feature distinguishing bats from the other remaining animals would be the presence of fur. Using a rule built around this feature, we have then correctly identified all the animals:

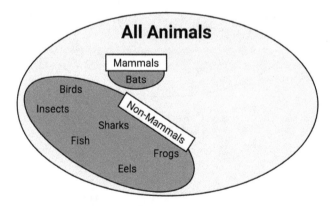

At this point, since all of the training instances have been classified, the rule learning process would stop. We learned a total of three rules:

- Animals that walk on land and have tails are mammals
- If the animal does not have fur, it is not a mammal
- Otherwise, the animal is a mammal

The previous example illustrates how rules gradually consume larger and larger segments of data to eventually classify all instances.

As the rules seem to cover portions of the data, separate and conquer algorithms are also known as **covering algorithms**, and the resulting rules are called covering rules. In the next section, we will learn how covering rules are applied in practice by examining a simple rule learning algorithm. We will then examine a more complex rule learner, and apply both to a real-world problem.

The 1R algorithm

Suppose a television game show has a wheel with ten evenly sized colored slices. Three of the segments were colored red, three were blue, and four were white. Prior to spinning the wheel, you are asked to choose one of these colors. When the wheel stops spinning, if the color shown matches your prediction, you will win a large cash prize. What color should you pick?

If you choose white, you are, of course, more likely to win the prize—this is the most common color on the wheel. Obviously, this game show is a bit ridiculous, but it demonstrates the simplest classifier, **ZeroR**, a rule learner that literally learns no rules (hence the name). For every unlabeled example, regardless of the values of its features, it predicts the most common class.

The **1R algorithm** (**One Rule** or **OneR**), improves over ZeroR by selecting a single rule. Although this may seem overly simplistic, it tends to perform better than you might expect. As demonstrated in empirical studies, the accuracy of this algorithm can approach that of much more sophisticated algorithms for many real-world tasks.

For an in-depth look at the surprising performance of 1R, see Holte RC. *Very simple classification rules perform well on most commonly used datasets.* Machine Learning. 1993; 11:63-91.

The strengths and weaknesses of the 1R algorithm are shown in the following table:

Strengths	Weaknesses
• Generates a single, easy-to-understand, human-readable rule of thumb • Often performs surprisingly well • Can serve as a benchmark for more complex algorithms	• Uses only a single feature • Probably overly simplistic

The way this algorithm works is simple. For each feature, 1R divides the data into groups based on similar values of the feature. Then, for each segment, the algorithm predicts the majority class. The error rate for the rule based on each feature is calculated and the rule with the fewest errors is chosen as the one rule.

The following tables show how this would work for the animal data we looked at earlier in this section:

Animal	Travels By	Has Fur	Mammal
Bats	Air	Yes	Yes
Bears	Land	Yes	Yes
Birds	Air	No	No
Cats	Land	Yes	Yes
Dogs	Land	Yes	Yes
Eels	Sea	No	No
Elephants	Land	No	Yes
Fish	Sea	No	No
Frogs	Land	No	No
Insects	Air	No	No
Pigs	Land	No	Yes
Rabbits	Land	Yes	Yes
Rats	Land	Yes	Yes
Rhinos	Land	No	Yes
Sharks	Sea	No	No

Full Dataset

Travels By	Predicted	Mammal	
Air	No	Yes	✖
Air	No	No	
Air	No	No	
Land	Yes	Yes	
Land	Yes	Yes	
Land	Yes	Yes	
Land	Yes	Yes	
Land	Yes	No	✖
Land	Yes	Yes	
Land	Yes	Yes	
Land	Yes	Yes	
Land	Yes	Yes	
Sea	No	No	
Sea	No	No	
Sea	No	No	

Rule for "Travels By"
Error Rate = 2 / 15

Has Fur	Predicted	Mammal	
No	No	No	
No	No	No	
No	No	Yes	✖
No	No	No	
No	No	No	
No	No	No	
No	No	Yes	✖
No	No	Yes	✖
No	No	No	
Yes	Yes	Yes	
Yes	Yes	Yes	
Yes	Yes	Yes	
Yes	Yes	Yes	
Yes	Yes	Yes	
Yes	Yes	Yes	

Rule for "Has Fur"
Error Rate = 3 / 15

For the **Travels By** feature, the dataset was divided into three groups: **Air**, **Land**, and **Sea**. Animals in the **Air** and **Sea** groups were predicted to be non-mammal, while animals in the **Land** group were predicted to be mammals. This resulted in two errors: bats and frogs. The **Has Fur** feature divided animals into two groups. Those with fur were predicted to be mammals, while those without fur were not predicted to be mammals. Three errors were counted: pigs, elephants, and rhinos. As the **Travels By** feature results in fewer errors, the 1R algorithm will return the following "one rule" based on **Travels By**:

- If the animal travels by air, it is not a mammal
- If the animal travels by land, it is a mammal
- If the animal travels by sea, it is not a mammal

The algorithm stops here, having found the single most important rule.

Obviously, this rule learning algorithm may be too basic for some tasks. Would you want a medical diagnosis system to consider only a single symptom, or an automated driving system to stop or accelerate your car based on only a single factor? For these types of tasks, a more sophisticated rule learner might be useful. We'll learn about one in the following section.

The RIPPER algorithm

Early rule learning algorithms were plagued by a couple of problems. First, they were notorious for being slow, which made them ineffective for the increasing number of large datasets. Secondly, they were often prone to being inaccurate on noisy data.

A first step toward solving these problems was proposed in 1994 by Johannes Furnkranz and Gerhard Widmer. Their **Incremental Reduced Error Pruning (IREP) algorithm** uses a combination of pre-pruning and post-pruning methods that grow very complex rules and prune them before separating the instances from the full dataset. Although this strategy helped the performance of rule learners, decision trees often still performed better.

 For more information on IREP, see Furnkranz J, Widmer G. *Incremental Reduced Error Pruning*. Proceedings of the 11th International Conference on Machine Learning. 1994: 70-77.

Rule learners took another step forward in 1995 when William W. Cohen introduced the **Repeated Incremental Pruning to Produce Error Reduction (RIPPER) algorithm**, which improved upon IREP to generate rules that match or exceed the performance of decision trees.

For more detail on RIPPER, see Cohen WW. *Fast effective rule induction*. Proceedings of the 12th International Conference on Machine Learning. 1995:115-123.

As outlined in the following table, the strengths and weaknesses of RIPPER are generally comparable to decision trees. The chief benefit is that they may result in a slightly more parsimonious model:

Strengths	Weaknesses
• Generates easy-to-understand, human-readable rules • Efficient on large and noisy datasets • Generally produces a simpler model than a comparable decision tree	• May result in rules that seem to defy common sense or expert knowledge • Not ideal for working with numeric data • Might not perform as well as more complex models

Having evolved from several iterations of rule learning algorithms, the RIPPER algorithm is a patchwork of efficient heuristics for rule learning. Due to its complexity, a discussion of the technical implementation details is beyond the scope of this book. However, it can be understood in general terms as a three-step process:

1. Grow

2. Prune

3. Optimize

The growing phase uses the separate and conquer technique to greedily add conditions to a rule until it perfectly classifies a subset of data or runs out of attributes for splitting. Similar to decision trees, the information gain criterion is used to identify the next splitting attribute. When increasing a rule's specificity no longer reduces entropy, the rule is immediately pruned. Steps one and two are repeated until it reaches a stopping criterion, at which point the entire set of rules is optimized using a variety of heuristics.

The RIPPER algorithm can create much more complex rules than can the 1R algorithm, as in can consider more than one feature. This means that it can create rules with multiple antecedents such as "if an animal flies and has fur, then it is a mammal." This improves the algorithm's ability to model complex data, but just like decision trees, it means that the rules can quickly become more difficult to comprehend.

The evolution of classification rule learners didn't stop with RIPPER. New rule learning algorithms are being proposed rapidly. A survey of literature shows algorithms called IREP++, SLIPPER, TRIPPER, among many others.

Rules from decision trees

Classification rules can also be obtained directly from decision trees. Beginning at a leaf node and following the branches back to the root, you will have obtained a series of decisions. These can be combined into a single rule. The following figure shows how rules could be constructed from the decision tree to predict movie success:

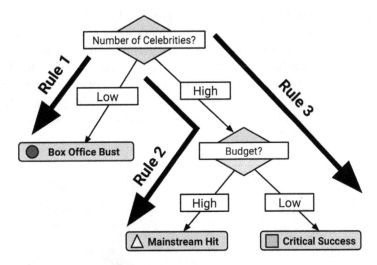

Following the paths from the root node down to each leaf, the rules would be:

1. If the number of celebrities is low, then the movie will be a **Box Office Bust**.

2. If the number of celebrities is high and the budget is high, then the movie will be a **Mainstream Hit**.

3. If the number of celebrities is high and the budget is low, then the movie will be a **Critical Success**.

For reasons that will be made clear in the following section, the chief downside to using a decision tree to generate rules is that the resulting rules are often more complex than those learned by a rule learning algorithm. The divide and conquer strategy employed by decision trees biases the results differently than that of a rule learner. On the other hand, it is sometimes more computationally efficient to generate rules from trees.

The C5.0() function in the C50 package will generate a model using classification rules if you specify rules = TRUE when training the model.

What makes trees and rules greedy?

Decision trees and rule learners are known as **greedy learners** because they use data on a first-come, first-served basis. Both the divide and conquer heuristic used by decision trees and the separate and conquer heuristic used by rule learners attempt to make partitions one at a time, finding the most homogeneous partition first, followed by the next best, and so on, until all examples have been classified.

The downside to the greedy approach is that greedy algorithms are not guaranteed to generate the optimal, most accurate, or smallest number of rules for a particular dataset. By taking the low-hanging fruit early, a greedy learner may quickly find a single rule that is accurate for one subset of data; however, in doing so, the learner may miss the opportunity to develop a more nuanced set of rules with better overall accuracy on the entire set of data. However, without using the greedy approach to rule learning, it is likely that for all but the smallest of datasets, rule learning would be computationally infeasible.

Though both trees and rules employ greedy learning heuristics, there are subtle differences in how they build rules. Perhaps the best way to distinguish them is to note that once divide and conquer splits on a feature, the partitions created by the split may not be re-conquered, only further subdivided. In this way, a tree is permanently limited by its history of past decisions. In contrast, once separate and conquer finds a rule, any examples not covered by all of the rule's conditions may be re-conquered.

To illustrate this contrast, consider the previous case in which we built a rule learner to determine whether an animal was a mammal. The rule learner identified three rules that perfectly classify the example animals:

- Animals that walk on land and have tails are mammals (bears, cats, dogs, elephants, pigs, rabbits, rats, rhinos)
- If the animal does not has fur, it is not a mammal (birds, eels, fish, frogs, insects, sharks)
- Otherwise, the animal is a mammal (bats)

In contrast, a decision tree built on the same data might have come up with four rules to achieve the same perfect classification:

- If an animal walks on land and has fur, then it is a mammal (bears, cats, dogs, elephants, pigs, rabbits, rats, rhinos)
- If an animal walks on land and does not have fur, then it is not a mammal (frogs)
- If the animal does not walk on land and has fur, then it is a mammal (bats)
- If the animal does not walk on land and does not have fur, then it is not a mammal (birds, insects, sharks, fish, eels)

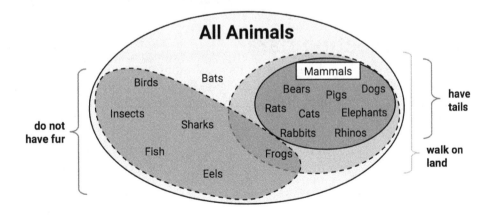

The different result across these two approaches has to do with what happens to the frogs after they are separated by the "walk on land" decision. Where the rule learner allows frogs to be re-conquered by the "does not have fur" decision, the decision tree cannot modify the existing partitions, and therefore must place the frog into its own rule.

On one hand, because rule learners can reexamine cases that were considered but ultimately not covered as part of prior rules, rule learners often find a more parsimonious set of rules than those generated from decision trees. On the other hand, this reuse of data means that the computational cost of rule learners may be somewhat higher than for decision trees.

Example – identifying poisonous mushrooms with rule learners

Each year, many people fall ill and sometimes even die from ingesting poisonous wild mushrooms. Since many mushrooms are very similar to each other in appearance, occasionally even experienced mushroom gatherers are poisoned.

Unlike the identification of harmful plants such as a poison oak or poison ivy, there are no clear rules such as "leaves of three, let them be" to identify whether a wild mushroom is poisonous or edible. Complicating matters, many traditional rules, such as "poisonous mushrooms are brightly colored," provide dangerous or misleading information. If simple, clear, and consistent rules were available to identify poisonous mushrooms, they could save the lives of foragers.

Because one of the strengths of rule learning algorithms is the fact that they generate easy-to-understand rules, they seem like an appropriate fit for this classification task. However, the rules will only be as useful as they are accurate.

Step 1 – collecting data

To identify rules for distinguishing poisonous mushrooms, we will utilize the Mushroom dataset by Jeff Schlimmer of Carnegie Mellon University. The raw dataset is available freely at the UCI Machine Learning Repository (http://archive.ics. uci.edu/ml).

The dataset includes information on 8,124 mushroom samples from 23 species of gilled mushrooms listed in *Audubon Society Field Guide to North American Mushrooms* (1981). In the Field Guide, each of the mushroom species is identified "definitely edible," "definitely poisonous," or "likely poisonous, and not recommended to be eaten." For the purposes of this dataset, the latter group was combined with the "definitely poisonous" group to make two classes: poisonous and nonpoisonous. The data dictionary available on the UCI website describes the 22 features of the mushroom samples, including characteristics such as cap shape, cap color, odor, gill size and color, stalk shape, and habitat.

> This chapter uses a slightly modified version of the mushroom data. If you plan on following along with the example, download the mushrooms.csv file from the Packt Publishing website and save it in your R working directory.

Step 2 – exploring and preparing the data

We begin by using read.csv(), to import the data for our analysis. Since all the 22 features and the target class are nominal, in this case, we will set stringsAsFactors = TRUE and take advantage of the automatic factor conversion:

```
> mushrooms <- read.csv("mushrooms.csv", stringsAsFactors = TRUE)
```

The output of the str(mushrooms) command notes that the data contain 8,124 observations of 23 variables as the data dictionary had described. While most of the str() output is unremarkable, one feature is worth mentioning. Do you notice anything peculiar about the veil_type variable in the following line?

```
$ veil_type : Factor w/ 1 level "partial": 1 1 1 1 1 1 ...
```

If you think it is odd that a factor has only one level, you are correct. The data dictionary lists two levels for this feature: partial and universal. However, all the examples in our data are classified as partial. It is likely that this data element was somehow coded incorrectly. In any case, since the veil type does not vary across samples, it does not provide any useful information for prediction. We will drop this variable from our analysis using the following command:

```
> mushrooms$veil_type <- NULL
```

By assigning NULL to the veil type vector, R eliminates the feature from the mushrooms data frame.

Before going much further, we should take a quick look at the distribution of the mushroom type class variable in our dataset:

```
> table(mushrooms$type)

  edible poisonous
    4208      3916
```

About 52 percent of the mushroom samples (*N = 4,208*) are edible, while 48 percent (*N = 3,916*) are poisonous.

For the purposes of this experiment, we will consider the 8,214 samples in the mushroom data to be an exhaustive set of all the possible wild mushrooms. This is an important assumption, because it means that we do not need to hold some samples out of the training data for testing purposes. We are not trying to develop rules that cover unforeseen types of mushrooms; we are merely trying to find rules that accurately depict the complete set of known mushroom types. Therefore, we can build and test the model on the same data.

Step 3 – training a model on the data

If we trained a hypothetical ZeroR classifier on this data, what would it predict? Since ZeroR ignores all of the features and simply predicts the target's mode, in plain language, its rule would state that all the mushrooms are edible. Obviously, this is not a very helpful classifier, because it would leave a mushroom gatherer sick or dead with nearly half of the mushroom samples bearing the possibility of being poisonous. Our rules will need to do much better than this in order to provide safe advice that can be published. At the same time, we need simple rules that are easy to remember.

Since simple rules can often be extremely predictive, let's see how a very simple rule learner performs on the mushroom data. Toward the end, we will apply the 1R classifier, which will identify the most predictive single feature of the target class and use it to construct a set of rules.

We will use the 1R implementation in the RWeka package called OneR().
You may recall that we had installed RWeka in *Chapter 1, Introducing Machine Learning*, as a part of the tutorial on installing and loading packages. If you haven't installed the package per these instructions, you will need to use the install.packages("RWeka") command and have Java installed on your system (refer to the installation instructions for more details). With these steps complete, load the package by typing library(RWeka):

1R classification rule syntax

using the OneR() function in the RWeka package

Building the classifier:

```
m <- OneR(class ~ predictors, data = mydata)
```

- class is the column in the mydata data frame to be predicted
- predictors is an R formula specifying the features in the mydata data frame to use for prediction
- data is the data frame in which class and predictors can be found

The function will return a 1R model object that can be used to make predictions.

Making predictions:

```
p <- predict(m, test)
```

- m is a model trained by the OneR() function
- test is a data frame containing test data with the same features as the training data used to build the classifier.

The function will return a vector of predicted class values.

Example:

```
mushroom_classifier <- OneR(type ~ odor + cap_color,
                            data = mushroom_train)
mushroom_prediction <- predict(mushroom_classifier,
                               mushroom_test)
```

The OneR() implementation uses the R formula syntax to specify the model to be trained. The formula syntax uses the ~ operator (known as the tilde) to express the relationship between a target variable and its predictors. The class variable to be learned goes to the left of the tilde, and the predictor features are written on the right, separated by + operators. If you like to model the relationship between the y class and predictors x1 and x2, you could write the formula as y ~ x1 + x2. If you like to include all the variables in the model, the special term . can be used. For example, y ~ . specifies the relationship between y and all the other features in the dataset.

The R formula syntax is used across many R functions and offers some powerful features to describe the relationships among predictor variables. We will explore some of these features in the later chapters. However, if you're eager for a sneak peek, feel free to read the documentation using the ?formula command.

Using the `type ~ .` formula, we will allow our first `OneR()` rule learner to consider all the possible features in the mushroom data while constructing its rules to predict type:

```
> mushroom_1R <- OneR(type ~ ., data = mushrooms)
```

To examine the rules it created, we can type the name of the classifier object, in this case, `mushroom_1R`:

```
> mushroom_1R

odor:
  almond   -> edible
  anise   -> edible
  creosote  -> poisonous
  fishy  -> poisonous
  foul   -> poisonous
  musty  -> poisonous
  none   -> edible
  pungent   -> poisonous
  spicy  -> poisonous
(8004/8124 instances correct)
```

In the first line of the output, we see that the odor feature was selected for rule generation. The categories of odor, such as almond, anise, and so on, specify rules for whether the mushroom is likely to be edible or poisonous. For instance, if the mushroom smells fishy, foul, musty, pungent, spicy, or like creosote, the mushroom is likely to be poisonous. On the other hand, mushrooms with more pleasant smells like almond and anise, and those with no smell at all are predicted to be edible. For the purposes of a field guide for mushroom gathering, these rules could be summarized in a simple rule of thumb: "if the mushroom smells unappetizing, then it is likely to be poisonous."

Step 4 – evaluating model performance

The last line of the output notes that the rules correctly predicted the edibility of 8,004 of the 8,124 mushroom samples or nearly 99 percent of the mushroom samples. We can obtain additional details about the classifier using the `summary()` function, as shown in the following example:

```
> summary(mushroom_1R)
```

```
=== Summary ===
Correctly Classified Instances         8004    98.5229 %
Incorrectly Classified Instances        120     1.4771 %
Kappa statistic                           0.9704
Mean absolute error                       0.0148
Root mean squared error                   0.1215
Relative absolute error                   2.958  %
Root relative squared error              24.323  %
Coverage of cases (0.95 level)           98.5229 %
Mean rel. region size (0.95 level)       50      %
Total Number of Instances              8124
```

```
=== Confusion Matrix ===
    a    b    <-- classified as
 4208    0 |   a = edible
  120 3796 |   b = poisonous
```

The section labeled `Summary` lists a number of different ways to measure the performance of our 1R classifier. We will cover many of these statistics later on in *Chapter 10, Evaluating Model Performance*, so we will ignore them for now.

The section labeled `Confusion Matrix` is similar to those used before. Here, we can see where our rules went wrong. The key is displayed on the right, with a = edible and b = poisonous. Table columns indicate the predicted class of the mushroom while the table rows separate the 4,208 edible mushrooms from the 3,916 poisonous mushrooms. Examining the table, we can see that although the 1R classifier did not classify any edible mushrooms as poisonous, it did classify 120 poisonous mushrooms as edible—which makes for an incredibly dangerous mistake!

Considering that the learner utilized only a single feature, it did reasonably well; if one avoids unappetizing smells when foraging for mushrooms, they will almost avoid a trip to the hospital. That said, close does not cut it when lives are involved, not to mention the field guide publisher might not be happy about the prospect of a lawsuit when its readers fall ill. Let's see if we can add a few more rules and develop an even better classifier.

Step 5 – improving model performance

For a more sophisticated rule learner, we will use JRip(), a Java-based implementation of the RIPPER rule learning algorithm. As with the 1R implementation we used previously, JRip() is included in the RWeka package. If you have not done so yet, be sure to load the package using the library(RWeka) command:

RIPPER classification rule syntax

using the JRip() function in the RWeka package

Building the classifier:

```
m <- JRip(class ~ predictors, data = mydata)
```

- class is the column in the mydata data frame to be predicted
- predictors is an R formula specifying the features in the mydata data frame to use for prediction
- data is the data frame in which class and predictors can be found

The function will return a RIPPER model object that can be used to make predictions.

Making predictions:

```
p <- predict(m, test)
```

- m is a model trained by the JRip() function
- test is a data frame containing test data with the same features as the training data used to build the classifier.

The function will return a vector of predicted class values.

Example:

```
mushroom_classifier <- JRip(type ~ odor + cap_color,
                            data = mushroom_train)
mushroom_prediction <- predict(mushroom_classifier,
                               mushroom_test)
```

As shown in the syntax box, the process of training a JRip() model is very similar to how we previously trained a OneR() model. This is one of the pleasant benefits of the functions in the RWeka package; the syntax is consistent across algorithms, which makes the process of comparing a number of different models very simple.

Let's train the JRip() rule learner as we did with OneR(), allowing it to choose rules from all the available features:

```
> mushroom_JRip <- JRip(type ~ ., data = mushrooms)
```

To examine the rules, type the name of the classifier:

```
> mushroom_JRip
```

```
JRIP rules:
===========
(odor = foul) => type=poisonous (2160.0/0.0)
(gill_size = narrow) and (gill_color = buff) => type=poisonous
(1152.0/0.0)
(gill_size = narrow) and (odor = pungent) => type=poisonous (256.0/0.0)
(odor = creosote) => type=poisonous (192.0/0.0)
(spore_print_color = green) => type=poisonous (72.0/0.0)
(stalk_surface_below_ring = scaly) and (stalk_surface_above_ring = silky)
=> type=poisonous (68.0/0.0)
(habitat = leaves) and (cap_color = white) => type=poisonous (8.0/0.0)
(stalk_color_above_ring = yellow) => type=poisonous (8.0/0.0)
 => type=edible (4208.0/0.0)
Number of Rules : 9
```

The JRip() classifier learned a total of nine rules from the mushroom data. An easy way to read these rules is to think of them as a list of if-else statements, similar to programming logic. The first three rules could be expressed as:

- If the odor is foul, then the mushroom type is poisonous
- If the gill size is narrow and the gill color is buff, then the mushroom type is poisonous
- If the gill size is narrow and the odor is pungent, then the mushroom type is poisonous

Finally, the ninth rule implies that any mushroom sample that was not covered by the preceding eight rules is edible. Following the example of our programming logic, this can be read as:

- Else, the mushroom is edible

Divide and Conquer – Classification Using Decision Trees and Rules

The numbers next to each rule indicate the number of instances covered by the rule and a count of misclassified instances. Notably, there were no misclassified mushroom samples using these nine rules. As a result, the number of instances covered by the last rule is exactly equal to the number of edible mushrooms in the data ($N = 4,208$).

The following figure provides a rough illustration of how the rules are applied to the mushroom data. If you imagine everything within the oval as all the species of mushroom, the rule learner identified features or sets of features, which separate homogeneous segments from the larger group. First, the algorithm found a large group of poisonous mushrooms uniquely distinguished by their foul odor. Next, it found smaller and more specific groups of poisonous mushrooms. By identifying covering rules for each of the varieties of poisonous mushrooms, all of the remaining mushrooms were found to be edible. Thanks to Mother Nature, each variety of mushrooms was unique enough that the classifier was able to achieve 100 percent accuracy.

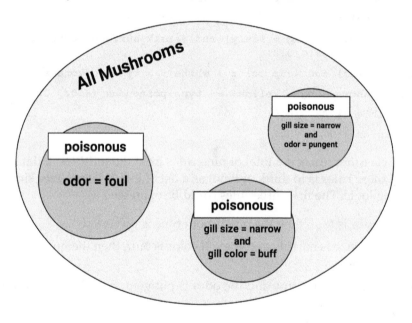

Summary

This chapter covered two classification methods that use so-called "greedy" algorithms to partition the data according to feature values. Decision trees use a divide and conquer strategy to create flowchart-like structures, while rule learners separate and conquer data to identify logical if-else rules. Both methods produce models that can be interpreted without a statistical background.

One popular and highly configurable decision tree algorithm is C5.0. We used the C5.0 algorithm to create a tree to predict whether a loan applicant will default. Using options for boosting and cost-sensitive errors, we were able to improve our accuracy and avoid risky loans that would cost the bank more money.

We also used two rule learners, 1R and RIPPER, to develop rules to identify poisonous mushrooms. The 1R algorithm used a single feature to achieve 99 percent accuracy in identifying potentially fatal mushroom samples. On the other hand, the set of nine rules generated by the more sophisticated RIPPER algorithm correctly identified the edibility of each mushroom.

This chapter merely scratched the surface of how trees and rules can be used. In *Chapter 6*, *Forecasting Numeric Data – Regression Methods*, we will learn techniques known as regression trees and model trees, which use decision trees for numeric prediction rather than classification. In *Chapter 11*, *Improving Model Performance*, we will discover how the performance of decision trees can be improved by grouping them together in a model known as a random forest. In *Chapter 8*, *Finding Patterns – Market Basket Analysis Using Association Rules*, we will see how association rules—a relative of classification rules—can be used to identify groups of items in transactional data.

6
Forecasting Numeric Data – Regression Methods

Mathematical relationships help us to understand many aspects of everyday life. For example, body weight is a function of one's calorie intake, income is often related to education and job experience, and poll numbers help us estimate a presidential candidate's odds of being re-elected.

When such relationships are expressed with exact numbers, we gain additional clarity. For example, an additional 250 kilocalories consumed daily may result in nearly a kilogram of weight gain per month; each year of job experience may be worth an additional $1,000 in yearly salary; and a president is more likely to be re-elected when the economy is strong. Obviously, these equations do not perfectly fit every situation, but we expect that they are reasonably correct, on average.

This chapter extends our machine learning toolkit by going beyond the classification methods covered previously and introducing techniques for estimating relationships among numeric data. While examining several real-world numeric prediction tasks, you will learn:

- The basic statistical principles used in regression, a technique that models the size and the strength of numeric relationships
- How to prepare data for regression analysis, and estimate and interpret a regression model
- A pair of hybrid techniques known as regression trees and model trees, which adapt decision tree classifiers for numeric prediction tasks

Based on a large body of work in the field of statistics, the methods used in this chapter are a bit heavier on math than those covered previously, but don't worry! Even if your algebra skills are a bit rusty, R takes care of the heavy lifting.

Understanding regression

Regression is concerned with specifying the relationship between a single numeric **dependent variable** (the value to be predicted) and one or more numeric **independent variables** (the predictors). As the name implies, the dependent variable depends upon the value of the independent variable or variables. The simplest forms of regression assume that the relationship between the independent and dependent variables follows a straight line.

The origin of the term "regression" to describe the process of fitting lines to data is rooted in a study of genetics by Sir Francis Galton in the late 19th century. He discovered that fathers who were extremely short or extremely tall tended to have sons whose heights were closer to the average height. He called this phenomenon "regression to the mean".

You might recall from basic algebra that lines can be defined in a **slope-intercept form** similar to $y = a + bx$. In this form, the letter y indicates the dependent variable and x indicates the independent variable. The **slope** term b specifies how much the line rises for each increase in x. Positive values define lines that slope upward while negative values define lines that slope downward. The term a is known as the **intercept** because it specifies the point where the line crosses, or intercepts, the vertical y axis. It indicates the value of y when $x = 0$.

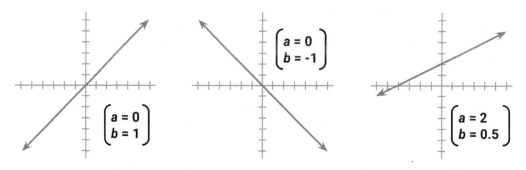

Regression equations model data using a similar slope-intercept format. The machine's job is to identify values of a and b so that the specified line is best able to relate the supplied x values to the values of y. There may not always be a single function that perfectly relates the values, so the machine must also have some way to quantify the margin of error. We'll discuss this in depth shortly.

Regression analysis is commonly used for modeling complex relationships among data elements, estimating the impact of a treatment on an outcome, and extrapolating into the future. Although it can be applied to nearly any task, some specific use cases include:

- Examining how populations and individuals vary by their measured characteristics, for use in scientific research across fields as diverse as economics, sociology, psychology, physics, and ecology
- Quantifying the causal relationship between an event and the response, such as those in clinical drug trials, engineering safety tests, or marketing research
- Identifying patterns that can be used to forecast future behavior given known criteria, such as predicting insurance claims, natural disaster damage, election results, and crime rates

Regression methods are also used for **statistical hypothesis testing**, which determines whether a premise is likely to be true or false in light of the observed data. The regression model's estimates of the strength and consistency of a relationship provide information that can be used to assess whether the observations are due to chance alone.

 Hypothesis testing is extremely nuanced and falls outside the scope of machine learning. If you are interested in this topic, an introductory statistics textbook is a good place to get started.

Regression analysis is not synonymous with a single algorithm. Rather, it is an umbrella for a large number of methods that can be adapted to nearly any machine learning task. If you were limited to choosing only a single method, regression would be a good choice. One could devote an entire career to nothing else and perhaps still have much to learn.

In this chapter, we'll focus only on the most basic **linear regression** models — those that use straight lines. When there is only a single independent variable it is known as **simple linear regression**. In the case of two or more independent variables, this is known as **multiple linear regression**, or simply "multiple regression". Both of these techniques assume that the dependent variable is measured on a continuous scale.

Regression can also be used for other types of dependent variables and even for some classification tasks. For instance, **logistic regression** is used to model a binary categorical outcome, while **Poisson regression** — named after the French mathematician Siméon Poisson — models integer count data. The method known as **multinomial logistic regression** models a categorical outcome; thus, it can be used for classification. The same basic principles apply across all the regression methods, so after understanding the linear case, it is fairly simple to learn the others.

Many of the specialized regression methods fall into a class of **Generalized Linear Models** (**GLM**). Using a GLM, linear models can be generalized to other patterns via the use of a **link function**, which specifies more complex forms for the relationship between x and y. This allows regression to be applied to almost any type of data.

We'll begin with the basic case of simple linear regression. Despite the name, this method is not too simple to address complex problems. In the next section, we'll see how the use of a simple linear regression model might have averted a tragic engineering disaster.

Simple linear regression

On January 28, 1986, seven crew members of the United States space shuttle *Challenger* were killed when a rocket booster failed, causing a catastrophic disintegration. In the aftermath, experts focused on the launch temperature as a potential culprit. The rubber O-rings responsible for sealing the rocket joints had never been tested below 40°F (4°C) and the weather on the launch day was unusually cold and below freezing.

With the benefit of hindsight, the accident has been a case study for the importance of data analysis and visualization. Although it is unclear what information was available to the rocket engineers and decision makers leading up to the launch, it is undeniable that better data, utilized carefully, might very well have averted this disaster.

This section's analysis is based on data presented in Dalal SR, Fowlkes EB, Hoadley B. *Risk analysis of the space shuttle: pre-Challenger prediction of failure*. Journal of the American Statistical Association. 1989; 84:945-957. For one perspective on how data may have changed the result, see Tufte ER. *Visual Explanations: Images and Quantities, Evidence and Narrative*. Graphics Press; 1997. For a counterpoint, see Robison W, Boisioly R, Hoeker D, Young, S. *Representation and misrepresentation: Tufte and the Morton Thiokol engineers on the Challenger*. Science and Engineering Ethics. 2002; 8:59-81.

The rocket engineers almost certainly knew that cold temperatures could make the components more brittle and less able to seal properly, which would result in a higher chance of a dangerous fuel leak. However, given the political pressure to continue with the launch, they needed data to support this hypothesis. A regression model that demonstrated a link between temperature and O-ring failure, and could forecast the chance of failure given the expected temperature at launch, might have been very helpful.

To build the regression model, scientists might have used the data on launch temperature and component distresses from 23 previous successful shuttle launches. A component distress indicates one of the two types of problems. The first problem, called erosion, occurs when excessive heat burns up the O-ring. The second problem, called blowby, occurs when hot gases leak through or "blow by" a poorly sealed O-ring. Since the shuttle has a total of six primary O-rings, up to six distresses can occur per flight. Though the rocket can survive one or more distress events, or fail with as few as one, each additional distress increases the probability of a catastrophic failure.

The following scatterplot shows a plot of primary O-ring distresses detected for the previous 23 launches, as compared to the temperature at launch:

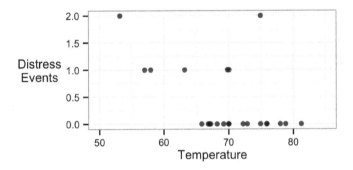

Examining the plot, there is an apparent trend. Launches occurring at higher temperatures tend to have fewer O-ring distress events.

Additionally, the coldest launch (53° F) had two distress events, a level which had only been reached in one other launch. With this information at hand, the fact that the Challenger was scheduled to launch at a temperature over 20 degrees colder seems concerning. But exactly how concerned should we be? To answer this question, we can turn to simple linear regression.

A simple linear regression model defines the relationship between a dependent variable and a single independent predictor variable using a line defined by an equation in the following form:

$$y = \alpha + \beta x$$

Don't be alarmed by the Greek characters, this equation can still be understood using the slope-intercept form described previously. The intercept, *a* (alpha), describes where the line crosses the *y* axis, while the slope, *β* (beta), describes the change in *y* given an increase of *x*. For the shuttle launch data, the slope would tell us the expected reduction in the number of O-ring failures for each degree the launch temperature increases.

Greek characters are often used in the field of statistics to indicate variables that are parameters of a statistical function. Therefore, performing a regression analysis involves finding **parameter estimates** for *a* and *β*. The parameter estimates for alpha and beta are often denoted using *a* and *b*, although you may find that some of this terminology and notation is used interchangeably.

Suppose we know that the estimated regression parameters in the equation for the shuttle launch data are: *a = 3.70* and *b = -0.048*.

Hence, the full linear equation is *y = 3.70 – 0.048x*. Ignoring for a moment how these numbers were obtained, we can plot the line on the scatterplot like this:

As the line shows, at 60 degrees Fahrenheit, we predict just under one O-ring distress. At 70 degrees Fahrenheit, we expect around 0.3 failures. If we extrapolate our model, all the way to 31 degrees—the forecasted temperature for the Challenger launch—we would expect about *3.70 - 0.048 * 31 = 2.21* O-ring distress events. Assuming that each O-ring failure is equally likely to cause a catastrophic fuel leak means that the Challenger launch at 31 degrees was nearly three times more risky than the typical launch at 60 degrees, and over eight times more risky than a launch at 70 degrees.

Notice that the line doesn't pass through each data point exactly. Instead, it cuts through the data somewhat evenly, with some predictions lower or higher than the line. In the next section, we will learn about why this particular line was chosen.

Ordinary least squares estimation

In order to determine the optimal estimates of a and β, an estimation method known as **Ordinary Least Squares (OLS)** was used. In OLS regression, the slope and intercept are chosen so that they minimize the sum of the squared errors, that is, the vertical distance between the predicted y value and the actual y value. These errors are known as **residuals**, and are illustrated for several points in the following diagram:

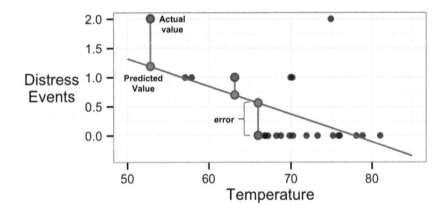

In mathematical terms, the goal of OLS regression can be expressed as the task of minimizing the following equation:

$$\sum (y_i - \hat{y}_i)^2 = \sum e_i^2$$

In plain language, this equation defines e (the error) as the difference between the actual y value and the predicted y value. The error values are squared and summed across all the points in the data.

 The caret character (^) above the y term is a commonly used feature of statistical notation. It indicates that the term is an estimate for the true y value. This is referred to as the y-hat, and is pronounced exactly like the hat you'd wear on your head.

The solution for a depends on the value of b. It can be obtained using the following formula:

$$a = \bar{y} - b\bar{x}$$

 To understand these equations, you'll need to know another bit of statistical notation. The horizontal bar appearing over the x and y terms indicates the mean value of x or y. This is referred to as the x-bar or y-bar, and is pronounced just like the establishment you'd go to for an alcoholic drink.

Though the proof is beyond the scope of this book, it can be shown using calculus that the value of b that results in the minimum squared error is:

$$b = \frac{\sum(x_i - \bar{x})(y_i - \bar{y})}{\sum(x_i - \bar{x})^2}$$

If we break this equation apart into its component pieces, we can simplify it a bit. The denominator for b should look familiar; it is very similar to the variance of x, which is denoted as *Var(x)*. As we learned in *Chapter 2, Managing and Understanding Data*, the variance involves finding the average squared deviation from the mean of x. This can be expressed as:

$$\text{Var}(x) = \frac{\sum(x_i - \bar{x})^2}{n}$$

The numerator involves taking the sum of each data point's deviation from the mean x value multiplied by that point's deviation away from the mean y value. This is similar to the **covariance** function for x and y, denoted as *Cov(x, y)*. The covariance formula is:

$$\text{Cov}(x, y) = \frac{\sum(x_i - \bar{x})(y_i - \bar{y})}{n}$$

If we divide the covariance function by the variance function, the n terms get cancelled and we can rewrite the formula for b as:

$$b = \frac{\text{Cov}(x, y)}{\text{Var}(x)}$$

Given this restatement, it is easy to calculate the value of b using built-in R functions. Let's apply it to the rocket launch data to estimate the regression line.

 If you would like to follow along with these examples, download the `challenger.csv` file from the Packt Publishing website and load to a data frame using the `launch <- read.csv("challenger.csv")` command.

Assume that our shuttle launch data is stored in a data frame named `launch`, the independent variable x is temperature, and the dependent variable y is `distress_ct`. We can then use R's `cov()` and `var()` functions to estimate b:

```
> b <- cov(launch$temperature, launch$distress_ct) /
        var(launch$temperature)
> b
[1] -0.04753968
```

From here we can estimate a using the `mean()` function:

```
> a <- mean(launch$distress_ct) - b * mean(launch$temperature)
> a
[1] 3.698413
```

Estimating the regression equation by hand is not ideal, so R provides functions for performing this calculation automatically. We will use such methods shortly. First, we will expand our understanding of regression by learning a method for measuring the strength of a linear relationship, and then we will see how linear regression can be applied to data having more than one independent variable.

Correlations

The **correlation** between two variables is a number that indicates how closely their relationship follows a straight line. Without additional qualification, correlation typically refers to **Pearson's correlation coefficient**, which was developed by the 20th century mathematician Karl Pearson. The correlation ranges between -1 and +1. The extreme values indicate a perfectly linear relationship, while a correlation close to zero indicates the absence of a linear relationship.

The following formula defines Pearson's correlation:

$$\rho_{x,y} = \text{Corr}(x, y) = \frac{\text{Cov}(x, y)}{\sigma_x \sigma_y}$$

 More Greek notation has been introduced here. The first symbol (which looks like a lowercase p) is *rho*, and it is used to denote the Pearson correlation statistic. The characters that look like q turned sideways are the Greek letter *sigma*, and they indicate the standard deviation of *x* or *y*.

Using this formula, we can calculate the correlation between the launch temperature and the number of O-ring distress events. Recall that the covariance function is `cov()` and the standard deviation function is `sd()`. We'll store the result in `r`, a letter that is commonly used to indicate the estimated correlation:

```
> r <- cov(launch$temperature, launch$distress_ct) /
        (sd(launch$temperature) * sd(launch$distress_ct))
> r
[1] -0.5111264
```

Alternatively, we can use R's correlation function, `cor()`:

```
> cor(launch$temperature, launch$distress_ct)
[1] -0.5111264
```

The correlation between the temperature and the number of distressed O-rings is -0.51. The negative correlation implies that increases in temperature are related to decreases in the number of distressed O-rings. To the NASA engineers studying the O-ring data, this would have been a very clear indicator that a low temperature launch could be problematic. The correlation also tells us about the relative strength of the relationship between temperature and O-ring distress. Because -0.51 is halfway to the maximum negative correlation of -1, this implies that there is a moderately strong negative linear association.

There are various rules of thumb used to interpret correlation strength. One method assigns a status of "weak" to values between 0.1 and 0.3, "moderate" to the range of 0.3 to 0.5, and "strong" to values above 0.5 (these also apply to similar ranges of negative correlations). However, these thresholds may be too lax for some purposes. Often, the correlation must be interpreted in context. For data involving human beings, a correlation of 0.5 may be considered extremely high, while for data generated by mechanical processes, a correlation of 0.5 may be weak.

You have probably heard the expression "correlation does not imply causation." This is rooted in the fact that a correlation only describes the association between a pair of variables, yet there could be other unmeasured explanations. For example, there may be a strong association between mortality and time per day spent matching movies, but before doctors should start recommending that we all watch more movies, we need to rule out another explanation— younger people watch more movies and are less likely to die.

Measuring the correlation between two variables gives us a way to quickly gauge the relationships among the independent and dependent variables. This will be increasingly important as we start defining the regression models with a larger number of predictors.

Multiple linear regression

Most real-world analyses have more than one independent variable. Therefore, it is likely that you will be using **multiple linear regression** for most numeric prediction tasks. The strengths and weaknesses of multiple linear regression are shown in the following table:

Strengths	Weaknesses
• By far the most common approach for modeling numeric data • Can be adapted to model almost any modeling task • Provides estimates of both the strength and size of the relationships among features and the outcome	• Makes strong assumptions about the data • The model's form must be specified by the user in advance • Does not handle missing data • Only works with numeric features, so categorical data requires extra processing • Requires some knowledge of statistics to understand the model

We can understand multiple regression as an extension of simple linear regression. The goal in both cases is similar—find values of beta coefficients that minimize the prediction error of a linear equation. The key difference is that there are additional terms for additional independent variables.

Multiple regression equations generally follow the form of the following equation. The dependent variable y is specified as the sum of an intercept term a plus the product of the estimated β value and the x values for each of the i features. An error term (denoted by the Greek letter *epsilon*) has been added here as a reminder that the predictions are not perfect. This represents the **residual** term noted previously:

$$y = \alpha + \beta_1 x_1 + \beta_2 x_2 + \ldots + \beta_i x_i + \varepsilon$$

Let's consider for a moment the interpretation of the estimated regression parameters. You will note that in the preceding equation, a coefficient is provided for each feature. This allows each feature to have a separate estimated effect on the value of y. In other words, y changes by the amount β_i for each unit increase in x_i. The intercept a is then the expected value of y when the independent variables are all zero.

Since the intercept term a is really no different than any other regression parameter, it is also sometimes denoted as β_0 (pronounced beta-naught), as shown in the following equation:

$$y = \beta_0 + \beta_1 x_1 + \beta_2 x_2 + \ldots + \beta_i x_i + \varepsilon$$

Just like before, the intercept is unrelated to any of the independent x variables. However, for reasons that will become clear shortly, it helps to imagine β_0 as if it were being multiplied by a term x_0, which is a constant with the value 1:

$$y = \beta_0 x_0 + \beta_1 x_1 + \beta_2 x_2 + \ldots + \beta_i x_i + \varepsilon$$

In order to estimate the values of the regression parameters, each observed value of the dependent variable y must be related to the observed values of the independent x variables using the regression equation in the previous form. The following figure illustrates this structure:

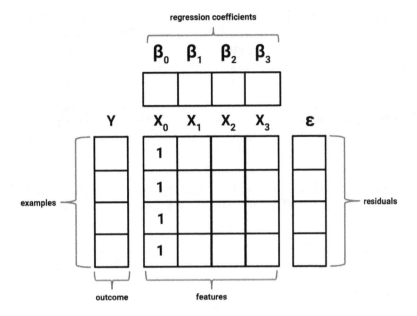

The many rows and columns of data illustrated in the preceding figure can be described in a condensed formulation using bold font **matrix notation** to indicate that each of the terms represents multiple values:

$$\mathbf{Y} = \beta\mathbf{X} + \varepsilon$$

The dependent variable is now a vector, $\mathbf{Y}$, with a row for every example. The independent variables have been combined into a matrix, $\mathbf{X}$, with a column for each feature plus an additional column of '1' values for the intercept term. Each column has a row for every example. The regression coefficients β and residual errors ε are also now vectors.

The goal is now to solve for β, the vector of regression coefficients that minimizes the sum of the squared errors between the predicted and actual $\mathbf{Y}$ values. Finding the optimal solution requires the use of matrix algebra; therefore, the derivation deserves more careful attention than can be provided in this text. However, if you're willing to trust the work of others, the best estimate of the vector β can be computed as:

$$\hat{\beta} = (\mathbf{X}^\mathbf{T}\mathbf{X})^{-1}\mathbf{X}^\mathbf{T}\mathbf{Y}$$

This solution uses a pair of matrix operations — the T indicates the **transpose** of matrix **X**, while the negative exponent indicates the **matrix inverse**. Using R's built-in matrix operations, we can thus implement a simple multiple regression learner. Let's apply this formula to the Challenger launch data.

If you are unfamiliar with the preceding matrix operations, the Wikipedia pages for transpose and matrix inverse provide a thorough introduction and are quite understandable, even without a strong mathematics background.

Using the following code, we can create a basic regression function named `reg()`, which takes a parameter y and a parameter x and returns a vector of estimated beta coefficients:

```
reg <- function(y, x) {
  x <- as.matrix(x)
  x <- cbind(Intercept = 1, x)
  b <- solve(t(x) %*% x) %*% t(x) %*% y
  colnames(b) <- "estimate"
  print(b)
}
```

The `reg()` function created here uses several R commands that we have not used previously. First, since we will be using the function with sets of columns from a data frame, the `as.matrix()` function is used to convert the data frame into matrix form. Next, the `cbind()` function is used to bind an additional column onto the x matrix; the command `Intercept = 1` instructs R to name the new column `Intercept` and to fill the column with repeating 1 values. Then, a number of matrix operations are performed on the x and y objects:

- `solve()` takes the inverse of a matrix
- `t()` is used to transpose a matrix
- `%*%` multiplies two matrices

By combining these as shown, our function will return a vector b, which contains the estimated parameters for the linear model relating x to y. The final two lines in the function give the b vector a name and print the result on screen.

Let's apply our function to the shuttle launch data. As shown in the following code, the dataset includes three features and the distress count (`distress_ct`), which is the outcome of interest:

```
> str(launch)
'data.frame':       23 obs. of  4 variables:
 $ distress_ct         : int  0 1 0 0 0 0 0 0 1 1 ...
 $ temperature         : int  66 70 69 68 67 72 73 70 57 63 ...
 $ field_check_pressure: int  50 50 50 50 50 50 100 100 200 ...
 $ flight_num          : int  1 2 3 4 5 6 7 8 9 10 ...
```

We can confirm that our function is working correctly by comparing its result to the simple linear regression model of O-ring failures versus temperature, which we found earlier to have parameters $a = 3.70$ and $b = -0.048$. Since temperature is in the third column of the launch data, we can run the `reg()` function as follows:

```
> reg(y = launch$distress_ct, x = launch[2])
               estimate
Intercept     3.69841270
temperature  -0.04753968
```

These values exactly match our prior result, so let's use the function to build a multiple regression model. We'll apply it just as before, but this time specifying three columns of data instead of just one:

```
> reg(y = launch$distress_ct, x = launch[2:4])
                        estimate
Intercept             3.527093383
temperature          -0.051385940
field_check_pressure  0.001757009
flight_num            0.014292843
```

This model predicts the number of O-ring distress events versus temperature, field check pressure, and the launch ID number. As with the simple linear regression model, the coefficient for the temperature variable is negative, which suggests that as temperature increases, the number of expected O-ring events decreases. The field check pressure refers to the amount of pressure applied to the O-ring to test it prior to launch. Although the check pressure had originally been 50 psi, it was raised to 100 and 200 psi for some launches, which led some to believe that it may be responsible for O-ring erosion. The coefficient is positive, but small. The flight number is included to account for the shuttle's age. As it gets older, its parts may be more brittle or prone to fail. The small positive association between flight number and distress count may reflect this fact.

So far we've only scratched the surface of linear regression modeling. Although our work was useful to help us understand exactly how regression models are built, R's functions also include some additional functionality necessary for the more complex modeling tasks and diagnostic output that are needed to aid model interpretation and assess fit. Let's apply our knowledge of regression to a more challenging learning task.

Example – predicting medical expenses using linear regression

In order for a health insurance company to make money, it needs to collect more in yearly premiums than it spends on medical care to its beneficiaries. As a result, insurers invest a great deal of time and money in developing models that accurately forecast medical expenses for the insured population.

Medical expenses are difficult to estimate because the most costly conditions are rare and seemingly random. Still, some conditions are more prevalent for certain segments of the population. For instance, lung cancer is more likely among smokers than non-smokers, and heart disease may be more likely among the obese.

The goal of this analysis is to use patient data to estimate the average medical care expenses for such population segments. These estimates can be used to create actuarial tables that set the price of yearly premiums higher or lower, depending on the expected treatment costs.

Step 1 – collecting data

For this analysis, we will use a simulated dataset containing hypothetical medical expenses for patients in the United States. This data was created for this book using demographic statistics from the US Census Bureau, and thus, approximately reflect real-world conditions.

 If you would like to follow along interactively, download the insurance.csv file from the Packt Publishing website and save it to your R working folder.

The `insurance.csv` file includes 1,338 examples of beneficiaries currently enrolled in the insurance plan, with features indicating characteristics of the patient as well as the total medical expenses charged to the plan for the calendar year. The features are:

- `age`: An integer indicating the age of the primary beneficiary (excluding those above 64 years, since they are generally covered by the government).

- `sex`: The policy holder's gender, either male or female.

- `bmi`: The body mass index (BMI), which provides a sense of how over- or under-weight a person is relative to their height. BMI is equal to weight (in kilograms) divided by height (in meters) squared. An ideal BMI is within the range of 18.5 to 24.9.

- `children`: An integer indicating the number of children/dependents covered by the insurance plan.

- `smoker`: A yes or no categorical variable that indicates whether the insured regularly smokes tobacco.

- `region`: The beneficiary's place of residence in the US, divided into four geographic regions: northeast, southeast, southwest, or northwest.

It is important to give some thought to how these variables may be related to billed medical expenses. For instance, we might expect that older people and smokers are at higher risk of large medical expenses. Unlike many other machine learning methods, in regression analysis, the relationships among the features are typically specified by the user rather than being detected automatically. We'll explore some of these potential relationships in the next section.

Step 2 – exploring and preparing the data

As we have done before, we will use the `read.csv()` function to load the data for analysis. We can safely use `stringsAsFactors = TRUE` because it is appropriate to convert the three nominal variables to factors:

```
> insurance <- read.csv("insurance.csv", stringsAsFactors = TRUE)
```

The `str()` function confirms that the data is formatted as we had expected:

```
> str(insurance)
'data.frame':    1338 obs. of  7 variables:
 $ age      : int  19 18 28 33 32 31 46 37 37 60 ...
 $ sex      : Factor w/ 2 levels "female","male": 1 2 2 2 2 1 ...
 $ bmi      : num  27.9 33.8 33 22.7 28.9 25.7 33.4 27.7 ...
 $ children: int  0 1 3 0 0 0 1 3 2 0 ...
```

```
$ smoker  : Factor w/ 2 levels "no","yes": 2 1 1 1 1 1 1 1 ...
$ region  : Factor w/ 4 levels "northeast","northwest",..: ...
$ expenses: num  16885 1726 4449 21984 3867 ...
```

Our model's dependent variable is `expenses`, which measures the medical costs each person charged to the insurance plan for the year. Prior to building a regression model, it is often helpful to check for normality. Although linear regression does not strictly require a normally distributed dependent variable, the model often fits better when this is true. Let's take a look at the summary statistics:

```
> summary(insurance$expenses)
   Min. 1st Qu.  Median    Mean 3rd Qu.    Max.
   1122    4740    9382   13270   16640   63770
```

Because the mean value is greater than the median, this implies that the distribution of insurance expenses is right-skewed. We can confirm this visually using a histogram:

```
> hist(insurance$expenses)
```

The output is shown as follows:

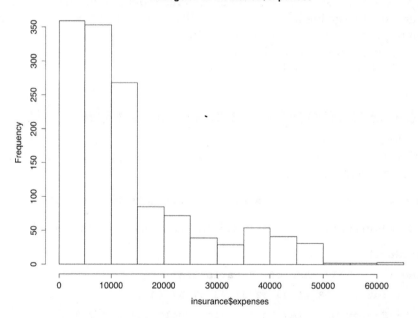

As expected, the figure shows a right-skewed distribution. It also shows that the majority of people in our data have yearly medical expenses between zero and $15,000, in spite of the fact that the tail of the distribution extends far past these peaks. Although this distribution is not ideal for a linear regression, knowing this weakness ahead of time may help us design a better-fitting model later on.

Before we address that issue, another problem is at hand. Regression models require that every feature is numeric, yet we have three factor-type features in our data frame. For instance, the sex variable is divided into male and female levels, while smoker is divided into yes and no. From the summary() output, we know that the region variable has four levels, but we need to take a closer look to see how they are distributed:

```
> table(insurance$region)

northeast northwest southeast southwest
      324       325       364       325
```

Here, we see that the data has been divided nearly evenly among four geographic regions. We will see how R's linear regression function handles these factor variables shortly.

Exploring relationships among features – the correlation matrix

Before fitting a regression model to data, it can be useful to determine how the independent variables are related to the dependent variable and each other. A **correlation matrix** provides a quick overview of these relationships. Given a set of variables, it provides a correlation for each pairwise relationship.

To create a correlation matrix for the four numeric variables in the insurance data frame, use the cor() command:

```
> cor(insurance[c("age", "bmi", "children", "expenses")])
               age        bmi   children    expenses
age      1.0000000 0.10934101 0.04246900 0.29900819
bmi      0.1093410 1.00000000 0.01264471 0.19857626
children 0.0424690 0.01264471 1.00000000 0.06799823
expenses 0.2990082 0.19857626 0.06799823 1.00000000
```

At the intersection of each row and column pair, the correlation is listed for the variables indicated by that row and column. The diagonal is always 1.0000000 since there is always a perfect correlation between a variable and itself. The values above and below the diagonal are identical since correlations are symmetrical. In other words, cor(x, y) is equal to cor(y, x).

None of the correlations in the matrix are considered strong, but there are some notable associations. For instance, age and bmi appear to have a weak positive correlation, meaning that as someone ages, their body mass tends to increase. There is also a moderate positive correlation between age and expenses, bmi and expenses, and children and expenses. These associations imply that as age, body mass, and number of children increase, the expected cost of insurance goes up. We'll try to tease out these relationships more clearly when we build our final regression model.

Visualizing relationships among features – the scatterplot matrix

It can also be helpful to visualize the relationships among numeric features by using a scatterplot. Although we could create a scatterplot for each possible relationship, doing so for a large number of features might become tedious.

An alternative is to create a **scatterplot matrix** (sometimes abbreviated as **SPLOM**), which is simply a collection of scatterplots arranged in a grid. It is used to detect patterns among three or more variables. The scatterplot matrix is not a true multidimensional visualization because only two features are examined at a time. Still, it provides a general sense of how the data may be interrelated.

We can use R's graphical capabilities to create a scatterplot matrix for the four numeric features: age, bmi, children, and expenses. The pairs() function is provided in a default R installation and provides basic functionality for producing scatterplot matrices. To invoke the function, simply provide it the data frame to present. Here, we'll limit the insurance data frame to the four numeric variables of interest:

```
> pairs(insurance[c("age", "bmi", "children", "expenses")])
```

This produces the following diagram:

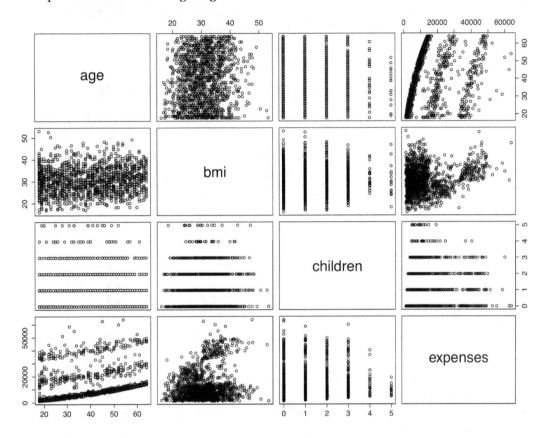

In the scatterplot matrix, the intersection of each row and column holds the scatterplot of the variables indicated by the row and column pair. The diagrams above and below the diagonal are transpositions since the *x* axis and *y* axis have been swapped.

Do you notice any patterns in these plots? Although some look like random clouds of points, a few seem to display some trends. The relationship between age and expenses displays several relatively straight lines, while the bmi versus expenses plot has two distinct groups of points. It is difficult to detect trends in any of the other plots.

If we add more information to the plot, it can be even more useful. An enhanced scatterplot matrix can be created with the `pairs.panels()` function in the `psych` package. If you do not have this package installed, type `install.packages("psych")` to install it on your system and load it using the `library(psych)` command. Then, we can create a scatterplot matrix as we had done previously:

```
> pairs.panels(insurance[c("age", "bmi", "children", "expenses")])
```

This produces a slightly more informative scatterplot matrix, as shown here:

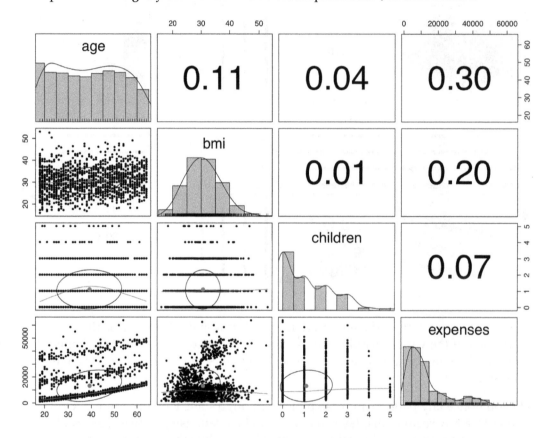

Above the diagonal, the scatterplots have been replaced with a correlation matrix. On the diagonal, a histogram depicting the distribution of values for each feature is shown. Finally, the scatterplots below the diagonal are now presented with additional visual information.

The oval-shaped object on each scatterplot is a **correlation ellipse**. It provides a visualization of correlation strength. The dot at the center of the ellipse indicates the point at the mean values for the *x* and *y* axis variables. The correlation between the two variables is indicated by the shape of the ellipse; the more it is stretched, the stronger the correlation. An almost perfectly round oval, as with bmi and children, indicates a very weak correlation (in this case, it is 0.01).

The curve drawn on the scatterplot is called a **loess curve**. It indicates the general relationship between the *x* and *y* axis variables. It is best understood by example. The curve for age and children is an upside-down U, peaking around middle age. This means that the oldest and youngest people in the sample have fewer children on the insurance plan than those around middle age. Because this trend is non-linear, this finding could not have been inferred from the correlations alone. On the other hand, the loess curve for age and bmi is a line sloping gradually up, implying that body mass increases with age, but we had already inferred this from the correlation matrix.

Step 3 – training a model on the data

To fit a linear regression model to data with R, the lm() function can be used. This is included in the stats package, which should be included and loaded by default with your R installation. The lm() syntax is as follows:

Multiple regression modeling syntax

using the lm() function in the **stats** package

Building the model:

```
m <- lm(dv ~ iv, data = mydata)
```

- dv is the dependent variable in the mydata data frame to be modeled
- iv is an R formula specifying the independent variables in the mydata data frame to use in the model
- data specifies the data frame in which the dv and iv variables can be found

The function will return a regression model object that can be used to make predictions. Interactions between independent variables can be specified using the * operator.

Making predictions:

```
p <- predict(m, test)
```

- m is a model trained by the lm() function
- test is a data frame containing test data with the same features as the training data used to build the model.

The function will return a vector of predicted values.

Example:

```
ins_model <- lm(charges ~ age + sex + smoker,
                data = insurance)
ins_pred <- predict(ins_model, insurance_test)
```

The following command fits a linear regression model relating the six independent variables to the total medical expenses. The R formula syntax uses the tilde character ~ to describe the model; the dependent variable expenses goes to the left of the tilde while the independent variables go to the right, separated by + signs. There is no need to specify the regression model's intercept term as it is assumed by default:

```
> ins_model <- lm(expenses ~ age + children + bmi + sex +
    smoker + region, data = insurance)
```

Because the . character can be used to specify all the features (excluding those already specified in the formula), the following command is equivalent to the preceding command:

```
> ins_model <- lm(expenses ~ ., data = insurance)
```

After building the model, simply type the name of the model object to see the estimated beta coefficients:

```
> ins_model
```

```
Call:
lm(formula = expenses ~ ., data = insurance)

Coefficients:
      (Intercept)                age             sexmale
         -11941.6              256.8              -131.4
              bmi           children           smokeryes
            339.3              475.7             23847.5
  regionnorthwest    regionsoutheast     regionsouthwest
           -352.8            -1035.6              -959.3
```

Understanding the regression coefficients is fairly straightforward. The intercept is the predicted value of expenses when the independent variables are equal to zero. As is the case here, quite often the intercept is of little value alone because it is impossible to have values of zero for all features. For example, since no person exists with age zero and BMI zero, the intercept has no real-world interpretation. For this reason, in practice, the intercept is often ignored.

The beta coefficients indicate the estimated increase in expenses for an increase of one in each of the features, assuming all other values are held constant. For instance, for each additional year of age, we would expect $256.80 higher medical expenses on average, assuming everything else is equal. Similarly, each additional child results in an average of $475.70 in additional medical expenses each year, and each unit increase in BMI is associated with an average increase of $339.30 in yearly medical expenses, all else equal.

You might notice that although we only specified six features in our model formula, there are eight coefficients reported in addition to the intercept. This happened because the `lm()` function automatically applied a technique known as **dummy coding** to each of the factor-type variables we included in the model.

Dummy coding allows a nominal feature to be treated as numeric by creating a binary variable, often called a **dummy variable**, for each category of the feature. The dummy variable is set to `1` if the observation falls into the specified category or `0` otherwise. For instance, the `sex` feature has two categories: `male` and `female`. This will be split into two binary variables, which R names `sexmale` and `sexfemale`. For observations where `sex = male`, then `sexmale = 1` and `sexfemale = 0`; conversely, if `sex = female`, then `sexmale = 0` and `sexfemale = 1`. The same coding applies to variables with three or more categories. For example, R split the four-category feature `region` into four dummy variables: `regionnorthwest`, `regionsoutheast`, `regionsouthwest`, and `regionnortheast`.

When adding a dummy variable to a regression model, one category is always left out to serve as the reference category. The estimates are then interpreted relative to the reference. In our model, R automatically held out the `sexfemale`, `smokerno`, and `regionnortheast` variables, making female non-smokers in the northeast region the reference group. Thus, males have $131.40 less medical expenses each year relative to females and smokers cost an average of $23,847.50 more than non-smokers per year. The coefficient for each of the three regions in the model is negative, which implies that the reference group, the northeast region, tends to have the highest average expenses.

> By default, R uses the first level of the factor variable as the reference. If you would prefer to use another level, the `relevel()` function can be used to specify the reference group manually. Use the `?relevel` command in R for more information.

The results of the linear regression model make logical sense: old age, smoking, and obesity tend to be linked to additional health issues, while additional family member dependents may result in an increase in physician visits and preventive care such as vaccinations and yearly physical exams. However, we currently have no sense of how well the model is fitting the data. We'll answer this question in the next section.

Step 4 – evaluating model performance

The parameter estimates we obtained by typing `ins_model` tell us about how the independent variables are related to the dependent variable, but they tell us nothing about how well the model fits our data. To evaluate the model performance, we can use the `summary()` command on the stored model:

```
> summary(ins_model)
```

This produces the following output. Note that the output has been labeled for illustrative purposes:

```
Call:
lm(formula = expenses ~ ., data = insurance)

Residuals:
      Min       1Q   Median       3Q      Max
 -11302.7  -2850.9   -979.6   1383.9  29981.7        ( 1 )

Coefficients:
                   Estimate Std. Error t value Pr(>|t|)
(Intercept)        -11941.6      987.8 -12.089  < 2e-16 ***
age                   256.8       11.9  21.586  < 2e-16 ***        ( 2 )
sexmale              -131.3      332.9  -0.395 0.693255
bmi                   339.3       28.6  11.864  < 2e-16 ***
children              475.7      137.8   3.452 0.000574 ***
smokeryes           23847.5      413.1  57.723  < 2e-16 ***
regionnorthwest      -352.8      476.3  -0.741 0.458976
regionsoutheast     -1035.6      478.7  -2.163 0.030685 *
regionsouthwest      -959.3      477.9  -2.007 0.044921 *
---
Signif. codes:  0 '***' 0.001 '**' 0.01 '*' 0.05 '.' 0.1 ' ' 1

Residual standard error: 6062 on 1329 degrees of freedom
Multiple R-squared:  0.7509,  Adjusted R-squared:  0.7494        ( 3 )
F-statistic: 500.9 on 8 and 1329 DF,  p-value: < 2.2e-16
```

The `summary()` output may seem confusing at first, but the basics are easy to pick up. As indicated by the numbered labels in the preceding output, the output provides three key ways to evaluate the performance, or fit, of our model:

1. The **residuals** section provides summary statistics for the errors in our predictions, some of which are apparently quite substantial. Since a residual is equal to the true value minus the predicted value, the maximum error of 29981.7 suggests that the model under-predicted expenses by nearly $30,000 for at least one observation. On the other hand, 50 percent of errors fall within the 1Q and 3Q values (the first and third quartile), so the majority of predictions were between $2,850.90 over the true value and $1,383.90 under the true value.

2. For each estimated regression coefficient, the **p-value**, denoted `Pr(>|t|)`, provides an estimate of the probability that the true coefficient is zero given the value of the estimate. Small p-values suggest that the true coefficient is very unlikely to be zero, which means that the feature is extremely unlikely to have no relationship with the dependent variable. Note that some of the p-values have stars (***), which correspond to the footnotes to indicate the **significance level** met by the estimate. This level is a threshold, chosen prior to building the model, which will be used to indicate "real" findings, as opposed to those due to chance alone; p-values less than the significance level are considered **statistically significant**. If the model had few such terms, it may be cause for concern, since this would indicate that the features used are not very predictive of the outcome. Here, our model has several highly significant variables, and they seem to be related to the outcome in logical ways.

3. The **multiple R-squared value** (also called the coefficient of determination) provides a measure of how well our model as a whole explains the values of the dependent variable. It is similar to the correlation coefficient, in that the closer the value is to 1.0, the better the model perfectly explains the data. Since the R-squared value is 0.7494, we know that the model explains nearly 75 percent of the variation in the dependent variable. Because models with more features always explain more variation, the **adjusted R-squared value** corrects R-squared by penalizing models with a large number of independent variables. It is useful for comparing the performance of models with different numbers of explanatory variables.

Given the preceding three performance indicators, our model is performing fairly well. It is not uncommon for regression models of real-world data to have fairly low R-squared values; a value of 0.75 is actually quite good. The size of some of the errors is a bit concerning, but not surprising given the nature of medical expense data. However, as shown in the next section, we may be able to improve the model's performance by specifying the model in a slightly different way.

Step 5 – improving model performance

As mentioned previously, a key difference between the regression modeling and other machine learning approaches is that regression typically leaves feature selection and model specification to the user. Consequently, if we have subject matter knowledge about how a feature is related to the outcome, we can use this information to inform the model specification and potentially improve the model's performance.

Model specification – adding non-linear relationships

In linear regression, the relationship between an independent variable and the dependent variable is assumed to be linear, yet this may not necessarily be true. For example, the effect of age on medical expenditure may not be constant throughout all the age values; the treatment may become disproportionately expensive for oldest populations.

If you recall, a typical regression equation follows a form similar to this:

$$y = \alpha + \beta_1 x$$

To account for a non-linear relationship, we can add a higher order term to the regression model, treating the model as a polynomial. In effect, we will be modeling a relationship like this:

$$y = \alpha + \beta_1 x + \beta_2 x^2$$

The difference between these two models is that an additional beta will be estimated, which is intended to capture the effect of the x-squared term. This allows the impact of age to be measured as a function of age squared.

To add the non-linear age to the model, we simply need to create a new variable:

```
> insurance$age2 <- insurance$age^2
```

Then, when we produce our improved model, we'll add both age and age2 to the lm() formula using the expenses ~ age + age2 form. This will allow the model to separate the linear and non-linear impact of age on medical expenses.

Transformation – converting a numeric variable to a binary indicator

Suppose we have a hunch that the effect of a feature is not cumulative, rather it has an effect only after a specific threshold has been reached. For instance, BMI may have zero impact on medical expenditures for individuals in the normal weight range, but it may be strongly related to higher costs for the obese (that is, BMI of 30 or above).

We can model this relationship by creating a binary obesity indicator variable that is 1 if the BMI is at least 30, and 0 if less. The estimated beta for this binary feature would then indicate the average net impact on medical expenses for individuals with BMI of 30 or above, relative to those with BMI less than 30.

To create the feature, we can use the `ifelse()` function, which for each element in a vector tests a specified condition and returns a value depending on whether the condition is true or false. For BMI greater than or equal to 30, we will return 1, otherwise 0:

```
> insurance$bmi30 <- ifelse(insurance$bmi >= 30, 1, 0)
```

We can then include the `bmi30` variable in our improved model, either replacing the original `bmi` variable or in addition, depending on whether or not we think the effect of obesity occurs in addition to a separate linear BMI effect. Without good reason to do otherwise, we'll include both in our final model.

 If you have trouble deciding whether or not to include a variable, a common practice is to include it and examine the p-value. If the variable is not statistically significant, you have evidence to support excluding it in the future.

Model specification – adding interaction effects

So far, we have only considered each feature's individual contribution to the outcome. What if certain features have a combined impact on the dependent variable? For instance, smoking and obesity may have harmful effects separately, but it is reasonable to assume that their combined effect may be worse than the sum of each one alone.

When two features have a combined effect, this is known as an **interaction**. If we suspect that two variables interact, we can test this hypothesis by adding their interaction to the model. Interaction effects are specified using the R formula syntax. To have the obesity indicator (`bmi30`) and the smoking indicator (`smoker`) interact, we would write a formula in the form `expenses ~ bmi30*smoker`.

The `*` operator is shorthand that instructs R to model `expenses ~ bmi30 + smokeryes + bmi30:smokeryes`. The `:` (colon) operator in the expanded form indicates that `bmi30:smokeryes` is the interaction between the two variables. Note that the expanded form also automatically included the `bmi30` and `smoker` variables as well as the interaction.

 Interactions should never be included in a model without also adding each of the interacting variables. If you always create interactions using the `*` operator, this will not be a problem since R will add the required components automatically.

Putting it all together – an improved regression model

Based on a bit of subject matter knowledge of how medical costs may be related to patient characteristics, we developed what we think is a more accurately specified regression formula. To summarize the improvements, we:

- Added a non-linear term for age
- Created an indicator for obesity
- Specified an interaction between obesity and smoking

We'll train the model using the `lm()` function as before, but this time we'll add the newly constructed variables and the interaction term:

```
> ins_model2 <- lm(expenses ~ age + age2 + children + bmi + sex +
                   bmi30*smoker + region, data = insurance)
```

Next, we summarize the results:

```
> summary(ins_model2)
```

The output is shown as follows:

```
Call:
lm(formula = expenses ~ age + age2 + children + bmi + sex + bmi30 *
    smoker + region, data = insurance)

Residuals:
     Min       1Q   Median       3Q      Max
-17297.1  -1656.0  -1262.7   -727.8  24161.6

Coefficients:
                   Estimate Std. Error t value Pr(>|t|)
(Intercept)        139.0053 1363.1359    0.102 0.918792
age                -32.6181   59.8250   -0.545 0.585690
age2                 3.7307    0.7463    4.999 6.54e-07 ***
children           678.6017  105.8855    6.409 2.03e-10 ***
bmi                119.7715   34.2796    3.494 0.000492 ***
sexmale           -496.7690  244.3713   -2.033 0.042267 *
bmi30             -997.9355  422.9607   -2.359 0.018449 *
smokeryes        13404.5952  439.9591   30.468  < 2e-16 ***
regionnorthwest   -279.1661  349.2826   -0.799 0.424285
regionsoutheast   -828.0345  351.6484   -2.355 0.018682 *
regionsouthwest  -1222.1619  350.5314   -3.487 0.000505 ***
bmi30:smokeryes  19810.1534  604.6769   32.762  < 2e-16 ***
---
Signif. codes:  0 '***' 0.001 '**' 0.01 '*' 0.05 '.' 0.1 ' ' 1

Residual standard error: 4445 on 1326 degrees of freedom
Multiple R-squared:  0.8664,  Adjusted R-squared:  0.8653
F-statistic: 781.7 on 11 and 1326 DF,  p-value: < 2.2e-16
```

The model fit statistics help to determine whether our changes improved the performance of the regression model. Relative to our first model, the R-squared value has improved from 0.75 to about 0.87. Similarly, the adjusted R-squared value, which takes into account the fact that the model grew in complexity, also improved from 0.75 to 0.87. Our model is now explaining 87 percent of the variation in medical treatment costs. Additionally, our theories about the model's functional form seem to be validated. The higher-order `age2` term is statistically significant, as is the obesity indicator, `bmi30`. The interaction between obesity and smoking suggests a massive effect; in addition to the increased costs of over $13,404 for smoking alone, obese smokers spend another $19,810 per year. This may suggest that smoking exacerbates diseases associated with obesity.

Strictly speaking, regression modeling makes some strong assumptions about the data. These assumptions are not as important for numeric forecasting, as the model's worth is not based upon whether it truly captures the underlying process — we simply care about the accuracy of its predictions. However, if you would like to make firm inferences from the regression model coefficients, it is necessary to run diagnostic tests to ensure that the regression assumptions have not been violated. For an excellent introduction to this topic, see Allison PD. *Multiple regression: A primer*. Pine Forge Press; 1998.

Understanding regression trees and model trees

If you recall from *Chapter 5, Divide and Conquer – Classification Using Decision Trees and Rules*, a decision tree builds a model much like a flowchart in which decision nodes, leaf nodes, and branches define a series of decisions that are used to classify examples. Such trees can also be used for numeric prediction by making only small adjustments to the tree-growing algorithm. In this section, we will consider only the ways in which trees for numeric prediction differ from trees used for classification.

Trees for numeric prediction fall into two categories. The first, known as **regression trees**, were introduced in the 1980s as part of the seminal **Classification and Regression Tree (CART)** algorithm. Despite the name, regression trees do not use linear regression methods as described earlier in this chapter, rather they make predictions based on the average value of examples that reach a leaf.

The CART algorithm is described in detail in Breiman L, Friedman JH, Stone CJ, Olshen RA. *Classification and Regression Trees*. Belmont, CA: Chapman and Hall; 1984.

The second type of trees for numeric prediction are known as **model trees**. Introduced several years later than regression trees, they are lesser-known, but perhaps more powerful. Model trees are grown in much the same way as regression trees, but at each leaf, a multiple linear regression model is built from the examples reaching that node. Depending on the number of leaf nodes, a model tree may build tens or even hundreds of such models. This may make model trees more difficult to understand than the equivalent regression tree, with the benefit that they may result in a more accurate model.

The earliest model tree algorithm, **M5**, is described in Quinlan JR. *Learning with continuous classes*. Proceedings of the 5th Australian Joint Conference on Artificial Intelligence. 1992:343-348.

Adding regression to trees

Trees that can perform numeric prediction offer a compelling yet often overlooked alternative to regression modeling. The strengths and weaknesses of regression trees and model trees relative to the more common regression methods are listed in the following table:

Strengths	Weaknesses
• Combines the strengths of decision trees with the ability to model numeric data • Does not require the user to specify the model in advance • Uses automatic feature selection, which allows the approach to be used with a very large number of features • May fit some types of data much better than linear regression • Does not require knowledge of statistics to interpret the model	• Not as well-known as linear regression • Requires a large amount of training data • Difficult to determine the overall net effect of individual features on the outcome • Large trees can become more difficult to interpret than a regression model

Though traditional regression methods are typically the first choice for numeric prediction tasks, in some cases, numeric decision trees offer distinct advantages. For instance, decision trees may be better suited for tasks with many features or many complex, non-linear relationships among features and outcome. These situations present challenges for regression. Regression modeling also makes assumptions about how numeric data is distributed that are often violated in real-world data. This is not the case for trees.

Trees for numeric prediction are built in much the same way as they are for classification. Beginning at the root node, the data is partitioned using a divide-and-conquer strategy according to the feature that will result in the greatest increase in homogeneity in the outcome after a split is performed. In classification trees, you will recall that homogeneity is measured by entropy, which is undefined for numeric data. Instead, for numeric decision trees, homogeneity is measured by statistics such as variance, standard deviation, or absolute deviation from the mean.

One common splitting criterion is called the **Standard Deviation Reduction (SDR)**. It is defined by the following formula:

$$\text{SDR} = sd(T) - \sum_i \frac{|T_i|}{|T|} \times sd(T_i)$$

In this formula, the $sd(T)$ function refers to the standard deviation of the values in set T, while $T_1, T_2, ..., T_n$ are the sets of values resulting from a split on a feature. The $|T|$ term refers to the number of observations in set T. Essentially, the formula measures the reduction in standard deviation by comparing the standard deviation pre-split to the weighted standard deviation post-split.

For example, consider the following case in which a tree is deciding whether or not to perform a split on binary feature A or B:

original data	1	1	1	2	2	3	4	5	5	6	6	7	7	7	7
split on feature A	1	1	1	2	2	3	4	5	5	6	6	7	7	7	7
split on feature B	1	1	1	2	2	3	4	5	5	6	6	7	7	7	7

$$T_1 \qquad\qquad\qquad T_2$$

Using the groups that would result from the proposed splits, we can compute the SDR for A and B as follows. The length() function used here returns the number of elements in a vector. Note that the overall group T is named tee to avoid overwriting R's built-in T() and t() functions:

```
> tee <- c(1, 1, 1, 2, 2, 3, 4, 5, 5, 6, 6, 7, 7, 7, 7)
> at1 <- c(1, 1, 1, 2, 2, 3, 4, 5, 5)
> at2 <- c(6, 6, 7, 7, 7, 7)
> bt1 <- c(1, 1, 1, 2, 2, 3, 4)
> bt2 <- c(5, 5, 6, 6, 7, 7, 7, 7)
> sdr_a <- sd(tee) - (length(at1) / length(tee) * sd(at1) +
            length(at2) / length(tee) * sd(at2))
> sdr_b <- sd(tee) - (length(bt1) / length(tee) * sd(bt1) +
            length(bt2) / length(tee) * sd(bt2))
```

Let's compare the SDR of A against the SDR of B:

```
> sdr_a
[1] 1.202815
> sdr_b
[1] 1.392751
```

The SDR for the split on feature A was about 1.2 versus 1.4 for the split on feature B. Since the standard deviation was reduced more for the split on B, the decision tree would use B first. It results in slightly more homogeneous sets than with A.

Suppose that the tree stopped growing here using this one and only split. A regression tree's work is done. It can make predictions for new examples depending on whether the example's value on feature B places the example into group T_1 or T_2. If the example ends up in T_1, the model would predict *mean(bt1)* = 2, otherwise it would predict *mean(bt2)* = 6.25.

In contrast, a model tree would go one step further. Using the seven training examples falling in group T_1 and the eight in T_2, the model tree could build a linear regression model of the outcome versus feature A. Note that Feature B is of no help in building the regression model because all examples at the leaf have the same value of B—they were placed into T_1 or T_2 according to their value of B. The model tree can then make predictions for new examples using either of the two linear models.

To further illustrate the differences between these two approaches, let's work through a real-world example.

Example – estimating the quality of wines with regression trees and model trees

Winemaking is a challenging and competitive business that offers the potential for great profit. However, there are numerous factors that contribute to the profitability of a winery. As an agricultural product, variables as diverse as the weather and the growing environment impact the quality of a varietal. The bottling and manufacturing can also affect the flavor for better or worse. Even the way the product is marketed, from the bottle design to the price point, can affect the customer's perception of taste.

As a consequence, the winemaking industry has heavily invested in data collection and machine learning methods that may assist with the decision science of winemaking. For example, machine learning has been used to discover key differences in the chemical composition of wines from different regions, or to identify the chemical factors that lead a wine to taste sweeter.

More recently, machine learning has been employed to assist with rating the quality of wine – a notoriously difficult task. A review written by a renowned wine critic often determines whether the product ends up on the top or bottom shelf, in spite of the fact that even the expert judges are inconsistent when rating a wine in a blinded test.

In this case study, we will use regression trees and model trees to create a system capable of mimicking expert ratings of wine. Because trees result in a model that is readily understood, this can allow the winemakers to identify the key factors that contribute to better-rated wines. Perhaps more importantly, the system does not suffer from the human elements of tasting, such as the rater's mood or palate fatigue. Computer-aided wine testing may therefore result in a better product as well as more objective, consistent, and fair ratings.

Step 1 – collecting data

To develop the wine rating model, we will use data donated to the UCI Machine Learning Data Repository (http://archive.ics.uci.edu/ml) by P. Cortez, A. Cerdeira, F. Almeida, T. Matos, and J. Reis. The data include examples of red and white Vinho Verde wines from Portugal – one of the world's leading wine-producing countries. Because the factors that contribute to a highly rated wine may differ between the red and white varieties, for this analysis we will examine only the more popular white wines.

To follow along with this example, download the `whitewines.csv` file from the Packt Publishing website and save it to your R working directory. The `redwines.csv` file is also available in case you would like to explore this data on your own.

The white wine data includes information on 11 chemical properties of 4,898 wine samples. For each wine, a laboratory analysis measured characteristics such as acidity, sugar content, chlorides, sulfur, alcohol, pH, and density. The samples were then rated in a blind tasting by panels of no less than three judges on a quality scale ranging from zero (very bad) to 10 (excellent). In the case of judges disagreeing on the rating, the median value was used.

The study by Cortez evaluated the ability of three machine learning approaches to model the wine data: multiple regression, artificial neural networks, and support vector machines. We covered multiple regression earlier in this chapter, and we will learn about neural networks and support vector machines in *Chapter 7, Black Box Methods – Neural Networks and Support Vector Machines*. The study found that the support vector machine offered significantly better results than the linear regression model. However, unlike regression, the support vector machine model is difficult to interpret. Using regression trees and model trees, we may be able to improve the regression results while still having a model that is easy to understand.

To read more about the wine study described here, please refer to Cortez P, Cerdeira A, Almeida F, Matos T, Reis J. *Modeling wine preferences by data mining from physicochemical properties*. Decision Support Systems. 2009; 47:547-553.

Step 2 – exploring and preparing the data

As usual, we will use the `read.csv()` function to load the data into R. Since all of the features are numeric, we can safely ignore the `stringsAsFactors` parameter:

```
> wine <- read.csv("whitewines.csv")
```

The wine data includes 11 features and the quality outcome, as follows:

```
> str(wine)
'data.frame':  4898 obs. of  12 variables:
 $ fixed.acidity      : num  6.7 5.7 5.9 5.3 6.4 7 7.9 ...
 $ volatile.acidity   : num  0.62 0.22 0.19 0.47 0.29 0.12 ...
 $ citric.acid        : num  0.24 0.2 0.26 0.1 0.21 0.41 ...
 $ residual.sugar     : num  1.1 16 7.4 1.3 9.65 0.9 ...
```

```
$ chlorides           : num  0.039 0.044 0.034 0.036 0.041 ...
$ free.sulfur.dioxide : num  6 41 33 11 36 22 33 17 34 40 ...
$ total.sulfur.dioxide: num  62 113 123 74 119 95 152 ...
$ density             : num  0.993 0.999 0.995 0.991 0.993 ...
$ pH                  : num  3.41 3.22 3.49 3.48 2.99 3.25 ...
$ sulphates           : num  0.32 0.46 0.42 0.54 0.34 0.43 ...
$ alcohol             : num  10.4 8.9 10.1 11.2 10.9 ...
$ quality             : int  5 6 6 4 6 6 6 6 6 7 ...
```

Compared with other types of machine learning models, one of the advantages of trees is that they can handle many types of data without preprocessing. This means we do not need to normalize or standardize the features.

However, a bit of effort to examine the distribution of the outcome variable is needed to inform our evaluation of the model's performance. For instance, suppose that there was a very little variation in quality from wine-to-wine, or that wines fell into a bimodal distribution: either very good or very bad. To check for such extremes, we can examine the distribution of quality using a histogram:

```
> hist(wine$quality)
```

This produces the following figure:

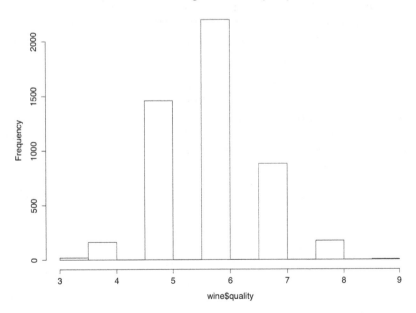

The wine quality values appear to follow a fairly normal, bell-shaped distribution, centered around a value of six. This makes sense intuitively because most wines are of average quality; few are particularly bad or good. Although the results are not shown here, it is also useful to examine the `summary(wine)` output for outliers or other potential data problems. Even though trees are fairly robust with messy data, it is always prudent to check for severe problems. For now, we'll assume that the data is reliable.

Our last step then is to divide into training and testing datasets. Since the `wine` data set was already sorted into random order, we can partition into two sets of contiguous rows as follows:

```
> wine_train <- wine[1:3750, ]
> wine_test <- wine[3751:4898, ]
```

In order to mirror the conditions used by Cortez, we used sets of 75 percent and 25 percent for training and testing, respectively. We'll evaluate the performance of our tree-based models on the testing data to see if we can obtain results comparable to the prior research study.

Step 3 – training a model on the data

We will begin by training a regression tree model. Although almost any implementation of decision trees can be used to perform regression tree modeling, the `rpart` (recursive partitioning) package offers the most faithful implementation of regression trees as they were described by the CART team. As the classic R implementation of CART, the `rpart` package is also well-documented and supported with functions for visualizing and evaluating the `rpart` models.

Install the `rpart` package using the `install.packages("rpart")` command. It can then be loaded into your R session using the `library(rpart)` command. The following syntax will train a tree using the default settings, which typically work fairly well. If you need more finely-tuned settings, refer to the documentation for the control parameters using the `?rpart.control` command.

Regression trees syntax

using the `rpart()` function in the `rpart` package

Building the model:

```
m <- rpart(dv ~ iv, data = mydata)
```

- dv is the dependent variable in the `mydata` data frame to be modeled
- iv is an R formula specifying the independent variables in the `mydata` data frame to use in the model
- data specifies the data frame in which the dv and iv variables can be found

The function will return a regression tree model object that can be used to make predictions.

Making predictions:

```
p <- predict(m, test, type = "vector")
```

- m is a model trained by the `rpart()` function
- test is a data frame containing test data with the same features as the training data used to build the model
- type specifies the type of prediction to return, either `"vector"` (for predicted numeric values), `"class"` for predicted classes, or `"prob"` (for predicted class probabilities)

The function will return a vector of predictions depending on the type parameter.

Example:

```
wine_model <- rpart(quality ~ alcohol + sulfates,
                    data = wine_train)
wine_predictions <- predict(wine_model, wine_test)
```

Using the R formula interface, we can specify quality as the outcome variable and use the dot notation to allow all the other columns in the wine_train data frame to be used as predictors. The resulting regression tree model object is named m.rpart to distinguish it from the model tree that we will train later:

```
> m.rpart <- rpart(quality ~ ., data = wine_train)
```

For basic information about the tree, simply type the name of the model object:

```
> m.rpart
n= 3750


node), split, n, deviance, yval
      * denotes terminal node


 1) root 3750 2945.53200 5.870933
   2) alcohol< 10.85 2372 1418.86100 5.604975
     4) volatile.acidity>=0.2275 1611  821.30730 5.432030
```

```
    8) volatile.acidity>=0.3025 688   278.97670 5.255814 *
    9) volatile.acidity< 0.3025 923   505.04230 5.563380 *
  5) volatile.acidity< 0.2275 761   447.36400 5.971091 *
3) alcohol>=10.85 1378 1070.08200 6.328737
  6) free.sulfur.dioxide< 10.5 84    95.55952 5.369048 *
  7) free.sulfur.dioxide>=10.5 1294   892.13600 6.391036
   14) alcohol< 11.76667 629   430.11130 6.173291
     28) volatile.acidity>=0.465 11    10.72727 4.545455 *
     29) volatile.acidity< 0.465 618   389.71680 6.202265 *
   15) alcohol>=11.76667 665   403.99400 6.596992 *
```

For each node in the tree, the number of examples reaching the decision point is listed. For instance, all 3,750 examples begin at the root node, of which 2,372 have `alcohol < 10.85` and 1,378 have `alcohol >= 10.85`. Because alcohol was used first in the tree, it is the single most important predictor of wine quality.

Nodes indicated by * are terminal or leaf nodes, which means that they result in a prediction (listed here as `yval`). For example, node 5 has a `yval` of 5.971091. When the tree is used for predictions, any wine samples with `alcohol < 10.85` and `volatile.acidity < 0.2275` would therefore be predicted to have a quality value of 5.97.

A more detailed summary of the tree's fit, including the mean squared error for each of the nodes and an overall measure of feature importance, can be obtained using the `summary(m.rpart)` command.

Visualizing decision trees

Although the tree can be understood using only the preceding output, it is often more readily understood using visualization. The `rpart.plot` package by Stephen Milborrow provides an easy-to-use function that produces publication-quality decision trees.

> For more information on `rpart.plot`, including additional examples of the types of decision tree diagrams that the function can produce, refer to the author's website at http://www.milbo.org/rpart-plot/.

After installing the package using the `install.packages("rpart.plot")` command, the `rpart.plot()` function produces a tree diagram from any `rpart` model object. The following commands plot the regression tree we built earlier:

```
> library(rpart.plot)
> rpart.plot(m.rpart, digits = 3)
```

The resulting tree diagram is as follows:

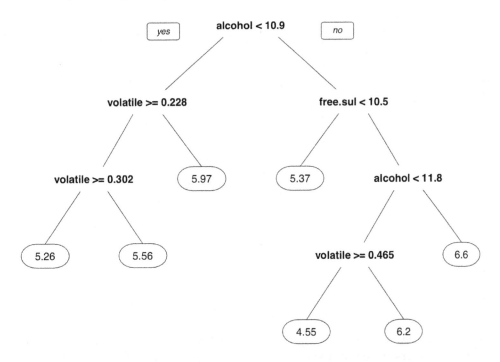

In addition to the `digits` parameter that controls the number of numeric digits to include in the diagram, many other aspects of the visualization can be adjusted. The following command shows just a few of the useful options: The `fallen.leaves` parameter forces the leaf nodes to be aligned at the bottom of the plot, while the `type` and `extra` parameters affect the way the decisions and nodes are labeled:

```
> rpart.plot(m.rpart, digits = 4, fallen.leaves = TRUE,
             type = 3, extra = 101)
```

The result of these changes is a very different looking tree diagram:

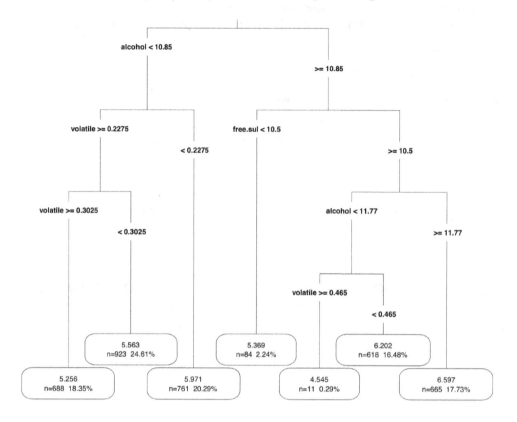

Visualizations like these may assist with the dissemination of regression tree results, as they are readily understood even without a mathematics background. In both cases, the numbers shown in the leaf nodes are the predicted values for the examples reaching that node. Showing the diagram to the wine producers may thus help to identify the key factors that predict the higher rated wines.

Step 4 – evaluating model performance

To use the regression tree model to make predictions on the test data, we use the `predict()` function. By default, this returns the estimated numeric value for the outcome variable, which we'll save in a vector named `p.rpart`:

```
> p.rpart <- predict(m.rpart, wine_test)
```

A quick look at the summary statistics of our predictions suggests a potential problem; the predictions fall on a much narrower range than the true values:

```
> summary(p.rpart)
   Min. 1st Qu.  Median    Mean 3rd Qu.    Max.
  4.545   5.563   5.971   5.893   6.202   6.597
> summary(wine_test$quality)
   Min. 1st Qu.  Median    Mean 3rd Qu.    Max.
  3.000   5.000   6.000   5.901   6.000   9.000
```

This finding suggests that the model is not correctly identifying the extreme cases, in particular the best and worst wines. On the other hand, between the first and third quartile, we may be doing well.

The correlation between the predicted and actual quality values provides a simple way to gauge the model's performance. Recall that the cor() function can be used to measure the relationship between two equal-length vectors. We'll use this to compare how well the predicted values correspond to the true values:

```
> cor(p.rpart, wine_test$quality)
[1] 0.5369525
```

A correlation of 0.54 is certainly acceptable. However, the correlation only measures how strongly the predictions are related to the true value; it is not a measure of how far off the predictions were from the true values.

Measuring performance with the mean absolute error

Another way to think about the model's performance is to consider how far, on average, its prediction was from the true value. This measurement is called the **mean absolute error** (MAE). The equation for MAE is as follows, where n indicates the number of predictions and e_i indicates the error for prediction i:

$$\mathrm{MAE} = \frac{1}{n} \sum_{i=1}^{n} |e_i|$$

As the name implies, this equation takes the mean of the absolute value of the errors. Since the error is just the difference between the predicted and actual values, we can create a simple `MAE()` function as follows:

```
> MAE <- function(actual, predicted) {
    mean(abs(actual - predicted))
}
```

The MAE for our predictions is then:

```
> MAE(p.rpart, wine_test$quality)
[1] 0.5872652
```

This implies that, on average, the difference between our model's predictions and the true quality score was about 0.59. On a quality scale from zero to 10, this seems to suggest that our model is doing fairly well.

On the other hand, recall that most wines were neither very good nor very bad; the typical quality score was around five to six. Therefore, a classifier that did nothing but predict the mean value may still do fairly well according to this metric.

The mean quality rating in the training data is as follows:

```
> mean(wine_train$quality)
[1] 5.870933
```

If we predicted the value 5.87 for every wine sample, we would have a mean absolute error of only about 0.67:

```
> MAE(5.87, wine_test$quality)
[1] 0.6722474
```

Our regression tree ($MAE = 0.59$) comes closer on average to the true quality score than the imputed mean ($MAE = 0.67$), but not by much. In comparison, Cortez reported an MAE of 0.58 for the neural network model and an MAE of 0.45 for the support vector machine. This suggests that there is room for improvement.

Step 5 – improving model performance

To improve the performance of our learner, let's try to build a model tree. Recall that a model tree improves on regression trees by replacing the leaf nodes with regression models. This often results in more accurate results than regression trees, which use only a single value for prediction at the leaf nodes.

The current state-of-the-art in model trees is the **M5' algorithm** (M5-prime) by Y. Wang and I.H. Witten, which is a variant of the original M5 model tree algorithm proposed by J.R. Quinlan in 1992.

 For more information on the M5' algorithm, see Wang Y, Witten IH. *Induction of model trees for predicting continuous classes*. Proceedings of the Poster Papers of the European Conference on Machine Learning. 1997.

The M5 algorithm is available in R via the RWeka package and the M5P() function. The syntax of this function is shown in the following table. Be sure to install the RWeka package if you haven't already. Because of its dependence on Java, the installation instructions are included in *Chapter 1, Introducing Machine Learning*.

Model trees syntax

using the M5P() function in the **RWeka** package

Building the model:

```
m <- M5P(dv ~ iv, data = mydata)
```

- dv is the dependent variable in the mydata data frame to be modeled
- iv is an R formula specifying the independent variables in the mydata data frame to use in the model
- data specifies the data frame in which the dv and iv variables can be found

The function will return a model tree object that can be used to make predictions.

Making predictions:

```
p <- predict(m, test)
```

- m is a model trained by the M5P() function
- test is a data frame containing test data with the same features as the training data used to build the model

The function will return a vector of predicted numeric values.

Example:

```
wine_model <- M5P(quality ~ alcohol + sulfates,
                  data = wine_train)
wine_predictions <- predict(wine_model, wine_test)
```

We'll fit the model tree using essentially the same syntax as we used for the regression tree:

```
> library(RWeka)
> m.m5p <- M5P(quality ~ ., data = wine_train)
```

The tree itself can be examined by typing its name. In this case, the tree is very large and only the first few lines of output are shown:

```
> m.m5p
M5 pruned model tree:
(using smoothed linear models)


alcohol <= 10.85 :
|    volatile.acidity <= 0.238 :
|    |    fixed.acidity <= 6.85 : LM1 (406/66.024%)
|    |    fixed.acidity >  6.85 :
|    |    |    free.sulfur.dioxide <= 24.5 : LM2 (113/87.697%)
```

You will note that the splits are very similar to the regression tree that we built earlier. Alcohol is the most important variable, followed by volatile acidity and free sulfur dioxide. A key difference, however, is that the nodes terminate not in a numeric prediction, but a linear model (shown here as LM1 and LM2).

The linear models themselves are shown later in the output. For instance, the model for LM1 is shown in the forthcoming output. The values can be interpreted exactly the same as the multiple regression models we built earlier in this chapter. Each number is the net effect of the associated feature on the predicted wine quality. The coefficient of 0.266 for fixed acidity implies that for an increase of 1 unit of acidity, the wine quality is expected to increase by 0.266:

```
LM num: 1
quality =
  0.266 * fixed.acidity
  - 2.3082 * volatile.acidity
  - 0.012 * citric.acid
  + 0.0421 * residual.sugar
  + 0.1126 * chlorides
  + 0 * free.sulfur.dioxide
  - 0.0015 * total.sulfur.dioxide
  - 109.8813 * density
```

```
+ 0.035 * pH
+ 1.4122 * sulphates
- 0.0046 * alcohol
+ 113.1021
```

It is important to note that the effects estimated by LM1 apply only to wine samples reaching this node; a total of 36 linear models were built in this model tree, each with different estimates of the impact of fixed acidity and the other 10 features.

For statistics on how well the model fits the training data, the summary() function can be applied to the M5P model. However, note that since these statistics are based on the training data, they should be used only as a rough diagnostic:

```
> summary(m.m5p)


=== Summary ===


Correlation coefficient                    0.6666
Mean absolute error                        0.5151
Root mean squared error                    0.6614
Relative absolute error               76.4921 %
Root relative squared error           74.6259 %
Total Number of Instances               3750
```

Instead, we'll look at how well the model performs on the unseen test data. The predict() function gets us a vector of predicted values:

```
> p.m5p <- predict(m.m5p, wine_test)
```

The model tree appears to be predicting a wider range of values than the regression tree:

```
> summary(p.m5p)
  Min. 1st Qu.  Median    Mean 3rd Qu.    Max.
 4.389   5.430   5.863   5.874   6.305   7.437
```

The correlation also seems to be substantially higher:

```
> cor(p.m5p, wine_test$quality)
[1] 0.6272973
```

Furthermore, the model has slightly reduced the mean absolute error:

```
> MAE(wine_test$quality, p.m5p)
[1] 0.5463023
```

Although we did not improve a great deal beyond the regression tree, we surpassed the performance of the neural network model published by Cortez, and we are getting closer to the published mean absolute error value of 0.45 for the support vector machine model, all by using a much simpler learning method.

> Not surprisingly, we have confirmed that predicting the quality of wines is a difficult problem; wine tasting, after all, is inherently subjective. If you would like additional practice, you may try revisiting this problem after reading *Chapter 11, Improving Model Performance*, which covers additional techniques that may lead to better results.

Summary

In this chapter, we studied two methods for modeling numeric data. The first method, linear regression, involves fitting straight lines to data. The second method uses decision trees for numeric prediction. The latter comes in two forms: regression trees, which use the average value of examples at leaf nodes to make numeric predictions; and model trees, which build a regression model at each leaf node in a hybrid approach that is, in some ways, the best of both worlds.

We used linear regression modeling to calculate the expected medical costs for various segments of the population. Because the relationship between the features and the target variable are well-described by the estimated regression model, we were able to identify certain demographics, such as smokers and the obese, who may need to be charged higher insurance rates to cover the higher-than-average medical expenses.

Regression trees and model trees were used to model the subjective quality of wines from measureable characteristics. In doing so, we learned how regression trees offer a simple way to explain the relationship between features and a numeric outcome, but the more complex model trees may be more accurate. Along the way, we learned several methods for evaluating the performance of numeric models.

In stark contrast to this chapter, which covered machine learning methods that result in a clear understanding of the relationships between the input and the output, the next chapter covers methods that result in nearly-incomprehensible models. The upside is that they are extremely powerful techniques — among the most powerful stock classifiers — that can be applied to both classification and numeric prediction problems.

Black Box Methods – Neural Networks and Support Vector Machines

The late science fiction author Arthur C. Clarke wrote, "any sufficiently advanced technology is indistinguishable from magic."This chapter covers a pair of machine learning methods that may appear at first glance to be magic. Though they are extremely powerful, their inner workings can be difficult to understand.

In engineering, these are referred to as **black box** processes because the mechanism that transforms the input into the output is obfuscated by an imaginary box. For instance, the black box of closed-source software intentionally conceals proprietary algorithms, the black box of political lawmaking is rooted in the bureaucratic processes, and the black box of sausage-making involves a bit of purposeful (but tasty) ignorance. In the case of machine learning, the black box is due to the complex mathematics allowing them to function.

Although they may not be easy to understand, it is dangerous to apply black box models blindly. Thus, in this chapter, we'll peek inside the box and investigate the statistical sausage-making involved in fitting such models. You'll discover:

- Neural networks mimic the structure of animal brains to model arbitrary functions
- Support vector machines use multidimensional surfaces to define the relationship between features and outcomes
- Despite their complexity, these can be applied easily to real-world problems

With any luck, you'll realize that you don't need a black belt in statistics to tackle black box machine's learning methods—there's no need to be intimidated!

Understanding neural networks

An **Artificial Neural Network (ANN)** models the relationship between a set of input signals and an output signal using a model derived from our understanding of how a biological brain responds to stimuli from sensory inputs. Just as a brain uses a network of interconnected cells called **neurons** to create a massive parallel processor, ANN uses a network of artificial neurons or **nodes** to solve learning problems.

The human brain is made up of about 85 billion neurons, resulting in a network capable of representing a tremendous amount of knowledge. As you might expect, this dwarfs the brains of other living creatures. For instance, a cat has roughly a billion neurons, a mouse has about 75 million neurons, and a cockroach has only about a million neurons. In contrast, many ANNs contain far fewer neurons, typically only several hundred, so we're in no danger of creating an artificial brain anytime in the near future—even a fruit fly brain with 100,000 neurons far exceeds the current state-of-the-art ANN.

Though it may be unfeasible to completely model a cockroach's brain, a neural network may still provide an adequate heuristic model of its behavior. Suppose that we develop an algorithm that can mimic how a roach flees when discovered. If the behavior of the robot roach is convincing, does it matter whether its brain is as sophisticated as the living creature's? This question is the basis of the controversial **Turing test**, proposed in 1950 by the pioneering computer scientist Alan Turing, proposed in 1950 by the pioneering computer scientist Alan Turing, which grades a machine as intelligent if a human being cannot distinguish its behavior from a living creature's.

Rudimentary ANNs have been used for over 50 years to simulate the brain's approach to problem-solving. At first, this involved learning simple functions like the logical AND function or the logical OR function. These early exercises were used primarily to help scientists understand how biological brains might operate. However, as computers have become increasingly powerful in the recent years, the complexity of ANNs has likewise increased so much that they are now frequently applied to more practical problems including:

- Speech and handwriting recognition programs like those used by voicemail transcription services and postal mail sorting machines
- The automation of smart devices like an office building's environmental controls or self-driving cars and self-piloting drones
- Sophisticated models of weather and climate patterns, tensile strength, fluid dynamics, and many other scientific, social, or economic phenomena

Broadly speaking, ANNs are versatile learners that can be applied to nearly any learning task: classification, numeric prediction, and even unsupervised pattern recognition.

 Whether deserving or not, ANN learners are often reported in the media with great fanfare. For instance, an *"artificial brain"* developed by Google was recently touted for its ability to identify cat videos on YouTube. Such hype may have less to do with anything unique to ANNs and more to do with the fact that ANNs are captivating because of their similarities to living minds.

ANNs are best applied to problems where the input data and output data are well-defined or at least fairly simple, yet the process that relates the input to output is extremely complex. As a black box method, they work well for these types of black box problems.

From biological to artificial neurons

Because ANNs were intentionally designed as conceptual models of human brain activity, it is helpful to first understand how biological neurons function. As illustrated in the following figure, incoming signals are received by the cell's **dendrites** through a biochemical process. The process allows the impulse to be weighted according to its relative importance or frequency. As the **cell body** begins accumulating the incoming signals, a threshold is reached at which the cell fires and the output signal is transmitted via an electrochemical process down the **axon**. At the axon's terminals, the electric signal is again processed as a chemical signal to be passed to the neighboring neurons across a tiny gap known as a **synapse**.

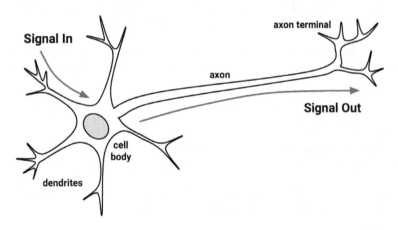

The model of a single artificial neuron can be understood in terms very similar to the biological model. As depicted in the following figure, a directed network diagram defines a relationship between the input signals received by the dendrites (*x* variables), and the output signal (*y* variable). Just as with the biological neuron, each dendrite's signal is weighted (*w* values) according to its importance — ignore, for now, how these weights are determined. The input signals are summed by the cell body and the signal is passed on according to an **activation function** denoted by *f*:

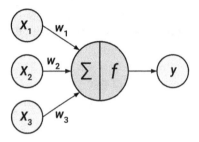

A typical artificial neuron with *n* input dendrites can be represented by the formula that follows. The *w* weights allow each of the *n* inputs (denoted by x_i) to contribute a greater or lesser amount to the sum of input signals. The net total is used by the activation function *f(x)*, and the resulting signal, *y(x)*, is the output axon:

$$y(x) = f\left(\sum_{i=1}^{n} w_i x_i\right)$$

Neural networks use neurons defined this way as building blocks to construct complex models of data. Although there are numerous variants of neural networks, each can be defined in terms of the following characteristics:

- An **activation function**, which transforms a neuron's combined input signals into a single output signal to be broadcasted further in the network

- A **network topology** (or architecture), which describes the number of neurons in the model as well as the number of layers and manner in which they are connected

- The **training algorithm** that specifies how connection weights are set in order to inhibit or excite neurons in proportion to the input signal

Let's take a look at some of the variations within each of these categories to see how they can be used to construct typical neural network models.

Activation functions

The activation function is the mechanism by which the artificial neuron processes incoming information and passes it throughout the network. Just as the artificial neuron is modeled after the biological version, so is the activation function modeled after nature's design.

In the biological case, the activation function could be imagined as a process that involves summing the total input signal and determining whether it meets the firing threshold. If so, the neuron passes on the signal; otherwise, it does nothing. In ANN terms, this is known as a **threshold activation function**, as it results in an output signal only once a specified input threshold has been attained.

The following figure depicts a typical threshold function; in this case, the neuron fires when the sum of input signals is at least zero. Because its shape resembles a stair, it is sometimes called a **unit step activation function**.

$$f(x) = \begin{cases} 0 \text{ if } x < 0 \\ 1 \text{ if } x \geq 0 \end{cases}$$

Although the threshold activation function is interesting due to its parallels with biology, it is rarely used in artificial neural networks. Freed from the limitations of biochemistry, the ANN activation functions can be chosen based on their ability to demonstrate desirable mathematical characteristics and accurately model relationships among data.

Perhaps the most commonly used alternative is the **sigmoid activation function** (more specifically, the *logistic* sigmoid) shown in the following figure. Note that in the formula shown, *e* is the base of the natural logarithm (approximately 2.72). Although it shares a similar step or "S" shape with the threshold activation function, the output signal is no longer binary; output values can fall anywhere in the range from 0 to 1. Additionally, the sigmoid is **differentiable**, which means that it is possible to calculate the derivative across the entire range of inputs. As you will learn later, this feature is crucial to create efficient ANN optimization algorithms.

Although sigmoid is perhaps the most commonly used activation function and is often used by default, some neural network algorithms allow a choice of alternatives. A selection of such activation functions is shown in the following figure:

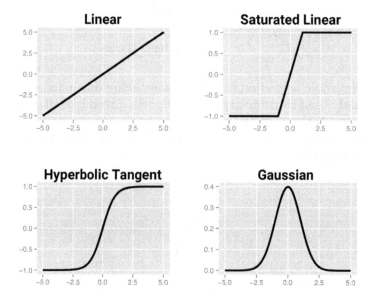

The primary detail that differentiates these activation functions is the output signal range. Typically, this is one of (0, 1), (-1, +1), or (-inf, +inf). The choice of activation function biases the neural network such that it may fit certain types of data more appropriately, allowing the construction of specialized neural networks. For instance, a linear activation function results in a neural network very similar to a linear regression model, while a Gaussian activation function results in a model called a **Radial Basis Function** (**RBF**) network. Each of these has strengths better suited for certain learning tasks and not others.

It's important to recognize that for many of the activation functions, the range of input values that affect the output signal is relatively narrow. For example, in the case of sigmoid, the output signal is always nearly 0 or 1 for an input signal below -5 or above +5, respectively. The compression of signal in this way results in a saturated signal at the high and low ends of very dynamic inputs, just as turning a guitar amplifier up too high results in a distorted sound due to clipping of the peaks of sound waves. Because this essentially squeezes the input values into a smaller range of outputs, activation functions like the sigmoid are sometimes called **squashing functions**.

The solution to the squashing problem is to transform all neural network inputs such that the features' values fall within a small range around 0. Typically, this involves standardizing or normalizing the features. By restricting the range of input values, the activation function will have action across the entire range, preventing large-valued features such as household income from dominating small-valued features such as the number of children in the household. A side benefit is that the model may also be faster to train, since the algorithm can iterate more quickly through the actionable range of input values.

> Although theoretically a neural network can adapt to a very dynamic feature by adjusting its weight over many iterations. In extreme cases, many algorithms will stop iterating long before this occurs. If your model is making predictions that do not make sense, double-check whether you've correctly standardized the input data.

Network topology

The ability of a neural network to learn is rooted in its **topology**, or the patterns and structures of interconnected neurons. Although there are countless forms of network architecture, they can be differentiated by three key characteristics:

- The number of layers
- Whether information in the network is allowed to travel backward
- The number of nodes within each layer of the network

The topology determines the complexity of tasks that can be learned by the network. Generally, larger and more complex networks are capable of identifying more subtle patterns and complex decision boundaries. However, the power of a network is not only a function of the network size, but also the way units are arranged.

The number of layers

To define topology, we need a terminology that distinguishes artificial neurons based on their position in the network. The figure that follows illustrates the topology of a very simple network. A set of neurons called **input nodes** receives unprocessed signals directly from the input data. Each input node is responsible for processing a single feature in the dataset; the feature's value will be transformed by the corresponding node's activation function. The signals sent by the input nodes are received by the output node, which uses its own activation function to generate a final prediction (denoted here as p).

The input and output nodes are arranged in groups known as **layers**. Because the input nodes process the incoming data exactly as it is received, the network has only one set of connection weights (labeled here as w_1, w_2, and w_3). It is therefore termed a **single-layer network**. Single-layer networks can be used for basic pattern classification, particularly for patterns that are linearly separable, but more sophisticated networks are required for most learning tasks.

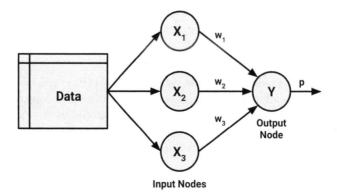

As you might expect, an obvious way to create more complex networks is by adding additional layers. As depicted here, a **multilayer network** adds one or more **hidden layers** that process the signals from the input nodes prior to it reaching the output node. Most multilayer networks are **fully connected**, which means that every node in one layer is connected to every node in the next layer, but this is not required.

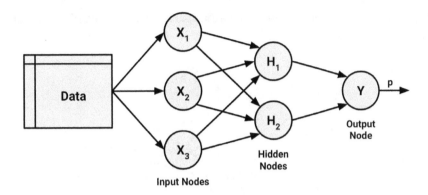

The direction of information travel

You may have noticed that in the prior examples, arrowheads were used to indicate signals traveling in only one direction. Networks in which the input signal is fed continuously in one direction from connection to connection until it reaches the output layer are called **feedforward** networks.

In spite of the restriction on information flow, feedforward networks offer a surprising amount of flexibility. For instance, the number of levels and nodes at each level can be varied, multiple outcomes can be modeled simultaneously, or multiple hidden layers can be applied. A neural network with multiple hidden layers is called a **Deep Neural Network (DNN)** and the practice of training such network is sometimes referred to as **deep learning**.

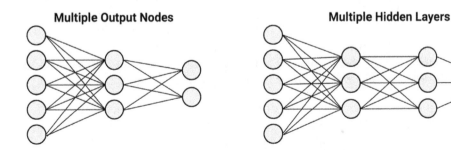

In contrast, a **recurrent network** (or **feedback network**) allows signals to travel in both directions using loops. This property, which more closely mirrors how a biological neural network works, allows extremely complex patterns to be learned. The addition of a short-term memory, or **delay**, increases the power of recurrent networks immensely. Notably, this includes the capability to understand the sequences of events over a period of time. This could be used for stock market prediction, speech comprehension, or weather forecasting. A simple recurrent network is depicted as follows:

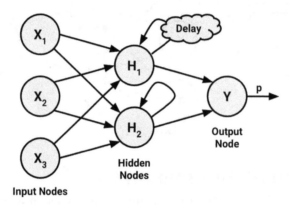

In spite of their potential, recurrent networks are still largely theoretical and are rarely used in practice. On the other hand, feedforward networks have been extensively applied to real-world problems. In fact, the multilayer feedforward network, sometimes called the **Multilayer Perceptron (MLP)**, is the de facto standard ANN topology. If someone mentions that they are fitting a neural network, they are most likely referring to a MLP.

The number of nodes in each layer

In addition to the variations in the number of layers and the direction of information travel, neural networks can also vary in complexity by the number of nodes in each layer. The number of input nodes is predetermined by the number of features in the input data. Similarly, the number of output nodes is predetermined by the number of outcomes to be modeled or the number of class levels in the outcome. However, the number of hidden nodes is left to the user to decide prior to training the model.

Unfortunately, there is no reliable rule to determine the number of neurons in the hidden layer. The appropriate number depends on the number of input nodes, the amount of training data, the amount of noisy data, and the complexity of the learning task, among many other factors.

In general, more complex network topologies with a greater number of network connections allow the learning of more complex problems. A greater number of neurons will result in a model that more closely mirrors the training data, but this runs a risk of overfitting; it may generalize poorly to future data. Large neural networks can also be computationally expensive and slow to train.

The best practice is to use the fewest nodes that result in adequate performance in a validation dataset. In most cases, even with only a small number of hidden nodes— often as few as a handful—the neural network can offer a tremendous amount of learning ability.

It has been proven that a neural network with at least one hidden layer of sufficient neurons is a **universal function approximator**. This means that neural networks can be used to approximate any continuous function to an arbitrary precision over a finite interval.

Training neural networks with backpropagation

The network topology is a blank slate that by itself has not learned anything. Like a newborn child, it must be trained with experience. As the neural network processes the input data, connections between the neurons are strengthened or weakened, similar to how a baby's brain develops as he or she experiences the environment. The network's connection weights are adjusted to reflect the patterns observed over time.

Training a neural network by adjusting connection weights is very computationally intensive. Consequently, though they had been studied for decades prior, ANNs were rarely applied to real-world learning tasks until the mid-to-late 1980s, when an efficient method of training an ANN was discovered. The algorithm, which used a strategy of back-propagating errors, is now known simply as **backpropagation**.

Coincidentally, several research teams independently discovered and published the backpropagation algorithm around the same time. Among them, perhaps the most often cited work is: Rumelhart DE, Hinton GE, Williams RJ. Learning representations by back-propagating errors. *Nature*. 1986; 323:533-566.

Although still notoriously slow relative to many other machine learning algorithms, the backpropagation method led to a resurgence of interest in ANNs. As a result, multilayer feedforward networks that use the backpropagation algorithm are now common in the field of data mining. Such models offer the following strengths and weaknesses:

Strengths	Weaknesses
• Can be adapted to classification or numeric prediction problems • Capable of modeling more complex patterns than nearly any algorithm • Makes few assumptions about the data's underlying relationships	• Extremely computationally intensive and slow to train, particularly if the network topology is complex • Very prone to overfitting training data • Results in a complex black box model that is difficult, if not impossible, to interpret

In its most general form, the backpropagation algorithm iterates through many cycles of two processes. Each cycle is known as an **epoch**. Because the network contains no *a priori* (existing) knowledge, the starting weights are typically set at random. Then, the algorithm iterates through the processes, until a stopping criterion is reached. Each epoch in the backpropagation algorithm includes:

- A **forward phase** in which the neurons are activated in sequence from the input layer to the output layer, applying each neuron's weights and activation function along the way. Upon reaching the final layer, an output signal is produced.

- A **backward phase** in which the network's output signal resulting from the forward phase is compared to the true target value in the training data. The difference between the network's output signal and the true value results in an error that is propagated backwards in the network to modify the connection weights between neurons and reduce future errors.

Over time, the network uses the information sent backward to reduce the total error of the network. Yet one question remains: because the relationship between each neuron's inputs and outputs is complex, how does the algorithm determine how much a weight should be changed? The answer to this question involves a technique called **gradient descent**. Conceptually, it works similarly to how an explorer trapped in the jungle might find a path to water. By examining the terrain and continually walking in the direction with the greatest downward slope, the explorer will eventually reach the lowest valley, which is likely to be a riverbed.

In a similar process, the backpropagation algorithm uses the derivative of each neuron's activation function to identify the gradient in the direction of each of the incoming weights—hence the importance of having a differentiable activation function. The gradient suggests how steeply the error will be reduced or increased for a change in the weight. The algorithm will attempt to change the weights that result in the greatest reduction in error by an amount known as the **learning rate**. The greater the learning rate, the faster the algorithm will attempt to descend down the gradients, which could reduce the training time at the risk of overshooting the valley.

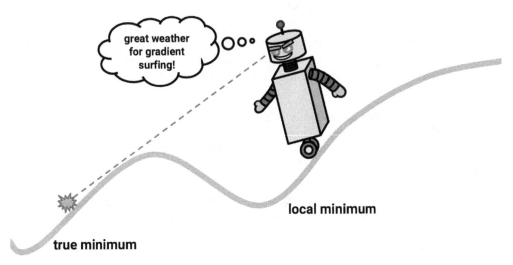

Although this process seems complex, it is easy to apply in practice. Let's apply our understanding of multilayer feedforward networks to a real-world problem.

Example – Modeling the strength of concrete with ANNs

In the field of engineering, it is crucial to have accurate estimates of the performance of building materials. These estimates are required in order to develop safety guidelines governing the materials used in the construction of buildings, bridges, and roadways.

Estimating the strength of concrete is a challenge of particular interest. Although it is used in nearly every construction project, concrete performance varies greatly due to a wide variety of ingredients that interact in complex ways. As a result, it is difficult to accurately predict the strength of the final product. A model that could reliably predict concrete strength given a listing of the composition of the input materials could result in safer construction practices.

Step 1 – collecting data

For this analysis, we will utilize data on the compressive strength of concrete donated to the UCI Machine Learning Data Repository (http://archive.ics.uci.edu/ml) by I-Cheng Yeh. As he found success using neural networks to model these data, we will attempt to replicate his work using a simple neural network model in R.

For more information on Yeh's approach to this learning task, refer to: Yeh IC. Modeling of strength of high performance concrete using artificial neural networks. *Cement and Concrete Research*. 1998; 28:1797-1808.

According to the website, the concrete dataset contains 1,030 examples of concrete with eight features describing the components used in the mixture. These features are thought to be related to the final compressive strength and they include the amount (in kilograms per cubic meter) of cement, slag, ash, water, superplasticizer, coarse aggregate, and fine aggregate used in the product in addition to the aging time (measured in days).

To follow along with this example, download the concrete.csv file from the Packt Publishing website and save it to your R working directory.

Step 2 – exploring and preparing the data

As usual, we'll begin our analysis by loading the data into an R object using the read.csv() function, and confirming that it matches the expected structure:

```
> concrete <- read.csv("concrete.csv")
> str(concrete)
'data.frame':   1030 obs. of  9 variables:
 $ cement    : num  141 169 250 266 155 ...
 $ slag      : num  212 42.2 0 114 183.4 ...
 $ ash       : num  0 124.3 95.7 0 0 ...
```

```
$ water       : num   204 158 187 228 193 ...
$ superplastic: num   0 10.8 5.5 0 9.1 0 0 6.4 0 9 ...
$ coarseagg   : num   972 1081 957 932 1047 ...
$ fineagg     : num   748 796 861 670 697 ...
$ age         : int   28 14 28 28 28 90 7 56 28 28 ...
$ strength    : num   29.9 23.5 29.2 45.9 18.3 ...
```

The nine variables in the data frame correspond to the eight features and one outcome we expected, although a problem has become apparent. Neural networks work best when the input data are scaled to a narrow range around zero, and here, we see values ranging anywhere from zero up to over a thousand.

Typically, the solution to this problem is to rescale the data with a normalizing or standardization function. If the data follow a bell-shaped curve (a normal distribution as described in *Chapter 2, Managing and Understanding Data*), then it may make sense to use standardization via R's built-in scale() function. On the other hand, if the data follow a uniform distribution or are severely nonnormal, then normalization to a 0-1 range may be more appropriate. In this case, we'll use the latter.

In *Chapter 3, Lazy Learning – Classification Using Nearest Neighbors*, we defined our own normalize() function as:

```
> normalize <- function(x) {
    return((x - min(x)) / (max(x) - min(x)))
  }
```

After executing this code, our normalize() function can be applied to every column in the concrete data frame using the lapply() function as follows:

```
> concrete_norm <- as.data.frame(lapply(concrete, normalize))
```

To confirm that the normalization worked, we can see that the minimum and maximum strength are now 0 and 1, respectively:

```
> summary(concrete_norm$strength)
   Min. 1st Qu.  Median    Mean 3rd Qu.    Max.
 0.0000  0.2664  0.4001  0.4172  0.5457  1.0000
```

In comparison, the original minimum and maximum values were 2.33 and 82.60:

```
> summary(concrete$strength)
   Min. 1st Qu.  Median    Mean 3rd Qu.    Max.
   2.33   23.71   34.44   35.82   46.14   82.60
```

Any transformation applied to the data prior to training the model will have to be applied in reverse later on, in order to convert back to the original units of measurement. To facilitate the rescaling, it is wise to save the original data or at least the summary statistics of the original data.

Following Yeh's precedent in the original publication, we will partition the data into a training set with 75 percent of the examples and a testing set with 25 percent. The CSV file we used was already sorted in random order, so we simply need to divide it into two portions:

```
> concrete_train <- concrete_norm[1:773, ]
> concrete_test <- concrete_norm[774:1030, ]
```

We'll use the training dataset to build the neural network and the testing dataset to evaluate how well the model generalizes to future results. As it is easy to overfit a neural network, this step is very important.

Step 3 – training a model on the data

To model the relationship between the ingredients used in concrete and the strength of the finished product, we will use a multilayer feedforward neural network. The neuralnet package by Stefan Fritsch and Frauke Guenther provides a standard and easy-to-use implementation of such networks. It also offers a function to plot the network topology. For these reasons, the neuralnet implementation is a strong choice for learning more about neural networks, though this is not to say that it cannot be used to accomplish real work as well—it's quite a powerful tool, as you will soon see.

There are several other commonly used packages to train ANN models in R, each with unique strengths and weaknesses. Because it ships as a part of the standard R installation, the nnet package is perhaps the most frequently cited ANN implementation. It uses a slightly more sophisticated algorithm than standard backpropagation. Another strong option is the RSNNS package, which offers a complete suite of neural network functionality with the downside being that it is more difficult to learn.

As `neuralnet` is not included in base R, you will need to install it by typing `install.packages("neuralnet")` and load it with the `library(neuralnet)` command. The included `neuralnet()` function can be used for training neural networks for numeric prediction using the following syntax:

Neural network syntax

using the `neuralnet()` function in the `neuralnet` package

Building the model:

```
m <- neuralnet(target ~ predictors, data = mydata,
               hidden = 1)
```

- `target` is the outcome in the `mydata` data frame to be modeled
- `predictors` is an R formula specifying the features in the `mydata` data frame to use for prediction
- `data` specifies the data frame in which the `target` and `predictors` variables can be found
- `hidden` specifies the number of neurons in the hidden layer (by default, 1)

The function will return a neural network object that can be used to make predictions.

Making predictions:

```
p <- compute(m, test)
```

- `m` is a model trained by the `neuralnet()` function
- `test` is a data frame containing test data with the same features as the training data used to build the classifier

The function will return a list with two components: `$neurons`, which stores the neurons for each layer in the network, and `$net.result`, which stores the model's predicted values.

Example:

```
concrete_model <- neuralnet(strength ~ cement + slag
  + ash, data = concrete)
model_results <- compute(concrete_model,
  concrete_data)
strength_predictions <- model_results$net.result
```

We'll begin by training the simplest multilayer feedforward network with only a single hidden node:

```
> concrete_model <- neuralnet(strength ~ cement + slag
+ ash + water + superplastic + coarseagg + fineagg + age,
  data = concrete_train)
```

We can then visualize the network topology using the `plot()` function on the resulting model object:

```
> plot(concrete_model)
```

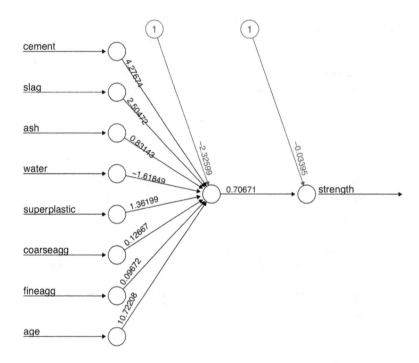

Error: 5.077438   Steps: 4882

In this simple model, there is one input node for each of the eight features, followed by a single hidden node and a single output node that predicts the concrete strength. The weights for each of the connections are also depicted, as are the **bias terms** (indicated by the nodes labeled with the number **1**). The bias terms are numeric constants that allow the value at the indicated nodes to be shifted upward or downward, much like the intercept in a linear equation.

> A neural network with a single hidden node can be thought of as a distant cousin of the linear regression models we studied in *Chapter 6, Forecasting Numeric Data – Regression Methods*. The weight between each input node and the hidden node is similar to the regression coefficients, and the weight for the bias term is similar to the intercept.

At the bottom of the figure, R reports the number of training steps and an error measure called the **Sum of Squared Errors (SSE)**, which as you might expect, is the sum of the squared predicted minus actual values. A lower SSE implies better predictive performance. This is helpful for estimating the model's performance on the training data, but tells us little about how it will perform on unseen data.

Step 4 – evaluating model performance

The network topology diagram gives us a peek into the black box of the ANN, but it doesn't provide much information about how well the model fits future data. To generate predictions on the test dataset, we can use the `compute()` as follows:

```
> model_results <- compute(concrete_model, concrete_test[1:8])
```

The `compute()` function works a bit differently from the `predict()` functions we've used so far. It returns a list with two components: `$neurons`, which stores the neurons for each layer in the network, and `$net.result`, which stores the predicted values. We'll want the latter:

```
> predicted_strength <- model_results$net.result
```

Because this is a numeric prediction problem rather than a classification problem, we cannot use a confusion matrix to examine model accuracy. Instead, we must measure the correlation between our predicted concrete strength and the true value. This provides insight into the strength of the linear association between the two variables.

Recall that the `cor()` function is used to obtain a correlation between two numeric vectors:

```
> cor(predicted_strength, concrete_test$strength)
            [,1]
[1,] 0.8064655576
```

 Don't be alarmed if your result differs. Because the neural network begins with random weights, the predictions can vary from model to model. If you'd like to match these results exactly, try using `set.seed(12345)` before building the neural network.

Correlations close to 1 indicate strong linear relationships between two variables. Therefore, the correlation here of about 0.806 indicates a fairly strong relationship. This implies that our model is doing a fairly good job, even with only a single hidden node.

Given that we only used one hidden node, it is likely that we can improve the performance of our model. Let's try to do a bit better.

Step 5 – improving model performance

As networks with more complex topologies are capable of learning more difficult concepts, let's see what happens when we increase the number of hidden nodes to five. We use the `neuralnet()` function as before, but add the `hidden = 5` parameter:

```
> concrete_model2 <- neuralnet(strength ~ cement + slag +
                               ash + water + superplastic +
                               coarseagg + fineagg + age,
                               data = concrete_train, hidden = 5)
```

Plotting the network again, we see a drastic increase in the number of connections. We can see how this impacted the performance as follows:

```
> plot(concrete_model2)
```

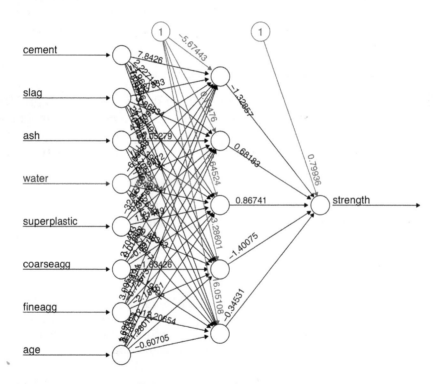

Error: 1.626684   Steps: 86849

Notice that the reported error (measured again by SSE) has been reduced from 5.08 in the previous model to 1.63 here. Additionally, the number of training steps rose from 4,882 to 86,849, which should come as no surprise given how much more complex the model has become. More complex networks take many more iterations to find the optimal weights.

Applying the same steps to compare the predicted values to the true values, we now obtain a correlation around 0.92, which is a considerable improvement over the previous result of 0.80 with a single hidden node:

```
> model_results2 <- compute(concrete_model2, concrete_test[1:8])
> predicted_strength2 <- model_results2$net.result
> cor(predicted_strength2, concrete_test$strength)
            [,1]
[1,]  0.9244533426
```

Interestingly, in the original publication, Yeh reported a mean correlation of 0.885 using a very similar neural network. This means that with relatively little effort, we were able to match the performance of a subject-matter expert. If you'd like more practice with neural networks, you might try applying the principles learned earlier in this chapter to see how it impacts model performance. Perhaps try using different numbers of hidden nodes, applying different activation functions, and so on. The ?neuralnet help page provides more information on the various parameters that can be adjusted.

Understanding Support Vector Machines

A **Support Vector Machine (SVM)** can be imagined as a surface that creates a boundary between points of data plotted in multidimensional that represent examples and their feature values. The goal of a SVM is to create a flat boundary called a **hyperplane**, which divides the space to create fairly homogeneous partitions on either side. In this way, the SVM learning combines aspects of both the instance-based nearest neighbor learning presented in *Chapter 3, Lazy Learning – Classification Using Nearest Neighbors*, and the linear regression modeling described in *Chapter 6, Forecasting Numeric Data – Regression Methods*. The combination is extremely powerful, allowing SVMs to model highly complex relationships.

Although the basic mathematics that drive SVMs have been around for decades, they have recently exploded in popularity. This is, of course, rooted in their state-of-the-art performance, but perhaps also due to the fact that award winning SVM algorithms have been implemented in several popular and well-supported libraries across many programming languages, including R. SVMs have thus been adopted by a much wider audience, might have otherwise been unable to apply the somewhat complex math needed to implement a SVM. The good news is that although the math may be difficult, the basic concepts are understandable.

SVMs can be adapted for use with nearly any type of learning task, including both classification and numeric prediction. Many of the algorithm's key successes have come in pattern recognition. Notable applications include:

- Classification of microarray gene expression data in the field of bioinformatics to identify cancer or other genetic diseases

- Text categorization such as identification of the language used in a document or the classification of documents by subject matter

- The detection of rare yet important events like combustion engine failure, security breaches, or earthquakes

SVMs are most easily understood when used for binary classification, which is how the method has been traditionally applied. Therefore, in the remaining sections, we will focus only on SVM classifiers. Don't worry, however, as the same principles you learn here will apply while adapting SVMs to other learning tasks such as numeric prediction.

Classification with hyperplanes

As noted previously, SVMs use a boundary called a hyperplane to partition data into groups of similar class values. For example, the following figure depicts hyperplanes that separate groups of circles and squares in two and three dimensions. Because the circles and squares can be separated perfectly by the straight line or flat surface, they are said to be **linearly separable**. At first, we'll consider only the simple case where this is true, but SVMs can also be extended to problems where the points are not linearly separable.

Two Dimensions

Three Dimensions

 For convenience, the hyperplane is traditionally depicted as a line in 2D space, but this is simply because it is difficult to illustrate space in greater than two dimensions. In reality, the hyperplane is a flat surface in a high-dimensional space – a concept that can be difficult to get your mind around.

In two dimensions, the task of the SVM algorithm is to identify a line that separates the two classes. As shown in the following figure, there is more than one choice of dividing line between the groups of circles and squares. Three such possibilities are labeled **a**, **b**, and **c**. How does the algorithm choose?

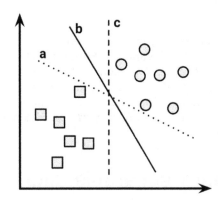

The answer to that question involves a search for the **Maximum Margin Hyperplane** (**MMH**) that creates the greatest separation between the two classes. Although any of the three lines separating the circles and squares would correctly classify all the data points, it is likely that the line that leads to the greatest separation will generalize the best to the future data. The maximum margin will improve the chance that, in spite of random noise, the points will remain on the correct side of the boundary.

The **support vectors** (indicated by arrows in the figure that follows) are the points from each class that are the closest to the MMH; each class must have at least one support vector, but it is possible to have more than one. Using the support vectors alone, it is possible to define the MMH. This is a key feature of SVMs; the support vectors provide a very compact way to store a classification model, even if the number of features is extremely large.

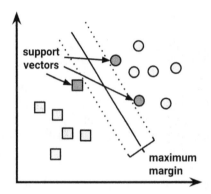

The algorithm to identify the support vectors relies on vector geometry and involves some fairly tricky math that is outside the scope of this book. However, the basic principles of the process are fairly straightforward.

> More information on the mathematics of SVMs can be found in the classic paper: Cortes C, Vapnik V. Support-vector network. *Machine Learning*. 1995; 20:273-297. A beginner level discussion can be found in: Bennett KP, Campbell C. Support vector machines: hype or hallelujah. SIGKDD Explorations. 2003; 2:1-13. A more in-depth look can be found in: Steinwart I, Christmann A. *Support Vector Machines*. New York: Springer; 2008.

The case of linearly separable data

It is easiest to understand how to find the maximum margin under the assumption that the classes are linearly separable. In this case, the MMH is as far away as possible from the outer boundaries of the two groups of data points. These outer boundaries are known as the **convex hull**. The MMH is then the perpendicular bisector of the shortest line between the two convex hulls. Sophisticated computer algorithms that use a technique known as **quadratic optimization** are capable of finding the maximum margin in this way.

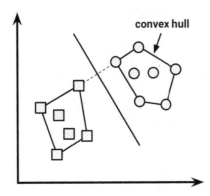

An alternative (but equivalent) approach involves a search through the space of every possible hyperplane in order to find a set of two parallel planes that divide the points into homogeneous groups yet themselves are as far apart as possible. To use a metaphor, one can imagine this process as similar to trying to find the thickest mattress that can fit up a stairwell to your bedroom.

To understand this search process, we'll need to define exactly what we mean by a hyperplane. In *n*-dimensional space, the following equation is used:

$$\vec{w} \cdot \vec{x} + b = 0$$

If you aren't familiar with this notation, the arrows above the letters indicate that they are vectors rather than single numbers. In particular, *w* is a vector of *n* weights, that is, $\{w_1, w_2 ..., w_n\}$, and *b* is a single number known as the **bias**. The bias is conceptually equivalent to the intercept term in the slope-intercept form discussed in *Chapter 6, Forecasting Numeric Data – Regression Methods*.

If you're having trouble imagining the plane, don't worry about the details. Simply think of the equation as a way to specify a surface, much like when the slope-intercept form ($y = mx + b$) is used to specify lines in 2D space.

Using this formula, the goal of the process is to find a set of weights that specify two hyperplanes, as follows:

$$\vec{w} \cdot \vec{x} + b \geq +1$$
$$\vec{w} \cdot \vec{x} + b \leq -1$$

We will also require that these hyperplanes are specified such that all the points of one class fall above the first hyperplane and all the points of the other class fall beneath the second hyperplane. This is possible so long as the data are linearly separable.

Vector geometry defines the distance between these two planes as:

$$\frac{2}{||\vec{w}||}$$

Here, $||w||$ indicates the **Euclidean norm** (the distance from the origin to vector w). Because $||w||$ is in the denominator, to maximize distance, we need to minimize $||w||$. The task is typically reexpressed as a set of constraints, as follows:

$$\min\frac{1}{2}\,||\vec{w}||^2$$
$$s.t.\ \ y_i(\vec{w}\cdot\vec{x}_i - b) \geq 1, \forall\vec{x}_i$$

Although this looks messy, it's really not too complicated to understand conceptually. Basically, the first line implies that we need to minimize the Euclidean norm (squared and divided by two to make the calculation easier). The second line notes that this is subject to (*s.t.*), the condition that each of the y_i data points is correctly classified. Note that y indicates the class value (transformed to either +1 or -1) and the upside down "A" is shorthand for "for all."

As with the other method for finding the maximum margin, finding a solution to this problem is a task best left for quadratic optimization software. Although it can be processor-intensive, specialized algorithms are capable of solving these problems quickly even on fairly large datasets.

The case of nonlinearly separable data

As we've worked through the theory behind SVMs, you may be wondering about the elephant in the room: what happens if the data are not linearly separable? The solution to this problem is the use of a **slack variable**, which creates a soft margin that allows some points to fall on the incorrect side of the margin. The figure that follows illustrates two points falling on the wrong side of the line with the corresponding slack terms (denoted with the Greek letter Xi):

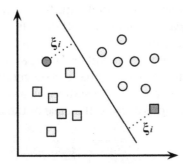

A cost value (denoted as *C*) is applied to all points that violate the constraints, and rather than finding the maximum margin, the algorithm attempts to minimize the total cost. We can therefore revise the optimization problem to:

$$\min \frac{1}{2} \|\vec{w}\|^2 + C \sum_{i=1}^{n} \xi_i$$

$$s.t. \ y_i(\vec{w} \cdot \vec{x}_i - b) \geq 1 - \xi_i, \forall \vec{x}_i, \xi_i \geq 0$$

If you're still confused, don't worry, you're not alone. Luckily, SVM packages will happily optimize this for you without you having to understand the technical details. The important piece to understand is the addition of the cost parameter *C*. Modifying this value will adjust the penalty, for example, the fall on the wrong side of the hyperplane. The greater the cost parameter, the harder the optimization will try to achieve 100 percent separation. On the other hand, a lower cost parameter will place the emphasis on a wider overall margin. It is important to strike a balance between these two in order to create a model that generalizes well to future data.

Using kernels for non-linear spaces

In many real-world applications, the relationships between variables are nonlinear. As we just discovered, a SVM can still be trained on such data through the addition of a slack variable, which allows some examples to be misclassified. However, this is not the only way to approach the problem of nonlinearity. A key feature of SVMs is their ability to map the problem into a higher dimension space using a process known as the **kernel trick**. In doing so, a nonlinear relationship may suddenly appear to be quite linear.

Though this seems like nonsense, it is actually quite easy to illustrate by example. In the following figure, the scatterplot on the left depicts a nonlinear relationship between a weather class (sunny or snowy) and two features: latitude and longitude. The points at the center of the plot are members of the snowy class, while the points at the margins are all sunny. Such data could have been generated from a set of weather reports, some of which were obtained from stations near the top of a mountain, while others were obtained from stations around the base of the mountain.

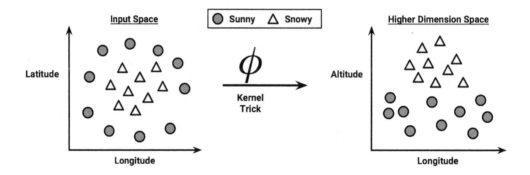

On the right side of the figure, after the kernel trick has been applied, we look at the data through the lens of a new dimension: altitude. With the addition of this feature, the classes are now perfectly linearly separable. This is possible because we have obtained a new perspective on the data. In the left figure, we are viewing the mountain from a bird's eye view, while in the right one, we are viewing the mountain from a distance at the ground level. Here, the trend is obvious: snowy weather is found at higher altitudes.

SVMs with nonlinear kernels add additional dimensions to the data in order to create separation in this way. Essentially, the kernel trick involves a process of constructing new features that express mathematical relationships between measured characteristics. For instance, the altitude feature can be expressed mathematically as an interaction between latitude and longitude—the closer the point is to the center of each of these scales, the greater the altitude. This allows SVM to learn concepts that were not explicitly measured in the original data.

SVMs with nonlinear kernels are extremely powerful classifiers, although they do have some downsides, as shown in the following table:

Strengths	Weaknesses
• Can be used for classification or numeric prediction problems • Not overly influenced by noisy data and not very prone to overfitting • May be easier to use than neural networks, particularly due to the existence of several well-supported SVM algorithms • Gaining popularity due to its high accuracy and high-profile wins in data mining competitions	• Finding the best model requires testing of various combinations of kernels and model parameters • Can be slow to train, particularly if the input dataset has a large number of features or examples • Results in a complex black box model that is difficult, if not impossible, to interpret

Kernel functions, in general, are of the following form. The function denoted by the Greek letter phi, that is, $\varphi(x)$, is a mapping of the data into another space. Therefore, the general kernel function applies some transformation to the feature vectors x_i and x_j and combines them using the **dot product**, which takes two vectors and returns a single number.

$$K(\vec{x_i}, \vec{x_j}) = \phi(\vec{x_i}) \cdot \phi(\vec{x_j})$$

Using this form, kernel functions have been developed for many different domains of data. A few of the most commonly used kernel functions are listed as follows. Nearly all SVM software packages will include these kernels, among many others.

The **linear kernel** does not transform the data at all. Therefore, it can be expressed simply as the dot product of the features:

$$K(\vec{x_i}, \vec{x_j}) = \vec{x_i} \cdot \vec{x_j}$$

The **polynomial kernel** of degree d adds a simple nonlinear transformation of the data:

$$K(\vec{x_i}, \vec{x_j}) = (\vec{x_i} \cdot \vec{x_j} + 1)^d$$

The **sigmoid kernel** results in a SVM model somewhat analogous to a neural network using a sigmoid activation function. The Greek letters kappa and delta are used as kernel parameters:

$$K(\vec{x_i}, \vec{x_j}) = \tanh(\kappa \; \vec{x_i} \cdot \vec{x_j} - \delta)$$

The **Gaussian RBF kernel** is similar to a RBF neural network. The RBF kernel performs well on many types of data and is thought to be a reasonable starting point for many learning tasks:

$$K(\vec{x_i}, \vec{x_j}) = e^{\frac{-||\vec{x_i} - \vec{x_j}||^2}{2\sigma^2}}$$

There is no reliable rule to match a kernel to a particular learning task. The fit depends heavily on the concept to be learned as well as the amount of training data and the relationships among the features. Often, a bit of trial and error is required by training and evaluating several SVMs on a validation dataset. This said, in many cases, the choice of kernel is arbitrary, as the performance may vary slightly. To see how this works in practice, let's apply our understanding of SVM classification to a real-world problem.

Example – performing OCR with SVMs

Image processing is a difficult task for many types of machine learning algorithms. The relationships linking patterns of pixels to higher concepts are extremely complex and hard to define. For instance, it's easy for a human being to recognize a face, a cat, or the letter "A", but defining these patterns in strict rules is difficult. Furthermore, image data is often noisy. There can be many slight variations in how the image was captured, depending on the lighting, orientation, and positioning of the subject.

SVMs are well-suited to tackle the challenges of image data. Capable of learning complex patterns without being overly sensitive to noise, they are able to recognize visual patterns with a high degree of accuracy. Moreover, the key weakness of SVMs—the black box model representation—is less critical for image processing. If an SVM can differentiate a cat from a dog, it does not matter much how it is doing so.

In this section, we will develop a model similar to those used at the core of the **Optical Character Recognition (OCR)** software often bundled with desktop document scanners. The purpose of such software is to process paper-based documents by converting printed or handwritten text into an electronic form to be saved in a database. Of course, this is a difficult problem due to the many variants in handwritten style and printed fonts. Even so, software users expect perfection, as errors or typos can result in embarrassing or costly mistakes in a business environment. Let's see whether our SVM is up to the task.

Step 1 – collecting data

When OCR software first processes a document, it divides the paper into a matrix such that each cell in the grid contains a single **glyph**, which is just a term referring to a letter, symbol, or number. Next, for each cell, the software will attempt to match the glyph to a set of all characters it recognizes. Finally, the individual characters would be combined back together into words, which optionally could be spell-checked against a dictionary in the document's language.

In this exercise, we'll assume that we have already developed the algorithm to partition the document into rectangular regions each consisting of a single character. We will also assume the document contains only alphabetic characters in English. Therefore, we'll simulate a process that involves matching glyphs to one of the 26 letters, A through Z.

To this end, we'll use a dataset donated to the UCI Machine Learning Data Repository (http://archive.ics.uci.edu/ml) by W. Frey and D. J. Slate. The dataset contains 20,000 examples of 26 English alphabet capital letters as printed using 20 different randomly reshaped and distorted black and white fonts.

 For more information on this dataset, refer to Slate DJ, Frey W. Letter recognition using Holland-style adaptive classifiers. *Machine Learning*. 1991; 6:161-182.

The following figure, published by Frey and Slate, provides an example of some of the printed glyphs. Distorted in this way, the letters are challenging for a computer to identify, yet are easily recognized by a human being:

Step 2 – exploring and preparing the data

According to the documentation provided by Frey and Slate, when the glyphs are scanned into the computer, they are converted into pixels and 16 statistical attributes are recorded.

The attributes measure such characteristics as the horizontal and vertical dimensions of the glyph, the proportion of black (versus white) pixels, and the average horizontal and vertical position of the pixels. Presumably, differences in the concentration of black pixels across various areas of the box should provide a way to differentiate among the 26 letters of the alphabet.

 To follow along with this example, download the `letterdata.csv` file from the Packt Publishing website, and save it to your R working directory.

Reading the data into R, we confirm that we have received the data with the 16 features that define each example of the letter class. As expected, letter has 26 levels:

```
> letters <- read.csv("letterdata.csv")
> str(letters)
'data.frame':   20000 obs. of 17 variables:
 $ letter: Factor w/ 26 levels "A","B","C","D",..
 $ xbox  : int  2 5 4 7 2 4 4 1 2 11 ...
 $ ybox  : int  8 12 11 11 1 11 2 1 2 15 ...
 $ width : int  3 3 6 6 3 5 5 3 4 13 ...
 $ height: int  5 7 8 6 1 8 4 2 4 9 ...
```

```
$ onpix : int   1 2 6 3 1 3 4 1 2 7 ...
$ xbar  : int   8 10 10 5 8 8 8 8 10 13 ...
$ ybar  : int   13 5 6 9 6 8 7 2 6 2 ...
$ x2bar : int   0 5 2 4 6 6 6 2 2 6 ...
$ y2bar : int   6 4 6 6 6 9 6 2 6 2 ...
$ xybar : int   6 13 10 4 6 5 7 8 12 12 ...
$ x2ybar: int   10 3 3 4 5 6 6 2 4 1 ...
$ xy2bar: int   8 9 7 10 9 6 6 8 8 9 ...
$ xedge : int   0 2 3 6 1 0 2 1 1 8 ...
$ xedgey: int   8 8 7 10 7 8 8 6 6 1 ...
$ yedge : int   0 4 3 2 5 9 7 2 1 1 ...
$ yedgex: int   8 10 9 8 10 7 10 7 7 8 ...
```

Recall that SVM learners require all features to be numeric, and moreover, that each feature is scaled to a fairly small interval. In this case, every feature is an integer, so we do not need to convert any factors into numbers. On the other hand, some of the ranges for these integer variables appear fairly wide. This indicates that we need to normalize or standardize the data. However, we can skip this step for now, because the R package that we will use for fitting the SVM model will perform the rescaling automatically.

Given that the data preparation has been largely done for us, we can move directly to the training and testing phases of the machine learning process. In the previous analyses, we randomly divided the data between the training and testing sets. Although we could do so here, Frey and Slate have already randomized the data, and therefore suggest using the first 16,000 records (80 percent) to build the model and the next 4,000 records (20 percent) to test. Following their advice, we can create training and testing data frames as follows:

```
> letters_train <- letters[1:16000, ]
> letters_test  <- letters[16001:20000, ]
```

With our data ready to go, let's start building our classifier.

Step 3 – training a model on the data

When it comes to fitting an SVM model in R, there are several outstanding packages to choose from. The e1071 package from the Department of Statistics at the Vienna University of Technology (TU Wien) provides an R interface to the award winning LIBSVM library, a widely used open source SVM program written in C++. If you are already familiar with LIBSVM, you may want to start here.

 For more information on LIBSVM, refer to the authors' website at http://www.csie.ntu.edu.tw/~cjlin/libsvm/.

Similarly, if you're already invested in the SVMlight algorithm, the klaR package from the Department of Statistics at the Dortmund University of Technology (TU Dortmund) provides functions to work with this SVM implementation directly within R.

 For information on SVMlight, have a look at http://svmlight.joachims.org/.

Finally, if you are starting from scratch, it is perhaps best to begin with the SVM functions in the kernlab package. An interesting advantage of this package is that it was developed natively in R rather than C or C++, which allows it to be easily customized; none of the internals are hidden behind the scenes. Perhaps even more importantly, unlike the other options, kernlab can be used with the caret package, which allows SVM models to be trained and evaluated using a variety of automated methods (covered in *Chapter 11, Improving Model Performance*).

 For a more thorough introduction to kernlab, please refer to the authors' paper at http://www.jstatsoft.org/v11/i09/.

The syntax for training SVM classifiers with `kernlab` is as follows. If you do happen to be using one of the other packages, the commands are largely similar. By default, the `ksvm()` function uses the Gaussian RBF kernel, but a number of other options are provided.

Support vector machine syntax

using the `ksvm()` function in the `kernlab` package

Building the model:

```
m <- ksvm(target ~ predictors, data = mydata,
          kernel = "rbfdot", C = 1)
```

- `target` is the outcome in the `mydata` data frame to be modeled
- `predictors` is an R formula specifying the features in the `mydata` data frame to use for prediction
- `data` specifies the data frame in which the `target` and `predictors` variables can be found
- `kernel` specifies a nonlinear mapping such as `"rbfdot"` (radial basis), `"polydot"` (polynomial), `"tanhdot"` (hyperbolic tangent sigmoid), or `"vanilladot"` (linear)
- `C` is a number that specifies the cost of violating the constraints, i.e., how big of a penalty there is for the "soft margin." Larger values will result in narrower margins

The function will return a SVM object that can be used to make predictions.

Making predictions:

```
p <- predict(m, test, type = "response")
```

- `m` is a model trained by the `ksvm()` function
- `test` is a data frame containing test data with the same features as the training data used to build the classifier
- `type` specifies whether the predictions should be `"response"` (the predicted class) or `"probabilities"` (the predicted probability, one column per class level).

The function will return a vector (or matrix) of predicted classes (or probabilities) depending on the value of the type parameter.

Example:

```
letter_classifier <- ksvm(letter ~ ., data =
    letters_train, kernel = "vanilladot")
letter_prediction <- predict(letter_classifier,
    letters_test)
```

To provide a baseline measure of SVM performance, let's begin by training a simple linear SVM classifier. If you haven't already, install the `kernlab` package to your library, using the `install.packages("kernlab")` command. Then, we can call the `ksvm()` function on the training data and specify the linear (that is, vanilla) kernel using the `vanilladot` option, as follows:

```
> library(kernlab)

> letter_classifier <- ksvm(letter ~ ., data = letters_train,
                            kernel = "vanilladot")
```

Depending on the performance of your computer, this operation may take some time to complete. When it finishes, type the name of the stored model to see some basic information about the training parameters and the fit of the model.

```
> letter_classifier
Support Vector Machine object of class "ksvm"

SV type: C-svc  (classification)
 parameter : cost C = 1

Linear (vanilla) kernel function.

Number of Support Vectors : 7037

Objective Function Value : -14.1746 -20.0072 -23.5628 -6.2009 -7.5524
-32.7694 -49.9786 -18.1824 -62.1111 -32.7284 -16.2209...

Training error : 0.130062
```

This information tells us very little about how well the model will perform in the real world. We'll need to examine its performance on the testing dataset to know whether it generalizes well to unseen data.

Step 4 – evaluating model performance

The predict() function allows us to use the letter classification model to make predictions on the testing dataset:

```
> letter_predictions <- predict(letter_classifier, letters_test)
```

Because we didn't specify the type parameter, the type = "response" default was used. This returns a vector containing a predicted letter for each row of values in the test data. Using the head() function, we can see that the first six predicted letters were U, N, V, X, N, and H:

```
> head(letter_predictions)
[1] U N V X N H
Levels: A B C D E F G H I J K L M N O P Q R S T U V W X Y Z
```

To examine how well our classifier performed, we need to compare the predicted letter to the true letter in the testing dataset. We'll use the `table()` function for this purpose (only a portion of the full table is shown here):

```
> table(letter_predictions, letters_test$letter)
letter_predictions    A    B    C    D    E
                 A  144    0    0    0    0
                 B    0  121    0    5    2
                 C    0    0  120    0    4
                 D    2    2    0  156    0
                 E    0    0    5    0  127
```

The diagonal values of `144`, `121`, `120`, `156`, and `127` indicate the total number of records where the predicted letter matches the true value. Similarly, the number of mistakes is also listed. For example, the value of `5` in row B and column D indicates that there were five cases where the letter D was misidentified as a B.

Looking at each type of mistake individually may reveal some interesting patterns about the specific types of letters the model has trouble with, but this is time consuming. We can simplify our evaluation instead by calculating the overall accuracy. This considers only whether the prediction was correct or incorrect, and ignores the type of error.

The following command returns a vector of TRUE or FALSE values, indicating whether the model's predicted letter agrees with (that is, matches) the actual letter in the test dataset:

```
> agreement <- letter_predictions == letters_test$letter
```

Using the `table()` function, we see that the classifier correctly identified the letter in 3,357 out of the 4,000 test records:

```
> table(agreement)
agreement
FALSE   TRUE
 643   3357
```

In percentage terms, the accuracy is about 84 percent:

```
> prop.table(table(agreement))
agreement
  FALSE     TRUE
0.16075  0.83925
```

Note that when Frey and Slate published the dataset in 1991, they reported a recognition accuracy of about 80 percent. Using just a few lines of R code, we were able to surpass their result, although we also have the benefit of over two decades of additional machine learning research. With this in mind, it is likely that we are able to do even better.

Step 5 – improving model performance

Our previous SVM model used the simple linear kernel function. By using a more complex kernel function, we can map the data into a higher dimensional space, and potentially obtain a better model fit.

It can be challenging, however, to choose from the many different kernel functions. A popular convention is to begin with the Gaussian RBF kernel, which has been shown to perform well for many types of data. We can train an RBF-based SVM, using the `ksvm()` function as shown here:

```
> letter_classifier_rbf <- ksvm(letter ~ ., data = letters_train,
                            kernel = "rbfdot")
```

Next, we make predictions as done earlier:

```
> letter_predictions_rbf <- predict(letter_classifier_rbf,
                            letters_test)
```

Finally, we'll compare the accuracy to our linear SVM:

```
> agreement_rbf <- letter_predictions_rbf == letters_test$letter
> table(agreement_rbf)
agreement_rbf
FALSE   TRUE
 275   3725
> prop.table(table(agreement_rbf))
agreement_rbf
  FALSE     TRUE
0.06875 0.93125
```

 Your results may differ from those shown here due to randomness in the `ksvm` RBF kernel. If you'd like them to match exactly, use `set.seed(12345)` prior to running the ksvm() function.

By simply changing the kernel function, we were able to increase the accuracy of our character recognition model from 84 percent to 93 percent. If this level of performance is still unsatisfactory for the OCR program, other kernels could be tested, or the cost of constraints parameter C could be varied to modify the width of the decision boundary. As an exercise, you should experiment with these parameters to see how they impact the success of the final model.

Summary

In this chapter, we examined two machine learning methods that offer a great deal of potential, but are often overlooked due to their complexity. Hopefully, you now see that this reputation is at least somewhat undeserved. The basic concepts that drive ANNs and SVMs are fairly easy to understand.

On the other hand, because ANNs and SVMs have been around for many decades, each of them has numerous variations. This chapter just scratches the surface of what is possible with these methods. By utilizing the terminology you learned here, you should be capable of picking up the nuances that distinguish the many advancements that are being developed every day.

Now that we have spent some time learning about many different types of predictive models from simple to sophisticated; in the next chapter, we will begin to consider methods for other types of learning tasks. These unsupervised learning techniques will bring to light fascinating patterns within the data.

8

Finding Patterns – Market Basket Analysis Using Association Rules

Think back to the last time you made an impulse purchase. Maybe you were waiting in the grocery store checkout lane and bought a pack of chewing gum or a candy bar. Perhaps on a late-night trip for diapers and formula you picked up a caffeinated beverage or a six-pack of beer. You might have even bought this book on a whim on a bookseller's recommendation. These impulse buys are no coincidence, as retailers use sophisticated data analysis techniques to identify patterns that will drive retail behavior.

In years past, such recommendation systems were based on the subjective intuition of marketing professionals and inventory managers or buyers. More recently, as barcode scanners, computerized inventory systems, and online shopping trends have built a wealth of transactional data, machine learning has been increasingly applied to learn purchasing patterns. The practice is commonly known as **market basket analysis** due to the fact that it has been so frequently applied to supermarket data.

Although the technique originated with shopping data, it is useful in other contexts as well. By the time you finish this chapter, you will be able to apply market basket analysis techniques to your own tasks, whatever they may be. Generally, the work involves:

- Using simple performance measures to find associations in large databases
- Understanding the peculiarities of transactional data
- Knowing how to identify the useful and actionable patterns

The results of a market basket analysis are actionable patterns. Thus, as we apply the technique, you are likely to identify applications to your work, even if you have no affiliation with a retail chain.

Understanding association rules

The building blocks of a market basket analysis are the items that may appear in any given transaction. Groups of one or more items are surrounded by brackets to indicate that they form a set, or more specifically, an **itemset** that appears in the data with some regularity. Transactions are specified in terms of itemsets, such as the following transaction that might be found in a typical grocery store:

$$\{\text{bread, peanut butter, jelly}\}$$

The result of a market basket analysis is a collection of **association rules** that specify patterns found in the relationships among items he itemsets. Association rules are always composed from subsets of itemsets and are denoted by relating one itemset on the left-hand side (LHS) of the rule to another itemset on the right-hand side (RHS) of the rule. The LHS is the condition that needs to be met in order to trigger the rule, and the RHS is the expected result of meeting that condition. A rule identified from the example transaction might be expressed in the form:

$$\{\text{peanut butter, jelly}\} \rightarrow \{\text{bread}\}$$

In plain language, this association rule states that if peanut butter and jelly are purchased together, then bread is also likely to be purchased. In other words, "peanut butter and jelly imply bread."

Developed in the context of retail transaction databases, association rules are not used for prediction, but rather for unsupervised knowledge discovery in large databases. This is unlike the classification and numeric prediction algorithms presented in previous chapters. Even so, you will find that association rule learners are closely related to and share many features of the classification rule learners presented in *Chapter 5, Divide and Conquer – Classification Using Decision Trees and Rules.*

Because association rule learners are unsupervised, there is no need for the algorithm to be trained; data does not need to be labeled ahead of time. The program is simply unleashed on a dataset in the hope that interesting associations are found. The downside, of course, is that there isn't an easy way to objectively measure the performance of a rule learner, aside from evaluating them for qualitative usefulness—typically, an eyeball test of some sort.

Although association rules are most often used for market basket analysis, they are helpful for finding patterns in many different types of data. Other potential applications include:

- Searching for interesting and frequently occurring patterns of DNA and protein sequences in cancer data

- Finding patterns of purchases or medical claims that occur in combination with fraudulent credit card or insurance use

- Identifying combinations of behavior that precede customers dropping their cellular phone service or upgrading their cable television package

Association rule analysis is used to search for interesting connections among a very large number of elements. Human beings are capable of such insight quite intuitively, but it often takes expert-level knowledge or a great deal of experience to do what a rule learning algorithm can do in minutes or even seconds. Additionally, some datasets are simply too large and complex for a human being to find the needle in the haystack.

The Apriori algorithm for association rule learning

Just as it is challenging for humans, transactional data makes association rule mining a challenging task for machines as well. Transactional datasets are typically extremely large, both in terms of the number of transactions as well as the number of items or features that are monitored. The problem is that the number of potential itemsets grows exponentially with the number of features. Given k items that can appear or not appear in a set, there are 2^k possible itemsets that could be potential rules. A retailer that sells only 100 different items could have on the order of $2^{100} = 1.27e+30$ itemsets that an algorithm must evaluate—a seemingly impossible task.

Rather than evaluating each of these itemsets one by one, a smarter rule learning algorithm takes advantage of the fact that, in reality, many of the potential combinations of items are rarely, if ever, found in practice. For instance, even if a store sells both automotive items and women's cosmetics, a set of *{motor oil, lipstick}* is likely to be extraordinarily uncommon. By ignoring these rare (and, perhaps, less important) combinations, it is possible to limit the scope of the search for rules to a more manageable size.

Much work has been done to identify heuristic algorithms for reducing the number of itemsets to search. Perhaps the most-widely used approach for efficiently searching large databases for rules is known as **Apriori**. Introduced in 1994 by Rakesh Agrawal and Ramakrishnan Srikant, the Apriori algorithm has since become somewhat synonymous with association rule learning. The name is derived from the fact that the algorithm utilizes a simple prior (that is, *a priori*) belief about the properties of frequent itemsets.

Before we discuss that in more depth, it's worth noting that this algorithm, like all learning algorithms, is not without its strengths and weaknesses. Some of these are listed as follows:

Strengths	Weaknesses
• Is capable of working with large amounts of transactional data • Results in rules that are easy to understand • Useful for "data mining" and discovering unexpected knowledge in databases	• Not very helpful for small datasets • Requires effort to separate the true insight from common sense • Easy to draw spurious conclusions from random patterns

As noted earlier, the Apriori algorithm employs a simple *a priori* belief to reduce the association rule search space: all subsets of a frequent itemset must also be frequent. This heuristic is known as the **Apriori property**. Using this astute observation, it is possible to dramatically limit the number of rules to be searched. For example, the set *{motor oil, lipstick}* can only be frequent if both *{motor oil}* and *{lipstick}* occur frequently as well. Consequently, if either motor oil or lipstick is infrequent, any set containing these items can be excluded from the search.

 For additional details on the Apriori algorithm, refer to: Agrawal R, Srikant R. Fast algorithms for mining association rules. *Proceedings of the 20th International Conference on Very Large Databases.* 1994:487-499.

To see how this principle can be applied in a more realistic setting, let's consider a simple transaction database. The following table shows five completed transactions in an imaginary hospital's gift shop:

Transaction number	Purchased items
1	{flowers, get well card, soda}
2	{plush toy bear, flowers, balloons, candy bar}
3	{get well card, candy bar, flowers}
4	{plush toy bear, balloons, soda}
5	{flowers, get well card, soda}

By looking at the sets of purchases, one can infer that there are a couple of typical buying patterns. A person visiting a sick friend or family member tends to buy a get well card and flowers, while visitors to new mothers tend to buy plush toy bears and balloons. Such patterns are notable because they appear frequently enough to catch our interest; we simply apply a bit of logic and subject matter experience to explain the rule.

In a similar fashion, the Apriori algorithm uses statistical measures of an itemset's "interestingness" to locate association rules in much larger transaction databases. In the sections that follow, we will discover how Apriori computes such measures of interest and how they are combined with the Apriori property to reduce the number of rules to be learned.

Measuring rule interest – support and confidence

Whether or not an association rule is deemed interesting is determined by two statistical measures: support and confidence measures. By providing minimum thresholds for each of these metrics and applying the Apriori principle, it is easy to drastically limit the number of rules reported, perhaps even to the point where only the obvious or common sense rules are identified. For this reason, it is important to carefully understand the types of rules that are excluded under these criteria.

The **support** of an itemset or rule measures how frequently it occurs in the data. For instance the itemset *{get well card, flowers}*, has support of $3/5 = 0.6$ in the hospital gift shop data. Similarly, the support for *{get well card}* → *{flowers}* is also 0.6. The support can be calculated for any itemset or even a single item; for instance, the support for *{candy bar}* is $2/5 = 0.4$, since candy bars appear in 40 percent of purchases. A function defining support for the itemset X can be defined as follows:

$$\text{support}(X) = \frac{\text{count}(X)}{N}$$

Here, N is the number of transactions in the database and *count(X)* is the number of transactions containing itemset X.

A rule's **confidence** is a measurement of its predictive power or accuracy. It is defined as the support of the itemset containing both X and Y divided by the support of the itemset containing only X:

$$\text{confidence}(X \to Y) = \frac{\text{support}(X, Y)}{\text{support}(X)}$$

Essentially, the confidence tells us the proportion of transactions where the presence of item or itemset X results in the presence of item or itemset Y. Keep in mind that the confidence that X leads to Y is not the same as the confidence that Y leads to X. For example, the confidence of *{flowers}* → *{get well card}* is $0.6/0.8 = 0.75$. In comparison, the confidence of *{get well card}* → *{flowers}* is $0.6/0.6 = 1.0$. This means that a purchase involving flowers is accompanied by a purchase of a get well card 75 percent of the time, while a purchase of a get well card is associated with flowers 100 percent of the time. This information could be quite useful to the gift shop management.

> You may have noticed similarities between support, confidence, and the Bayesian probability rules covered in *Chapter 4, Probabilistic Learning – Classification Using Naive Bayes*. In fact, *support(A, B)* is the same as $P(A \cap B)$ and *confidence(A → B)* is the same as $P(B | A)$. It is just the context that differs.

Rules like *{get well card}* → *{flowers}* are known as **strong rules**, because they have both high support and confidence. One way to find more strong rules would be to examine every possible combination of the items in the gift shop, measure the support and confidence value, and report back only those rules that meet certain levels of interest. However, as noted before, this strategy is generally not feasible for anything but the smallest of datasets.

In the next section, you will see how the Apriori algorithm uses the minimum levels of support and confidence with the Apriori principle to find strong rules quickly by reducing the number of rules to a more manageable level.

Building a set of rules with the Apriori principle

Recall that the Apriori principle states that all subsets of a frequent itemset must also be frequent. In other words, if {A, B} is frequent, then {A} and {B} must both be frequent. Recall also that by definition, the support indicates how frequently an itemset appears in the data. Therefore, if we know that {A} does not meet a desired support threshold, there is no reason to consider {A, B} or any itemset containing {A}; it cannot possibly be frequent.

The Apriori algorithm uses this logic to exclude potential association rules prior to actually evaluating them. The actual process of creating rules occurs in two phases:

1. Identifying all the itemsets that meet a minimum support threshold.
2. Creating rules from these itemsets using those meeting a minimum confidence threshold.

The first phase occurs in multiple iterations. Each successive iteration involves evaluating the support of a set of increasingly large itemsets. For instance, iteration 1 involves evaluating the set of 1-item itemsets (1-itemsets), iteration 2 evaluates 2-itemsets, and so on. The result of each iteration i is a set of all the i-itemsets that meet the minimum support threshold.

All the itemsets from iteration i are combined in order to generate candidate itemsets for the evaluation in iteration $i + 1$. But the Apriori principle can eliminate some of them even before the next round begins. If {A}, {B}, and {C} are frequent in iteration 1 while {D} is not frequent, iteration 2 will consider only {A, B}, {A, C}, and {B, C}. Thus, the algorithm needs to evaluate only three itemsets rather than the six that would have been evaluated if the sets containing D had not been eliminated *a priori*.

Continuing with this thought, suppose during iteration 2, it is discovered that {A, B} and {B, C} are frequent, but {A, C} is not. Although iteration 3 would normally begin by evaluating the support for {A, B, C}, it is not mandatory that this step should occur at all. Why not? The Apriori principle states that {A, B, C} cannot possibly be frequent, since the subset {A, C} is not. Therefore, having generated no new itemsets in iteration 3, the algorithm may stop.

At this point, the second phase of the Apriori algorithm may begin. Given the set of frequent itemsets, association rules are generated from all possible subsets. For instance, {A, B} would result in candidate rules for {A} → {B} and {B} → {A}. These are evaluated against a minimum confidence threshold, and any rule that does not meet the desired confidence level is eliminated.

Example – identifying frequently purchased groceries with association rules

As noted in this chapter's introduction, market basket analysis is used behind the scenes for the recommendation systems used in many brick-and-mortar and online retailers. The learned association rules indicate the combinations of items that are often purchased together. Knowledge of these patterns provides insight into new ways a grocery chain might optimize the inventory, advertise promotions, or organize the physical layout of the store. For instance, if shoppers frequently purchase coffee or orange juice with a breakfast pastry, it may be possible to increase profit by relocating pastries closer to coffee and juice.

In this tutorial, we will perform a market basket analysis of transactional data from a grocery store. However, the techniques could be applied to many different types of problems, from movie recommendations, to dating sites, to finding dangerous interactions among medications. In doing so, we will see how the Apriori algorithm is able to efficiently evaluate a potentially massive set of association rules.

Step 1 – collecting data

Our market basket analysis will utilize the purchase data collected from one month of operation at a real-world grocery store. The data contains 9,835 transactions or about 327 transactions per day (roughly 30 transactions per hour in a 12-hour business day), suggesting that the retailer is not particularly large, nor is it particularly small.

 The dataset used here was adapted from the Groceries dataset in the arules R package. For more information, see: Hahsler M, Hornik K, Reutterer T. Implications of probabilistic data modeling for mining association rules. In: Gaul W, Vichi M, Weihs C, ed. *Studies in Classification, Data Analysis, and Knowledge Organization: from Data and Information Analysis to Knowledge Engineering*. New York: Springer; 2006:598–605.

The typical grocery store offers a huge variety of items. There might be five brands of milk, a dozen different types of laundry detergent, and three brands of coffee. Given the moderate size of the retailer, we will assume that they are not terribly concerned with finding rules that apply only to a specific brand of milk or detergent. With this in mind, all brand names can be removed from the purchases. This reduces the number of groceries to a more manageable 169 types, using broad categories such as chicken, frozen meals, margarine, and soda.

> If you hope to identify highly specific association rules — such as whether customers prefer grape or strawberry jelly with their peanut butter — you will need a tremendous amount of transactional data. Large chain retailers use databases of many millions of transactions in order to find associations among particular brands, colors, or flavors of items.

Do you have any guesses about which types of items might be purchased together? Will wine and cheese be a common pairing? Bread and butter? Tea and honey? Let's dig into this data and see whether we can confirm our guesses.

Step 2 – exploring and preparing the data

Transactional data is stored in a slightly different format than that we used previously. Most of our prior analyses utilized data in the matrix form where rows indicated example instances and columns indicated features. Given the structure of the matrix format, all examples are required to have exactly the same set of features.

In comparison, transactional data is a more free form. As usual, each row in the data specifies a single example — in this case, a transaction. However, rather than having a set number of features, each record comprises a comma-separated list of any number of items, from one to many. In essence, the features may differ from example to example.

> To follow along with this analysis, download the `groceries.csv` file from the Packt Publishing website and save it in your R working directory.

The first five rows of the raw `grocery.csv` file are as follows:

```
citrus fruit,semi-finished bread,margarine,ready soups
tropical fruit,yogurt,coffee
whole milk
pip fruit,yogurt,cream cheese,meat spreads
other vegetables,whole milk,condensed milk,long life bakery
product
```

These lines indicate five separate grocery store transactions. The first transaction included four items: citrus fruit, semi-finished bread, margarine, and ready soups. In comparison, the third transaction included only one item: whole milk.

Suppose we try to load the data using the `read.csv()` function as we did in the prior analyses. R would happily comply and read the data into a matrix form as follows:

	V1	V2	V3	V4
1	citrus fruit	semi-finished bread	margarine	ready soups
2	tropical fruit	yogurt	coffee	
3	whole milk			
4	pip fruit	yogurt	cream cheese	meat spreads
5	other vegetables	whole milk	condensed milk	long life bakery product

You will notice that R created four columns to store the items in the transactional data: V1, V2, V3, and V4. Although this may seem reasonable this, if we use the data in this form, we will encounter problems later may seem reasonable, R chose to create four variables because the first line had exactly four comma-separated values. However, we know that grocery purchases can contain more than four items; in the four column design such transactions will be broken across multiple rows in the matrix. We could try to remedy this by putting the transaction with the largest number of items at the top of the file, but this ignores another more problematic issue.

By structuring data this way, R has constructed a set of features that record not just the items in the transactions, but also the order in which they appear. If we imagine our learning algorithm as an attempt to find a relationship among V1, V2, V3, and V4, then whole milk in V1 might be treated differently than the whole milk appearing in V2. Instead, we need a dataset that does not treat a transaction as a set of positions to be filled (or not filled) with specific items, but rather as a market basket that either contains or does not contain each particular item.

Data preparation – creating a sparse matrix for transaction data

The solution to this problem utilizes a data structure called a **sparse matrix**. You may recall that we used a sparse matrix to process text data in *Chapter 4, Probabilistic Learning – Classification Using Naive Bayes*. Just as with the preceding dataset, each row in the sparse matrix indicates a transaction. However, the sparse matrix has a column (that is, feature) for every item that could possibly appear in someone's shopping bag. Since there are 169 different items in our grocery store data, our sparse matrix will contain 169 columns.

Why not just store this as a data frame as we did in most of our analyses? The reason is that as additional transactions and items are added, a conventional data structure quickly becomes too large to fit in the available memory. Even with the relatively small transactional dataset used here, the matrix contains nearly 1.7 million cells, most of which contain zeros (hence, the name "sparse" matrix—there are very few nonzero values). Since there is no benefit to storing all these zero values, a sparse matrix does not actually store the full matrix in memory; it only stores the cells that are occupied by an item. This allows the structure to be more memory efficient than an equivalently sized matrix or data frame.

In order to create the sparse matrix data structure from the transactional data, we can use the functionality provided by the arules package. Install and load the package using the install.packages("arules") and library(arules) commands.

> For more information on the arules package, refer to: Hahsler M, Gruen B, Hornik K. arules – a computational environment for mining association rules and frequent item sets. *Journal of Statistical Software*. 2005; 14.

Since we're loading the transactional data, we cannot simply use the read.csv() function used previously. Instead, arules provides a read.transactions() function that is similar to read.csv() with the exception that it results in a sparse matrix suitable for transactional data. The sep = "," parameter specifies that items in the input file are separated by a comma. To read the groceries.csv data into a sparse matrix named groceries, type the following line:

```
> groceries <- read.transactions("groceries.csv", sep = ",")
```

To see some basic information about the groceries matrix we just created, use the summary() function on the object:

```
> summary(groceries)
transactions as itemMatrix in sparse format with
 9835 rows (elements/itemsets/transactions) and
 169 columns (items) and a density of 0.02609146
```

The first block of information in the output (as shown previously) provides a summary of the sparse matrix we created. The output 9835 rows refers to the number of transactions, and the output 169 columns refers to the 169 different items that might appear in someone's grocery basket. Each cell in the matrix is 1 if the item was purchased for the corresponding transaction, or 0 otherwise.

The **density** value of 0.02609146 (2.6 percent) refers to the proportion of nonzero matrix cells. Since there are *9,835 * 169 = 1,662,115* positions in the matrix, we can calculate that a total of *1,662,115 * 0.02609146 = 43,367* items were purchased during the store's 30 days of operation (ignoring the fact that duplicates of the same items might have been purchased). With an additional step, we can determine that the average transaction contained *43,367 / 8,835 = 4.409* distinct grocery items. Of course, if we look a little further down the output, we'll see that the mean number of items per transaction has already been provided.

The next block of the summary() output lists the items that were most commonly found in the transactional data. Since *2,513 / 9,835 = 0.2555*, we can determine that whole milk appeared in 25.6 percent of the transactions. The other vegetables, rolls/buns, soda, and yogurt round out the list of other common items, as follows:

```
most frequent items:
      whole milk other vegetables       rolls/buns
            2513             1903             1809
            soda           yogurt          (Other)
            1715             1372            34055
```

Finally, we are presented with a set of statistics about the size of the transactions. A total of 2,159 transactions contained only a single item, while one transaction had 32 items. The first quartile and median purchase sizes are two and three items, respectively, implying that 25 percent of the transactions contained two or fewer items and the transactions were split in half between those with less than three items and those with more. The mean of 4.409 items per transaction matches the value we calculated by hand.

```
element (itemset/transaction) length distribution:
sizes
   1    2    3    4    5    6    7    8    9   10   11   12
2159 1643 1299 1005  855  645  545  438  350  246  182  117
  13   14   15   16   17   18   19   20   21   22   23   24
  78   77   55   46   29   14   14    9   11    4    6    1
  26   27   28   29   32
   1    1    1    3    1

  Min. 1st Qu.  Median    Mean 3rd Qu.    Max.
 1.000   2.000   3.000   4.409   6.000  32.000
```

The `arules` package includes some useful features for examining transaction data. To look at the contents of the sparse matrix, use the `inspect()` function in combination with the vector operators. The first five transactions can be viewed as follows:

```
> inspect(groceries[1:5])
  items
1 {citrus fruit,
   margarine,
   ready soups,
   semi-finished bread}
2 {coffee,
   tropical fruit,
   yogurt}
3 {whole milk}
4 {cream cheese,
   meat spreads,
   pip fruit,
   yogurt}
5 {condensed milk,
   long life bakery product,
   other vegetables,
   whole milk}
```

These transactions match our look at the original CSV file. To examine a particular item (that is, a column of data), it is possible use the `[row, column]` matrix notion. Using this with the `itemFrequency()` function allows us to see the proportion of transactions that contain the item. This allows us, for instance, to view the support level for the first three items in the grocery data:

```
> itemFrequency(groceries[, 1:3])
abrasive cleaner artif. sweetener    baby cosmetics
    0.0035587189      0.0032536858      0.0006100661
```

Note that the items in the sparse matrix are sorted in columns by alphabetical order. Abrasive cleaner and artificial sweeteners are found in about 0.3 percent of the transactions, while baby cosmetics are found in about 0.06 percent of the transactions.

Visualizing item support – item frequency plots

To present these statistics visually, use the `itemFrequencyPlot()` function. This allows you to produce a bar chart depicting the proportion of transactions containing certain items. Since the transactional data contains a very large number of items, you will often need to limit the ones appearing in the plot in order to produce a legible chart.

If you require these items to appear in a minimum proportion of transactions, use `itemFrequencyPlot()` with the `support` parameter:

```
> itemFrequencyPlot(groceries, support = 0.1)
```

As shown in the following plot, this results in a histogram showing the eight items in the `groceries` data with at least 10 percent support:

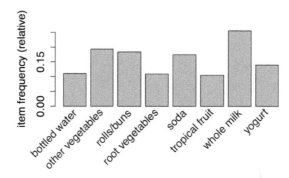

If you would rather limit the plot to a specific number of items, the `topN` parameter can be used with `itemFrequencyPlot()`:

```
> itemFrequencyPlot(groceries, topN = 20)
```

The histogram is then sorted by decreasing support, as shown in the following diagram of the top 20 items in the `groceries` data:

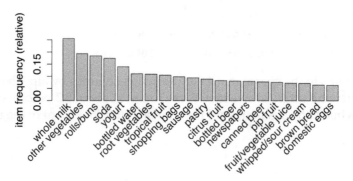

Visualizing the transaction data – plotting the sparse matrix

In addition to looking at the items, it's also possible to visualize the entire sparse matrix. To do so, use the image() function. The command to display the sparse matrix for the first five transactions is as follows:

```
> image(groceries[1:5])
```

The resulting diagram depicts a matrix with 5 rows and 169 columns, indicating the 5 transactions and 169 possible items we requested. Cells in the matrix are filled with black for transactions (rows) where the item (column) was purchased.

Although the preceding diagram is small and may be slightly hard to read, you can see that the first, fourth, and fifth transactions contained four items each, since their rows have four cells filled in. You can also see that rows three, five, two, and four have an item in common (on the right side of the diagram).

This visualization can be a useful tool for exploring data. For one, it may help with the identification of potential data issues. Columns that are filled all the way down could indicate items that are purchased in every transaction—a problem that could arise, perhaps, if a retailer's name or identification number was inadvertently included in the transaction dataset.

Additionally, patterns in the diagram may help reveal actionable insights within the transactions and items, particularly if the data is sorted in interesting ways. For example, if the transactions are sorted by date, the patterns in black dots could reveal seasonal effects in the number or types of items purchased. Perhaps around Christmas or Hanukkah, toys are more common; around Halloween, perhaps candies become popular. This type of visualization could be especially powerful if the items were also sorted into categories. In most cases, however, the plot will look fairly random, like static on a television screen.

Keep in mind that this visualization will not be as useful for extremely large transaction databases, because the cells will be too small to discern. Still, by combining it with the `sample()` function, you can view the sparse matrix for a randomly sampled set of transactions. The command to create random selection of 100 transactions is as follows:

```
> image(sample(groceries, 100))
```

This creates a matrix diagram with 100 rows and 169 columns:

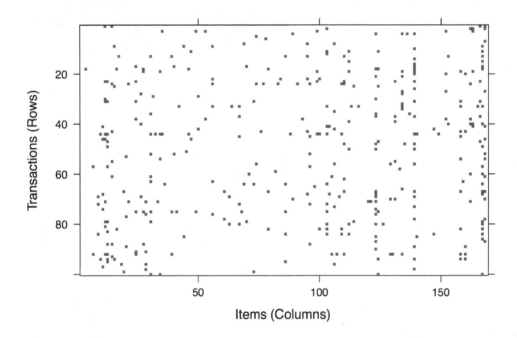

A few columns seem fairly heavily populated, indicating some very popular items at the store. But overall, the distribution of dots seems fairly random. Given nothing else of note, let's continue with our analysis.

Step 3 – training a model on the data

With data preparation completed, we can now work at finding associations among shopping cart items. We will use an implementation of the Apriori algorithm in the `arules` package we've been using to explore and prepare the groceries data. You'll need to install and load this package if you have not done so already. The following table shows the syntax to create sets of rules with the `apriori()` function:

Association rule syntax

using the `apriori()` function in the `arules` package

Finding association rules:

```
myrules <- apriori(data = mydata, parameter =
   list(support = 0.1, confidence = 0.8, minlen = 1))
```

- `data` is a sparse item matrix holding transactional data
- `support` specifies the minimum required rule support
- `confidence` specifies the minimum required rule confidence
- `minlen` specifies the minimum required rule items

The function will return a rules object storing all rules that meet the minimum criteria.

Examining association rules:

```
inspect(myrules)
```

- `myrules` is a set of association rules from the `apriori()` function

This will output the association rules to the screen. Vector operators can be used on myrules to choose a specific rule or rules to view.

Example:

```
groceryrules <- apriori(groceries, parameter =
   list(support = 0.01, confidence = 0.25, minlen = 2))
inspect(groceryrules[1:3])
```

Although running the `apriori()` function is straightforward, there can sometimes be a fair amount of trial and error needed to find the `support` and `confidence` parameters that produce a reasonable number of association rules. If you set these levels too high, you might find no rules or rules that are too generic to be very useful. On the other hand, a threshold too low might result in an unwieldy number of rules, or worse, the operation might take a very long time or run out of memory during the learning phase.

In this case, if we attempt to use the default settings of `support = 0.1` and `confidence = 0.8`, we will end up with a set of zero rules:

```
> apriori(groceries)
set of 0 rules
```

Obviously, we need to widen the search a bit.

 If you think about it, this outcome should not have been terribly surprising. Because `support = 0.1` by default, in order to generate a rule, an item must have appeared in at least *0.1 * 9,385 = 938.5* transactions. Since only eight items appeared this frequently in our data, it's no wonder that we didn't find any rules.

One way to approach the problem of setting a minimum support threshold is to think about the smallest number of transactions you would need before you would consider a pattern interesting. For instance, you could argue that if an item is purchased twice a day (about 60 times in a month of data), it may be an interesting pattern. From there, it is possible to calculate the support level needed to find only the rules matching at least that many transactions. Since 60 out of 9,835 equals 0.006, we'll try setting the support there first.

Setting the minimum confidence involves a delicate balance. On one hand, if confidence is too low, we might be overwhelmed with a large number of unreliable rules—such as dozens of rules indicating the items commonly purchased with batteries. How would we know where to target our advertising budget then? On the other hand, if we set confidence too high, we will be limited to the rules that are obvious or inevitable—similar to the fact that smoke detectors are always purchased in combination with batteries. In this case, moving the smoke detectors closer to the batteries is unlikely to generate additional revenue, since the two items already were almost always purchased together.

> The appropriate minimum confidence level depends a great deal on the goals of your analysis. If you start with a conservative value, you can always reduce it to broaden the search if you aren't finding actionable intelligence.

We'll start with a confidence threshold of 0.25, which means that in order to be included in the results, the rule has to be correct at least 25 percent of the time. This will eliminate the most unreliable rules, while allowing some room for us to modify behavior with targeted promotions.

We are now ready to generate some rules. In addition to the minimum `support` and `confidence` parameters, it is helpful to set `minlen = 2` to eliminate rules that contain fewer than two items. This prevents uninteresting rules from being created simply because the item is purchased frequently, for instance, *{} → whole milk*. This rule meets the minimum support and confidence because whole milk is purchased in over 25 percent of the transactions, but it isn't a very actionable insight.

The full command to find a set of association rules using the Apriori algorithm is as follows:

```
> groceryrules <- apriori(groceries, parameter = list(support =
                  0.006, confidence = 0.25, minlen = 2))
```

This saves our rules in a `rules` object, can take a peek into by typing its name:

```
> groceryrules
set of 463 rules
```

Our `groceryrules` object contains a set of 463 association rules. To determine whether any of them are useful, we'll have to dig deeper.

Step 4 – evaluating model performance

To obtain a high-level overview of the association rules, we can use `summary()` as follows. The rule length distribution tells us how many rules have each count of items. In our rule set, 150 rules have only two items, while 297 have three, and 16 have four. The `summary` statistics associated with this distribution are also given:

```
> summary(groceryrules)
set of 463 rules


rule length distribution (lhs + rhs):sizes
  2   3   4
150 297  16


   Min. 1st Qu.  Median    Mean 3rd Qu.    Max.
  2.000   2.000   3.000   2.711   3.000   4.000
```

 As noted in the previous output, the size of the rule is calculated as the total of both the left-hand side (`lhs`) and right-hand side (`rhs`) of the rule. This means that a rule like *{bread}* → *{butter}* is two items and *{peanut butter, jelly}* → *{bread}* is three.

Next, we see the summary statistics of the rule quality measures: support, confidence, and lift. The support and confidence measures should not be very surprising, since we used these as selection criteria for the rules. We might be alarmed if most or all of the rules had support and confidence very near the minimum thresholds, as this would mean that we may have set the bar too high. This is not the case here, as there are many rules with much higher values of each.

```
summary of quality measures:
    support            confidence          lift
 Min.    :0.006101   Min.    :0.2500   Min.    :0.9932
 1st Qu.:0.007117   1st Qu.:0.2971   1st Qu.:1.6229
```

```
Median :0.008744    Median :0.3554    Median :1.9332

Mean   :0.011539    Mean    :0.3786    Mean    :2.0351

3rd Qu.:0.012303    3rd Qu.:0.4495    3rd Qu.:2.3565

Max.   :0.074835    Max.    :0.6600    Max.    :3.9565
```

The third column is a metric we have not considered yet. The *lift* of a rule measures how much more likely one item or itemset is purchased relative to its typical rate of purchase, given that you know another item or itemset has been purchased. This is defined by the following equation:

$$\text{lift}(X \to Y) = \frac{\text{confidence}(X \to Y)}{\text{support}(Y)}$$

Unlike confidence where the item order matters, *lift(X → Y)* is the same as *lift(Y → X)*.

For example, suppose at a grocery store, most people purchase milk and bread. By chance alone, we would expect to find many transactions with both milk and bread. However, if *lift(milk → bread)* is greater than one, it implies that the two items are found together more often than one would expect by chance. A large lift value is therefore a strong indicator that a rule is important, and reflects a true connection between the items.

In the final section of the summary() output, we receive mining information, telling us about how the rules were chosen. Here, we see that the groceries data, which contained 9,835 transactions, was used to construct rules with a minimum support of 0.0006 and minimum confidence of 0.25:

```
mining info:
        data ntransactions support confidence
groceries         9835     0.006       0.25
```

We can take a look at specific rules using the inspect() function. For instance, the first three rules in the groceryrules object can be viewed as follows:

```
> inspect(groceryrules[1:3])
```

```
    lhs                  rhs                   support    confidence     lift
1 {potted plants} => {whole milk}       0.006914082  0.4000000  1.565460
2 {pasta}         => {whole milk}       0.006100661  0.4054054  1.586614
3 {herbs}         => {root vegetables}  0.007015760  0.4312500  3.956477
```

The first rule can be read in plain language as, "if a customer buys potted plants, they will also buy whole milk." With support of 0.007 and confidence of 0.400, we can determine that this rule covers 0.7 percent of the transactions and is correct in 40 percent of purchases involving potted plants. The lift value tells us how much more likely a customer is to buy whole milk relative to the average customer, given that he or she bought a potted plant. Since we know that about 25.6 percent of the customers bought whole milk (`support`), while 40 percent of the customers buying a potted plant bought whole milk (`confidence`), we can compute the lift value as *0.40 / 0.256 = 1.56*, which matches the value shown.

Note that the column labeled `support` indicates the support value for the rule, not the support value for the `lhs` or `rhs` alone).

In spite of the fact that the confidence and lift are high, does *{potted plants}* → *{whole milk}* seem like a very useful rule? Probably not, as there doesn't seem to be a logical reason why someone would be more likely to buy milk with a potted plant. Yet our data suggests otherwise. How can we make sense of this fact?

A common approach is to take the association rules and divide them into the following three categories:

- Actionable
- Trivial
- Inexplicable

Obviously, the goal of a market basket analysis is to find **actionable** rules that provide a clear and useful insight. Some rules are clear, others are useful; it is less common to find a combination of both of these factors.

So-called **trivial rules** include any rules that are so obvious that they are not worth mentioning—they are clear, but not useful. Suppose you were a marketing consultant being paid large sums of money to identify new opportunities for cross-promoting items. If you report the finding that *{diapers}* → *{formula}*, you probably won't be invited back for another consulting job.

Trivial rules can also sneak in disguised as more interesting results. For instance, say you found an association between a particular brand of children's cereal and a certain DVD movie. This finding is not very insightful if the movie's main character is on the front of the cereal box.

Rules are **inexplicable** if the connection between the items is so unclear that figuring out how to use the information is impossible or nearly impossible. The rule may simply be a random pattern in the data, for instance, a rule stating that *{pickles}* → *{chocolate ice cream}* may be due to a single customer, whose pregnant wife had regular cravings for strange combinations of foods.

The best rules are hidden gems — those undiscovered insights into patterns that seem obvious once discovered. Given enough time, one could evaluate each and every rule to find the gems. However, we (the one performing the market basket analysis) may not be the best judge of whether a rule is actionable, trivial, or inexplicable. In the next section, we'll improve the utility of our work by employing methods to sort and share the learned rules so that the most interesting results might float to the top.

Step 5 – improving model performance

Subject matter experts may be able to identify useful rules very quickly, but it would be a poor use of their time to ask them to evaluate hundreds or thousands of rules. Therefore, it's useful to be able to sort rules according to different criteria, and get them out of R into a form that can be shared with marketing teams and examined in more depth. In this way, we can improve the performance of our rules by making the results more actionable.

Sorting the set of association rules

Depending upon the objectives of the market basket analysis, the most useful rules might be the ones with the highest support, confidence, or lift. The arules package includes a sort() function that can be used to reorder the list of rules so that the ones with the highest or lowest values of the quality measure come first.

To reorder the groceryrules object, we can apply sort() while specifying a "support", "confidence", or "lift" value to the by parameter. By combining the sort function with vector operators, we can obtain a specific number of interesting rules. For instance, the best five rules according to the lift statistic can be examined using the following command:

```
> inspect(sort(groceryrules, by = "lift")[1:5])
```

These output is shown as follows:

```
      lhs                      rhs                     support confidence    lift
1 {herbs}                => {root vegetables}    0.007015760  0.4312500 3.956477
2 {berries}              => {whipped/sour cream} 0.009049314  0.2721713 3.796886
3 {other vegetables,
   tropical fruit,
   whole milk}           => {root vegetables}    0.007015760  0.4107143 3.768074
4 {beef,
   other vegetables}     => {root vegetables}    0.007930859  0.4020619 3.688692
5 {other vegetables,
   tropical fruit}       => {pip fruit}          0.009456024  0.2634561 3.482649
```

These rules appear to be more interesting than the ones we looked at previously. The first rule, with a `lift` of about 3.96, implies that people who buy herbs are nearly four times more likely to buy root vegetables than the typical customer—perhaps for a stew of some sort? Rule two is also interesting. Whipped cream is over three times more likely to be found in a shopping cart with berries versus other carts, suggesting perhaps a dessert pairing?

> [By default, the sort order is decreasing, meaning the largest values come first. To reverse this order, add an additional line, `parameterdecreasing = FALSE`.]

Taking subsets of association rules

Suppose that given the preceding rule, the marketing team is excited about the possibilities of creating an advertisement to promote berries, which are now in season. Before finalizing the campaign, however, they ask you to investigate whether berries are often purchased with other items. To answer this question, we'll need to find all the rules that include berries in some form.

The `subset()` function provides a method to search for subsets of transactions, items, or rules. To use it to find any rules with `berries` appearing in the rule, use the following command. It will store the rules in a new object titled `berryrules`:

```
> berryrules <- subset(groceryrules, items %in% "berries")
```

We can then inspect the rules as we did with the larger set:

```
> inspect(berryrules)
```

The result is the following set of rules:

```
    lhs              rhs                      support confidence       lift
1 {berries} => {whipped/sour cream} 0.009049314  0.2721713 3.796886
2 {berries} => {yogurt}             0.010574479  0.3180428 2.279848
3 {berries} => {other vegetables}   0.010269446  0.3088685 1.596280
4 {berries} => {whole milk}         0.011794611  0.3547401 1.388328
```

There are four rules involving berries, two of which seem to be interesting enough to be called actionable. In addition to whipped cream, berries are also purchased frequently with yogurt—a pairing that could serve well for breakfast or lunch as well as dessert.

The subset() function is very powerful. The criteria for choosing the subset can be defined with several keywords and operators:

- The keyword items explained previously, matches an item appearing anywhere in the rule. To limit the subset to where the match occurs only on the left- or right-hand side, use lhs and rhs instead.

- The operator %in% means that at least one of the items must be found in the list you defined. If you want any rules matching either berries or yogurt, you could write items %in%c("berries", "yogurt").

- Additional operators are available for partial matching (%pin%) and complete matching (%ain%). Partial matching allows you to find both citrus fruit and tropical fruit using one search: items %pin% "fruit". Complete matching requires that all the listed items are present. For instance, items %ain% c("berries", "yogurt") finds only rules with both berries and yogurt.

- Subsets can also be limited by support, confidence, or lift. For instance, confidence > 0.50 would limit you to the rules with confidence greater than 50 percent.

- Matching criteria can be combined with the standard R logical operators such as and (&), or (|), and not (!).

Using these options, you can limit the selection of rules to be as specific or general as you would like.

Saving association rules to a file or data frame

To share the results of your market basket analysis, you can save the rules to a CSV file with the `write()` function. This will produce a CSV file that can be used in most spreadsheet programs including Microsoft Excel:

```
> write(groceryrules, file = "groceryrules.csv",

        sep = ",", quote = TRUE, row.names = FALSE)
```

Sometimes it is also convenient to convert the rules into an R data frame. This can be accomplished easily using the `as()` function, as follows:

```
> groceryrules_df <- as(groceryrules, "data.frame")
```

This creates a data frame with the rules in the factor format, and numeric vectors for `support`, `confidence`, and `lift`:

```
> str(groceryrules_df)
'data.frame':463 obs. of 4 variables:
 $ rules      : Factor w/ 463 levels "{baking powder} => {other
vegetables}",..: 340 302 207 206 208 341 402 21 139 140 ...
 $ support    : num  0.00691 0.0061 0.00702 0.00773 0.00773 ...
 $ confidence: num  0.4 0.405 0.431 0.475 0.475 ...
 $ lift       : num  1.57 1.59 3.96 2.45 1.86 ...
```

You might choose to do this if you want to perform additional processing on the rules or need to export them to another database.

Summary

Association rules are frequently used to find provide useful insights in the massive transaction databases of large retailers. As an unsupervised learning process, association rule learners are capable of extracting knowledge from large databases without any prior knowledge of what patterns to seek. The catch is that it takes some effort to reduce the wealth of information into a smaller and more manageable set of results. The Apriori algorithm, which we studied in this chapter, does so by setting minimum thresholds of interestingness, and reporting only the associations meeting these criteria.

We put the Apriori algorithm to work while performing a market basket analysis for a month's worth of transactions at a moderately sized supermarket. Even in this small example, a wealth of associations was identified. Among these, we noted several patterns that may be useful for future marketing campaigns. The same methods we applied are used at much larger retailers on databases many times this size.

In the next chapter, we will examine another unsupervised learning algorithm. Much like association rules, it is intended to find patterns within data. But unlike association rules that seek patterns within the features, the methods in the next chapter are concerned with finding connections among the examples.

9
Finding Groups of Data – Clustering with k-means

Have you ever spent time watching a large crowd? If so, you are likely to have seen some recurring personalities. Perhaps a certain type of person, identified by a freshly pressed suit and a briefcase, comes to typify the "fat cat" business executive. A twenty-something wearing skinny jeans, a flannel shirt, and sunglasses might be dubbed a "hipster," while a woman unloading children from a minivan may be labeled a "soccer mom."

Of course, these types of stereotypes are dangerous to apply to individuals, as no two people are exactly alike. Yet understood as a way to describe a collective, the labels capture some underlying aspect of similarity among the individuals within the group.

As you will soon learn, the act of clustering, or spotting patterns in data, is not much different from spotting patterns in groups of people. In this chapter, you will learn:

- The ways clustering tasks differ from the classification tasks we examined previously

- How clustering defines a group, and how such groups are identified by k-means, a classic and easy-to-understand clustering algorithm

- The steps needed to apply clustering to a real-world task of identifying marketing segments among teenage social media users

Before jumping into action, we'll begin by taking an in-depth look at exactly what clustering entails.

Understanding clustering

Clustering is an unsupervised machine learning task that automatically divides the data into **clusters,** or groups of similar items. It does this without having been told how the groups should look ahead of time. As we may not even know what we're looking for, clustering is used for knowledge discovery rather than prediction. It provides an insight into the natural groupings found within data.

Without advance knowledge of what comprises a cluster, how can a computer possibly know where one group ends and another begins? The answer is simple. Clustering is guided by the principle that items inside a cluster should be very similar to each other, but very different from those outside. The definition of similarity might vary across applications, but the basic idea is always the same—group the data so that the related elements are placed together.

The resulting clusters can then be used for action. For instance, you might find clustering methods employed in the following applications:

- Segmenting customers into groups with similar demographics or buying patterns for targeted marketing campaigns
- Detecting anomalous behavior, such as unauthorized network intrusions, by identifying patterns of use falling outside the known clusters
- Simplifying extremely large datasets by grouping features with similar values into a smaller number of homogeneous categories

Overall, clustering is useful whenever diverse and varied data can be exemplified by a much smaller number of groups. It results in meaningful and actionable data structures that reduce complexity and provide insight into patterns of relationships.

Clustering as a machine learning task

Clustering is somewhat different from the classification, numeric prediction, and pattern detection tasks we examined so far. In each of these cases, the result is a model that relates features to an outcome or features to other features; conceptually, the model describes the existing patterns within data. In contrast, clustering creates new data. Unlabeled examples are given a cluster label that has been inferred entirely from the relationships within the data. For this reason, you will, sometimes, see the clustering task referred to as **unsupervised classification** because, in a sense, it classifies unlabeled examples.

The catch is that the class labels obtained from an unsupervised classifier are without intrinsic meaning. Clustering will tell you which groups of examples are closely related — for instance, it might return the groups A, B, and C — but it's up to you to apply an actionable and meaningful label. To see how this impacts the clustering task, let's consider a hypothetical example.

Suppose you were organizing a conference on the topic of data science. To facilitate professional networking and collaboration, you planned to seat people in groups according to one of three research specialties: computer and/or database science, math and statistics, and machine learning. Unfortunately, after sending out the conference invitations, you realize that you had forgotten to include a survey asking which discipline the attendee would prefer to be seated with.

In a stroke of brilliance, you realize that you might be able to infer each scholar's research specialty by examining his or her publication history. To this end, you begin collecting data on the number of articles each attendee published in computer science-related journals and the number of articles published in math or statistics-related journals. Using the data collected for several scholars, you create a scatterplot:

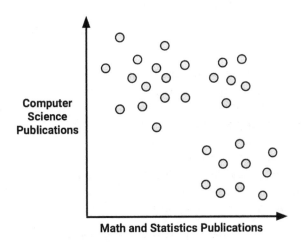

As expected, there seems to be a pattern. We might guess that the upper-left corner, which represents people with many computer science publications but few articles on math, could be a cluster of computer scientists. Following this logic, the lower-right corner might be a group of mathematicians. Similarly, the upper-right corner, those with both math and computer science experience, may be machine learning experts.

Our groupings were formed visually; we simply identified clusters as closely grouped data points. Yet in spite of the seemingly obvious groupings, we unfortunately have no way to know whether they are truly homogeneous without personally asking each scholar about his/her academic specialty. The labels we applied required us to make qualitative, presumptive judgments about the types of people that would fall into the group. For this reason, you might imagine the cluster labels in uncertain terms, as follows:

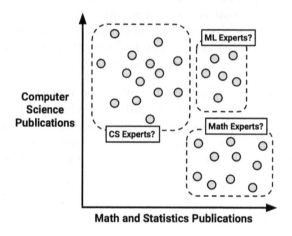

Rather than defining the group boundaries subjectively, it would be nice to use machine learning to define them objectively. Given the axis-parallel splits in the preceding diagram, our problem seems like an obvious application for the decision trees described in *Chapter 5, Divide and Conquer – Classification Using Decision Trees and Rules*. This might provide us with a rule in the form "if a scholar has few math publications, then he/she is a computer science expert." Unfortunately, there's a problem with this plan. As we do not have data on the true class value for each point, a supervised learning algorithm would have no ability to learn such a pattern, as it would have no way of knowing what splits would result in homogenous groups.

On the other hand, clustering algorithms use a process very similar to what we did by visually inspecting the scatterplot. Using a measure of how closely the examples are related, homogeneous groups can be identified. In the next section, we'll start looking at how clustering algorithms are implemented.

 This example highlights an interesting application of clustering. If you begin with unlabeled data, you can use clustering to create class labels. From there, you could apply a supervised learner such as decision trees to find the most important predictors of these classes. This is called **semi-supervised learning**.

The k-means clustering algorithm

The **k-means algorithm** is perhaps the most commonly used clustering method. Having been studied for several decades, it serves as the foundation for many more sophisticated clustering techniques. If you understand the simple principles it uses, you will have the knowledge needed to understand nearly any clustering algorithm in use today. Many such methods are listed on the following site, the **CRAN Task View** for clustering at `http://cran.r-project.org/web/views/Cluster.html`.

 As k-means has evolved over time, there are many implementations of the algorithm. One popular approach is described in : Hartigan JA, Wong MA. A k-means clustering algorithm. Applied *Statistics*. 1979; 28:100-108.

Even though clustering methods have advanced since the inception of k-means, this is not to imply that k-means is obsolete. In fact, the method may be more popular now than ever. The following table lists some reasons why k-means is still used widely:

Strengths	Weaknesses
• Uses simple principles that can be explained in non-statistical terms	• Not as sophisticated as more modern clustering algorithms
• Highly flexible, and can be adapted with simple adjustments to address nearly all of its shortcomings	• Because it uses an element of random chance, it is not guaranteed to find the optimal set of clusters
• Performs well enough under many real-world use cases	• Requires a reasonable guess as to how many clusters naturally exist in the data
	• Not ideal for non-spherical clusters or clusters of widely varying density

If the name k-means sounds familiar to you, you may be recalling the k-NN algorithm discussed in *Chapter 3, Lazy Learning – Classification Using Nearest Neighbors*. As you will soon see, k-means shares more in common with the k-nearest neighbors than just the letter k.

The k-means algorithm assigns each of the n examples to one of the k clusters, where k is a number that has been determined ahead of time. The goal is to minimize the differences within each cluster and maximize the differences between the clusters.

Unless *k* and *n* are extremely small, it is not feasible to compute the optimal clusters across all the possible combinations of examples. Instead, the algorithm uses a heuristic process that finds **locally optimal** solutions. Put simply, this means that it starts with an initial guess for the cluster assignments, and then modifies the assignments slightly to see whether the changes improve the homogeneity within the clusters.

We will cover the process in depth shortly, but the algorithm essentially involves two phases. First, it assigns examples to an initial set of *k* clusters. Then, it updates the assignments by adjusting the cluster boundaries according to the examples that currently fall into the cluster. The process of updating and assigning occurs several times until changes no longer improve the cluster fit. At this point, the process stops and the clusters are finalized.

Due to the heuristic nature of k-means, you may end up with somewhat different final results by making only slight changes to the starting conditions. If the results vary dramatically, this could indicate a problem. For instance, the data may not have natural groupings or the value of *k* has been poorly chosen. With this in mind, it's a good idea to try a cluster analysis more than once to test the robustness of your findings.

To see how the process of assigning and updating works in practice, let's revisit the case of the hypothetical data science conference. Though this is a simple example, it will illustrate the basics of how k-means operates under the hood.

Using distance to assign and update clusters

As with k-NN, k-means treats feature values as coordinates in a multidimensional feature space. For the conference data, there are only two features, so we can represent the feature space as a two-dimensional scatterplot as depicted previously.

The k-means algorithm begins by choosing *k* points in the feature space to serve as the cluster centers. These centers are the catalyst that spurs the remaining examples to fall into place. Often, the points are chosen by selecting *k* random examples from the training dataset. As we hope to identify three clusters, according to this method, *k* = 3 points will be selected at random. These points are indicated by the star, triangle, and diamond in the following diagram:

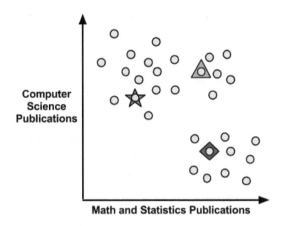

It's worth noting that although the three cluster centers in the preceding diagram happen to be widely spaced apart, this is not always necessarily the case. Since they are selected at random, the three centers could have just as easily been three adjacent points. As the k-means algorithm is highly sensitive to the starting position of the cluster centers, this means that random chance may have a substantial impact on the final set of clusters.

To address this problem, k-means can be modified to use different methods for choosing the initial centers. For example, one variant chooses random values occurring anywhere in the feature space (rather than only selecting among the values observed in the data). Another option is to skip this step altogether; by randomly assigning each example to a cluster, the algorithm can jump ahead immediately to the update phase. Each of these approaches adds a particular bias to the final set of clusters, which you may be able to use to improve your results.

In 2007, an algorithm called **k-means++** was introduced, which proposes an alternative method for selecting the initial cluster centers. It purports to be an efficient way to get much closer to the optimal clustering solution while reducing the impact of random chance. For more information, refer to *Arthur D, Vassilvitskii S. k-means++: The advantages of careful seeding. Proceedings of the eighteenth annual ACM-SIAM symposium on discrete algorithms. 2007:1027–1035.*

After choosing the initial cluster centers, the other examples are assigned to the cluster center that is nearest according to the distance function. You will remember that we studied distance functions while learning about k-Nearest Neighbors. Traditionally, k-means uses Euclidean distance, but Manhattan distance or Minkowski distance are also sometimes used.

Recall that if n indicates the number of features, the formula for Euclidean distance between example x and example y is:

$$\text{dist}(x, y) = \sqrt{\sum_{i=1}^{n}(x_i - y_i)^2}$$

For instance, if we are comparing a guest with five computer science publications and one math publication to a guest with zero computer science papers and two math papers, we could compute this in R as follows:

```
> sqrt((5 - 0)^2 + (1 - 2)^2)
[1] 5.09902
```

Using this distance function, we find the distance between each example and each cluster center. The example is then assigned to the nearest cluster center.

 Keep in mind that as we are using distance calculations, all the features need to be numeric, and the values should be normalized to a standard range ahead of time. The methods discussed in *Chapter 3, Lazy Learning – Classification Using Nearest Neighbors*, will prove helpful for this task.

As shown in the following diagram, the three cluster centers partition the examples into three segments labeled **Cluster A**, **Cluster B**, and **Cluster C**. The dashed lines indicate the boundaries for the **Voronoi diagram** created by the cluster centers. The Voronoi diagram indicates the areas that are closer to one cluster center than any other; the vertex where all the three boundaries meet is the maximal distance from all three cluster centers. Using these boundaries, we can easily see the regions claimed by each of the initial k-means seeds:

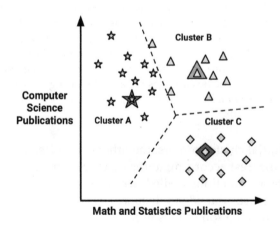

Now that the initial assignment phase has been completed, the k-means algorithm proceeds to the update phase. The first step of updating the clusters involves shifting the initial centers to a new location, known as the **centroid**, which is calculated as the average position of the points currently assigned to that cluster. The following diagram illustrates how as the cluster centers shift to the new centroids, the boundaries in the Voronoi diagram also shift and a point that was once in **Cluster B** (indicated by an arrow) is added to **Cluster A**:

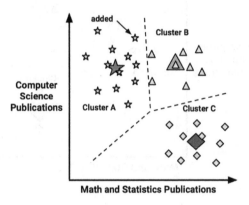

As a result of this reassignment, the k-means algorithm will continue through another update phase. After shifting the cluster centroids, updating the cluster boundaries, and reassigning points into new clusters (as indicated by arrows), the figure looks like this:

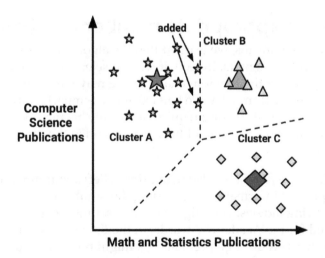

Because two more points were reassigned, another update must occur, which moves the centroids and updates the cluster boundaries. However, because these changes result in no reassignments, the k-means algorithm stops. The cluster assignments are now final:

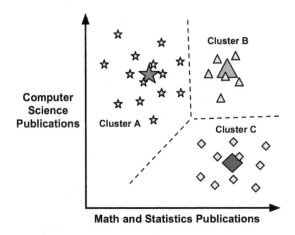

The final clusters can be reported in one of the two ways. First, you might simply report the cluster assignments such as A, B, or C for each example. Alternatively, you could report the coordinates of the cluster centroids after the final update. Given either reporting method, you are able to define the cluster boundaries by calculating the centroids or assigning each example to its nearest cluster.

Choosing the appropriate number of clusters

In the introduction to k-means, we learned that the algorithm is sensitive to the randomly-chosen cluster centers. Indeed, if we had selected a different combination of three starting points in the previous example, we may have found clusters that split the data differently from what we had expected. Similarly, k-means is sensitive to the number of clusters; the choice requires a delicate balance. Setting k to be very large will improve the homogeneity of the clusters, and at the same time, it risks overfitting the data.

Ideally, you will have *a priori* knowledge (a prior belief) about the true groupings and you can apply this information to choosing the number of clusters. For instance, if you were clustering movies, you might begin by setting k equal to the number of genres considered for the Academy Awards. In the data science conference seating problem that we worked through previously, k might reflect the number of academic fields of study that were invited.

Sometimes the number of clusters is dictated by business requirements or the motivation for the analysis. For example, the number of tables in the meeting hall could dictate how many groups of people should be created from the data science attendee list. Extending this idea to another business case, if the marketing department only has resources to create three distinct advertising campaigns, it might make sense to set $k = 3$ to assign all the potential customers to one of the three appeals.

Without any prior knowledge, one rule of thumb suggests setting k equal to the square root of $(n / 2)$, where n is the number of examples in the dataset. However, this rule of thumb is likely to result in an unwieldy number of clusters for large datasets. Luckily, there are other statistical methods that can assist in finding a suitable k-means cluster set.

A technique known as the **elbow method** attempts to gauge how the homogeneity or heterogeneity within the clusters changes for various values of k. As illustrated in the following diagrams, the homogeneity within clusters is expected to increase as additional clusters are added; similarly, heterogeneity will also continue to decrease with more clusters. As you could continue to see improvements until each example is in its own cluster, the goal is not to maximize homogeneity or minimize heterogeneity, but rather to find k so that there are diminishing returns beyond that point. This value of k is known as the **elbow point** because it looks like an elbow.

There are numerous statistics to measure homogeneity and heterogeneity within the clusters that can be used with the elbow method (the following information box provides a citation for more detail). Still, in practice, it is not always feasible to iteratively test a large number of k values. This is in part because clustering large datasets can be fairly time consuming; clustering the data repeatedly is even worse. Regardless, applications requiring the exact optimal set of clusters are fairly rare. In most clustering applications, it suffices to choose a k value based on convenience rather than strict performance requirements.

For a very thorough review of the vast assortment of cluster performance measures, refer to: *Halkidi M, Batistakis Y, Vazirgiannis M.* On clustering validation techniques. *Journal of Intelligent Information Systems.* 2001; 17:107-145.

The process of setting *k* itself can sometimes lead to interesting insights. By observing how the characteristics of the clusters change as *k* is varied, one might infer where the data have naturally defined boundaries. Groups that are more tightly clustered will change a little, while less homogeneous groups will form and disband over time.

In general, it may be wise to spend little time worrying about getting *k* exactly right. The next example will demonstrate how even a tiny bit of subject-matter knowledge borrowed from a Hollywood film can be used to set *k* such that actionable and interesting clusters are found. As clustering is unsupervised, the task is really about what you make of it; the value is in the insights you take away from the algorithm's findings.

Example – finding teen market segments using k-means clustering

Interacting with friends on a **social networking service** (**SNS**), such as Facebook, Tumblr, and Instagram has become a rite of passage for teenagers around the world. Having a relatively large amount of disposable income, these adolescents are a coveted demographic for businesses hoping to sell snacks, beverages, electronics, and hygiene products.

The many millions of teenage consumers using such sites have attracted the attention of marketers struggling to find an edge in an increasingly competitive market. One way to gain this edge is to identify segments of teenagers who share similar tastes, so that clients can avoid targeting advertisements to teens with no interest in the product being sold. For instance, sporting apparel is likely to be a difficult sell to teens with no interest in sports.

Given the text of teenagers' SNS pages, we can identify groups that share common interests such as sports, religion, or music. Clustering can automate the process of discovering the natural segments in this population. However, it will be up to us to decide whether or not the clusters are interesting and how we can use them for advertising. Let's try this process from start to finish.

Step 1 – collecting data

For this analysis, we will use a dataset representing a random sample of 30,000 U.S. high school students who had profiles on a well-known SNS in 2006. To protect the users' anonymity, the SNS will remain unnamed. However, at the time the data was collected, the SNS was a popular web destination for US teenagers. Therefore, it is reasonable to assume that the profiles represent a fairly wide cross section of American adolescents in 2006.

> This dataset was compiled by Brett Lantz while conducting sociological research on the teenage identities at the University of Notre Dame. If you use the data for research purposes, please cite this book chapter. The full dataset is available at the Packt Publishing website with the filename snsdata.csv. To follow along interactively, this chapter assumes that you have saved this file to your R working directory.

The data was sampled evenly across four high school graduation years (2006 through 2009) representing the senior, junior, sophomore, and freshman classes at the time of data collection. Using an automated web crawler, the full text of the SNS profiles were downloaded, and each teen's gender, age, and number of SNS friends was recorded.

A text mining tool was used to divide the remaining SNS page content into words. From the top 500 words appearing across all the pages, 36 words were chosen to represent five categories of interests: namely extracurricular activities, fashion, religion, romance, and antisocial behavior. The 36 words include terms such as *football*, *sexy*, *kissed*, *bible*, *shopping*, *death*, and *drugs*. The final dataset indicates, for each person, how many times each word appeared in the person's SNS profile.

Step 2 – exploring and preparing the data

We can use the default settings of read.csv() to load the data into a data frame:

```
> teens <- read.csv("snsdata.csv")
```

Let's also take a quick look at the specifics of the data. The first several lines of the str() output are as follows:

```
> str(teens)
'data.frame':	30000 obs. of  40 variables:
 $ gradyear   : int  2006 2006 2006 2006 2006 2006 2006 2006 ...
 $ gender     : Factor w/ 2 levels "F","M": 2 1 2 1 NA 1 1 2 ...
 $ age        : num  19 18.8 18.3 18.9 19 ...
```

```
$ friends     : int  7 0 69 0 10 142 72 17 52 39 ...
$ basketball  : int  0 0 0 0 0 0 0 0 0 0 ...
```

As we had expected, the data include 30,000 teenagers with four variables indicating personal characteristics and 36 words indicating interests.

Do you notice anything strange around the gender row? If you were looking carefully, you may have noticed the NA value, which is out of place compared to the 1 and 2 values. The NA is R's way of telling us that the record has a missing value—we do not know the person's gender. Until now, we haven't dealt with missing data, but it can be a significant problem for many types of analyses.

Let's see how substantial this problem is. One option is to use the table() command, as follows:

```
> table(teens$gender)

    F     M
22054  5222
```

Although this command tells us how many F and M values are present, the table() function excluded the NA values rather than treating it as a separate category. To include the NA values (if there are any), we simply need to add an additional parameter:

```
> table(teens$gender, useNA = "ifany")

    F     M  <NA>
22054  5222  2724
```

Here, we see that 2,724 records (9 percent) have missing gender data. Interestingly, there are over four times as many females as males in the SNS data, suggesting that males are not as inclined to use SNS websites as females.

If you examine the other variables in the data frame, you will find that besides gender, only age has missing values. For numeric data, the summary() command tells us the number of missing NA values:

```
> summary(teens$age)
   Min. 1st Qu.  Median    Mean 3rd Qu.    Max.    NA's
  3.086  16.310  17.290  17.990  18.260 106.900    5086
```

A total of 5,086 records (17 percent) have missing ages. Also concerning is the fact that the minimum and maximum values seem to be unreasonable; it is unlikely that a 3 year old or a 106 year old is attending high school. To ensure that these extreme values don't cause problems for the analysis, we'll need to clean them up before moving on.

A more reasonable range of ages for the high school students includes those who are at least 13 years old and not yet 20 years old. Any age value falling outside this range should be treated the same as missing data—we cannot trust the age provided. To recode the age variable, we can use the `ifelse()` function, assigning `teen$age` the value of `teen$age` if the age is at least 13 and less than 20 years; otherwise, it will receive the value `NA`:

```
> teens$age <- ifelse(teens$age >= 13 & teens$age < 20,
                       teens$age, NA)
```

By rechecking the `summary()` output, we see that the age range now follows a distribution that looks much more like an actual high school:

```
> summary(teens$age)
   Min. 1st Qu.  Median    Mean 3rd Qu.    Max.   NA's
  13.03   16.30   17.26   17.25   18.22   20.00    5523
```

Unfortunately, now we've created an even larger missing data problem. We'll need to find a way to deal with these values before continuing with our analysis.

Data preparation – dummy coding missing values

An easy solution for handling the missing values is to exclude any record with a missing value. However, if you think through the implications of this practice, you might think twice before doing so—just because it is easy does not mean it is a good idea! The problem with this approach is that even if the missingness is not extensive, you can easily exclude large portions of the data.

For example, suppose that in our data, the people with the NA values for gender are completely different from those with missing age data. This would imply that by excluding those missing either gender or age, you would exclude 9% + 17% = 26% of the data, or over 7,500 records. And this is for missing data on only two variables! The larger the number of missing values present in a dataset, the more likely it is that any given record will be excluded. Fairly soon, you will be left with a tiny subset of data, or worse, the remaining records will be systematically different or non-representative of the full population.

An alternative solution for categorical variables like gender is to treat a missing value as a separate category. For instance, rather than limiting to female and male, we can add an additional category for the unknown gender. This allows us to utilize dummy coding, which was covered in *Chapter 3, Lazy Learning – Classification Using Nearest Neighbors*.

If you recall, dummy coding involves creating a separate binary (1 or 0) valued dummy variable for each level of a nominal feature except one, which is held out to serve as the reference group. The reason one category can be excluded is because its status can be inferred from the other categories. For instance, if someone is not female and not unknown gender, they must be male. Therefore, in this case, we need to only create dummy variables for female and unknown gender:

```
> teens$female <- ifelse(teens$gender == "F" &
                         !is.na(teens$gender), 1, 0)
> teens$no_gender <- ifelse(is.na(teens$gender), 1, 0)
```

As you might expect, the is.na() function tests whether gender is equal to NA. Therefore, the first statement assigns teens$female the value 1 if gender is equal to F and the gender is not equal to NA; otherwise, it assigns the value 0. In the second statement, if is.na() returns TRUE, meaning the gender is missing, the teens$no_gender variable is assigned 1; otherwise, it is assigned the value 0. To confirm that we did the work correctly, let's compare our constructed dummy variables to the original gender variable:

```
> table(teens$gender, useNA = "ifany")
     F       M    <NA>
 22054    5222    2724
> table(teens$female, useNA = "ifany")
     0       1
  7946   22054
> table(teens$no_gender, useNA = "ifany")
     0       1
 27276    2724
```

The number of 1 values for teens$female and teens$no_gender matches the number of F and NA values, respectively, so we should be able to trust our work.

Data preparation – imputing the missing values

Next, let's eliminate the 5,523 missing age values. As age is numeric, it doesn't make sense to create an additional category for the unknown values—where would you rank "unknown" relative to the other ages? Instead, we'll use a different strategy known as **imputation**, which involves filling in the missing data with a guess as to the true value.

Can you think of a way we might be able to use the SNS data to make an informed guess about a teenager's age? If you are thinking of using the graduation year, you've got the right idea. Most people in a graduation cohort were born within a single calendar year. If we can identify the typical age for each cohort, we would have a fairly reasonable estimate of the age of a student in that graduation year.

One way to find a typical value is by calculating the average or mean value. If we try to apply the mean() function, as we did for previous analyses, there's a problem:

```
> mean(teens$age)
[1] NA
```

The issue is that the mean is undefined for a vector containing missing data. As our age data contains missing values, mean(teens$age) returns a missing value. We can correct this by adding an additional parameter to remove the missing values before calculating the mean:

```
> mean(teens$age, na.rm = TRUE)
[1] 17.25243
```

This reveals that the average student in our data is about 17 years old. This only gets us part of the way there; we actually need the average age for each graduation year. You might be tempted to calculate the mean four times, but one of the benefits of R is that there's usually a way to avoid repeating oneself. In this case, the aggregate() function is the tool for the job. It computes statistics for subgroups of data. Here, it calculates the mean age by graduation year after removing the NA values:

```
> aggregate(data = teens, age ~ gradyear, mean, na.rm = TRUE)
  gradyear      age
1     2006 18.65586
2     2007 17.70617
3     2008 16.76770
4     2009 15.81957
```

The mean age differs by roughly one year per change in graduation year. This is not at all surprising, but a helpful finding for confirming our data is reasonable.

The aggregate() output is a data frame. This is helpful for some purposes, but would require extra work to merge back onto our original data. As an alternative, we can use the ave() function, which returns a vector with the group means repeated so that the result is equal in length to the original vector:

```
> ave_age <- ave(teens$age, teens$gradyear, FUN =
                function(x) mean(x, na.rm = TRUE))
```

To impute these means onto the missing values, we need one more `ifelse()` call to use the `ave_age` value only if the original age value was NA:

```
> teens$age <- ifelse(is.na(teens$age), ave_age, teens$age)
```

The `summary()` results show that the missing values have now been eliminated:

```
> summary(teens$age)
   Min. 1st Qu.  Median    Mean 3rd Qu.    Max.
  13.03   16.28   17.24   17.24   18.21   20.00
```

With the data ready for analysis, we are ready to dive into the interesting part of this project. Let's see whether our efforts have paid off.

Step 3 – training a model on the data

To cluster the teenagers into marketing segments, we will use an implementation of k-means in the `stats` package, which should be included in your R installation by default. If by chance you do not have this package, you can install it as you would any other package and load it using the `library(stats)` command. Although there is no shortage of k-means functions available in various R packages, the `kmeans()` function in the `stats` package is widely used and provides a vanilla implementation of the algorithm.

Clustering syntax

using the `kmeans()` function in the `stats` package

Finding clusters:

```
myclusters <- kmeans(mydata, k)
```

- `mydata` is a matrix or data frame with the examples to be clustered
- `k` specifies the desired number of clusters

The function will return a cluster object that stores information about the clusters.

Examining clusters:

- `myclusters$cluster` is a vector of cluster assignments from the `kmeans()` function
- `myclusters$centers` is a matrix indicating the mean values for each feature and cluster combination
- `myclusters$size` lists the number of examples assigned to each cluster

Example:

```
teen_clusters <- kmeans(teens, 5)
teens$cluster_id <- teen_clusters$cluster
```

The `kmeans()` function requires a data frame containing only numeric data and a parameter specifying the desired number of clusters. If you have these two things ready, the actual process of building the model is simple. The trouble is that choosing the right combination of data and clusters can be a bit of an art; sometimes a great deal of trial and error is involved.

We'll start our cluster analysis by considering only the 36 features that represent the number of times various interests appeared on the teen SNS profiles. For convenience, let's make a data frame containing only these features:

```
> interests <- teens[5:40]
```

If you recall from *Chapter 3, Lazy Learning – Classification Using Nearest Neighbors*, a common practice employed prior to any analysis using distance calculations is to normalize or z-score standardize the features so that each utilizes the same range. By doing so, you can avoid a problem in which some features come to dominate solely because they have a larger range of values than the others.

The process of z-score standardization rescales features so that they have a mean of zero and a standard deviation of one. This transformation changes the interpretation of the data in a way that may be useful here. Specifically, if someone mentions football three times on their profile, without additional information, we have no idea whether this implies they like football more or less than their peers. On the other hand, if the z-score is three, we know that that they mentioned football many more times than the average teenager.

To apply the z-score standardization to the `interests` data frame, we can use the `scale()` function with `lapply()` as follows:

```
> interests_z <- as.data.frame(lapply(interests, scale))
```

Since `lapply()` returns a matrix, it must be coerced back to data frame form using the `as.data.frame()` function.

Our last decision involves deciding how many clusters to use for segmenting the data. If we use too many clusters, we may find them too specific to be useful; conversely, choosing too few may result in heterogeneous groupings. You should feel comfortable experimenting with the values of *k*. If you don't like the result, you can easily try another value and start over.

 Choosing the number of clusters is easier if you are familiar with the analysis population. Having a hunch about the true number of natural groupings can save you some trial and error.

To help us predict the number of clusters in the data, I'll defer to one of my favorite films, The *Breakfast Club*, a coming-of-age comedy released in 1985 and directed by John Hughes. The teenage characters in this movie are identified in terms of five stereotypes: a brain, an athlete, a basket case, a princess, and a criminal. Given that these identities prevail throughout popular teen fiction, five seems like a reasonable starting point for *k*.

To use the k-means algorithm to divide the teenagers' interest data into five clusters, we use the kmeans() function on the interests data frame. Because the k-means algorithm utilizes random starting points, the set.seed() function is used to ensure that the results match the output in the examples that follow. If you recall from the previous chapters, this command initializes R's random number generator to a specific sequence. In the absence of this statement, the results will vary each time the k-means algorithm is run:

```
> set.seed(2345)
> teen_clusters <- kmeans(interests_z, 5)
```

The result of the k-means clustering process is a list named teen_clusters that stores the properties of each of the five clusters. Let's dig in and see how well the algorithm has divided the teens' interest data.

 If you find that your results differ from those shown here, ensure that the set.seed(2345) command is run immediately prior to the kmeans() function.

Step 4 – evaluating model performance

Evaluating clustering results can be somewhat subjective. Ultimately, the success or failure of the model hinges on whether the clusters are useful for their intended purpose. As the goal of this analysis was to identify clusters of teenagers with similar interests for marketing purposes, we will largely measure our success in qualitative terms. For other clustering applications, more quantitative measures of success may be needed.

One of the most basic ways to evaluate the utility of a set of clusters is to examine the number of examples falling in each of the groups. If the groups are too large or too small, they are not likely to be very useful. To obtain the size of the kmeans() clusters, use the teen_clusters$size component as follows:

```
> teen_clusters$size
[1]   871   600  5981  1034 21514
```

Here, we see the five clusters we requested. The smallest cluster has 600 teenagers (2 percent) while the largest cluster has 21,514 (72 percent). Although the large gap between the number of people in the largest and smallest clusters is slightly concerning, without examining these groups more carefully, we will not know whether or not this indicates a problem. It may be the case that the clusters' size disparity indicates something real, such as a big group of teens that share similar interests, or it may be a random fluke caused by the initial k-means cluster centers. We'll know more as we start to look at each cluster's homogeneity.

Sometimes, k-means may find extremely small clusters — occasionally, as small as a single point. This can happen if one of the initial cluster centers happens to fall on an outlier far from the rest of the data. It is not always clear whether to treat such small clusters as a true finding that represents a cluster of extreme cases, or a problem caused by random chance. If you encounter this issue, it may be worth re-running the k-means algorithm with a different random seed to see whether the small cluster is robust to different starting points.

For a more in-depth look at the clusters, we can examine the coordinates of the cluster centroids using the `teen_clusters$centers` component, which is as follows for the first four interests:

```
> teen_clusters$centers
    basketball    football       soccer     softball
1   0.16001227   0.2364174   0.10385512   0.07232021
2  -0.09195886   0.0652625  -0.09932124  -0.01739428
3   0.52755083   0.4873480   0.29778605   0.37178877
4   0.34081039   0.3593965   0.12722250   0.16384661
5  -0.16695523  -0.1641499  -0.09033520  -0.11367669
```

The rows of the output (labeled 1 to 5) refer to the five clusters, while the numbers across each row indicate the cluster's average value for the interest listed at the top of the column. As the values are z-score standardized, positive values are above the overall mean level for all the teens and negative values are below the overall mean. For example, the third row has the highest value in the basketball column, which means that cluster 3 has the highest average interest in basketball among all the clusters.

By examining whether the clusters fall above or below the mean level for each interest category, we can begin to notice patterns that distinguish the clusters from each other. In practice, this involves printing the cluster centers and searching through them for any patterns or extreme values, much like a word search puzzle but with numbers. The following screenshot shows a highlighted pattern for each of the five clusters, for 19 of the 36 teen interests:

```
> teen_clusters$centers
    basketball    football      soccer    softball  volleyball    swimming
1   0.16001227   0.2364174  0.10385512  0.07232021  0.18897158  0.23970234
2  -0.09195886   0.0652625 -0.09932124 -0.01739428 -0.06219308  0.03339844
3   0.52755083   0.4873480  0.29778605  0.37178877  0.37986175  0.29628671
4   0.34081039   0.3593965  0.12722250  0.16384661  0.11032200  0.26943332
5  -0.16695523  -0.1641499 -0.09033520 -0.11367669 -0.11682181 -0.10595448
    cheerleading    baseball      tennis      sports        cute         sex
1     0.3931445  0.02993479  0.13532387  0.10257837  0.37884271  0.020042068
2    -0.1101103 -0.11487510  0.04062204 -0.09899231 -0.03265037 -0.042486141
3     0.3303485  0.35231971  0.14057808  0.32967130  0.54442929  0.002913623
4     0.1856664  0.27527088  0.10980958  0.79711920  0.47866008  2.028471066
5    -0.1136077 -0.10918483 -0.05097057 -0.13135334 -0.18878627 -0.097928345
          sexy         hot      kissed       dance        band    marching       music
1   0.11740551  0.41389104  0.06787768  0.22780899 -0.10257102 -0.10942590  0.1378306
2  -0.04329091 -0.03812345 -0.04554933  0.04573186  4.06726666  5.25757242  0.4981238
3   0.24040196  0.38551819 -0.03356121  0.45662534 -0.02120728 -0.10880541  0.2844999
4   0.51266080  0.31708549  2.97973077  0.45535061  0.38053621 -0.02014608  1.1367885
5  -0.09501817 -0.13810894 -0.13535855 -0.15932739 -0.12167214 -0.11098063 -0.1532006
```

Given this subset of the interest data, we can already infer some characteristics of the clusters. **Cluster 3** is substantially above the mean interest level on all the sports. This suggests that this may be a group of **Athletes** per *The Breakfast Club* stereotype. **Cluster 1** includes the most mentions of "cheerleading," the word "hot," and is above the average level of football interest. Are these the so-called **Princesses**?

By continuing to examine the clusters in this way, it is possible to construct a table listing the dominant interests of each of the groups. In the following table, each cluster is shown with the features that most distinguish it from the other clusters, and The *Breakfast Club* identity that most accurately captures the group's characteristics.

Interestingly, **Cluster 5** is distinguished by the fact that it is unexceptional; its members had lower-than-average levels of interest in every measured activity. It is also the single largest group in terms of the number of members. One potential explanation is that these users created a profile on the website but never posted any interests.

Cluster 1 (N = 3,376)	Cluster 2 (N = 601)	Cluster 3 (N = 1,036)	Cluster 4 (N = 3,279)	Cluster 5 (N = 21,708)
swimming cheerleading cute sexy hot dance dress hair mall hollister abercrombie shopping clothes	band marching music rock	sports sex sexy hot kissed dance music band die death drunk drugs	basketball football soccer softball volleyball baseball sports god church Jesus bible	???
Princesses	Brains	Criminals	Athletes	Basket Cases

When sharing the results of a segmentation analysis, it is often helpful to apply informative labels that simplify and capture the essence of the groups such as *The Breakfast Club* typology applied here. The risk in adding such labels is that they can obscure the groups' nuances by stereotyping the group members. As such labels can bias our thinking, important patterns can be missed if labels are taken as the whole truth.

Given the table, a marketing executive would have a clear depiction of five types of teenage visitors to the social networking website. Based on these profiles, the executive could sell targeted advertising impressions to businesses with products relevant to one or more of the clusters. In the next section, we will see how the cluster labels can be applied back to the original population for such uses.

Step 5 – improving model performance

Because clustering creates new information, the performance of a clustering algorithm depends at least somewhat on both the quality of the clusters themselves as well as what is done with that information. In the preceding section, we already demonstrated that the five clusters provided useful and novel insights into the interests of teenagers. By that measure, the algorithm appears to be performing quite well. Therefore, we can now focus our effort on turning these insights into action.

We'll begin by applying the clusters back onto the full dataset. The `teen_clusters` object created by the `kmeans()` function includes a component named `cluster` that contains the cluster assignments for all 30,000 individuals in the sample. We can add this as a column on the `teens` data frame with the following command:

```
> teens$cluster <- teen_clusters$cluster
```

Given this new data, we can start to examine how the cluster assignment relates to individual characteristics. For example, here's the personal information for the first five teens in the SNS data:

```
> teens[1:5, c("cluster", "gender", "age", "friends")]
  cluster gender    age friends
1       5      M 18.982       7
2       3      F 18.801       0
3       5      M 18.335      69
4       5      F 18.875       0
5       4   <NA> 18.995      10
```

Using the `aggregate()` function, we can also look at the demographic characteristics of the clusters. The mean age does not vary much by cluster, which is not too surprising as these teen identities are often determined before high school. This is depicted as follows:

```
> aggregate(data = teens, age ~ cluster, mean)
  cluster      age
1       1 16.86497
2       2 17.39037
3       3 17.07656
4       4 17.11957
5       5 17.29849
```

On the other hand, there are some substantial differences in the proportion of females by cluster. This is a very interesting finding as we didn't use gender data to create the clusters, yet the clusters are still predictive of gender:

```
> aggregate(data = teens, female ~ cluster, mean)
  cluster    female
1       1 0.8381171
2       2 0.7250000
3       3 0.8378198
4       4 0.8027079
5       5 0.6994515
```

Recall that overall about 74 percent of the SNS users are female. **Cluster 1**, the so-called **Princesses**, is nearly 84 percent female, while **Cluster 2** and **Cluster 5** are only about 70 percent female. These disparities imply that there are differences in the interests that teen boys and girls discuss on their social networking pages.

Given our success in predicting gender, you might also suspect that the clusters are predictive of the number of friends the users have. This hypothesis seems to be supported by the data, which is as follows:

```
> aggregate(data = teens, friends ~ cluster, mean)
  cluster  friends
1       1 41.43054
2       2 32.57333
3       3 37.16185
4       4 30.50290
5       5 27.70052
```

On an average, **Princesses** have the most friends (41.4), followed by **Athletes** (37.2) and **Brains** (32.6). On the low end are **Criminals** (30.5) and **Basket Cases** (27.7). As with gender, the connection between a teen's number of friends and their predicted cluster is remarkable, given that we did not use the friendship data as an input to the clustering algorithm. Also interesting is the fact that the number of friends seems to be related to the stereotype of each clusters' high school popularity; the stereotypically popular groups tend to have more friends.

The association among group membership, gender, and number of friends suggests that the clusters can be useful predictors of behavior. Validating their predictive ability in this way may make the clusters an easier sell when they are pitched to the marketing team, ultimately improving the performance of the algorithm.

Summary

Our findings support the popular adage that "birds of a feather flock together." By using machine learning methods to cluster teenagers with others who have similar interests, we were able to develop a typology of teen identities that was predictive of personal characteristics, such as gender and the number of friends. These same methods can be applied to other contexts with similar results.

This chapter covered only the fundamentals of clustering. As a very mature machine learning method, there are many variants of the k-means algorithm as well as many other clustering algorithms that bring unique biases and heuristics to the task. Based on the foundation in this chapter, you will be able to understand and apply other clustering methods to new problems.

In the next chapter, we will begin to look at methods for measuring the success of a learning algorithm, which are applicable across many machine learning tasks. While our process has always devoted some effort to evaluating the success of learning, in order to obtain the highest degree of performance, it is crucial to be able to define and measure it in the strictest terms.

10
Evaluating Model Performance

When only the wealthy could afford education, tests and exams did not evaluate students' potential. Instead, teachers were judged for parents who wanted to know whether their children had learned enough to justify the instructors' wages. Obviously, this has changed over the years. Now, such evaluations are used to distinguish between high- and low-achieving students, filtering them into careers and other opportunities.

Given the significance of this process, a great deal of effort is invested in developing accurate student assessments. Fair assessments have a large number of questions that cover a wide breadth of topics and reward true knowledge over lucky guesses. They also require students to think about problems they have never faced before. Correct responses therefore indicate that students can generalize their knowledge more broadly.

The process of evaluating machine learning algorithms is very similar to the process of evaluating students. Since algorithms have varying strengths and weaknesses, tests should distinguish among the learners. It is also important to forecast how a learner will perform on future data.

This chapter provides the information needed to assess machine learners, such as:

- The reasons why predictive accuracy is not sufficient to measure performance, and the performance measures you might use instead
- Methods to ensure that the performance measures reasonably reflect a model's ability to predict or forecast unseen cases
- How to use R to apply these more useful measures and methods to the predictive models covered in the previous chapters

Just as the best way to learn a topic is to attempt to teach it to someone else, the process of teaching and evaluating machine learners will provide you with greater insight into the methods you've learned so far.

Measuring performance for classification

In the previous chapters, we measured classifier accuracy by dividing the proportion of correct predictions by the total number of predictions. This indicates the percentage of cases in which the learner is right or wrong. For example, suppose that for 99,990 out of 100,000 newborn babies a classifier correctly predicted whether they were a carrier of a treatable but potentially fatal genetic defect. This would imply an accuracy of 99.99 percent and an error rate of only 0.01 percent.

At first glance, this appears to be an extremely accurate classifier. However, it would be wise to collect additional information before trusting your child's life to the test. What if the genetic defect is found in only 10 out of every 100,000 babies? A test that predicts *no defect* regardless of the circumstances will be correct for 99.99 percent of all cases, but incorrect for 100 percent of the cases that matter most. In other words, even though the predictions are extremely accurate, the classifier is not very useful to prevent treatable birth defects.

This is one consequence of the **class imbalance problem**, which refers to the trouble associated with data having a large majority of records belonging to a single class.

Though there are many ways to measure a classifier's performance, the best measure is always the one that captures whether the classifier is successful at its intended purpose. It is crucial to define the performance measures for utility rather than raw accuracy. To this end, we will begin exploring a variety of alternative performance measures derived from the confusion matrix. Before we get started, however, we need to consider how to prepare a classifier for evaluation.

Working with classification prediction data in R

The goal of evaluating a classification model is to have a better understanding of how its performance will extrapolate to future cases. Since it is usually unfeasible to test a still-unproven model in a live environment, we typically simulate future conditions by asking the model to classify a dataset made of cases that resemble what it will be asked to do in the future. By observing the learner's responses to this examination, we can learn about its strengths and weaknesses.

Though we've evaluated classifiers in the prior chapters, it's worth reflecting on the types of data at our disposal:

- Actual class values
- Predicted class values
- Estimated probability of the prediction

The actual and predicted class values may be self-evident, but they are the key to evaluation. Just like a teacher uses an answer key to assess the student's answers, we need to know the correct answer for a machine learner's predictions. The goal is to maintain two vectors of data: one holding the correct or actual class values, and the other holding the predicted class values. Both vectors must have the same number of values stored in the same order. The predicted and actual values may be stored as separate R vectors or columns in a single R data frame.

Obtaining this data is easy. The actual class values come directly from the target feature in the test dataset. Predicted class values are obtained from the classifier built upon the training data, and applied to the test data. For most machine learning packages, this involves applying the `predict()` function to a model object and a data frame of test data, such as: `predicted_outcome <- predict(model, test_data)`.

Until now, we have only examined classification predictions using these two vectors of data. Yet most models can supply another piece of useful information. Even though the classifier makes a single prediction about each example, it may be more confident about some decisions than others. For instance, a classifier may be 99 percent certain that an SMS with the words "free" and "ringtones" is spam, but is only 51 percent certain that an SMS with the word "tonight" is spam. In both cases, the classifier classifies the message as spam, but it is far more certain about one decision than the other.

Studying these internal prediction probabilities provides useful data to evaluate a model's performance. If two models make the same number of mistakes, but one is more capable of accurately assessing its uncertainty, then it is a smarter model. It's ideal to fid a learner that is extremely confident when making a correct prediction, but timid in the face of doubt. The balance between confidence and caution is a key part of model evaluation.

Unfortunately, obtaining internal prediction probabilities can be tricky because the method to do so varies across classifiers. In general, for most classifiers, the predict() function is used to specify the desired type of prediction. To obtain a single predicted class, such as spam or ham, you typically set the type = "class" parameter. To obtain the prediction probability, the type parameter should be set to one of "prob", "posterior", "raw", or "probability" depending on the classifier used.

Nearly all of the classifiers presented in this book will provide prediction probabilities. The type parameter is included in the syntax box introducing each model.

For example, to output the predicted probabilities for the C5.0 classifier built in *Chapter 5, Divide and Conquer – Classification Using Decision Trees and Rules*, use the predict() function with type = "prob" as follows:

```
> predicted_prob <- predict(credit_model, credit_test, type = "prob")
```

To further illustrate the process of evaluating learning algorithms, let's look more closely at the performance of the SMS spam classification model developed in *Chapter 4, Probabilistic Learning – Classification Using Naive Bayes*. To output the naive Bayes predicted probabilities, use predict() with type = "raw" as follows:

```
> sms_test_prob <- predict(sms_classifier, sms_test, type = "raw")
```

In most cases, the predict() function returns a probability for each category of the outcome. For example, in the case of a two-outcome model like the SMS classifier, the predicted probabilities might be a matrix or data frame as shown here:

```
> head(sms_test_prob)
            ham            spam
[1,] 9.999995e-01 4.565938e-07
[2,] 9.999995e-01 4.540489e-07
[3,] 9.998418e-01 1.582360e-04
[4,] 9.999578e-01 4.223125e-05
[5,] 4.816137e-10 1.000000e+00
[6,] 9.997970e-01 2.030033e-04
```

Each line in this output shows the classifier's predicted probability of spam and ham, which always sum up to 1 because these are the only two outcomes. While constructing an evaluation dataset, it is important to ensure that you are using the correct probability for the class level of interest. To avoid confusion, in the case of a binary outcome, you might even consider dropping the vector for one of the two alternatives.

For convenience during the evaluation process, it can be helpful to construct a data frame containing the predicted class values, actual class values, as well as the estimated probabilities of interest.

The steps required to construct the evaluation dataset have been omitted for brevity, but are included in this chapter's code on the Packt Publishing website. To follow along with the examples here, download the sms_results.csv file, and load to a data frame using the sms_results <- read.csv("sms_results.csv") command.

The sms_results data frame is simple. It contains four vectors of 1,390 values. One vector contains values indicating the actual type of SMS message (spam or ham), one vector indicates the naive Bayes model's predicted type, and the third and fourth vectors indicate the probability that the message was spam or ham, respectively:

```
> head(sms_results)
  actual_type predict_type prob_spam prob_ham
1         ham          ham   0.00000  1.00000
2         ham          ham   0.00000  1.00000
3         ham          ham   0.00016  0.99984
4         ham          ham   0.00004  0.99996
5        spam         spam   1.00000  0.00000
6         ham          ham   0.00020  0.99980
```

For these six test cases, the predicted and actual SMS message types agree; the model predicted their status correctly. Furthermore, the prediction probabilities suggest that model was extremely confident about these predictions, because they all fall close to zero or one.

What happens when the predicted and actual values are further from zero and one? Using the subset() function, we can identify a few of these records. The following output shows test cases where the model estimated the probability of spam somewhere between 40 and 60 percent:

```
> head(subset(sms_results, prob_spam > 0.40 & prob_spam < 0.60))
     actual_type predict_type prob_spam prob_ham
377         spam          ham   0.47536  0.52464
717          ham         spam   0.56188  0.43812
1311         ham         spam   0.57917  0.42083
```

By the model's own admission, these were cases in which a correct prediction was virtually a coin flip. Yet all three predictions were wrong—an unlucky result. Let's look at a few more cases where the model was wrong:

```
> head(subset(sms_results, actual_type != predict_type))
    actual_type predict_type prob_spam prob_ham
```

53	spam	ham	0.00071	0.99929
59	spam	ham	0.00156	0.99844
73	spam	ham	0.01708	0.98292
76	spam	ham	0.00851	0.99149
184	spam	ham	0.01243	0.98757
332	spam	ham	0.00003	0.99997

These cases illustrate the important fact that a model can be extremely confident and yet it can be extremely wrong. All six of these test cases were spam that the classifier believed to have no less than a 98 percent chance of being ham.

In spite of such mistakes, is the model still useful? We can answer this question by applying various error metrics to the evaluation data. In fact, many such metrics are based on a tool we've already used extensively in the previous chapters.

A closer look at confusion matrices

A **confusion matrix** is a table that categorizes predictions according to whether they match the actual value. One of the table's dimensions indicates the possible categories of predicted values, while the other dimension indicates the same for actual values. Although we have only seen 2 x 2 confusion matrices so far, a matrix can be created for models that predict any number of class values. The following figure depicts the familiar confusion matrix for a two-class binary model as well as the 3 x 3 confusion matrix for a three-class model.

When the predicted value is the same as the actual value, it is a correct classification. Correct predictions fall on the diagonal in the confusion matrix (denoted by **O**). The off-diagonal matrix cells (denoted by **X**) indicate the cases where the predicted value differs from the actual value. These are incorrect predictions. The performance measures for classification models are based on the counts of predictions falling on and off the diagonal in these tables:

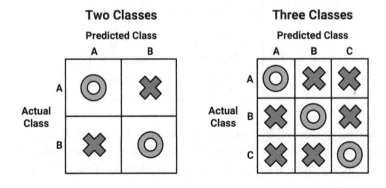

The most common performance measures consider the model's ability to discern one class versus all others. The class of interest is known as the **positive** class, while all others are known as **negative**.

 The use of the terms positive and negative is not intended to imply any value judgment (that is, good versus bad), nor does it necessarily suggest that the outcome is present or absent (such as birth defect versus none). The choice of the positive outcome can even be arbitrary, as in cases where a model is predicting categories such as sunny versus rainy or dog versus cat.

The relationship between the positive class and negative class predictions can be depicted as a 2 x 2 confusion matrix that tabulates whether predictions fall into one of the four categories:

- **True Positive (TP)**: Correctly classified as the class of interest
- **True Negative (TN)**: Correctly classified as not the class of interest
- **False Positive (FP)**: Incorrectly classified as the class of interest
- **False Negative (FN)**: Incorrectly classified as not the class of interest

For the spam classifier, the positive class is spam, as this is the outcome we hope to detect. We can then imagine the confusion matrix as shown in the following diagram:

Predicted to be Spam

	no	yes
no	**TN** True Negative	**FP** False Positive
Actually Spam **yes**	**FN** False Negative	**TP** True Positive

The confusion matrix, presented in this way, is the basis for many of the most important measures of model's performance. In the next section, we'll use this matrix to have a better understanding of what is meant by accuracy.

Using confusion matrices to measure performance

With the 2 x 2 confusion matrix, we can formalize our definition of prediction **accuracy** (sometimes called the **success rate**) as:

$$\text{accuracy} = \frac{TP + TN}{TP + TN + FP + FN}$$

In this formula, the terms *TP*, *TN*, *FP*, and *FN* refer to the number of times the model's predictions fell into each of these categories. The accuracy is therefore a proportion that represents the number of true positives and true negatives, divided by the total number of predictions.

The **error rate** or the proportion of the incorrectly classified examples is specified as:

$$\text{error rate} = \frac{FP + FN}{TP + TN + FP + FN} = 1 - \text{accuracy}$$

Notice that the error rate can be calculated as one minus the accuracy. Intuitively, this makes sense; a model that is correct 95 percent of the time is incorrect 5 percent of the time.

An easy way to tabulate a classifier's predictions into a confusion matrix is to use R's `table()` function. The command to create a confusion matrix for the SMS data is shown as follows. The counts in this table could then be used to calculate accuracy and other statistics:

```
> table(sms_results$actual_type, sms_results$predict_type)

        ham spam
  ham  1203    4
  spam   31  152
```

If you like to create a confusion matrix with a more informative output, the `CrossTable()` function in the `gmodels` package offers a customizable solution. If you recall, we first used this function in *Chapter 2, Managing and Understanding Data*. If you didn't install the package at that time, you will need to do so using the `install.packages("gmodels")` command.

By default, the `CrossTable()` output includes proportions in each cell that indicate the cell count as a percentage of table's row, column, or overall total counts. The output also includes row and column totals. As shown in the following code, the syntax is similar to the `table()` function:

```
> library(gmodels)
> CrossTable(sms_results$actual_type, sms_results$predict_type)
```

The result is a confusion matrix with a wealth of additional detail:

```
   Cell Contents
|-------------------------|
|                       N |
|   Chi-square contribution |
|             N / Row Total |
|             N / Col Total |
|           N / Table Total |
|-------------------------|


Total Observations in Table:  1390


                         | sms_results$predict_type
   sms_results$actual_type |      ham |     spam | Row Total |
-------------------------|----------|----------|-----------|
                     ham |     1203 |        4 |      1207 |
                         |   16.128 |  127.580 |           |
                         |    0.997 |    0.003 |     0.868 |
                         |    0.975 |    0.026 |           |
                         |    0.865 |    0.003 |           |
-------------------------|----------|----------|-----------|
                    spam |       31 |      152 |       183 |
                         |  106.377 |  841.470 |           |
                         |    0.169 |    0.831 |     0.132 |
                         |    0.025 |    0.974 |           |
                         |    0.022 |    0.109 |           |
-------------------------|----------|----------|-----------|
            Column Total |     1234 |      156 |      1390 |
                         |    0.888 |    0.112 |           |
-------------------------|----------|----------|-----------|
```

We've used `CrossTable()` in several of the previous chapters, so by now you should be familiar with the output. If you ever forget how to interpret the output, simply refer to the key (labeled `Cell Contents`), which provides the definition of each number in the table cells.

We can use the confusion matrix to obtain the accuracy and error rate. Since the accuracy is *(TP + TN) / (TP + TN + FP + FN)*, we can calculate it using following command:

```
> (152 + 1203) / (152 + 1203 + 4 + 31)
[1] 0.9748201
```

We can also calculate the error rate *(FP + FN) / (TP + TN + FP + FN)* as:

```
> (4 + 31) / (152 + 1203 + 4 + 31)
[1] 0.02517986
```

This is the same as one minus accuracy:

```
> 1 - 0.9748201
[1] 0.0251799
```

Although these calculations may seem simple, it is important to practice thinking about how the components of the confusion matrix relate to one another. In the next section, you will see how these same pieces can be combined in different ways to create a variety of additional performance measures.

Beyond accuracy – other measures of performance

Countless performance measures have been developed and used for specific purposes in disciplines as diverse as medicine, information retrieval, marketing, and signal detection theory, among others. Covering all of them could fill hundreds of pages and makes a comprehensive description infeasible here. Instead, we'll consider only some of the most useful and commonly cited measures in the machine learning literature.

The Classification and Regression Training package `caret` by Max Kuhn includes functions to compute many such performance measures. This package provides a large number of tools to prepare, train, evaluate, and visualize machine learning models and data. In addition to its use here, we will also employ `caret` extensively in *Chapter 11, Improving Model Performance*. Before proceeding, you will need to install the package using the `install.packages("caret")` command.

 For more information on `caret`, please refer to: Kuhn M. Building predictive models in R using the caret package. *Journal of Statistical Software*. 2008; 28.

The caret package adds yet another function to create a confusion matrix. As shown in the following command, the syntax is similar to table(), but with a minor difference. Because caret provides measures of model performance that consider the ability to classify the positive class, a positive parameter should be specified. In this case, since the SMS classifier is intended to detect spam, we will set positive = "spam" as follows:

```
> library(caret)
> confusionMatrix(sms_results$predict_type,
    sms_results$actual_type, positive = "spam")
```

This results in the following output:

```
Confusion Matrix and Statistics

          Reference
Prediction  ham spam
      ham  1203   31
      spam    4  152

               Accuracy : 0.9748
                 95% CI : (0.9652, 0.9824)
    No Information Rate : 0.8683
    P-Value [Acc > NIR] : < 2.2e-16

                  Kappa : 0.8825
 Mcnemar's Test P-Value : 1.109e-05

            Sensitivity : 0.8306
            Specificity : 0.9967
         Pos Pred Value : 0.9744
         Neg Pred Value : 0.9749
             Prevalence : 0.1317
         Detection Rate : 0.1094
   Detection Prevalence : 0.1122
      Balanced Accuracy : 0.9136

       'Positive' Class : spam
```

At the top of the output is a confusion matrix much like the one produced by the table() function, but transposed. The output also includes a set of performance measures. Some of these, like accuracy, are familiar, while many others are new. Let's take a look at few of the most important metrics.

The kappa statistic

The **kappa statistic** (labeled Kappa in the previous output) adjusts accuracy by accounting for the possibility of a correct prediction by chance alone. This is especially important for datasets with a severe class imbalance, because a classifier can obtain high accuracy simply by always guessing the most frequent class. The kappa statistic will only reward the classifier if it is correct more often than this simplistic strategy.

Kappa values range from 0 to a maximum of 1, which indicates perfect agreement between the model's predictions and the true values. Values less than one indicate imperfect agreement. Depending on how a model is to be used, the interpretation of the kappa statistic might vary. One common interpretation is shown as follows:

- Poor agreement = less than 0.20
- Fair agreement = 0.20 to 0.40
- Moderate agreement = 0.40 to 0.60
- Good agreement = 0.60 to 0.80
- Very good agreement = 0.80 to 1.00

It's important to note that these categories are subjective. While a "good agreement" may be more than adequate to predict someone's favorite ice cream flavor, "very good agreement" may not suffice if your goal is to identify birth defects.

 For more information on the previous scale, refer to: Landis JR, Koch GG. The measurement of observer agreement for categorical data. *Biometrics*. 1997; 33:159-174.

The following is the formula to calculate the kappa statistic. In this formula, *Pr(a)* refers to the proportion of the actual agreement and *Pr(e)* refers to the expected agreement between the classifier and the true values, under the assumption that they were chosen at random:

$$\kappa = \frac{\Pr(a) - \Pr(e)}{1 - \Pr(e)}$$

 There is more than one way to define the kappa statistic. The most common method described here uses **Cohen's kappa coefficient**, as described in the paper: Cohen J. A coefficient of agreement for nominal scales. *Education and Psychological Measurement*. 1960; 20:37-46.

These proportions are easy to obtain from a confusion matrix once you know where to look. Let's consider the confusion matrix for the SMS classification model created with the `CrossTable()` function, which is repeated here for convenience:

```
                        | sms_results$predict_type
  sms_results$actual_type |      ham |      spam | Row Total |
------------------------|----------|-----------|-----------|
                    ham |     1203 |         4 |      1207 |
                        |   16.128 |   127.580 |           |
                        |    0.997 |     0.003 |     0.868 |
                        |    0.975 |     0.026 |           |
                        |    0.865 |     0.003 |           |
------------------------|----------|-----------|-----------|
                   spam |       31 |       152 |       183 |
                        |  106.377 |   841.470 |           |
                        |    0.169 |     0.831 |     0.132 |
                        |    0.025 |     0.974 |           |
                        |    0.022 |     0.109 |           |
------------------------|----------|-----------|-----------|
           Column Total |     1234 |       156 |      1390 |
                        |    0.888 |     0.112 |           |
------------------------|----------|-----------|-----------|
```

Remember that the bottom value in each cell indicates the proportion of all instances falling into that cell. Therefore, to calculate the observed agreement *Pr(a)*, we simply add the proportion of all instances where the predicted type and actual SMS type agree. Thus, we can calculate *Pr(a)* as:

```
> pr_a <- 0.865 + 0.109
> pr_a
[1] 0.974
```

For this classifier, the observed and actual values agree 97.4 percent of the time — you will note that this is the same as the accuracy. The kappa statistic adjusts the accuracy relative to the expected agreement *Pr(e)*, which is the probability that the chance alone would lead the predicted and actual values to match, under the assumption that both are selected randomly according to the observed proportions.

To find these observed proportions, we can use the probability rules we learned in *Chapter 4, Probabilistic Learning – Classification Using Naive Bayes*. Assuming two events are independent (meaning that one does not affect the other), probability rules note that the probability of both occurring is equal to the product of the probabilities of each one occurring. For instance, we know that the probability of both choosing ham is:

*Pr(actual type is ham) * Pr(predicted type is ham)*

The probability of both choosing spam is:

*Pr(actual type is spam) * Pr(predicted type is spam)*

The probability that the predicted or actual type is spam or ham can be obtained from the row or column totals. For instance, *Pr(actual type is ham) = 0.868* and *Pr(predicted type is ham) = 0.888*.

Pr(e) is calculated as the sum of the probabilities that by chance the predicted and actual values agree that the message is either spam or ham. Recall that for mutually exclusive events (events that cannot happen simultaneously), the probability of either occurring is equal to the sum of their probabilities. Therefore, to obtain the final *Pr(e)*, we simply add both products, as shown in the following commands:

```
> pr_e <- 0.868 * 0.888 + 0.132 * 0.112

> pr_e

[1] 0.785568
```

Since *Pr(e)* is 0.786, by chance alone, we would expect the observed and actual values to agree about 78.6 percent of the time.

This means that we now have all the information needed to complete the kappa formula. Plugging the *Pr(a)* and *Pr(e)* values into the kappa formula, we find:

```
> k <- (pr_a - pr_e) / (1 - pr_e)

> k

[1] 0.8787494
```

The kappa is about 0.88, which agrees with the previous `confusionMatrix()` output from `caret` (the small difference is due to rounding). Using the suggested interpretation, we note that there is very good agreement between the classifier's predictions and the actual values.

There are a couple of R functions to calculate kappa automatically. The `Kappa()` function (be sure to note the capital 'K') in the Visualizing Categorical Data (`vcd`) package uses a confusion matrix of predicted and actual values. After installing the package by typing `install.packages("vcd")`, the following commands can be used to obtain kappa:

```
> library(vcd)

> Kappa(table(sms_results$actual_type, sms_results$predict_type))
             value        ASE
Unweighted 0.8825203 0.01949315
Weighted   0.8825203 0.01949315
```

We're interested in the unweighted kappa. The value 0.88 matches what we expected.

> The weighted kappa is used when there are varying degrees of agreement. For example, using a scale of cold, cool, warm, and hot, a value of warm agrees more with hot than it does with the value of cold. In the case of a two-outcome event, such as spam and ham, the weighted and unweighted kappa statistics will be identical.

The kappa2() function in the Inter-Rater Reliability (irr) package can be used to calculate kappa from the vectors of predicted and actual values stored in a data frame. After installing the package using the install.packages("irr") command, the following commands can be used to obtain kappa:

```
> kappa2(sms_results[1:2])
 Cohen's Kappa for 2 Raters (Weights: unweighted)

 Subjects = 1390
   Raters = 2
    Kappa = 0.883

        z = 33
  p-value = 0
```

The Kappa() and kappa2() functions report the same kappa statistic, so use whichever option you are more comfortable with.

> Be careful not to use the built-in kappa() function. It is completely unrelated to the kappa statistic reported previously!

Sensitivity and specificity

Finding a useful classifier often involves a balance between predictions that are overly conservative and overly aggressive. For example, an e-mail filter could guarantee to eliminate every spam message by aggressively eliminating nearly every ham message at the same time. On the other hand, guaranteeing that no ham message is inadvertently filtered might require us to allow an unacceptable amount of spam to pass through the filter. A pair of performance measures captures this tradeoff: sensitivity and specificity.

The **sensitivity** of a model (also called the **true positive rate**) measures the proportion of positive examples that were correctly classified. Therefore, as shown in the following formula, it is calculated as the number of true positives divided by the total number of positives, both correctly classified (the true positives) as well as incorrectly classified (the false negatives):

$$\text{sensitivity} = \frac{TP}{TP + FN}$$

The **specificity** of a model (also called the **true negative rate**) measures the proportion of negative examples that were correctly classified. As with sensitivity, this is computed as the number of true negatives, divided by the total number of negatives—the true negatives plus the false positives:

$$\text{specificity} = \frac{TN}{TN + FP}$$

Given the confusion matrix for the SMS classifier, we can easily calculate these measures by hand. Assuming that spam is the positive class, we can confirm that the numbers in the `confusionMatrix()` output are correct. For example, the calculation for sensitivity is:

```
> sens <- 152 / (152 + 31)
> sens
[1] 0.8306011
```

Similarly, for specificity we can calculate:

```
> spec <- 1203 / (1203 + 4)
> spec
[1] 0.996686
```

The `caret` package provides functions to calculate sensitivity and specificity directly from the vectors of predicted and actual values. Be careful that you specify the `positive` or `negative` parameter appropriately, as shown in the following lines:

```
> library(caret)
> sensitivity(sms_results$predict_type, sms_results$actual_type,
              positive = "spam")
```

```
[1]  0.8306011


> specificity(sms_results$predict_type, sms_results$actual_type,
                negative = "ham")
```
`[1]  0.996686`

Sensitivity and specificity range from 0 to 1, with values close to 1 being more desirable. Of course, it is important to find an appropriate balance between the two—a task that is often quite context-specific.

For example, in this case, the sensitivity of 0.831 implies that 83.1 percent of the spam messages were correctly classified. Similarly, the specificity of 0.997 implies that 99.7 percent of the nonspam messages were correctly classified or, alternatively, 0.3 percent of the valid messages were rejected as spam. The idea of rejecting 0.3 percent of valid SMS messages may be unacceptable, or it may be a reasonable trade-off given the reduction in spam.

Sensitivity and specificity provide tools for thinking about such trade-offs. Typically, changes are made to the model and different models are tested until you find one that meets a desired sensitivity and specificity threshold. Visualizations, such as those discussed later in this chapter, can also assist with understanding the trade-off between sensitivity and specificity.

Precision and recall

Closely related to sensitivity and specificity are two other performance measures related to compromises made in classification: precision and recall. Used primarily in the context of information retrieval, these statistics are intended to provide an indication of how interesting and relevant a model's results are, or whether the predictions are diluted by meaningless noise.

The **precision** (also known as the **positive predictive value**) is defined as the proportion of positive examples that are truly positive; in other words, when a model predicts the positive class, how often is it correct? A precise model will only predict the positive class in cases that are very likely to be positive. It will be very trustworthy.

Consider what would happen if the model was very imprecise. Over time, the results would be less likely to be trusted. In the context of information retrieval, this would be similar to a search engine such as Google returning unrelated results. Eventually, users would switch to a competitor like Bing. In the case of the SMS spam filter, high precision means that the model is able to carefully target only the spam while ignoring the ham.

$$precision = \frac{TP}{TP + FP}$$

On the other hand, **recall** is a measure of how complete the results are. As shown in the following formula, this is defined as the number of true positives over the total number of positives. You may have already recognized this as the same as sensitivity. However, in this case, the interpretation differs slightly. A model with a high recall captures a large portion of the positive examples, meaning that it has wide breadth. For example, a search engine with a high recall returns a large number of documents pertinent to the search query. Similarly, the SMS spam filter has a high recall if the majority of spam messages are correctly identified.

$$recall = \frac{TP}{TP + FN}$$

We can calculate precision and recall from the confusion matrix. Again, assuming that spam is the positive class, the precision is:

```
> prec <- 152 / (152 + 4)
> prec
[1]  0.974359
```

The recall is:

```
> rec <- 152 / (152 + 31)
> rec
[1]  0.8306011
```

The caret package can be used to compute either of these measures from the vectors of predicted and actual classes. Precision uses the posPredValue() function:

```
> library(caret)
> posPredValue(sms_results$predict_type, sms_results$actual_type,
              positive = "spam")
[1]  0.974359
```

While recall uses the `sensitivity()` function that we used earlier:

```
> sensitivity(sms_results$predict_type, sms_results$actual_type,
              positive = "spam")
[1] 0.8306011
```

Similar to the inherent trade-off between sensitivity and specificity, for most of the real-world problems, it is difficult to build a model with both high precision and high recall. It is easy to be precise if you target only the low-hanging fruit — the easy to classify examples. Similarly, it is easy for a model to have high recall by casting a very wide net, meaning that the model is overly aggressive in identifying the positive cases. In contrast, having both high precision and recall at the same time is very challenging. It is therefore important to test a variety of models in order to find the combination of precision and recall that will meet the needs of your project.

The F-measure

A measure of model performance that combines precision and recall into a single number is known as the **F-measure** (also sometimes called the **F$_1$ score** or **F-score**). The F-measure combines precision and recall using the **harmonic mean**, a type of average that is used for rates of change. The harmonic mean is used rather than the common arithmetic mean since both precision and recall are expressed as proportions between zero and one, which can be interpreted as rates. The following is the formula for the F-measure:

$$\text{F-measure} = \frac{2 \times \text{precision} \times \text{recall}}{\text{recall} + \text{precision}} = \frac{2 \times \text{TP}}{2 \times \text{TP} + \text{FP} + \text{FN}}$$

To calculate the F-measure, use the precision and recall values computed previously:

```
> f <- (2 * prec * rec) / (prec + rec)
> f
[1] 0.8967552
```

This comes out exactly the same as using the counts from the confusion matrix:

```
> f <- (2 * 152) / (2 * 152 + 4 + 31)
> f
[1] 0.8967552
```

Since the F-measure describes the model performance in a single number, it provides a convenient way to compare several models side by side. However, this assumes that equal weight should be assigned to precision and recall, an assumption that is not always valid. It is possible to calculate F-scores using different weights for precision and recall, but choosing the weights could be tricky at the best and arbitrary at worst. A better practice is to use measures such as the F-score in combination with methods that consider a model's strengths and weaknesses more globally, such as those described in the next section.

Visualizing performance trade-offs

Visualizations are helpful to understand the performance of machine learning algorithms in greater detail. Where statistics such as sensitivity and specificity or precision and recall attempt to boil model performance down to a single number, visualizations depict how a learner performs across a wide range of conditions.

Because learning algorithms have different biases, it is possible that two models with similar accuracy could have drastic differences in how they achieve their accuracy. Some models may struggle with certain predictions that others make with ease, while breezing through the cases that others cannot get right. Visualizations provide a method to understand these trade-offs, by comparing learners side by side in a single chart.

The ROCR package provides an easy-to-use suite of functions for visualizing for visualizing the performance of classification models. It includes functions for computing large set of the most common performance measures and visualizations. The ROCR website at `http://rocr.bioinf.mpi-sb.mpg.de/` includes a list of the full set of features as well as several examples on visualization capabilities. Before continuing, install the package using the `install.packages("ROCR")` command.

> For more information on the development of ROCR, see : Sing T, Sander O, Beerenwinkel N, Lengauer T. ROCR: visualizing classifier performance in R. *Bioinformatics*. 2005; 21:3940-3941.

To create visualizations with ROCR, two vectors of data are needed. The first must contain the predicted class values, and the second must contain the estimated probability of the positive class. These are used to create a prediction object that can be examined with the plotting functions of ROCR.

The prediction object for the SMS classifier requires the classifier's estimated spam probabilities and the actual class labels. These are combined using the `prediction()` function in the following lines:

```
> library(ROCR)
> pred <- prediction(predictions = sms_results$prob_spam,
                     labels = sms_results$actual_type)
```

Next, the `performance()` function will allow us to compute measures of performance from the `prediction` object we just created, which can then be visualized using the R `plot()` function. Given these three steps, a large variety of useful visualizations can be created.

ROC curves

The **Receiver Operating Characteristic (ROC) curve** is commonly used to examine the trade-off between the detection of true positives, while avoiding the false positives. As you might suspect from the name, ROC curves were developed by engineers in the field of communications. Around the time of World War II, radar and radio operators used ROC curves to measure a receiver's ability to discriminate between true signals and false alarms. The same technique is useful today to visualize the efficacy of machine learning models.

The characteristics of a typical ROC diagram are depicted in the following plot. Curves are defined on a plot with the proportion of true positives on the vertical axis and the proportion of false positives on the horizontal axis. Because these values are equivalent to sensitivity and (1 – specificity), respectively, the diagram is also known as a sensitivity/specificity plot:

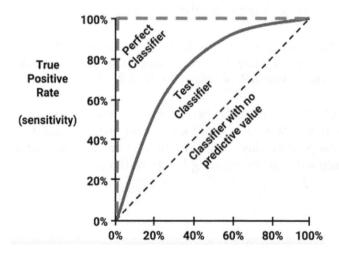

The points comprising ROC curves indicate the true positive rate at varying false positive thresholds. To create the curves, a classifier's predictions are sorted by the model's estimated probability of the positive class, with the largest values first. Beginning at the origin, each prediction's impact on the true positive rate and false positive rate will result in a curve tracing vertically (for a correct prediction) or horizontally (for an incorrect prediction).

To illustrate this concept, three hypothetical classifiers are contrasted in the previous plot. First, the diagonal line from the bottom-left to the top-right corner of the diagram represents a **classifier with no predictive value**. This type of classifier detects true positives and false positives at exactly the same rate, implying that the classifier cannot discriminate between the two. This is the baseline by which other classifiers may be judged. ROC curves falling close to this line indicate models that are not very useful. The **perfect classifier** has a curve that passes through the point at a 100 percent true positive rate and 0 percent false positive rate. It is able to correctly identify all of the positives before it incorrectly classifies any negative result. Most real-world classifiers are similar to the test classifier and they fall somewhere in the zone between perfect and useless.

The closer the curve is to the perfect classifier, the better it is at identifying positive values. This can be measured using a statistic known as the **area under the ROC curve** (abbreviated **AUC**). The AUC treats the ROC diagram as a two-dimensional square and measures the total area under the ROC curve. AUC ranges from 0.5 (for a classifier with no predictive value) to 1.0 (for a perfect classifier). A convention to interpret AUC scores uses a system similar to academic letter grades:

- **A**: Outstanding = 0.9 to 1.0
- **B**: Excellent/good = 0.8 to 0.9
- **C**: Acceptable/fair = 0.7 to 0.8
- **D**: Poor = 0.6 to 0.7
- **E**: No discrimination = 0.5 to 0.6

As with most scales similar to this, the levels may work better for some tasks than others; the categorization is somewhat subjective.

It's also worth noting that two ROC curves may be shaped very differently, yet have an identical AUC. For this reason, an AUC alone can be misleading. The best practice is to use AUC in combination with qualitative examination of the ROC curve.

Creating ROC curves with the `ROCR` package involves building a `performance` object from the `prediction` object we computed earlier. Since ROC curves plot true positive rates versus false positive rates, we simply call the `performance()` function while specifying the `tpr` and `fpr` measures, as shown in the following code:

```
> perf <- performance(pred, measure = "tpr", x.measure = "fpr")
```

Using the `perf` object, we can visualize the ROC curve with R's `plot()` function. As shown in the following code lines, many of the standard parameters to adjust the visualization can be used, such as `main` (to add a title), `col` (to change the line color), and `lwd` (to adjust the line width):

```
> plot(perf, main = "ROC curve for SMS spam filter",
        col = "blue", lwd = 3)
```

Although the `plot()` command is sufficient to create a valid ROC curve, it is helpful to add a reference line to indicate the performance of a classifier with no predictive value.

To plot such a line, we'll use the `abline()` function. This function can be used to specify a line in the slope-intercept form, where a is the intercept and b is the slope. Since we need an identity line that passes through the origin, we'll set the intercept to a = 0 and the slope to b = 1, as shown in the following plot. The `lwd` parameter adjusts the line thickness, while the `lty` parameter adjusts the type of line. For example, `lty = 2` indicates a dashed line:

```
> abline(a = 0, b = 1, lwd = 2, lty = 2)
```

The end result is an ROC plot with a dashed reference line:

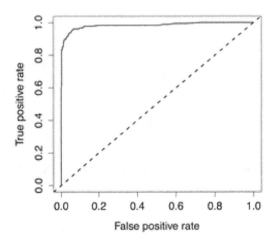

Qualitatively, we can see that this ROC curve appears to occupy the space at the top-left corner of the diagram, which suggests that it is closer to a perfect classifier than the dashed line representing a useless classifier. To confirm this quantitatively, we can use the ROCR package to calculate the AUC. To do so, we first need to create another `performance` object, this time specifying `measure = "auc"` as shown in the following code:

```
> perf.auc <- performance(pred, measure = "auc")
```

Since `perf.auc` is an R object (specifically known as an S4 object), we need to use a special type of notation to access the values stored within. S4 objects hold information in positions known as slots. The `str()` function can be used to see all of an object's slots:

```
> str(perf.auc)
Formal class 'performance' [package "ROCR"] with 6 slots
  ..@ x.name      : chr "None"
  ..@ y.name      : chr "Area under the ROC curve"
  ..@ alpha.name  : chr "none"
  ..@ x.values    : list()
  ..@ y.values    :List of 1
  .. ..$ : num 0.984
  ..@ alpha.values: list()
```

Notice that slots are prefixed with the @ symbol. To access the AUC value, which is stored as a list in the `y.values` slot, we can use the @ notation along with the `unlist()` function, which simplifies lists to a vector of numeric values:

```
> unlist(perf.auc@y.values)
[1] 0.9835862
```

The AUC for the SMS classifier is 0.98, which is extremely high. But how do we know whether the model is just as likely to perform well for another dataset? In order to answer such questions, we need to have a better understanding of how far we can extrapolate a model's predictions beyond the test data.

Estimating future performance

Some R machine learning packages present confusion matrices and performance measures during the model building process. The purpose of these statistics is to provide insight about the model's **resubstitution error**, which occurs when the training data is incorrectly predicted in spite of the model being built directly from this data. This information can be used as a rough diagnostic to identify obviously poor performers.

The resubstitution error is not a very useful marker of future performance. For example, a model that used rote memorization to perfectly classify every training instance with zero resubstitution error would be unable to generalize its predictions to data it has never seen before. For this reason, the error rate on the training data can be extremely optimistic about a model's future performance.

Instead of relying on resubstitution error, a better practice is to evaluate a model's performance on data it has not yet seen. We used this approach in previous chapters when we split the available data into a set for training and a set for testing. In some cases, however, it is not always ideal to create training and test datasets. For instance, in a situation where you have only a small pool of data, you might not want to reduce the sample any further.

Fortunately, there are other ways to estimate a model's performance on unseen data. The `caret` package we used to calculate performance measures also offers a number of functions to estimate future performance. If you are following the R code examples and haven't already installed the `caret` package, please do so. You will also need to load the package to the R session, using the `library(caret)` command.

The holdout method

The procedure of partitioning data into training and test datasets that we used in previous chapters is known as the **holdout method**. As shown in the following diagram, the **training dataset** is used to generate the model, which is then applied to the **test dataset** to generate predictions for evaluation. Typically, about one-third of the data is held out for testing, and two-thirds is used for training, but this proportion can vary depending on the amount of available data. To ensure that the training and test data do not have systematic differences, their examples are randomly divided into the two groups.

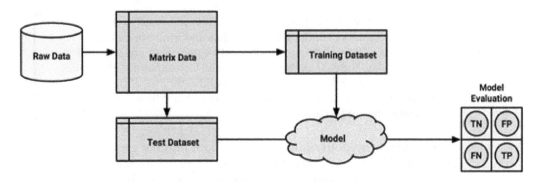

For the holdout method to result in a truly accurate estimate of the future performance, at no time should the performance on the test dataset be allowed to influence the model. It is easy to unknowingly violate this rule by choosing the best model based upon the results of repeated testing. For example, suppose we built several models on the training data, and selected the one with the highest accuracy on the test data. Because we have cherry-picked the best result, the test performance is not an unbiased measure of the performance on unseen data.

To avoid this problem, it is better to divide the original data so that in addition to the training datasets and the test datasets, a **validation dataset** is available. The validation dataset would be used for iterating and refining the model or models chosen, leaving the test dataset to be used only once as a final step to report an estimated error rate for future predictions. A typical split between training, test, and validation would be 50 percent, 25 percent, and 25 percent, respectively.

A keen reader will note that holdout test data was used in the previous chapters to both evaluate models and improve model performance. This was done for illustrative purposes, but it would indeed violate the rule as stated previously. Consequently, the model performance statistics shown were not valid estimates of future performance on unseen data and the process could have been more accurately termed validation.

A simple method to create holdout samples uses random number generators to assign records to partitions. This technique was first used in *Chapter 5, Divide and Conquer – Classification Using Decision Trees and Rules* to create training and test datasets.

If you'd like to follow along with the following examples, download the credit.csv dataset from the Packt Publishing website, and load to a data frame using the credit <- read.csv("credit.csv") command.

Suppose we have a data frame named credit with 1000 rows of data. We can divide it into three partitions as follows. First, we create a vector of randomly ordered row IDs from 1 to 1000 using the runif() function, which by default generates a specified number of random values between 0 and 1. The runif() function gets its name from the random uniform distribution, which was discussed in *Chapter 2, Managing and Understanding Data*.

```
> random_ids <- order(runif(1000))
```

The order() used here returns a vector indicating the rank order of the 1,000 random numbers. For example, order(c(0.5, 0.25, 0.75, 0.1)) returns the sequence 4 2 1 3 because the smallest number (0.1) appears fourth, the second smallest (0.25) appears second, and so on.

We can use the resulting random IDs to divide the credit data frame into 500, 250, and 250 records comprising the training, validation, and test datasets:

```
> credit_train <- credit[random_ids[1:500], ]
> credit_validate <- credit[random_ids[501:750], ]
> credit_test <- credit[random_ids[751:1000], ]
```

One problem with holdout sampling is that each partition may have a larger or smaller proportion of some classes. In certain cases, particularly those in which a class is a very small proportion of the dataset, this can lead a class to be omitted from the training dataset. This is a significant problem, because the model will not be able to learn this class.

In order to reduce the chance of this occurring, a technique called **stratified random sampling** can be used. Although in the long run a random sample should contain roughly the same proportion of each class value as the full dataset, stratified random sampling guarantees that the random partitions have nearly the same proportion of each class as the full dataset, even when some classes are small.

The `caret` package provides a `createDataPartition()` function that will create partitions based on stratified holdout sampling. The code to create a stratified sample of training and test data for the `credit` dataset is shown in the following commands. To use the function, a vector of the class values must be specified (here, `default` refers to whether a loan went into default) in addition to a parameter `p`, which specifies the proportion of instances to be included in the partition. The `list = FALSE` parameter prevents the result from being stored in the list format:

```
> in_train <- createDataPartition(credit$default, p = 0.75,
    list = FALSE)
> credit_train <- credit[in_train, ]
> credit_test <- credit[-in_train, ]
```

The `in_train` vector indicates row numbers included in the training sample. We can use these row numbers to select examples for the `credit_train` data frame. Similarly, by using a negative symbol, we can use the rows not found in the `in_train` vector for the `credit_test` dataset.

Although it distributes the classes evenly, stratified sampling does not guarantee other types of representativeness. Some samples may have too many or few difficult cases, easy-to-predict cases, or outliers. This is especially true for smaller datasets, which may not have a large enough portion of such cases to be divided among training and test sets.

In addition to potentially biased samples, another problem with the holdout method is that substantial portions of data must be reserved to test and validate the model. Since these data cannot be used to train the model until its performance has been measured, the performance estimates are likely to be overly conservative.

> Since models trained on larger datasets generally perform better, a common practice is to retrain the model on the full set of data (that is, training plus test and validation) after a final model has been selected and evaluated.

A technique called **repeated holdout** is sometimes used to mitigate the problems of randomly composed training datasets. The repeated holdout method is a special case of the holdout method that uses the average result from several random holdout samples to evaluate a model's performance. As multiple holdout samples are used, it is less likely that the model is trained or tested on nonrepresentative data. We'll expand on this idea in the next section.

Cross-validation

The repeated holdout is the basis of a technique known as **k-fold cross-validation** (or **k-fold CV**), which has become the industry standard for estimating model performance. Rather than taking repeated random samples that could potentially use the same record more than once, k-fold CV randomly divides the data into *k* to completely separate random partitions called **folds**.

Although *k* can be set to any number, by far, the most common convention is to use **10-fold cross-validation** (10-fold CV). Why 10 folds? The reason is that the empirical evidence suggests that there is little added benefit in using a greater number. For each of the 10 folds (each comprising 10 percent of the total data), a machine learning model is built on the remaining 90 percent of data. The fold's matching 10 percent sample is then used for model evaluation. After the process of training and evaluating the model has occurred for 10 times (with 10 different training/testing combinations), the average performance across all the folds is reported.

> An extreme case of k-fold CV is the **leave-one-out method**, which performs k-fold CV using a fold for each of the data's examples. This ensures that the greatest amount of data is used to train the model. Although this may seem useful, it is so computationally expensive that it is rarely used in practice.

Datasets for cross-validation can be created using the createFolds() function in the caret package. Similar to the stratified random holdout sampling, this function will attempt to maintain the same class balance in each of the folds as in the original dataset. The following is the command to create 10 folds:

```
> folds <- createFolds(credit$default, k = 10)
```

The result of the createFolds() function is a list of vectors storing the row numbers for each of the requested k = 10 folds. We can peek at the contents, using str():

```
> str(folds)
List of 10
 $ Fold01: int [1:100] 1 5 12 13 19 21 25 32 36 38 ...
 $ Fold02: int [1:100] 16 49 78 81 84 93 105 108 128 134 ...
```

```
$ Fold03: int [1:100] 15 48 60 67 76 91 102 109 117 123 ...
$ Fold04: int [1:100] 24 28 59 64 75 85 95 97 99 104 ...
$ Fold05: int [1:100] 9 10 23 27 29 34 37 39 53 61 ...
$ Fold06: int [1:100] 4 8 41 55 58 103 118 121 144 146 ...
$ Fold07: int [1:100] 2 3 7 11 14 33 40 45 51 57 ...
$ Fold08: int [1:100] 17 30 35 52 70 107 113 129 133 137 ...
$ Fold09: int [1:100] 6 20 26 31 42 44 46 63 79 101 ...
$ Fold10: int [1:100] 18 22 43 50 68 77 80 88 106 111 ...
```

Here, we see that the first fold is named `Fold01` and stores `100` integers, indicating the 100 rows in the credit data frame for the first fold. To create training and test datasets to build and evaluate a model, an additional step is needed. The following commands show how to create data for the first fold. We'll assign the selected 10 percent to the test dataset, and use the negative symbol to assign the remaining 90 percent to the training dataset:

```
> credit01_test <- credit[folds$Fold01, ]
> credit01_train <- credit[-folds$Fold01, ]
```

To perform the full 10-fold CV, this step would need to be repeated a total of 10 times; building a model and then calculating the model's performance each time. At the end, the performance measures would be averaged to obtain the overall performance. Thankfully, we can automate this task by applying several of the techniques we've learned earlier.

To demonstrate the process, we'll estimate the kappa statistic for a C5.0 decision tree model of the credit data using 10-fold CV. First, we need to load some R packages: `caret` (to create the folds), `C50` (for the decision tree), and `irr` (to calculate kappa). The latter two packages were chosen for illustrative purposes; if you desire, you can use a different model or a different performance measure along with the same series of steps.

```
> library(caret)
> library(C50)
> library(irr)
```

Next, we'll create a list of 10 folds as we have done previously. The `set.seed()` function is used here to ensure that the results are consistent if the same code is run again:

```
> set.seed(123)
> folds <- createFolds(credit$default, k = 10)
```

Finally, we will apply a series of identical steps to the list of folds using the `lapply()` function. As shown in the following code, because there is no existing function that does exactly what we need, we must define our own function to pass to `lapply()`. Our custom function divides the credit data frame into training and test data, builds a decision tree using the `C5.0()` function on the training data, generates a set of predictions from the test data, and compares the predicted and actual values using the `kappa2()` function:

```
> cv_results <- lapply(folds, function(x) {
    credit_train <- credit[-x, ]
    credit_test <- credit[x, ]
    credit_model <- C5.0(default ~ ., data = credit_train)
    credit_pred <- predict(credit_model, credit_test)
    credit_actual <- credit_test$default
    kappa <- kappa2(data.frame(credit_actual, credit_pred))$value
    return(kappa)
  })
```

The resulting kappa statistics are compiled into a list stored in the `cv_results` object, which we can examine using `str()`:

```
> str(cv_results)
List of 10
 $ Fold01: num 0.343
 $ Fold02: num 0.255
 $ Fold03: num 0.109
 $ Fold04: num 0.107
 $ Fold05: num 0.338
 $ Fold06: num 0.474
 $ Fold07: num 0.245
 $ Fold08: num 0.0365
 $ Fold09: num 0.425
 $ Fold10: num 0.505
```

There's just one more step remaining in the 10-fold CV process: we must calculate the average of these 10 values. Although you will be tempted to type `mean(cv_results)`, because `cv_results` is not a numeric vector, the result would be an error. Instead, use the `unlist()` function, which eliminates the list structure, and reduces `cv_results` to a numeric vector. From here, we can calculate the mean kappa as expected:

```
> mean(unlist(cv_results))
[1] 0.283796
```

This kappa statistic is fairly low, corresponding to "fair" on the interpretation scale, which suggests that the credit scoring model performs only marginally better than random chance. In the next chapter, we'll examine automated methods based on 10-fold CV that can assist us in improving the performance of this model.

Perhaps the current gold standard method to reliably estimate model performance is **repeated k-fold CV**. As you might guess from the name, this involves repeatedly applying k-fold CV and averaging the results. A common strategy is to perform 10-fold CV ten times. Although it is computationally intensive, it provides a very robust estimate.

Bootstrap sampling

A slightly less frequently used alternative to k-fold CV is known as **bootstrap sampling**, the **bootstrap** or **bootstrapping** for short. Generally speaking, these refer to the statistical methods of using random samples of data to estimate the properties of a larger set. When this principle is applied to machine learning model performance, it implies the creation of several randomly selected training and test datasets, which are then used to estimate performance statistics. The results from the various random datasets are then averaged to obtain a final estimate of future performance.

So, what makes this procedure different from k-fold CV? Whereas cross-validation divides the data into separate partitions in which each example can appear only once, the bootstrap allows examples to be selected multiple times through a process of **sampling with replacement**. This means that from the original dataset of n examples, the bootstrap procedure will create one or more new training datasets that will also contain n examples, some of which are repeated. The corresponding test datasets are then constructed from the set of examples that were not selected for the respective training datasets.

Using sampling with replacement as described previously, the probability that any given instance is included in the training dataset is 63.2 percent. Consequently, the probability of any instance being in the test dataset is 36.8 percent. In other words, the training data represents only 63.2 percent of available examples, some of which are repeated. In contrast to 10-fold CV, which uses 90 percent of the examples for training, the bootstrap sample is less representative of the full dataset.

Because a model trained on only 63.2 percent of the training data is likely to perform worse than a model trained on a larger training set, the bootstrap's performance estimates may be substantially lower than what would be obtained when the model is later trained on the full dataset. A special case of bootstrapping known as the **0.632 bootstrap** accounts for this by calculating the final performance measure as a function of performance on both the training data (which is overly optimistic) and the test data (which is overly pessimistic). The final error rate is then estimated as:

$$\text{error} = 0.632 \times \text{error}_{\text{test}} + 0.368 \times \text{error}_{\text{train}}$$

One advantage of bootstrap over cross-validation is that it tends to work better with very small datasets. Additionally, bootstrap sampling has applications beyond performance measurement. In particular, in the next chapter we'll learn how the principles of bootstrap sampling can be used to improve model performance.

Summary

This chapter presented a number of the most common measures and techniques for evaluating the performance of machine learning classification models. Although accuracy provides a simple method to examine how often a model is correct, this can be misleading in the case of rare events because the real-life cost of such events may be inversely proportional to how frequently they appear.

A number of measures based on confusion matrices better capture the balance among the costs of various types of errors. Closely examining the tradeoffs between sensitivity and specificity, or precision and recall can be a useful tool for thinking about the implications of errors in the real world. Visualizations such as the ROC curve are also helpful to this end.

It is also worth mentioning that sometimes the best measure of a model's performance is to consider how well it meets, or doesn't meet, other objectives. For instance, you may need to explain a model's logic in simple language, which would eliminate some models from consideration. Additionally, even if it performs very well, a model that is too slow or difficult to scale to a production environment is completely useless.

An obvious extension of measuring performance is to identify automated ways to find the best models for a particular task. In the next chapter, we will build upon our work so far to investigate ways to make smarter models by systematically iterating, refining, and combining learning algorithms.

11
Improving Model Performance

When a sports team falls short of meeting its goal — whether the goal is to obtain an Olympic gold medal, a league championship, or a world record time — it must search for possible improvements. Imagine that you're the team's coach. How would you spend your practice sessions? Perhaps you'd direct the athletes to train harder or train differently in order to maximize every bit of their potential. Or, you might emphasize better teamwork, utilizing the athletes' strengths and weaknesses more smartly.

Now imagine that you're training a world champion machine learning algorithm. Perhaps you hope to compete in data mining competitions such as those posted on Kaggle (`http://www.kaggle.com/competitions`). Maybe you simply need to improve business results. Where do you begin? Although the context differs, the strategies one uses to improve sports team performance can also be used to improve the performance of statistical learners.

As the coach, it is your job to find the combination of training techniques and teamwork skills that allow you to meet your performance goals. This chapter builds upon the material covered throughout this book to introduce a set of techniques for improving the predictive performance of machine learners. You will learn:

- How to automate model performance tuning by systematically searching for the optimal set of training conditions
- The methods for combining models into groups that use teamwork to tackle tough learning tasks
- How to apply a variant of decision trees, which has quickly become popular due to its impressive performance

None of these methods will be successful for every problem. Yet, looking at the winning entries to machine learning competitions, you'll likely find that at least one of them has been employed. To be competitive, you too will need to add these skills to your repertoire.

Tuning stock models for better performance

Some learning problems are well-suited to the stock models presented in the previous chapters. In such cases, it may not be necessary to spend much time iterating and refining the model; it may perform well enough as it is. On the other hand, some problems are inherently more difficult. The underlying concepts to be learned may be extremely complex, requiring an understanding of many subtle relationships, or it may be affected by random variation, making it difficult to define the signal within the noise.

Developing models that perform extremely well on difficult problems is every bit an art as it is a science. Sometimes a bit of intuition is helpful when trying to identify areas where performance can be improved. In other cases, finding improvements will require a brute-force, trial and error approach. Of course, the process of searching numerous possible improvements can be aided by the use of automated programs.

In *Chapter 5, Divide and Conquer – Classification Using Decision Trees and Rules*, we attempted a difficult problem: identifying loans that were likely to enter into default. Although we were able to use performance tuning methods to obtain a respectable classification accuracy of about 82 percent, upon a more careful examination in *Chapter 10, Evaluating Model Performance*, we realized that the high accuracy was a bit misleading. In spite of the reasonable accuracy, the kappa statistic was only about 0.28, which suggested that the model was actually performing somewhat poorly. In this section, we'll revisit the credit scoring model to see whether we can improve the results.

 To follow along with the examples, download the credit. csv file from the Packt Publishing website and save it to your R working directory. Load the file into R using the command credit <- read.csv("credit.csv").

You will recall that we first used a stock C5.0 decision tree to build the classifier for the credit data. We then attempted to improve its performance by adjusting the `trials` parameter to increase the number of boosting iterations. By increasing the number of iterations from the default of 1 up to the value of 10, we were able to increase the model's accuracy. This process of adjusting the model options to identify the best fit is called **parameter tuning**.

Parameter tuning is not limited to decision trees. For instance, we tuned k-NN models when we searched for the best value of *k*. We also tuned neural networks and support vector machines as we adjusted the number of nodes or hidden layers, or chose different kernel functions. Most machine learning algorithms allow the adjustment of at least one parameter, and the most sophisticated models offer a large number of ways to tweak the model fit. Although this allows the model to be tailored closely to the learning task, the complexity of all the possible options can be daunting. A more systematic approach is warranted.

Using caret for automated parameter tuning

Rather than choosing arbitrary values for each of the model's parameters—a task that is not only tedious, but also somewhat unscientific—it is better to conduct a search through many possible parameter values to find the best combination.

The `caret` package, which we used extensively in *Chapter 10, Evaluating Model Performance*, provides tools to assist with automated parameter tuning. The core functionality is provided by a `train()` function that serves as a standardized interface for over 175 different machine learning models for both classification and regression tasks. By using this function, it is possible to automate the search for optimal models using a choice of evaluation methods and metrics.

 Do not feel overwhelmed by the large number of models—we've already covered many of them in the earlier chapters. Others are simple variants or extensions of the base concepts. Given what you've learned so far, you should be confident that you have the ability to understand all of the available methods.

Automated parameter tuning requires you to consider three questions:

- What type of machine learning model (and specific implementation) should be trained on the data?

- Which model parameters can be adjusted, and how extensively should they be tuned to find the optimal settings?

- What criteria should be used to evaluate the models to find the best candidate?

Answering the first question involves finding a well-suited match between the machine learning task and one of the 175 models. Obviously, this requires an understanding of the breadth and depth of machine learning models. It can also help to work through a process of elimination. Nearly half of the models can be eliminated depending on whether the task is classification or numeric prediction; others can be excluded based on the format of the data or the need to avoid black box models, and so on. In any case, there's also no reason you can't try several approaches and compare the best results of each.

Addressing the second question is a matter largely dictated by the choice of model, since each algorithm utilizes a unique set of parameters. The available tuning parameters for the predictive models covered in this book are listed in the following table. Keep in mind that although some models have additional options not shown, only those listed in the table are supported by `caret` for automatic tuning.

Model	Learning Task	Method name	Parameters
k-Nearest Neighbors	Classification	`knn`	`k`
Naive Bayes	Classification	`nb`	`fL, usekernel`
Decision Trees	Classification	`C5.0`	`model, trials, winnow`
OneR Rule Learner	Classification	`OneR`	None
RIPPER Rule Learner	Classification	`JRip`	`NumOpt`
Linear Regression	Regression	`lm`	None
Regression Trees	Regression	`rpart`	`cp`
Model Trees	Regression	`M5`	`pruned, smoothed, rules`
Neural Networks	Dual use	`nnet`	`size, decay`
Support Vector Machines (Linear Kernel)	Dual use	`svmLinear`	`C`
Support Vector Machines (Radial Basis Kernel)	Dual use	`svmRadial`	`C, sigma`
Random Forests	Dual use	`rf`	`mtry`

 For a complete list of the models and corresponding tuning parameters covered by `caret`, refer to the table provided by package author Max Kuhn at `http://topepo.github.io/caret/modelList.html`.

If you ever forget the tuning parameters for a particular model, the `modelLookup()` function can be used to find them. Simply supply the method name, as illustrated here for the C5.0 model:

```
> modelLookup("C5.0")
  model parameter                    label forReg forClass probModel
1  C5.0    trials # Boosting Iterations  FALSE     TRUE      TRUE
2  C5.0     model            Model Type  FALSE     TRUE      TRUE
3  C5.0    winnow                Winnow  FALSE     TRUE      TRUE
```

The goal of automatic tuning is to search a set of candidate models comprising a matrix, or **grid**, of parameter combinations. Because it is impractical to search every conceivable combination, only a subset of possibilities is used to construct the grid. By default, `caret` searches at most three values for each of the p parameters. This means that at most 3^p candidate models will be tested. For example, by default, the automatic tuning of k-Nearest Neighbors will compare $3^1 = 3$ candidate models with `k=5`, `k=7`, and `k=9`. Similarly, tuning a decision tree will result in a comparison of up to 27 different candidate models, comprising the grid of $3^3 = 27$ combinations of `model`, `trials`, and `winnow` settings. In practice, however, only 12 models are actually tested. This is because the `model` and `winnow` parameters can only take two values (`tree` versus `rules` and `TRUE` versus `FALSE`, respectively), which makes the grid size $3 * 2 * 2 = 12$.

 Since the default search grid may not be ideal for your learning problem, `caret` allows you to provide a custom search grid defined by a simple command, which we will cover later.

The third and final step in automatic model tuning involves identifying the best model among the candidates. This uses the methods discussed in *Chapter 10, Evaluating Model Performance*, such as the choice of resampling strategy for creating training and test datasets and the use of model performance statistics to measure the predictive accuracy.

All of the resampling strategies and many of the performance statistics we've learned are supported by `caret`. These include statistics such as accuracy and kappa (for classifiers) and R-squared or RMSE (for numeric models). Cost-sensitive measures such as sensitivity, specificity, and area under the ROC curve (AUC) can also be used, if desired.

By default, `caret` will select the candidate model with the largest value of the desired performance measure. As this practice sometimes results in the selection of models that achieve marginal performance improvements via large increases in model complexity, alternative model selection functions are provided.

Given the wide variety of options, it is helpful that many of the defaults are reasonable. For instance, `caret` will use prediction accuracy on a bootstrap sample to choose the best performer for classification models. Beginning with these default values, we can then tweak the `train()` function to design a wide variety of experiments.

Creating a simple tuned model

To illustrate the process of tuning a model, let's begin by observing what happens when we attempt to tune the credit scoring model using the `caret` package's default settings. From there, we will adjust the options to our liking.

The simplest way to tune a learner requires you to only specify a model type via the `method` parameter. Since we used C5.0 decision trees previously with the credit model, we'll continue our work by optimizing this learner. The basic `train()` command for tuning a C5.0 decision tree using the default settings is as follows:

```
> library(caret)
> set.seed(300)
> m <- train(default ~ ., data = credit, method = "C5.0")
```

First, the `set.seed()` function is used to initialize R's random number generator to a set starting position. You may recall that we used this function in several prior chapters. By setting the `seed` parameter (in this case to the arbitrary number 300), the random numbers will follow a predefined sequence. This allows simulations that use random sampling to be repeated with identical results—a very helpful feature if you are sharing code or attempting to replicate a prior result.

Next, we define a tree as `default ~ .` using the R formula interface. This models loan default status (`yes` or `no`) using all of the other features in the `credit` data frame. The parameter `method = "C5.0"` tells `caret` to use the C5.0 decision tree algorithm.

After you've entered the preceding command, there may be a significant delay (dependent upon your computer's capabilities) as the tuning process occurs. Even though this is a fairly small dataset, a substantial amount of calculation must occur. R must repeatedly generate random samples of data, build decision trees, compute performance statistics, and evaluate the result.

The result of the experiment is saved in an object named `m`. If you would like to examine the object's contents, the `str(m)` command will list all the associated data, but this can be quite overwhelming. Instead, simply type the name of the object for a condensed summary of the results. For instance, typing `m` yields the following output (note that labels have been added for clarity):

```
   1000 samples
     16 predictor
      2 classes: 'no', 'yes'

   No pre-processing
   Resampling: Bootstrapped (25 reps)

   Summary of sample sizes: 1000, 1000, 1000, 1000, 1000, 1000, ...

   Resampling results across tuning parameters:

   model  winnow  trials  Accuracy   Kappa      Accuracy SD  Kappa SD
   rules  FALSE   1       0.6847204  0.2578421  0.02558775   0.05622302
   rules  FALSE   10      0.7112829  0.3094601  0.02087257   0.04585890
   rules  FALSE   20      0.7221976  0.3260145  0.01977334   0.04512083
   rules  TRUE    1       0.6888432  0.2549192  0.02683844   0.05695277
   rules  TRUE    10      0.7113716  0.3038075  0.01947701   0.04484956
   rules  TRUE    20      0.7233222  0.3266866  0.01843672   0.03714053
   tree   FALSE   1       0.6769653  0.2285102  0.03027647   0.07001131
   tree   FALSE   10      0.7222552  0.2880662  0.02061900   0.05601918
   tree   FALSE   20      0.7297858  0.3067404  0.02007556   0.05616826
   tree   TRUE    1       0.6771020  0.2219533  0.02703456   0.05955907
   tree   TRUE    10      0.7173312  0.2777136  0.01700633   0.04358591
   tree   TRUE    20      0.7285714  0.3058474  0.01497973   0.04145128
```

```
   Accuracy was used to select the optimal model using  the largest value.
   The final values used for the model were trials = 20, model = tree
   and winnow = FALSE.
```

The labels highlight four main components in the output:

1. **A brief description of the input dataset**: If you are familiar with your data and have applied the `train()` function correctly, this information should not be surprising.

2. **A report of the preprocessing and resampling methods applied**: Here, we see that 25 bootstrap samples, each including 1,000 examples, were used to train the models.

3. **A list of the candidate models evaluated**: In this section, we can confirm that 12 different models were tested, based on the combinations of three C5.0 tuning parameters—`model`, `trials`, and `winnow`. The average and standard deviation of the accuracy and kappa statistics for each candidate model are also shown.

4. **The choice of the best model**: As the footnote describes, the model with the largest accuracy was selected. This was the model that used a decision tree with 20 trials and the setting `winnow = FALSE`.

After identifying the best model, the `train()` function uses its tuning parameters to build a model on the full input dataset, which is stored in the `m` list object as `m$finalModel`. In most cases, you will not need to work directly with the `finalModel` sub-object. Instead, simply use the `predict()` function with the `m` object as follows:

```
> p <- predict(m, credit)
```

The resulting vector of predictions works as expected, allowing us to create a confusion matrix that compares the predicted and actual values:

```
> table(p, credit$default)
```

```
p       no yes
  no   700   2
  yes    0 298
```

Of the 1,000 examples used for training the final model, only two were misclassified. However, it is very important to note that since the model was built on both the training and test data, this accuracy is optimistic and thus, should not be viewed as indicative of performance on unseen data. The bootstrap estimate of 73 percent (shown in the summary output) is a more realistic estimate of future performance.

Using the `train()` and `predict()` functions also offers a couple of benefits in addition to the automatic parameter tuning.

First, any data preparation steps applied by the `train()` function will be similarly applied to the data used for generating predictions. This includes transformations such as centering and scaling as well as imputation of missing values. Allowing `caret` to handle the data preparation will ensure that the steps that contributed to the best model's performance will remain in place when the model is deployed.

Second, the `predict()` function provides a standardized interface for obtaining predicted class values and class probabilities, even for model types that ordinarily would require additional steps to obtain this information. The predicted classes are provided by default:

```
> head(predict(m, credit))
[1] no  yes no  no  yes no
Levels: no yes
```

To obtain the estimated probabilities for each class, use the `type = "prob"` parameter:

```
> head(predict(m, credit, type = "prob"))
          no         yes
1 0.9606970 0.03930299
2 0.1388444 0.86115561
3 1.0000000 0.00000000
4 0.7720279 0.22797208
5 0.2948062 0.70519385
6 0.8583715 0.14162851
```

Even in cases where the underlying model refers to the prediction probabilities using a different string (for example, `"raw"` for a `naiveBayes` model), the `predict()` function will translate `type = "prob"` to the appropriate string behind the scenes.

Customizing the tuning process

The decision tree we created previously demonstrates the `caret` package's ability to produce an optimized model with minimal intervention. The default settings allow optimized models to be created easily. However, it is also possible to change the default settings to something more specific to a learning task, which may assist with unlocking the upper echelon of performance.

Each step in the model selection process can be customized. To illustrate this flexibility, let's modify our work on the credit decision tree to mirror the process we had used in *Chapter 10, Evaluating Model Performance*. If you remember, we had estimated the kappa statistic using 10-fold cross-validation. We'll do the same here, using kappa to optimize the boosting parameter of the decision tree. Note that decision tree boosting was previously covered in *Chapter 5, Divide and Conquer – Classification Using Decision Trees and Rules*, and will also be covered in greater detail later this chapter.

The `trainControl()` function is used to create a set of configuration options known as a **control object**, which guides the `train()` function. These options allow for the management of model evaluation criteria such as the resampling strategy and the measure used for choosing the best model. Although this function can be used to modify nearly every aspect of a tuning experiment, we'll focus on the two important parameters: `method` and `selectionFunction`.

 If you're eager for more details, you can use the `?trainControl` command for a list of all the parameters.

For the `trainControl()` function, the `method` parameter is used to set the resampling method, such as holdout sampling or k-fold cross-validation. The following table lists the possible method types as well as any additional parameters for adjusting the sample size and number of iterations. Although the default options for these resampling methods follow popular convention, you may choose to adjust these depending upon the size of your dataset and the complexity of your model.

Resampling method	Method name	Additional options and default values
Holdout sampling	LGOCV	`p = 0.75` (training data proportion)
k-fold cross-validation	cv	`number = 10` (number of folds)
Repeated k-fold cross-validation	repeatedcv	`number = 10` (number of folds)
		`repeats = 10` (number of iterations)
Bootstrap sampling	boot	`number = 25` (resampling iterations)
0.632 bootstrap	boot632	`number = 25` (resampling iterations)
Leave-one-out cross-validation	LOOCV	None

The `selectionFunction` parameter is used to specify the function that will choose the optimal model among the various candidates. Three such functions are included. The `best` function simply chooses the candidate with the best value on the specified performance measure. This is used by default. The other two functions are used to choose the most parsimonious, or simplest, model that is within a certain threshold of the best model's performance. The `oneSE` function chooses the simplest candidate within one standard error of the best performance, and `tolerance` uses the simplest candidate within a user-specified percentage.

 Some subjectivity is involved with the `caret` package's ranking of models by simplicity. For information on how models are ranked, see the help page for the selection functions by typing `?best` at the R command prompt.

To create a control object named `ctrl` that uses 10-fold cross-validation and the `oneSE` selection function, use the following command (note that `number = 10` is included only for clarity; since this is the default value for `method = "cv"`, it could have been omitted):

```
> ctrl <- trainControl(method = "cv", number = 10,
                       selectionFunction = "oneSE")
```

We'll use the result of this function shortly.

In the meantime, the next step in defining our experiment is to create the grid of parameters to optimize. The grid must include a column named for each parameter in the desired model, prefixed by a period. It must also include a row for each desired combination of parameter values. Since we are using a C5.0 decision tree, this means we'll need columns named .model, .trials, and .winnow. For other machine learning models, refer to the table presented earlier in this chapter or use the modelLookup() function to lookup the parameters as described previously.

Rather than filling this data frame cell by cell—a tedious task if there are many possible combinations of parameter values—we can use the expand.grid() function, which creates data frames from the combinations of all the values supplied. For example, suppose we would like to hold constant model = "tree" and winnow = "FALSE" while searching eight different values of trials. This can be created as:

```
> grid <- expand.grid(.model = "tree",
                       .trials = c(1, 5, 10, 15, 20, 25, 30, 35),
                       .winnow = "FALSE")
```

The resulting grid data frame contains *1 * 8 * 1 = 8* rows:

```
> grid
  .model .trials .winnow
1   tree       1   FALSE
2   tree       5   FALSE
3   tree      10   FALSE
4   tree      15   FALSE
5   tree      20   FALSE
6   tree      25   FALSE
7   tree      30   FALSE
8   tree      35   FALSE
```

The train() function will build a candidate model for evaluation using each row's combination of model parameters.

Given this search grid and the control list created previously, we are ready to run a thoroughly customized train() experiment. As we did earlier, we'll set the random seed to the arbitrary number 300 in order to ensure repeatable results. But this time, we'll pass our control object and tuning grid while adding a parameter metric = "Kappa", indicating the statistic to be used by the model evaluation function—in this case, "oneSE". The full command is as follows:

```
> set.seed(300)
> m <- train(default ~ ., data = credit, method = "C5.0",
```

```
        metric = "Kappa",
        trControl = ctrl,
        tuneGrid = grid)
```

This results in an object that we can view by typing its name:

```
> m
```

```
1000 samples
  16 predictor
   2 classes: 'no', 'yes'

No pre-processing
Resampling: Cross-Validated (10 fold)

Summary of sample sizes: 900, 900, 900, 900, 900, 900, ...

Resampling results across tuning parameters:

    trials  Accuracy  Kappa       Accuracy SD  Kappa SD
    1       0.724     0.3124461   0.02547330   0.05897140
    5       0.713     0.2921760   0.02110819   0.06018851
    10      0.719     0.2947271   0.03107339   0.06719720
    15      0.721     0.3009258   0.01969207   0.05105480
    20      0.717     0.2929875   0.02790858   0.07912362
    25      0.728     0.3150336   0.03224903   0.09367152
    30      0.729     0.3104144   0.02766867   0.08069045
    35      0.741     0.3389908   0.03142893   0.09352673

Tuning parameter 'model' was held constant at a value of tree
Tuning parameter 'winnow' was held constant at a value of FALSE
Kappa was used to select the optimal model using  the one SE rule.
The final values used for the model were trials = 1, model = tree
and winnow = FALSE.
```

Although much of the output is similar to the automatically tuned model, there are a few differences of note. As 10-fold cross-validation was used, the sample size to build each candidate model was reduced to 900 rather than the 1,000 used in the bootstrap. As we requested, eight candidate models were tested. Additionally, because model and winnow were held constant, their values are no longer shown in the results; instead, they are listed as a footnote.

The best model here differs quite significantly from the prior trial. Before, the best model used `trials = 20`, whereas here, it used `trials = 1`. This seemingly odd finding is due to the fact that we used the `oneSE` rule rather the `best` rule to select the optimal model. Even though the 35-trial model offers the best raw performance according to kappa, the 1-trial model offers nearly the same performance with a much simpler form. Not only are simple models more computationally efficient, but they also reduce the chance of overfitting the training data.

Improving model performance with meta-learning

As an alternative to increasing the performance of a single model, it is possible to combine several models to form a powerful team. Just as the best sports teams have players with complementary rather than overlapping skillsets, some of the best machine learning algorithms utilize teams of complementary models. Since a model brings a unique bias to a learning task, it may readily learn one subset of examples, but have trouble with another. Therefore, by intelligently using the talents of several diverse team members, it is possible to create a strong team of multiple weak learners.

This technique of combining and managing the predictions of multiple models falls into a wider set of **meta-learning** methods defining techniques that involve learning how to learn. This includes anything from simple algorithms that gradually improve performance by iterating over design decisions—for instance, the automated parameter tuning used earlier in this chapter—to highly complex algorithms that use concepts borrowed from evolutionary biology and genetics for self-modifying and adapting to learning tasks.

For the remainder of this chapter, we'll focus on meta-learning only as it pertains to modeling a relationship between the predictions of several models and the desired outcome. The teamwork-based techniques covered here are quite powerful, and are used quite often to build more effective classifiers.

Understanding ensembles

Suppose you were a contestant on a television trivia show that allowed you to choose a panel of five friends to assist you with answering the final question for the million-dollar prize. Most people would try to stack the panel with a diverse set of subject matter experts. A panel containing professors of literature, science, history, and art, along with a current pop-culture expert would be a safely well-rounded group. Given their breadth of knowledge, it would be unlikely to find a question that stumps the group.

The meta-learning approach that utilizes a similar principle of creating a varied team of experts is known as an **ensemble**. All the ensemble methods are based on the idea that by combining multiple weaker learners, a stronger learner is created. The various ensemble methods can be distinguished, in large part, by the answers to these two questions:

- How are the weak learning models chosen and/or constructed?
- How are the weak learners' predictions combined to make a single final prediction?

When answering these questions, it can be helpful to imagine the ensemble in terms of the following process diagram; nearly all ensemble approaches follow this pattern:

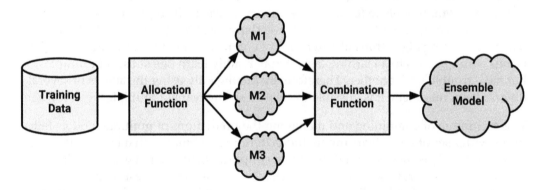

First, input training data is used to build a number of models. The **allocation function** dictates how much of the training data each model receives. Do they each receive the full training dataset or merely a sample? Do they each receive every feature or a subset?

Although the ideal ensemble includes a diverse set of models, the allocation function can increase diversity by artificially varying the input data to bias the resulting learners, even if they are the same type. For instance, it might use bootstrap sampling to construct unique training datasets or pass on a different subset of features or examples to each model. On the other hand, if the ensemble already includes a diverse set of algorithms—such as a neural network, a decision tree, and a k-NN classifier—the allocation function might pass the data on to each algorithm relatively unchanged.

After the models are constructed, they can be used to generate a set of predictions, which must be managed in some way. The **combination function** governs how disagreements among the predictions are reconciled. For example, the ensemble might use a majority vote to determine the final prediction, or it could use a more complex strategy such as weighting each model's votes based on its prior performance.

Some ensembles even utilize another model to learn a combination function from various combinations of predictions. For example, suppose that when *M1* and *M2* both vote yes, the actual class value is usually no. In this case, the ensemble could learn to ignore the vote of *M1* and *M2* when they agree. This process of using the predictions of several models to train a final arbiter model is known as **stacking**.

One of the benefits of using ensembles is that they may allow you to spend less time in pursuit of a single best model. Instead, you can train a number of reasonably strong candidates and combine them. Yet, convenience isn't the only reason why ensemble-based methods continue to rack up wins in machine learning competitions; ensembles also offer a number of performance advantages over single models:

- **Better generalizability to future problems**: As the opinions of several learners are incorporated into a single final prediction, no single bias is able to dominate. This reduces the chance of overfitting to a learning task.

- **Improved performance on massive or miniscule datasets**: Many models run into memory or complexity limits when an extremely large set of features or examples are used, making it more efficient to train several small models than a single full model. Conversely, ensembles also do well on the smallest datasets because resampling methods such as bootstrapping are inherently a part of many ensemble designs. Perhaps most importantly, it is often possible to train an ensemble in parallel using distributed computing methods.

- **The ability to synthesize data from distinct domains**: Since there is no one-size-fits-all learning algorithm, the ensemble's ability to incorporate evidence from multiple types of learners is increasingly important as complex phenomena rely on data drawn from diverse domains.

- **A more nuanced understanding of difficult learning tasks**: Real-world phenomena are often extremely complex with many interacting intricacies. Models that divide the task into smaller portions are likely to more accurately capture subtle patterns that a single global model might miss.

None of these benefits would be very helpful if you weren't able to easily apply ensemble methods in R, and there are many packages available to do just that. Let's take a look at several of the most popular ensemble methods and how they can be used to improve the performance of the credit model we've been working on.

Bagging

One of the first ensemble methods to gain widespread acceptance used a technique called **bootstrap aggregating** or **bagging** for short. As described by Leo Breiman in 1994, bagging generates a number of training datasets by bootstrap sampling the original training data. These datasets are then used to generate a set of models using a single learning algorithm. The models' predictions are combined using voting (for classification) or averaging (for numeric prediction).

 For additional information on bagging, refer to Breiman L. *Bagging predictors*. Machine Learning. 1996; 24:123-140.

Although bagging is a relatively simple ensemble, it can perform quite well as long as it is used with relatively **unstable** learners, that is, those generating models that tend to change substantially when the input data changes only slightly. Unstable models are essential in order to ensure the ensemble's diversity in spite of only minor variations between the bootstrap training datasets. For this reason, bagging is often used with decision trees, which have the tendency to vary dramatically given minor changes in the input data.

The `ipred` package offers a classic implementation of bagged decision trees. To train the model, the `bagging()` function works similar to many of the models used previously. The `nbagg` parameter is used to control the number of decision trees voting in the ensemble (with a default value of 25). Depending on the difficulty of the learning task and the amount of training data, increasing this number may improve the model's performance up to a limit. The downside is that this comes at the expense of additional computational expense because a large number of trees may take some time to train.

After installing the `ipred` package, we can create the ensemble as follows. We'll stick to the default value of 25 decision trees:

```
> library(ipred)
> set.seed(300)
> mybag <- bagging(default ~ ., data = credit, nbagg = 25)
```

The resulting model works as expected with the `predict()` function:

```
> credit_pred <- predict(mybag, credit)
> table(credit_pred, credit$default)


credit_pred  no yes
        no  699   2
       yes    1 298
```

Given the preceding results, the model seems to have fit the training data extremely well. To see how this translates into future performance, we can use the bagged trees with 10-fold CV using the `train()` function in the `caret` package. Note that the method name for the `ipred` bagged trees function is `treebag`:

```
> library(caret)
> set.seed(300)
> ctrl <- trainControl(method = "cv", number = 10)
> train(default ~ ., data = credit, method = "treebag",
        trControl = ctrl)


Bagged CART


1000 samples
  16 predictor
   2 classes: 'no', 'yes'


No pre-processing
Resampling: Cross-Validated (10 fold)


Summary of sample sizes: 900, 900, 900, 900, 900, 900, ...


Resampling results


  Accuracy  Kappa      Accuracy SD  Kappa SD
  0.735     0.3297726  0.03439961   0.08590462
```

The kappa statistic of 0.33 for this model suggests that the bagged tree model performs at least as well as the best C5.0 decision tree we tuned earlier in this chapter. This illustrates the power of ensemble methods; a set of simple learners working together can outperform very sophisticated models.

To get beyond bags of decision trees, the `caret` package also provides a more general `bag()` function. It includes native support for a handful of models, though it can be adapted to other types with a bit of additional effort. The `bag()` function uses a control object to configure the bagging process. It requires the specification of three functions: one for fitting the model, one for making predictions, and one for aggregating the votes.

For example, suppose we wanted to create a bagged support vector machine model, using the `ksvm()` function in the `kernlab` package we used in *Chapter 7, Black Box Methods – Neural Networks and Support Vector Machines*. The `bag()` function requires us to provide functionality for training the SVMs, making predictions, and counting votes.

Rather than writing these ourselves, the `caret` package's built-in `svmBag` list object supplies three functions we can use for this purpose:

```
> str(svmBag)
List of 3
 $ fit       :function (x, y, ...)
 $ pred      :function (object, x)
 $ aggregate:function (x, type = "class")
```

By looking at the `svmBag$fit` function, we see that it simply calls the `ksvm()` function from the `kernlab` package and returns the result:

```
> svmBag$fit
function (x, y, ...)
{
    library(kernlab)
    out <- ksvm(as.matrix(x), y, prob.model = is.factor(y), ...)
    out
}
<environment: namespace:caret>
```

The `pred` and `aggregate` functions for `svmBag` are also similarly straightforward. By studying these functions and creating your own in the same format, it is possible to use bagging with any machine learning algorithm you would like.

The caret package also includes example objects for bags of naive Bayes models (nbBag), decision trees (ctreeBag), and neural networks (nnetBag).

Applying the three functions in the svmBag list, we can create a bagging control object:

```
> bagctrl <- bagControl(fit = svmBag$fit,
                        predict = svmBag$pred,
                        aggregate = svmBag$aggregate)
```

By using this with the train() function and the training control object (ctrl), defined earlier, we can evaluate the bagged SVM model as follows (note that the kernlab package is required for this to work; you will need to install it if you have not done so previously):

```
> set.seed(300)
> svmbag <- train(default ~ ., data = credit, "bag",
                 trControl = ctrl, bagControl = bagctrl)
> svmbag


Bagged Model

1000 samples
  16 predictors
   2 classes: 'no', 'yes'


No pre-processing
Resampling: Cross-Validation (10 fold)


Summary of sample sizes: 900, 900, 900, 900, 900, 900, ...


Resampling results

  Accuracy  Kappa      Accuracy SD  Kappa SD
  0.728     0.2929505  0.04442222   0.1318101


Tuning parameter 'vars' was held constant at a value of 35
```

Given that the kappa statistic is below 0.30, it seems that the bagged SVM model performs worse than the bagged decision tree model. It's worth pointing out that the standard deviation of the kappa statistic is fairly large compared to the bagged decision tree model. This suggests that the performance varies substantially among the folds in the cross-validation. Such variation may imply that the performance might be improved further by upping the number of models in the ensemble.

Boosting

Another common ensemble-based method is called **boosting** because it boosts the performance of weak learners to attain the performance of stronger learners. This method is based largely on the work of Robert Schapire and Yoav Freund, who have published extensively on the topic.

> For additional information on boosting, refer to Schapire RE, Freund Y. *Boosting: Foundations and Algorithms*. Cambridge, MA, The MIT Press; 2012.

Similar to bagging, boosting uses ensembles of models trained on resampled data and a vote to determine the final prediction. There are two key distinctions. First, the resampled datasets in boosting are constructed specifically to generate complementary learners. Second, rather than giving each learner an equal vote, boosting gives each learner's vote a weight based on its past performance. Models that perform better have greater influence over the ensemble's final prediction.

Boosting will result in performance that is often quite better and certainly no worse than the best of the models in the ensemble. Since the models in the ensemble are built to be complementary, it is possible to increase ensemble performance to an arbitrary threshold simply by adding additional classifiers to the group, assuming that each classifier performs better than random chance. Given the obvious utility of this finding, boosting is thought to be one of the most significant discoveries in machine learning.

> Although boosting can create a model that meets an arbitrarily low error rate, this may not always be reasonable in practice. For one, the performance gains are incrementally smaller as additional learners are added, making some thresholds practically infeasible. Additionally, the pursuit of pure accuracy may result in the model being overfitted to the training data and not generalizable to unseen data.

A boosting algorithm called **AdaBoost** or **adaptive boosting** was proposed by Freund and Schapire in 1997. The algorithm is based on the idea of generating weak learners that iteratively learn a larger portion of the difficult-to-classify examples by paying more attention (that is, giving more weight) to frequently misclassified examples.

Beginning from an unweighted dataset, the first classifier attempts to model the outcome. Examples that the classifier predicted correctly will be less likely to appear in the training dataset for the following classifier, and conversely, the difficult-to-classify examples will appear more frequently. As additional rounds of weak learners are added, they are trained on data with successively more difficult examples. The process continues until the desired overall error rate is reached or performance no longer improves. At that point, each classifier's vote is weighted according to its accuracy on the training data on which it was built.

Though boosting principles can be applied to nearly any type of model, the principles are most commonly used with decision trees. We already used boosting in this way in *Chapter 5, Divide and Conquer – Classification Using Decision Trees and Rules*, as a method to improve the performance of a C5.0 decision tree.

The **AdaBoost.M1** algorithm provides another tree-based implementation of AdaBoost for classification. The AdaBoost.M1 algorithm can be found in the `adabag` package.

 For more information about the `adabag` package, refer to Alfaro E, Gamez M, Garcia N. *adabag – an R package for classification with boosting and bagging*. Journal of Statistical Software. 2013; 54:1-35.

Let's create an `AdaBoost.M1` classifier for the credit data. The general syntax for this algorithm is similar to other modeling techniques:

```
> set.seed(300)
> m_adaboost <- boosting(default ~ ., data = credit)
```

As usual, the `predict()` function is applied to the resulting object to make predictions:

```
> p_adaboost <- predict(m_adaboost, credit)
```

Departing from convention, rather than returning a vector of predictions, this returns an object with information about the model. The predictions are stored in a sub-object called `class`:

```
> head(p_adaboost$class)
[1] "no"  "yes" "no"  "no"  "yes" "no"
```

A confusion matrix can be found in the `confusion` sub-object:

```
> p_adaboost$confusion
                  Observed Class
Predicted Class   no yes
            no   700   0
            yes    0 300
```

Did you notice that the AdaBoost model made no mistakes? Before you get your hopes up, remember that the preceding confusion matrix is based on the model's performance on the training data. Since boosting allows the error rate to be reduced to an arbitrarily low level, the learner simply continued until it made no more errors. This likely resulted in overfitting on the training dataset.

For a more accurate assessment of performance on unseen data, we need to use another evaluation method. The `adabag` package provides a simple function to use 10-fold CV:

```
> set.seed(300)
> adaboost_cv <- boosting.cv(default ~ ., data = credit)
```

Depending on your computer's capabilities, this may take some time to run, during which it will log each iteration to screen. After it completes, we can view a more reasonable confusion matrix:

```
> adaboost_cv$confusion
                  Observed Class
Predicted Class   no yes
            no   594 151
            yes 106 149
```

We can find the kappa statistic using the `vcd` package as described in *Chapter 10, Evaluating Model Performance*.

```
> library(vcd)
> Kappa(adaboost_cv$confusion)
                value       ASE
Unweighted 0.3606965 0.0323002
Weighted   0.3606965 0.0323002
```

With a kappa of about 0.36, this is our best-performing credit scoring model yet. Let's see how it compares to one last ensemble method.

 The AdaBoost.M1 algorithm can be tuned in `caret` by specifying `method = "AdaBoost.M1"`.

Random forests

Another ensemble-based method called **random forests** (or **decision tree forests**) focuses only on ensembles of decision trees. This method was championed by Leo Breiman and Adele Cutler, and combines the base principles of bagging with random feature selection to add additional diversity to the decision tree models. After the ensemble of trees (the forest) is generated, the model uses a vote to combine the trees' predictions.

 For more detail on how random forests are constructed, refer to Breiman L. *Random Forests*. Machine Learning. 2001; 45:5-32.

Random forests combine versatility and power into a single machine learning approach. As the ensemble uses only a small, random portion of the full feature set, random forests can handle extremely large datasets, where the so-called "curse of dimensionality" might cause other models to fail. At the same time, its error rates for most learning tasks are on par with nearly any other method.

 Although the term "Random Forests" is trademarked by Breiman and Cutler, the term is sometimes used colloquially to refer to any type of decision tree ensemble. A pedant would use the more general term "decision tree forests" except when referring to the specific implementation by Breiman and Cutler.

It's worth noting that relative to other ensemble-based methods, random forests are quite competitive and offer key advantages relative to the competition. For instance, random forests tend to be easier to use and less prone to overfitting. The following table lists the general strengths and weaknesses of random forest models:

Strengths	Weaknesses
• An all-purpose model that performs well on most problems • Can handle noisy or missing data as well as categorical or continuous features • Selects only the most important features • Can be used on data with an extremely large number of features or examples	• Unlike a decision tree, the model is not easily interpretable • May require some work to tune the model to the data

Due to their power, versatility, and ease of use, random forests are quickly becoming one of the most popular machine learning methods. Later on in this chapter, we'll compare a random forest model head-to-head against the boosted C5.0 tree.

Training random forests

Though there are several packages to create random forests in R, the `randomForest` package is perhaps the implementation that is most faithful to the specification by Breiman and Cutler, and is also supported by `caret` for automated tuning. The syntax for training this model is as follows:

Random forest syntax

using the `randomForest()` function in the `randomForest` package

Building the classifier:

```
m <- randomForest(train, class, ntree = 500, mtry = sqrt(p))
```

- `train` is a data frame containing training data
- `class` is a factor vector with the class for each row in the training data
- `ntree` is an integer specifying the number of trees to grow
- `mtry` is an optional integer specifying the number of features to randomly select at each split (uses `sqrt(p)` by default, where p is the number of features in the data)

The function will return a random forest object that can be used to make predictions.

Making predictions:

```
p <- predict(m, test, type = "response")
```

- `m` is a model trained by the `randomForest()` function
- `test` is a data frame containing test data with the same features as the training data used to build the classifier
- `type` is either `"response"`, `"prob"`, or `"votes"` and is used to indicate whether the predictions vector should contain the predicted class, the predicted probabilities, or a matrix of vote counts, respectively.

The function will return predictions according to the value of the `type` parameter.

Example:

```
credit_model <- randomForest(credit_train, loan_default)
credit_prediction <- predict(credit_model, credit_test)
```

By default, the `randomForest()` function creates an ensemble of 500 trees that consider `sqrt(p)` random features at each split, where p is the number of features in the training dataset and `sqrt()` refers to R's square root function. Whether or not these default parameters are appropriate depends on the nature of the learning task and training data. Generally, more complex learning problems and larger datasets (either more features or more examples) work better with a larger number of trees, though this needs to be balanced with the computational expense of training more trees.

The goal of using a large number of trees is to train enough so that each feature has a chance to appear in several models. This is the basis of the `sqrt(p)` default value for the `mtry` parameter; using this value limits the features sufficiently so that substantial random variation occurs from tree-to-tree. For example, since the credit data has 16 features, each tree would be limited to splitting on four features at any time.

Let's see how the default `randomForest()` parameters work with the credit data. We'll train the model just as we did with other learners. Again, the `set.seed()` function ensures that the result can be replicated:

```
> library(randomForest)
> set.seed(300)
> rf <- randomForest(default ~ ., data = credit)
```

To look at a summary of the model's performance, we can simply type the resulting object's name:

```
> rf

Call:
 randomForest(formula = default ~ ., data = credit)
               Type of random forest: classification
                     Number of trees: 500
No. of variables tried at each split: 4

        OOB estimate of  error rate: 23.8%
Confusion matrix:
     no yes class.error
no   640  60  0.08571429
yes 178 122  0.59333333
```

The output notes that the random forest included 500 trees and tried four variables at each split, just as we expected. At first glance, you might be alarmed at the seemingly poor performance according to the confusion matrix—the error rate of 23.8 percent is far worse than the resubstitution error of any of the other ensemble methods so far. However, this confusion matrix does not show resubstitution error. Instead, it reflects the **out-of-bag error rate** (listed in the output as `OOB estimate of error rate`), which unlike resubstitution error, is an unbiased estimate of the test set error. This means that it should be a fairly reasonable estimate of future performance.

The out-of-bag estimate is computed during the construction of the random forest. Essentially, any example not selected for a single tree's bootstrap sample can be used to test the model's performance on unseen data. At the end of the forest construction, the predictions for each example each time it was held out are tallied, and a vote is taken to determine the final prediction for the example. The total error rate of such predictions becomes the out-of-bag error rate.

Evaluating random forest performance

As mentioned previously, the randomForest() function is supported by caret, which allows us to optimize the model while, at the same time, calculating performance measures beyond the out-of-bag error rate. To make things interesting, let's compare an auto-tuned random forest to the best auto-tuned boosted C5.0 model we've developed. We'll treat this experiment as if we were hoping to identify a candidate model for submission to a machine learning competition.

We must first load caret and set our training control options. For the most accurate comparison of model performance, we'll use repeated 10-fold cross-validation, or 10-fold CV repeated 10 times. This means that the models will take a much longer time to build and will be more computationally intensive to evaluate, but since this is our final comparison we should be *very* sure that we're making the right choice; the winner of this showdown will be our only entry into the machine learning competition.

```
> library(caret)
> ctrl <- trainControl(method = "repeatedcv",
                       number = 10, repeats = 10)
```

Next, we'll set up the tuning grid for the random forest. The only tuning parameter for this model is mtry, which defines how many features are randomly selected at each split. By default, we know that the random forest will use sqrt(16), or four features per tree. To be thorough, we'll also test values half of that, twice that, as well as the full set of 16 features. Thus, we need to create a grid with values of 2, 4, 8, and 16 as follows:

```
> grid_rf <- expand.grid(.mtry = c(2, 4, 8, 16))
```

> [A random forest that considers the full set of features at each split is essentially the same as a bagged decision tree model.]

We can supply the resulting grid to the train() function with the ctrl object as follows. We'll use the kappa metric to select the best model:

```
> set.seed(300)
> m_rf <- train(default ~ ., data = credit, method = "rf",
                metric = "Kappa", trControl = ctrl,
                tuneGrid = grid_rf)
```

The preceding command may take some time to complete as it has quite a bit of work to do! When it finishes, we'll compare that to a boosted tree using 10, 20, 30, and 40 iterations:

```
> grid_c50 <- expand.grid(.model = "tree",
                          .trials = c(10, 20, 30, 40),
                          .winnow = "FALSE")
> set.seed(300)
> m_c50 <- train(default ~ ., data = credit, method = "C5.0",
               metric = "Kappa", trControl = ctrl,
               tuneGrid = grid_c50)
```

When the C5.0 decision tree finally completes, we can compare the two approaches side-by-side. For the random forest model, the results are:

```
> m_rf
```

Resampling results across tuning parameters:

mtry	Accuracy	Kappa	Accuracy SD	Kappa SD
2	0.7247	0.1284142	0.01690466	0.06364740
4	0.7499	0.2933332	0.02989865	0.08768815
8	0.7539	0.3379986	0.03107160	0.08353988
16	0.7556	0.3613151	0.03379439	0.08891300

For the boosted C5.0 model, the results are:

```
> m_c50
```

Resampling results across tuning parameters:

trials	Accuracy	Kappa	Accuracy SD	Kappa SD
10	0.7325	0.3215655	0.04021093	0.09519817
20	0.7343	0.3268052	0.04033333	0.09711408
30	0.7381	0.3343137	0.03672709	0.08942323
40	0.7388	0.3335082	0.03934514	0.09746073

With a kappa of about 0.361, the random forest model with `mtry = 16` was the winner among these eight models. It was higher than the best C5.0 decision tree, which had a kappa of about 0.334, and slightly higher than the `AdaBoost.M1` model with a kappa of about 0.360. Based on these results, we would submit the random forest as our final model. Without actually evaluating the model on the competition data, we have no way of knowing for sure whether it will end up winning, but given our performance estimates, it's the safer bet. With a bit of luck, perhaps we'll come away with the prize.

Summary

After reading this chapter, you should now know the base techniques that are used to win data mining and machine learning competitions. Automated tuning methods can assist with squeezing every bit of performance out of a single model. On the other hand, performance gains are also possible by creating groups of machine learning models that work together.

Although this chapter was designed to help you prepare competition-ready models, note that your fellow competitors have access to the same techniques. You won't be able to get away with stagnancy; therefore, continue to add proprietary methods to your bag of tricks. Perhaps you can bring unique subject-matter expertise to the table, or perhaps your strengths include an eye for detail in data preparation. In any case, practice makes perfect, so take advantage of open competitions to test, evaluate, and improve your own machine learning skillset.

In the next chapter — the last in this book — we'll take a bird's eye look at ways to apply machine learning to some highly specialized and difficult domains using R. You'll gain the knowledge needed to apply machine learning to tasks at the cutting edge of the field.

12
Specialized Machine Learning Topics

Congratulations on reaching this point in your machine learning journey! If you have not already started work on your own projects, you will do so soon. And in doing so, you may find that the task of turning data into action is more difficult than it first appeared.

As you gathered data, you may have realized that the information was trapped in a proprietary format or spread across pages on the Web. Making matters worse, after spending hours reformatting the data, maybe your computer slowed to a crawl after running out of memory. Perhaps R even crashed or froze your machine. Hopefully, you were undeterred, as these issues can be remedied with a bit more effort.

This chapter covers techniques that may not apply to every project, but will prove useful for working around such specialized issues. You might find the information particularly useful if you tend to work with data that is:

- Stored in unstructured or proprietary formats such as web pages, web APIs, or spreadsheets
- From a specialized domain such as bioinformatics or social network analysis
- Too large to fit in memory or analyses take a very long time to complete

You're not alone if you suffer from any of these problems. Although there is no panacea—these issues are the bane of the data scientist as well as the reason data skills are in high demand—through the dedicated efforts of the R community, a number of R packages provide a head start toward solving the problem.

This chapter provides a cookbook of such solutions. Even if you are an experienced R veteran, you may discover a package that simplifies your workflow. Or, perhaps one day, you will author a package that makes work easier for everybody else!

Working with proprietary files and databases

Unlike the examples in this book, real-world data is rarely packaged in a simple CSV form that can be downloaded from a website. Instead, significant effort is needed to prepare data for analysis. Data must be collected, merged, sorted, filtered, or reformatted to meet the requirements of the learning algorithm. This process is informally known as **data munging** or **data wrangling**.

Data preparation has become even more important, as the size of typical datasets has grown from megabytes to gigabytes, and data is gathered from unrelated and messy sources, many of which are stored in massive databases. Several packages and resources for retrieving and working with proprietary data formats and databases are listed in the following sections.

Reading from and writing to Microsoft Excel, SAS, SPSS, and Stata files

A frustrating aspect of data analysis is the large amount of work required to pull and combine data from various proprietary formats. Vast troves of data exist in files and databases that simply need to be unlocked for use in R. Thankfully, packages exist for exactly this purpose.

What used to be a tedious and time-consuming process, requiring knowledge of specific tricks and tools across multiple R packages, has been made trivial by a relatively new R package called `rio` (an acronym for R input and output). This package, by Chung-hong Chan, Geoffrey CH Chan, Thomas J. Leeper, and Christopher Gandrud, is described as a "Swiss-army knife for data". It is capable of importing and exporting a large variety of file formats, including but not limited to: tab-separated (`.tsv`), comma-separated (`.csv`), JSON (`.json`), Stata (`.dta`), SPSS (`.sav` and `.por`), Microsoft Excel (`.xls` and `.xlsx`), Weka (`.arff`), and SAS (`.sas7bdat` and `.xpt`).

 For the complete list of file types `rio` can import and export, as well as more detailed usage examples, see http://cran.r-project.org/web/packages/rio/vignettes/rio.html.

The `rio` package consists of three functions for working with proprietary data formats: `import()`, `export()`, and `convert()`. Each does exactly what you'd expect, given their name. Consistent with the package's philosophy of keeping things simple, each function uses the filename extension to guess the type of file to import, export, or convert.

For example, to import the credit data from previous chapters, which is stored in CSV format, simply type:

```
> library(rio)
> credit <- import("credit.csv")
```

This creates the `credit` data frame as expected; as a bonus, not only did we not have to specify the CSV file type, `rio` automatically set `stringsAsFactors = FALSE` as well as other reasonable defaults.

To export the `credit` data frame to Microsoft Excel (.xlsx) format, use the `export()` function while specifying the desired filename, as follows. For other formats, simply change the file extension to the desired output type:

```
> export(credit, "credit.xlsx")
```

It is also possible to convert the CSV file to another format directly, without an import step, using the `convert()` function. For example, this converts the credit.csv file to Stata (.dta) format:

```
> convert("credit.csv", "credit.dta")
```

Though the `rio` package covers many common proprietary data formats, it does not do everything. The next section covers other ways to get data into R via database queries.

Querying data in SQL databases

Large datasets are often stored in **Database Management Systems (DBMSs)** such as Oracle, MySQL, PostgreSQL, Microsoft SQL, or SQLite. These systems allow the datasets to be accessed using a **Structured Query Language (SQL)**, a programming language designed to pull data from databases. If your DBMS is configured to allow **Open Database Connectivity (ODBC)**, the `RODBC` package by Brian Ripley can be used to import this data directly into an R data frame.

> If you have trouble using ODBC to connect to your database, you may try one of the DMBS-specific R packages. These include `ROracle`, `RMySQL`, `RPostgreSQL`, and `RSQLite`. Though they will function largely similar to the instructions here, refer to the package documentation on CRAN for instructions specific to each package.

ODBC is a standard protocol for connecting to databases regardless of operating system or DBMS. If you were previously connected to an ODBC database, you most likely would have referred to it via its **Data Source Name (DSN)**. You will need the DSN, plus a username and password (if your database requires it) to use `RODBC`.

The instructions to configure an ODBC connection are highly specific to the combination of the OS and DBMS. If you are having trouble setting up an ODBC connection, check with your database administrator. Another way to obtain help is via the RODBC package vignette, which can be accessed in R with the vignette ("RODBC") command after the RODBC package has been installed.

To open a connection called my_db for the database with the my_dsn DSN, use the odbcConnect() function:

```
> library(RODBC)
> my_db <- odbcConnect("my_dsn")
```

Alternatively, if your ODBC connection requires a username and password, they should be specified while calling the odbcConnect() function:

```
> my_db <- odbcConnect("my_dsn",
    uid = "my_username",
    pwd = "my_password")
```

With an open database connection, we can use the sqlQuery() function to create an R data frame from the database rows pulled by an SQL query. This function, like the many functions that create data frames, allows us to specify stringsAsFactors = FALSE to prevent R from automatically converting character data into factors.

The sqlQuery() function uses typical SQL queries, as shown in the following command:

```
> my_query <- "select * from my_table where my_value = 1"
> results_df <- sqlQuery(channel = my_db, query = sql_query,
    stringsAsFactors = FALSE)
```

The resulting results_df object is a data frame containing all of the rows selected using the SQL query stored in sql_query.

Once you are done using the database, the connection can be closed using the following command:

```
> odbcClose(my_db)
```

Although R will automatically close ODBC connections at the end of an R session, it is a better practice to do so explicitly.

Working with online data and services

With the growing amount of data available from web-based sources, it is increasingly important for machine learning projects to be able to access and interact with online services. R is able to read data from online sources natively, with some caveats. Firstly, by default, R cannot access secure websites (those using the `https://` rather than the `http://` protocol). Secondly, it is important to note that most web pages do not provide data in a form that R can understand. The data would need to be **parsed**, or broken apart and rebuilt into a structured form, before it can be useful. We'll discuss the workarounds shortly.

However, if neither of these caveats applies (that is, if data are already online on a nonsecure website and in a tabular form, like CSV, that R can understand natively), then R's `read.csv()` and `read.table()` functions will be able to access data from the Web just as if it were on your local machine. Simply supply the full URL for the dataset as follows:

```
> mydata <- read.csv("http://www.mysite.com/mydata.csv")
```

R also provides functionality to download other files from the Web, even if R cannot use them directly. For a text file, try the `readLines()` function as follows:

```
> mytext <- readLines("http://www.mysite.com/myfile.txt")
```

For other types of files, the `download.file()` function can be used. To download a file to R's current working directory, simply supply the URL and destination filename as follows:

```
> download.file("http://www.mysite.com/myfile.zip", "myfile.zip")
```

Beyond this base functionality, there are numerous packages that extend R's capabilities to work with online data. The most basic of them will be covered in the sections that follow. As the Web is massive and ever-changing, these sections are far from a comprehensive set of all the ways R can connect to online data. There are literally hundreds of packages for everything from niche projects to massive ones.

 For the most complete and up-to-date list of packages, refer to the regularly updated CRAN Web Technologies and Services task view at `http://cran.r-project.org/web/views/WebTechnologies.html`.

Downloading the complete text of web pages

The RCurl package by Duncan Temple Lang supplies a more robust way of accessing web pages by providing an R interface to the **curl** (client for URLs) utility, a command-line tool to transfer data over networks. The curl program acts much like a programmable web browser; given a set of commands, it can access and download the content of nearly anything available on the Web. Unlike R, it can access secure websites as well as post data to online forms. It is an incredibly powerful utility.

 Precisely because it is so powerful, a complete curl tutorial is outside the scope of this chapter. Instead, refer to the online RCurl documentation at http://www.omegahat.org/RCurl/.

After installing the RCurl package, downloading a page is as simple as typing:

```
> library(RCurl)

> packt_page <- ("https://www.packtpub.com/")
```

This will save the full text of the Packt Publishing homepage (including all the web markup) into the R character object named packt_page. As shown in the following lines, this is not very useful:

```
> str(packt_page, nchar.max=200)
 chr "<!DOCTYPE html>\n<html xmlns=\"http://www.w3.org/1999/xhtml\"
lang=\"en\" xml:lang=\"en\">\n\t<head>\n\t\t<title>Packt Publishing |
Technology Books, eBooks & Videos</title>\n\t\t<script>\n\t\t\tdata"|
__truncated__
```

The reason that the first 200 characters of the page look like nonsense is because the websites are written using **Hypertext Markup Language** (HTML), which combines the page text with special tags that tell web browsers how to display the text. The <title> and </title> tags here surround the page title, telling the browser that this is the Packt Publishing homepage. Similar tags are used to denote other portions of the page.

Though curl is the cross-platform standard to access online content, if you work with web data frequently in R, the httr package by Hadley Wickham builds upon the foundation of RCurl to make it more convenient and R-like. We can see some of the differences immediately by attempting to download the Packt Publishing homepage using the httr package's GET() function:

```
> library(httr)

> packt_page <- GET("https://www.packtpub.com")

> str(packt_page, max.level = 1)
```

```
List of 9
  $ url        : chr "https://www.packtpub.com/"
  $ status_code: int 200
  $ headers    : List of 11
  $ all_headers: List of 1
  $ cookies    : list()
  $ content    : raw [1:58560] 3c 21 44 4f ...
  $ date       : POSIXct[1:1], format: "2015-05-24 20:46:40"
  $ times      : Named num [1:6] 0 0.000071 0.000079 ...
  $ request    : List of 5
```

Where the `getURL()` function in `RCurl` downloaded only the HTML, the `GET()` function returns a list with site properties in addition to the HTML. To access the page content itself, we need to use the `content()` function:

```
> str(content(packt_page, type="text"), nchar.max=200)
 chr "<!DOCTYPE html>\n<html xmlns=\"http://www.w3.org/1999/xhtml\"
lang=\"en\" xml:lang=\"en\">\n\t<head>\n\t\t<title>Packt Publishing
Technology Books, eBooks & Videos</title>\n\t\t<script>\n\t\t\tdata"
__truncated__
```

In order to use this data in an R program, it is necessary to process the page to transform it into a structured format like a list or data frame. Functions to do so are discussed in the sections that follow.

> For detailed `httr` documentation and tutorials, visit the project GitHub page at `https://github.com/hadley/httr`. The quickstart guide is particularly helpful to learn the base functionality.

Scraping data from web pages

Because there is a consistent structure of the HTML tags of many web pages, it is possible to write programs that look for desired sections of the page and extract them in order to compile them into a dataset. This process practice of harvesting data from websites and transforming it into a structured form is known as **web scraping**.

Though it is frequently used, scraping should be considered a last resort to get data from the Web. This is because any changes to the underlying HTML structure may break your code, requiring efforts to be fixed. Even worse, it may introduce unnoticed errors into your data. Additionally, many websites' terms of use agreements explicitly forbid automated data extraction, not to mention the fact that your program's traffic may overload their servers. Always check the site's terms before you begin your project; you may even find that the site offers its data freely via a developer agreement.

The `rvest` package (a pun on the term "harvest") by Hadley Wickham makes web scraping a largely effortless process, assuming the data you want can be found in a consistent place within HTML.

Let's start with a simple example using the Packt Publishing homepage. We begin by downloading the page as before, using the `html()` function in the `rvest` package. Note that this function, when supplied with a URL, simply calls the `GET()` function in Hadley Wickham's `httr` package:

```
> library(rvest)
> packt_page <- html("https://www.packtpub.com")
```

Suppose we'd like to scrape the page title. Looking at the previous HTML code, we know that there is only one title per page wrapped within `<title>` and `</title>` tags. To pull the title, we supply the tag name to the `html_node()` function, as follows:

```
> html_node(packt_page, "title")
<title>Packt Publishing | Technology Books, eBooks &amp;
Videos</title>
```

This keeps the HTML formatting in place, including the `<title>` tags and the `&amp;` code, which is the HTML designation for the ampersand symbol. To translate this into plain text, we simply run it through the `html_text()` function, as shown:

```
> html_node(packt_page, "title") %>% html_text()
[1] "Packt Publishing | Technology Books, eBooks & Videos"
```

Notice the use of the `%>%` operator. This is known as a pipe, because it essentially "pipes" data from one function to another. The use of pipes allows the creation of powerful chains of functions to process HTML data.

The pipe operator is a part of the `magrittr` package by Stefan Milton Bache and Hadley Wickham, installed by default with the `rvest` package. The name is a play on René Magritte's famous painting of a pipe (you may recall seeing it in *Chapter 1, Introducing Machine Learning*). For more information on the project, visit its GitHub page at `https://github.com/smbache/magrittr`.

Let's try a slightly more interesting example. Suppose we'd like to scrape a list of all the packages on the CRAN machine learning task view. We begin as in the same way we did it earlier, by downloading the HTML page using the `html()` function. Since we don't know how the page is structured, we'll also peek into HTML by typing `cran_ml`, the name of the R object we created:

```
> library(rvest)
> cran_ml <- html("http://cran.r-project.org/web/views/MachineLearning.
html")
> cran_ml
```

Looking over the output, we find that one section appears to have the data we're interested in. Note that only a subset of the output is shown here:

```
<h3>CRAN packages:</h3>
<ul>
   <li><a href="../packages/ahaz/index.html">ahaz</a></li>
   <li><a href="../packages/arules/index.html">arules</a></li>
   <li><a href="../packages/bigrf/index.html">bigrf</a></li>
   <li><a href="../packages/bigRR/index.html">bigRR</a></li>
   <li><a href="../packages/bmrm/index.html">bmrm</a></li>
   <li><a href="../packages/Boruta/index.html">Boruta</a></li>
   <li><a href="../packages/bst/index.html">bst</a></li>
   <li><a href="../packages/C50/index.html">C50</a></li>
   <li><a href="../packages/caret/index.html">caret</a></li>
```

The `<h3>` tags imply a header of size 3, while the `<ul>` and `<li>` tags refer to the creation of an unordered list and list items, respectively. The data elements we want are surrounded by `<a>` tags, which are hyperlink anchor tags that link to the CRAN page for each package.

 Because the CRAN page is actively maintained and may be changed at any time, do not be surprised if your results differ from those shown here.

With this knowledge in hand, we can scrape the links much like we did previously. The one exception is that, because we expect to find more than one result, we need to use the `html_nodes()` function to return a vector of results rather than `html_node()`, which returns only a single item:

```
> ml_packages <- html_nodes(cran_ml, "a")
```

Let's peek at the result using the `head()` function:

```
> head(ml_packages, n = 7)
[[1]]
<a href="../packages/nnet/index.html">nnet</a>

[[2]]
<a href="../packages/RSNNS/index.html">RSNNS</a>

[[3]]
<a href="../packages/rpart/index.html">rpart</a>

[[4]]
<a href="../packages/tree/index.html">tree</a>

[[5]]
<a href="../packages/rpart/index.html">rpart</a>

[[6]]
<a href="http://www.cs.waikato.ac.nz/~ml/weka/">Weka</a>

[[7]]
<a href="../packages/RWeka/index.html">RWeka</a>
```

As we can see on line 6, it looks like the links to some other projects slipped in. This is because some packages are hyperlinked to additional websites; in this case, the RWeka package is linked to both CRAN and its homepage. To exclude these results, you might chain this output to another function that could look for the /packages string in the hyperlink.

> In general, web scraping is always a process of iterate-and-refine as you identify more specific criteria to exclude or include specific cases. The most difficult cases may even require a human eye to achieve 100 percent accuracy.

These are simple examples that merely scratch the surface of what is possible with the rvest package. Using the pipe functionality, it is possible to look for tags nested within tags or specific classes of HTML tags. For these types of complex examples, refer to the package documentation.

Parsing XML documents

XML is a plaintext, human-readable, structured markup language upon which many document formats have been based. It employs a tagging structure in some ways similar to HTML, but is far stricter about formatting. For this reason, it is a popular online format to store structured datasets.

The XML package by Duncan Temple Lang provides a suite of R functionality based on the popular C-based libxml2 parser to read and write XML documents. It is the grandfather of XML parsing packages in R and is still widely used.

> Information on the XML package, including simple examples to get you started quickly, can be found on the project's website at http://www.omegahat.org/RSXML/.

Recently, the xml2 package by Hadley Wickham has surfaced as an easier and more R-like interface to the libxml2 library. The rvest package, which was covered earlier in this chapter, utilizes xml2 behind the scenes to parse HTML. Moreover, rvest can be used to parse XML as well.

> The xml2 GitHub page is found at https://github.com/hadley/xml2.

Because parsing XML is so closely related to parsing HTML, the exact syntax is not covered here. Please refer to these packages' documentation for examples.

Parsing JSON from web APIs

Online applications communicate with one another using web-accessible functions known as **Application Programming Interfaces (APIs)**. These interfaces act much like a typical website; they receive a request from a client via a particular URL and return a response. The difference is that a normal website returns HTML meant for display in a web browser, while an API typically returns data in a structured form meant for processing by a machine.

Though it is not uncommon to find XML-based APIs, perhaps the most common API data structure today is **JavaScript Object Notation (JSON)**. Like XML, it is a standard, plaintext format, most often used for data structures and objects on the Web. The format has become popular recently due to its roots in browser-based JavaScript applications, but despite the pedigree, its utility is not limited to the Web. The ease in which JSON data structures can be understood by humans and parsed by machines makes it an appealing data structure for many types of projects.

JSON is based on a simple {key: value} format. The { } brackets denote a JSON object, and the key and value parameters denote a property of the object and the status of the property. An object can have any number of properties and the properties themselves may be objects. For example, a JSON object for this book might look something like this:

```
{
    "title": "Machine Learning with R",
    "author": "Brett Lantz",
    "publisher": {
        "name": "Packt Publishing",
        "url": "https://www.packtpub.com"
    },
    "topics": ["R", "machine learning", "data mining"],
    "MSRP": 54.99
}
```

This example illustrates the data types available to JSON: numeric, character, array (surrounded by [and] characters), and object. Not shown are the null and Boolean (true or false) values. The transmission of these types of objects from application to application and application to web browser, is what powers many of the most popular websites.

 For details on the JSON format, go to http://www.json.org/.

Public-facing APIs allow programs like R to systematically query websites to retrieve results in the JSON format, using packages like RCurl and httr. Though a full tutorial on using web APIs is worthy of a separate book, the basic process relies on only a couple of steps—it's the details that are tricky.

Suppose we wanted to query the Google Maps API to locate the latitude and longitude of the Eiffel Tower in France. We first need to review the Google Maps API documentation to determine the URL and parameters needed to make this query. We then supply this information to the httr package's GET() function, adding a list of query parameters in order to apply the search address:

```
> library(httr)
> map_search <-
    GET("https://maps.googleapis.com/maps/api/geocode/json",
        query = list(address = "Eiffel Tower"))
```

By typing the name of the resulting object, we can see some details about the request:

```
> map_search
Response [https://maps.googleapis.com/maps/api/geocode/
json?address=Eiffel%20T
ower]
  Status: 200
  Content-Type: application/json; charset=UTF-8
  Size: 2.34 kB
{
   "results" : [
      {
         "address_components" : [
            {
               "long_name" : "Eiffel Tower",
               "short_name" : "Eiffel Tower",
               "types" : [ "point_of_interest", "establishment" ]
            },
            {
...
```

To access the resulting JSON, which the `httr` package parsed automatically, we use the `content()` function. For brevity, only a handful of lines are shown here:

```
> content(map_search)
$results[[1]]$formatted_address
[1] "Eiffel Tower, Champ de Mars, 5 Avenue Anatole France, 75007
Paris, France"

$results[[1]]$geometry
$results[[1]]$geometry$location
$results[[1]]$geometry$location$lat
[1] 48.85837

$results[[1]]$geometry$location$lng
[1] 2.294481
```

To access these contents individually, simply refer to them using list syntax. The names are based on the JSON objects returned by the Google API. For instance, the entire set of results is in an object appropriately named `results` and each result is numbered. In this case, we will access the formatted address property of the first result, as well as the latitude and longitude:

```
> content(map_search)$results[[1]]$formatted_address
[1] "Eiffel Tower, Champ de Mars, 5 Avenue Anatole France, 75007
Paris, France"

> content(map_search)$results[[1]]$geometry$location$lat
[1] 48.85837

> content(map_search)$results[[1]]$geometry$location$lng
[1] 2.294481
```

These data elements could then be used in an R program as desired.

 Because the Google Maps API may be updated in the future, if you find that your results differ from those shown here, please check the Packt Publishing support page for updated code.

On the other hand, if you would like to do a conversion to and from the JSON format outside the `httr` package, there are a number of packages that add this functionality.

The `rjson` package by Alex Couture-Beil was one of the earliest packages to allow R data structures to be converted back and forth from the JSON format. The syntax is simple. After installing the `rjson` package, to convert from an R object to a JSON string, we use the `toJSON()` function. Notice that the quote characters have escaped using the `\"` notation:

```
> library(rjson)
> ml_book <- list(book_title = "Machine Learning with R",
                  author = "Brett Lantz")
> toJSON(ml_book)
[1] "{\"book_title\":\"Machine Learning with R\",
\"author\":\"Brett Lantz\"}"
```

To convert a JSON string into an R object, use the `fromJSON()` function. Quotation marks in the string need to be escaped, as shown:

```
> ml_book_json <- "{
  \"title\": \"Machine Learning with R\",
  \"author\": \"Brett Lantz\",
  \"publisher\": {
    \"name\": \"Packt Publishing\",
    \"url\": \"https://www.packtpub.com\"
  },
  \"topics\": [\"R\", \"machine learning\", \"data mining\"],
  \"MSRP\": 54.99
}"

> ml_book_r <- fromJSON(ml_book_json)
```

This results in a list structure in a form much like the original JSON:

```
> str(ml_book_r)
List of 5
 $ title    : chr "Machine Learning with R"
 $ author   : chr "Brett Lantz"
 $ publisher:List of 2
  ..$ name: chr "Packt Publishing"
```

```
..$ url    : chr "https://www.packtpub.com"
$ topics   : chr [1:3] "R" "machine learning" "data mining"
$ MSRP      : num 55
```

Recently, two new JSON packages have arrived on the scene. The first, RJSONIO, by Duncan Temple Lang was intended to be a faster and more extensible version of the rjson package, though they are now virtually identical. A second package, jsonlite, by Jeroen Ooms has quickly gained prominence as it creates data structures that are more consistent and R-like, especially while using data from web APIs. Which of these packages you use is a matter of preference; all three are virtually identical in practice as they each implement a fromJSON() and toJSON() function.

> For more information on the potential benefits of the jsonlite package, see: Ooms J. The jsonlite package: a practical and consistent mapping between JSON data and R objects. 2014. Available at: http://arxiv.org/abs/1403.2805

Working with domain-specific data

Machine learning has undoubtedly been applied to problems across every discipline. Although the basic techniques are similar across all domains, some are so specialized that communities are formed to develop solutions to the challenges unique to the field. This leads to the discovery of new techniques and new terminology that is relevant only to domain specific problems.

This section covers a pair of domains that use machine learning techniques extensively, but require specialized knowledge to unlock their full potential. Since entire books have been written on these topics, it will serve only as the briefest of introductions. For more details, seek out the help provided by the resources cited in each section.

Analyzing bioinformatics data

The field of **bioinformatics** is concerned with the application of computers and data analysis to the biological domain, particularly with regard to better understanding the genome. As genetic data is unique compared to many other types, data analysis in the field of bioinformatics offers a number of unique challenges. For example, because living creatures have a tremendous number of genes and genetic sequencing is still relatively expensive, typical datasets are much wider than they are long; that is, they have more features (genes) than examples (creatures that have been sequenced). This creates problems while attempting to apply conventional visualizations, statistical tests, and machine learning methods to such data. Additionally, the increasing use of proprietary **microarray** "lab-on-a-chip" techniques requires highly specialized knowledge simply to load the genetic data.

 A CRAN task view, which lists some of R's specialized packages for statistical genetics and bioinformatics, is available at
http://cran.r-project.org/web/views/Genetics.html.

The **Bioconductor** project of the Fred Hutchinson Cancer Research Center in Seattle, Washington, aims to solve some of these problems by providing a standardized set of methods for analyzing genomic data. Using R as its foundation, Bioconductor adds bioinformatics-specific packages and documentation on top of the base R software.

Bioconductor provides workflows to analyze DNA and protein microarray data from common microarray platforms such as Affymetrix, Illumina, Nimblegen, and Agilent. Additional functionality includes sequence annotation, multiple testing procedures, specialized visualizations, tutorials, documentation, and much more.

 For more information on the Bioconductor project, visit the project website at http://www.bioconductor.org.

Analyzing and visualizing network data

Social network data and graph datasets consist of structures that describe connections, or **links** (sometimes also called **edges**), between people or objects known as **nodes**. With N nodes, a $N \times N = N^2$ matrix of potential links can be created. This creates tremendous computational complexity as the number of nodes grows.

The field of **network analysis** is concerned with statistical measures and visualizations that identify meaningful patterns of connections. For example, the following figure shows three clusters of circular nodes, all connected via a square node at the center. A network analysis may reveal the importance of the square node, among other key metrics.

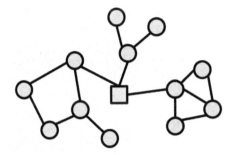

The `network` package by Carter T. Butts, David Hunter, and Mark S. Handcock offers a specialized data structure to work with networks. This data structure is necessary due to the fact that the matrix needed to store N^2 potential links will quickly exceed available memory; the `network` data structure uses a sparse representation to store only existent links, saving a great deal of memory if most relationships are nonexistent. A closely related package, `sna` (social network analysis), allows the analysis and visualization of the `network` objects.

 For more information on `network` and `sna`, including very detailed tutorials and documentation, refer to the project website hosted by the University of Washington at `http://www.statnet.org/`.

The `igraph` package by Gábor Csárdi provides another set of tools to visualize and analyze network data. It is capable of calculating metrics for very large networks. An additional benefit of `igraph` is the fact that it has analogous packages for the Python and C programming languages, allowing it to be used to perform analyses virtually anywhere. As we will demonstrate shortly, it is very easy to use.

 For more information on the `igraph` package, including demos and tutorials, visit the homepage at `http://igraph.org/r/`.

Using network data in R requires the use of specialized formats, as network data are not typically stored in typical tabular data structures like CSV files and data frames. As mentioned previously, because there are N^2 potential connections between N network nodes, a tabular structure would quickly grow to be unwieldy for all but the smallest N values. Instead, graph data are stored in a form that lists only the connections that are truly present; absent connections are inferred from the absence of data.

Perhaps the simplest of such formats is **edgelist**, which is a text file with one line per network connection. Each node must be assigned a unique identifier and the links between the nodes are defined by placing the connected nodes' identifiers together on a single line separated by a space. For instance, the following edgelist defines three connections between node 0 and nodes 1, 2, and 3:

```
0 1
0 2
0 3
```

To load network data into R, the `igraph` package provides a `read.graph()` function that can read edgelist files as well as other more sophisticated formats like **Graph Modeling Language** (GML). To illustrate this functionality, we'll use a dataset describing friendship among the members of a small karate club. To follow along, download the `karate.txt` file from the Packt Publishing website and save it in your R working directory. After you've installed the `igraph` package, the karate network can be read into R as follows:

```
> library(igraph)
> karate <- read.graph("karate.txt", "edgelist", directed = FALSE)
```

This will create a sparse matrix object that can be used for graphing and network analysis. Note that the `directed = FALSE` parameter forces the network to use undirected or bidirectional links between the nodes. Since the karate dataset describes friendship, it means that if person 1 is friends with person 2, then person 2 must be friends with person 1. On the other hand, if the dataset described fight outcomes, the fact that person 1 defeated person 2 would certainly not imply that person 2 defeated person 1. In this case, the `directed = TRUE` parameter should be set.

 The karate network dataset used here was compiled by *M.E.J. Newman* of the University of Michigan. It was first presented in Zachary WW. *An information flow model for conflict and fission in small groups.* Journal of Anthropological Research. 1977; 33:452-473.

To examine the graph, use the `plot()` function:

```
> plot(karate)
```

This produces the following figure:

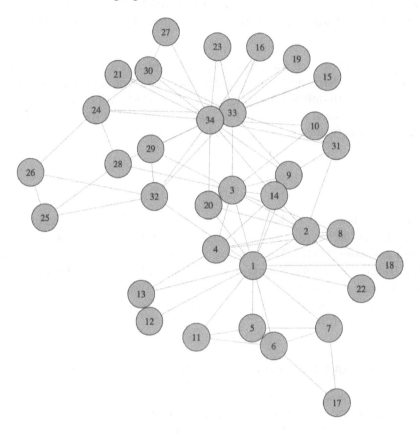

Examining the network visualization, it is apparent that there are a few highly connected members of the karate club. Nodes 1, 33, and 34 seem to be more central than the others, which remain at the club periphery.

Using `igraph` to calculate graph metrics, it is possible to demonstrate our hunch analytically. The **degree** of a node measures how many nodes it is linked to. The `degree()` function confirms our hunch that nodes 1, 33, and 34 are more connected than the others with `16`, `12`, and `17` connections, respectively:

```
> degree(karate)
 [1] 16  9 10  6  3  4  4  4  5  2  3  1  2  5  2  2  2  2
[19]  2  3  2  2  2  5  3  3  2  4  3  4  4  6 12 17
```

Because some connections are more important than others, a variety of network measures have been developed to measure node connectivity with this consideration. A network metric called **betweenness centrality** is intended to capture the number of shortest paths between nodes that pass through each node. Nodes that are truly more central to the entire graph will have a higher betweenness centrality value, because they act as a bridge between the other nodes. We obtain a vector of the centrality measures using the betweenness() function, as follows:

```
> betweenness(karate)
 [1] 231.0714286   28.4785714   75.8507937    6.2880952
 [5]   0.3333333   15.8333333   15.8333333    0.0000000
 [9]  29.5293651    0.4476190    0.3333333    0.0000000
[13]   0.0000000   24.2158730    0.0000000    0.0000000
[17]   0.0000000    0.0000000    0.0000000   17.1468254
[21]   0.0000000    0.0000000    0.0000000    9.3000000
[25]   1.1666667    2.0277778    0.0000000   11.7920635
[29]   0.9476190    1.5428571    7.6095238   73.0095238
[33]  76.6904762  160.5515873
```

As nodes 1 and 34 have much greater betweenness values than the others, they are more central to the karate club's friendship network. These two individuals, with extensive personal friendship networks, may be the "glue" that holds the network together.

 Betweenness centrality is only one of many metrics intended to capture a node's importance, and it isn't even the only measure of centrality. Refer to the igraph documentation for definitions of other network properties.

The sna and igraph packages are capable of computing many such graph metrics, which may then be used as inputs to machine learning functions. For example, suppose we were attempting to build a model predicting who would win an election for the club's president. The fact that nodes 1 and 34 are well-connected suggests that they may have the social capital needed for such a leadership role. These might be the highly valuable predictors of the election's results.

By combining network analysis with machine learning, services like Facebook, Twitter, and LinkedIn provide vast stores of network data to make predictions about the users' future behavior. A high-profile example is the 2012 U.S. Presidential campaign in which chief data scientist Rayid Ghani utilized Facebook data to identify people who might be persuaded to vote for Barack Obama.

Improving the performance of R

R has a reputation for being slow and memory-inefficient, a reputation that is at least somewhat earned. These faults are largely unnoticed on a modern PC for datasets of many thousands of records, but datasets with a million records or more can exceed the limits of what is currently possible with consumer-grade hardware. The problem worsens if the dataset contains many features or if complex learning algorithms are being used.

CRAN has a high-performance computing task view that lists packages pushing the boundaries of what is possible in R. It can be viewed at http://cran.r-project.org/web/views/HighPerformanceComputing.html.

Packages that extend R past the capabilities of the base software are being developed rapidly. This work comes primarily on two fronts: some packages add the capability to manage extremely large datasets by making data operations faster or allowing the size of the data to exceed the amount of available system memory; others allow R to work faster, perhaps by spreading the work over additional computers or processors, utilizing specialized computer hardware, or providing machine learning algorithms optimized for big data problems.

Managing very large datasets

Extremely large datasets can cause R to grind to a halt when the system runs out of memory to store data. Even if the entire dataset can fit into the available memory, additional memory overhead will be needed for data processing. Furthermore, very large datasets can take a long amount of time to analyze for no reason other than the sheer volume of records; even a quick operation can cause delays when performed many millions of times.

Years ago, many would perform data preparation outside R in another programming language, or use R but perform analyses on a smaller subset of data. However, this is no longer necessary, as several packages have been contributed to R to address these problems.

Generalizing tabular data structures with dplyr

The dplyr package introduced in 2014 by Hadley Wickham and Romain Francois is perhaps the most straightforward way to begin working with large datasets in R. Though other packages may exceed its capabilities in terms of raw speed or the raw size of the data, dplyr is still quite capable. More importantly, it is virtually transparent after the initial learning curve has passed.

> For more information on dplyr, including some very helpful tutorials, refer to the project's GitHub page at https://github.com/hadley/dplyr.

Put simply, the package provides an object called tbl, which is an abstraction of tabular data. It acts much like a data frame, with several important exceptions:

- Key functionality has been written in C++, which according to the authors results in a 20x to 1000x performance increase for many operations.

- R data frames are limited by available memory. The dplyr version of a data frame can be linked transparently to disk-based databases that can exceed what can be stored in memory.

- The dplyr package makes reasonable assumptions about data frames that optimize your effort as well as memory use. It doesn't automatically change data types. And, if possible, it avoids making copies of data by pointing to the original value instead.

- New operators are introduced that allow common data transformations to be performed with much less code while remaining highly readable.

Making the transition from data frames to dplyr is easy. To convert an existing data frame into a tbl object, use the as.tbl() function:

```
> library(dplyr)
> credit <- read.csv("credit.csv")
> credit_tbl <- as.tbl(credit)
```

Typing the name of the table provides information about the object. Even here, we see a distinction between `dplyr` and typical R behavior; where as a traditional data frame would have displayed many rows of data, `dplyr` objects are more considerate of real-world needs. For example, typing the name of the object provides output summarized in a form that fits a single screen:

```
> credit_tbl
```

```
Source: local data frame [1,000 x 17]

   checking_balance months_loan_duration credit_history          purpose amount
1           < 0 DM                     6         critical furniture/appliances   1169
2        1 - 200 DM                    48             good furniture/appliances   5951
3           unknown                    12         critical           education   2096
4           < 0 DM                     42             good furniture/appliances   7882
5           < 0 DM                     24             poor                 car   4870
6           unknown                    36             good           education   9055
7           unknown                    24             good furniture/appliances   2835
8        1 - 200 DM                    36             good                 car   6948
9           unknown                    12             good furniture/appliances   3059
10       1 - 200 DM                    30         critical                 car   5234
..              ...                   ...              ...                 ...    ...
Variables not shown: savings_balance (fctr), employment_duration (fctr),
   percent_of_income (int), years_at_residence (int), age (int), other_credit (fctr),
   housing (fctr), existing_loans_count (int), job (fctr), dependents (int), phone
   (fctr), default (fctr)
```

Connecting `dplyr` to an external database is straightforward as well. The `dplyr` package provides functions to connect to MySQL, PostgreSQL, and SQLite databases. These create a connection object that allows `tbl` objects to be pulled from the database.

Let's use the `src_sqlite()` function to create a SQLite database to store credit data. SQLite is a simple database that doesn't require a server. It simply connects to a database file, which we'll call `credit.sqlite3`. Since the file doesn't exist yet, we need to set the `create = TRUE` parameter to create the file. Note that for this step to work, you may require to install the `RSQLite` package if you have not already done so:

```
> credit_db_conn <- src_sqlite("credit.sqlite3", create = TRUE)
```

After creating the connection, we need to load the data into the database using the `copy_to()` function. This uses the `credit_tbl` object to create a database table within the database specified by `credit_db_conn`. The `temporary = FALSE` parameter forces the table to be created immediately. Since `dplyr` tries to avoid copying data unless it must, it will only create the table if it is explicitly asked to:

```
> copy_to(credit_db_conn, credit_tbl, temporary = FALSE)
```

Executing the `copy_to()` function will store the data in the `credit.sqlite3` file, which can be transported to other systems as needed. To access this file later, simply reopen the database connection and create a `tbl` object, as follows:

```
> credit_db_conn <- src_sqlite("credit.sqlite3")
> credit_tbl <- tbl(credit_db_conn, "credit_tbl")
```

In spite of the fact that `dplyr` is routed through a database, the `credit_tbl` object here will act exactly like any other `tbl` object and will gain all the other benefits of the `dplyr` package.

Making data frames faster with data.table

The `data.table` package by Matt Dowle, Tom Short, Steve Lianoglou, and Arun Srinivasan provides an enhanced version of a data frame called a **data table**. The `data.table` objects are typically much faster than data frames for subsetting, joining, and grouping operations. For the largest datasets — those with many millions of rows — these objects may be substantially faster than even `dplyr` objects. Yet, because it is essentially an improved data frame, the resulting objects can still be used by any R function that accepts a data frame.

> The `data.table` project can be found on GitHub at
> https://github.com/Rdatatable/data.table/wiki.

After installing the `data.table` package, the `fread()` function will read tabular files like CSVs into data table objects. For instance, to load the credit data used previously, type:

```
> library(data.table)
> credit <- fread("credit.csv")
```

The credit data table can then be queried using syntax similar to R's [row, col] form, but optimized for speed and some additional useful conveniences. In particular, the data table structure allows the row portion to select rows using an abbreviated subsetting command, and the col portion to use a function that does something with the selected rows. For example, the following command computes the mean requested loan amount for people with a good credit history:

```
> credit[credit_history == "good", mean(amount)]
[1] 3040.958
```

By building larger queries with this simple syntax, very complex operations can be performed on data tables. Since the data structure is optimized for speed, it can be used with large datasets.

One limitation of the data.table structures is that like data frames they are limited by the available system memory. The next two sections discuss packages that overcome this shortcoming at the expense of breaking compatibility with many R functions.

The dplyr and data.table packages each have unique strengths. For an in-depth comparison, check out the following Stack Overflow discussion at http://stackoverflow.com/questions/21435339/ data-table-vs-dplyr-can-one-do-something-well-the- other-cant-or-does-poorly. It is also possible to have the best of both worlds, as data.table structures can be loaded into dplyr using the tbl_dt() function.

Creating disk-based data frames with ff

The ff package by Daniel Adler, Christian Gläser, Oleg Nenadic, Jens Oehlschlägel, and Walter Zucchini provides an alternative to a data frame (ffdf) that allows datasets of over two billion rows to be created, even if this far exceeds the available system memory.

The ffdf structure has a physical component that stores the data on a disk in a highly efficient form, and a virtual component that acts like a typical R data frame, but transparently points to the data stored in the physical component. You can imagine the ffdf object as a map that points to a location of the data on a disk.

The ff project is on the Web at http://ff.r-forge.r-project.org/.

A downside of ffdf data structures is that they cannot be used natively by most R functions. Instead, the data must be processed in small chunks, and the results must be combined later on. The upside of chunking the data is that the task can be divided across several processors simultaneously using the parallel computing methods presented later in this chapter.

After installing the ff package, to read in a large CSV file, use the read.csv.ffdf() function, as follows:

```
> library(ff)
> credit <- read.csv.ffdf(file = "credit.csv", header = TRUE)
```

Unfortunately, we cannot work directly with the ffdf object, as attempting to treat it like a traditional data frame results in an error message:

```
> mean(credit$amount)
[1] NA
Warning message:
In mean.default(credit$amount) :
  argument is not numeric or logical: returning NA
```

The ffbase package by Edwin de Jonge, Jan Wijffels, and Jan van der Laan addresses this issue somewhat by adding capabilities for basic analyses using ff objects. This makes it possible to use ff objects directly for data exploration. For instance, after installing the ffbase package, the mean function works as expected:

```
> library(ffbase)
> mean(credit$amount)
[1] 3271.258
```

The package also provides other basic functionality such as mathematical operators, query functions, summary statistics, and wrappers to work with optimized machine learning algorithms like biglm (described later in this chapter). Though these do not completely eliminate the challenges of working with extremely large datasets, they make the process a bit more seamless.

 For more information on advanced functionality, visit the ffbase project site at http://github.com/edwindj/ffbase.

Using massive matrices with bigmemory

The bigmemory package by Michael J. Kane, John W. Emerson, and Peter Haverty allows the use of extremely large matrices that exceed the amount of available system memory. The matrices can be stored on a disk or in shared memory, allowing them to be used by other processes on the same computer or across a network. This facilitates parallel computing methods, such as the ones covered later in this chapter.

> Additional documentation on the bigmemory package can be found at http://www.bigmemory.org/.

Because bigmemory matrices are intentionally unlike data frames, they cannot be used directly with most of the machine learning methods covered in this book. They also can only be used with numeric data. That said, since they are similar to a typical R matrix, it is easy to create smaller samples or chunks that can be converted into standard R data structures.

The authors also provide the bigalgebra, biganalytics, and bigtabulate packages, which allow simple analyses to be performed on the matrices. Of particular note is the bigkmeans() function in the biganalytics package, which performs k-means clustering as described in *Chapter 9, Finding Groups of Data – Clustering with k-means*. Due to the highly specialized nature of these packages, use cases are outside the scope of this chapter.

Learning faster with parallel computing

In the early days of computing, processors executed instructions in **serial** which meant that they were limited to performing a single task at a time. The next instruction could not be started until the previous instruction was complete. Although it was widely known that many tasks could be completed more efficiently by completing the steps simultaneously, the technology simply did not exist yet.

Serial computing:

This was addressed by the development of **parallel computing** methods, which use a set of two or more processors or computers to solve a larger problem. Many modern computers are designed for parallel computing. Even in the cases in which they have a single processor, they often have two or more **cores** that are capable of working in parallel. This allows tasks to be accomplished independently of one another.

Parallel computing:

Networks of multiple computers called **clusters** can also be used for parallel computing. A large cluster may include a variety of hardware and be separated over large distances. In this case, the cluster is known as a **grid**. Taken to an extreme, a cluster or grid of hundreds or thousands of computers running commodity hardware could be a very powerful system.

The catch, however, is that not every problem can be parallelized. Certain problems are more conducive to parallel execution than others. One might expect that adding 100 processors would result in accomplishing 100 times the work in the same amount of time (that is, the overall execution time would be 1/100), but this is typically not the case. The reason is that it takes effort to manage the workers. Work must be divided into equal, nonoverlapping tasks, and each of the workers' results must be combined into one final answer.

So-called **embarrassingly parallel** problems are ideal. It is easy to reduce these tasks into nonoverlapping blocks of work and recombine the results. An example of an embarrassingly parallel machine learning task would be 10-fold cross-validation; once the 10 samples are divided, each of the 10 blocks of work is independent, meaning that they do not affect the others. As you will soon see, this task can be sped up quite dramatically using parallel computing.

Measuring execution time

Efforts to speed up R will be wasted if it is not possible to systematically measure how much time is saved. Although a stopwatch is one option, an easier solution would be to wrap the code in a system.time() function.

For example, on my laptop, the system.time() function notes that it takes about 0.093 seconds to generate a million random numbers:

```
> system.time(rnorm(1000000))
   user  system elapsed
  0.092   0.000   0.093
```

The same function can be used to evaluate the improvement in performance obtained by using the methods that were just described or any R function.

 For what it's worth, when the first edition was published, generating a million random numbers took 0.13 seconds. Although I'm now using a slightly more powerful computer, this reduction of about 30 percent of the processing time just two years later illustrates how quickly computer hardware and software are improving.

Working in parallel with multicore and snow

The parallel package, now included with R version 2.14.0 and higher, has lowered the entry barrier to deploy parallel algorithms by providing a standard framework to set up worker processes that can complete tasks simultaneously. It does this by including components of the multicore and snow packages, each taking a different approach towards multitasking.

If your computer is reasonably recent, you are likely to be able to use parallel processing. To determine the number of cores your machine has, use the detectCores() function as follows. Note that your output will differ depending on your hardware specifications:

```
> library(parallel)
> detectCores()
[1] 8
```

The multicore package was developed by Simon Urbanek and allows parallel processing on a single machine that has multiple processors or processor cores. It utilizes the multitasking capabilities of a computer's operating system to **fork** additional R sessions that share the same memory. It is perhaps the simplest way to get started with parallel processing in R. Unfortunately, because Windows does not support forking, this solution will not work everywhere.

An easy way to get started with the multicore functionality is to use the mclapply() function, which is a parallel version of lapply(). For instance, the following blocks of code illustrate how the task of generating a million random numbers can be divided across 1, 2, 4, and 8 cores. The unlist() function is used to combine the parallel results (a list) into a single vector after each core has completed its chunk of work:

```
> system.time(l1 <- rnorm(1000000))
   user  system elapsed
  0.094   0.003   0.097

> system.time(l2 <- unlist(mclapply(1:2, function(x) {
  rnorm(500000)}, mc.cores = 2)))
   user  system elapsed
  0.106   0.045   0.076

> system.time(l4 <- unlist(mclapply(1:4, function(x) {
  rnorm(250000) }, mc.cores = 4)))
   user  system elapsed
  0.135   0.055   0.063

> system.time(l8 <- unlist(mclapply(1:8, function(x) {
  rnorm(125000) }, mc.cores = 8)))
   user  system elapsed
  0.123   0.058   0.055
```

Notice how as the number of cores increases, the elapsed time decreases, and the benefit tapers off. Though this is a simple example, it can be adapted easily to many other tasks.

The snow package (simple networking of workstations) by Luke Tierney, A. J. Rossini, Na Li, and H. Sevcikova allows parallel computing on multicore or multiprocessor machines as well as on a network of multiple machines. It is slightly more difficult to use, but offers much more power and flexibility. After installing snow, to set up a cluster on a single machine, use the makeCluster() function with the number of cores to be used:

```
> library(snow)
> cl1 <- makeCluster(4)
```

Because snow communicates via network traffic, depending on your operating system, you may receive a message to approve access through your firewall.

To confirm whether the cluster is operational, we can ask each node to report back its hostname. The clusterCall() function executes a function on each machine in the cluster. In this case, we'll define a function that simply calls the Sys.info() function and returns the nodename parameter:

```
> clusterCall(cl1, function() { Sys.info()["nodename"] } )
[[1]]
                     nodename
"Bretts-Macbook-Pro.local"


[[2]]
                     nodename
"Bretts-Macbook-Pro.local"


[[3]]
                     nodename
"Bretts-Macbook-Pro.local"


[[4]]
                     nodename
"Bretts-Macbook-Pro.local"
```

Unsurprisingly, since all four nodes are running on a single machine, they report back the same hostname. To have the four nodes run a different command, supply them with a unique parameter via the `clusterApply()` function. Here, we'll supply each node with a different letter. Each node will then perform a simple function on its letter in parallel:

```
> clusterApply(cl1, c('A', 'B', 'C', 'D'),
                 function(x) { paste("Cluster", x, "ready!") })
[[1]]
[1] "Cluster A ready!"

[[2]]
[1] "Cluster B ready!"

[[3]]
[1] "Cluster C ready!"

[[4]]
[1] "Cluster D ready!"
```

Once we're done with the cluster, it's important to terminate the processes it spawned. This will free up the resources each node is using:

```
> stopCluster(cl1)
```

Using these simple commands, it is possible to speed up many machine learning tasks. For larger big data problems, much more complex snow configurations are possible. For instance, you may attempt to configure a **Beowulf cluster** — a network of many consumer-grade machines. In academic and industry research settings with dedicated computing clusters, snow can use the Rmpi package to access these high-performance **message-passing interface** (**MPI**) servers. Working with such clusters requires the knowledge of network configurations and computing hardware, which is outside the scope of this book.

> For a much more detailed introduction to snow, including some information on how to configure parallel computing on several computers over a network, see http://homepage.stat.uiowa.edu/~luke/classes/295-hpc/notes/snow.pdf.

Taking advantage of parallel with foreach and doParallel

The foreach package by Steve Weston of Revolution Analytics provides perhaps the easiest way to get started with parallel computing, particularly if you are running R on Windows, as some of the other packages are platform-specific.

The core of the package is a new foreach looping construct. If you have worked with other programming languages, you may be familiar with it. Essentially, it allows looping over a number of items in a set without explicitly counting the number of items; in other words, *for each* item in the set, *do* something.

> In addition to the foreach package, Revolution Analytics (recently acquired by Microsoft) has developed high-performance, enterprise-ready R builds. Free versions are available for trial and academic use. For more information, see their website at http://www.revolutionanalytics.com/.

If you're thinking that R already provides a set of apply functions to loop over the sets of items (for example, apply(), lapply(), sapply(), and so on), you are correct. However, the foreach loop has an additional benefit: iterations of the loop can be completed in parallel using a very simple syntax. Let's see how this works.

Recall the command we've been using to generate a million random numbers:

```
> system.time(11 <- rnorm(1000000))
   user  system elapsed
  0.096   0.000   0.096
```

After the foreach package has been installed, it can be expressed by a loop that generates four sets of 250,000 random numbers in parallel. The .combine parameter is an optional setting that tells foreach which function it should use to combine the final set of results from each loop iteration. In this case, since each iteration generates a set of random numbers, we simply use the c() concatenate function to create a single, combined vector:

```
> library(foreach)
> system.time(14 <- foreach(i = 1:4, .combine = 'c')
              %do% rnorm(250000))
   user  system elapsed
  0.106   0.003   0.109
```

If you noticed that this function didn't result in a speed improvement, good catch! The reason is that by default, the foreach package runs each loop iteration in serial. The doParallel sister package provides a parallel backend for foreach that utilizes the parallel package included with R, which was described earlier in this chapter. After installing the doParallel package, simply register the number of cores and swap the %do% command with %dopar%, as follows:

```
> library(doParallel)
> registerDoParallel(cores = 4)
> system.time(l4p <- foreach(i = 1:4, .combine = 'c')
                          %dopar% rnorm(250000))
   user  system elapsed
  0.062   0.030   0.054
```

As shown in the output, this code results in the expected performance improvement, nearly cutting the execution time in half.

To close the doParallel cluster, simply type:

```
> stopImplicitCluster()
```

Though the cluster will be closed automatically at the conclusion of the R session, it is better form to do so explicitly.

Parallel cloud computing with MapReduce and Hadoop

The **MapReduce** programming model was developed at Google as a way to process their data on a large cluster of networked computers. MapReduce defined parallel programming as a two-step process:

- A **map** step in which a problem is divided into smaller tasks that are distributed across the computers in the cluster
- A **reduce** step in which the results of the small chunks of work are collected and synthesized into a final solution to the original problem

A popular open source alternative to the proprietary MapReduce framework is **Apache Hadoop**. The Hadoop software comprises of the MapReduce concept, plus a distributed filesystem capable of storing large amounts of data across a cluster of computers.

Packt Publishing has published a large number of books on Hadoop. To search current offerings, visit `https://www.packtpub.com/all/?search=hadoop`.

Several R projects that provide an R interface to Hadoop are in development. The RHadoop project by Revolution Analytics provides an R interface to Hadoop. The project provides a package, `rmr`, intended to be an easy way for R developers to write MapReduce programs. Another companion package, `plyrmr`, provides functionality similar to the `dplyr` package to process large datasets. Additional RHadoop packages provide R functions to access Hadoop's distributed data stores.

 For more information on the RHadoop project, see `https://github.com/RevolutionAnalytics/RHadoop/wiki`.

Another similar project is RHIPE by Saptarshi Guha, which attempts to bring Hadoop's divide and recombine philosophy into R by managing the communication between R and Hadoop.

 The `RHIPE` package is not yet available at CRAN, but it can be built from the source available on the Web at `http://www.datadr.org`.

GPU computing

An alternative to parallel processing uses a computer's **Graphics Processing Unit (GPU)** to increase the speed of mathematical calculations. A GPU is a specialized processor that is optimized to rapidly display images on a computer screen. Because a computer often needs to display complex 3D graphics (particularly for video games), many GPUs use hardware designed for parallel processing and extremely efficient matrix and vector calculations. A side benefit is that they can be used to efficiently solve certain types of mathematical problems. Where a computer processor may have 16 cores, a GPU may have thousands.

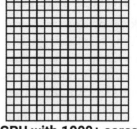

CPU with 16 cores   **GPU with 1000+ cores**

The downside of GPU computing is that it requires specific hardware that is not included in many computers. In most cases, a GPU from the manufacturer Nvidia is required, as they provide a proprietary framework called **Complete Unified Device Architecture (CUDA)** that makes the GPU programmable using common languages such as C++.

> For more information on Nvidia's role in GPU computing, go to http://www.nvidia.com/object/what-is-gpu-computing.html.

The gputools package by Josh Buckner, Mark Seligman, and Justin Wilson implements several R functions, such as matrix operations, clustering, and regression modeling using the Nvidia CUDA toolkit. The package requires a CUDA 1.3 or higher GPU and the installation of the Nvidia CUDA toolkit.

Deploying optimized learning algorithms

Some of the machine learning algorithms covered in this book are able to work on extremely large datasets with relatively minor modifications. For instance, it would be fairly straightforward to implement Naive Bayes or the Apriori algorithm using one of the data structures for big datasets described in the previous sections. Some types of learners, such as ensembles, lend themselves well to parallelization, because the work of each model can be distributed across processors or computers in a cluster. On the other hand, some require larger changes to the data or algorithm, or need to be rethought altogether, before they can be used with massive datasets.

The following sections examine packages that provide optimized versions of the learning algorithms we've worked with so far.

Building bigger regression models with biglm

The `biglm` package by Thomas Lumley provides functions to train regression models on datasets that may be too large to fit into memory. It works by using an iterative process in which the model is updated little by little using small chunks of data. In spite of it being a different approach, the results will be nearly identical to what would be obtained by running the conventional `lm()` function on the entire dataset.

For convenience while working with the largest datasets, the `biglm()` function allows the use of a SQL database in place of a data frame. The model can also be trained with chunks obtained from data objects created by the `ff` package described previously.

Growing bigger and faster random forests with bigrf

The `bigrf` package by Aloysius Lim implements the training of random forests for classification and regression on datasets that are too large to fit into memory. It uses the `bigmemory` objects as described earlier in this chapter. For speedier forest growth, the package can be used with the `foreach` and `doParallel` packages described previously to grow trees in parallel.

 For more information, including examples and Windows installation instructions, see the package's wiki, which is hosted on GitHub at `https://github.com/aloysius-lim/bigrf`.

Training and evaluating models in parallel with caret

The `caret` package by Max Kuhn (covered extensively in *Chapter 10, Evaluating Model Performance* and *Chapter 11, Improving Model Performance*) will transparently utilize a parallel backend if one has been registered with R using the `foreach` package described previously.

Let's take a look at a simple example in which we attempt to train a random forest model on the credit dataset. Without parallelization, the model takes about 109 seconds to be trained:

```
> library(caret)
> credit <- read.csv("credit.csv")
> system.time(train(default ~ ., data = credit, method = "rf"))
   user   system  elapsed
107.862   0.990  108.873
```

On the other hand, if we use the `doParallel` package to register the four cores to be used in parallel, the model takes under 32 seconds to build—less than a third of the time—and we didn't need to change even a single line of the `caret` code:

```
> library(doParallel)
> registerDoParallel(cores = 4)
> system.time(train(default ~ ., data = credit, method = "rf"))
   user   system  elapsed
114.578   2.037   31.362
```

Many of the tasks involved in training and evaluating models, such as creating random samples and repeatedly testing predictions for 10-fold cross-validation are embarrassingly parallel and ripe for performance improvements. With this in mind, it is wise to always register multiple cores before beginning a `caret` project.

Configuration instructions and a case study of the performance improvements needed to enable parallel processing in `caret` are available on the project's website at http://topepo.github.io/caret/parallel.html.

Summary

It is certainly an exciting time to be studying machine learning. Ongoing work on the relatively uncharted frontiers of parallel and distributed computing offers great potential for tapping the knowledge found in the deluge of big data. The burgeoning data science community is facilitated by the free and open source R programming language, which provides a very low barrier for entry — you simply need to be willing to learn.

The topics you have learned, both in this chapter and in the previous chapters, provide the foundation to understand more advanced machine learning methods. It is now your responsibility to keep learning and adding tools to your arsenal. Along the way, be sure to keep in mind the *No Free Lunch* theorem — no learning algorithm can rule them all, and they all have varying strengths and weaknesses. For this reason, there will always be a human element to machine learning, adding subject-specific knowledge and the ability to match the appropriate algorithm to the task at hand.

In the coming years, it will be interesting to see how the human side changes as the line between machine learning and human learning is blurred. Services such as Amazon's Mechanical Turk provide crowd-sourced intelligence, offering a cluster of human minds ready to perform simple tasks at a moment's notice. Perhaps one day, just as we have used computers to perform tasks that human beings cannot do easily, computers will employ human beings to do the reverse. What interesting food for thought!

Index

control object 355
convex hull 242
corpus 107
correlation 179, 180
cross-validation 340-343
CSV (Comma-Separated Values) file
  about 41
  data, importing from 41
curl utility 382
cut points 102

D

data
  importing, from CSV files 41
  managing, with R 39
Database Management
    Systems (DBMSs) 379
databases
  about 378
  data, querying in SQL databases 379, 380
data dictionary 43
data exploration 42
data frame 35, 36
data mining 3
data munging 378
data preparation, breast cancer example
  test datasets, creating 80, 81
  training, creating 80, 81
Data Source Name (DSN) 379
data storage 10
data structures, R
  about 28
  array 38, 39
  data frame 35-37
  exploring 43, 44
  factor 30, 31
  lists 32-34
  loading 39, 40
  matrix 37
  removing 39, 40
  saving 39, 40
  vector 28, 29
data.table package
  URL 401
  using 401, 402
data wrangling 378

decision nodes 126
decision tree
  about 127, 136
  accuracy, boosting 145-147
  classification rules, obtaining from 157
  divide and conquer 127-131
  potential uses 127
  pruning 135, 136
  used, for identifying risky bank loans 136
decision tree forests 369, 370
deep learning 227
Deep Neural Network (DNN) 227
delimiter 41
dendrites 221
dependent events 94
dependent variable 172
descriptive model 20
disk-based data frames
  creating, with ff package 402, 403
divide and conquer 127-131
domain-specific data
  bioinformatics data, analyzing 393
  network data, analyzing 393-397
  network data, visualizing 393-397
  working with 392
doParallel package
  using 410, 411
dplyr package
  URL 399
  used, for generalizing tabular data
    structures 399-401
dummy coding 73, 195
dummy variable 62, 195

E

early stopping 135
edgelist 395
elements 28
embarrassingly parallel problems 405
ensembles
  about 359, 362
  advantages 361, 362
  bagging 362-366
  boosting 366-368
  random forests 369, 370
entropy 133

optimized learning algorithms,
    deploying 413
parallel computing 404, 405
R-squared value 197
rudimentary ANNs 220
rvest package 384

S

scatterplot matrix (SPLOM) 190-192
Scoville scale 72
segmentation analysis 21
semi-supervised learning 288
separate and conquer 150-152
sigmoid kernel 248
simple linear regression 173-177
simple tuned model
    creating 352-355
slack variable 244
slope-intercept form 172
SMS Spam Collection
    URL 104
snowball
    URL 111
snow package
    URL 409
    using 406-409
social networking service (SNS) 296
sparse matrix 113, 268
SQL databases
    data, querying in 379, 380
squashing functions 225
stacking 361
standard deviation 54
standard deviation reduction (SDR) 203
statistical hypothesis testing 173
stock models
    tuning, for better performance 348, 349
Structured Query Language (SQL) 379
subtree raising 136
subtree replacement 136
summary statistics 44
supervised learning 19
Support Vector Machine (SVM)
    about 239, 364
    applications 240
    case of linearly separable data 242-244

case of nonlinearly separable data 244, 245
classifications, with hyperplanes 240-242
OCR, performing with 248
support vectors 242
SVMlight
    about 252
    URL 252
synapse 221

T

Tab-Separated Value (TSV) 42
tabular
    about 41
    data structures, generalizing with dplyr
        package 399-401
**teen market segments search, with k-means
    clustering**
    about 296
    data, collecting 297
    data, exploring 297-299
    data, preparing 297-301
    model performance, evaluating 304-307
    model performance, improving 308, 309
    model, training on data 302-304
terminal nodes 126
threshold activation function 223
training 12
trees
    regression, adding to 202-204
tree structure 126
tuning process
    customizing 355-359
two-way cross-tabulation 61

U

UCI Machine Learning Data Repository
    about 205
    URL 137
unimodal 58
unit of analysis 17
unit of observation 17
unit step activation function 223
univariate statistics 59
universal function approximator 229
unsupervised learning 20

Thank you for buying
Machine Learning with R
Second Edition

About Packt Publishing

Packt, pronounced 'packed', published its first book, *Mastering phpMyAdmin for Effective MySQL Management*, in April 2004, and subsequently continued to specialize in publishing highly focused books on specific technologies and solutions.

Our books and publications share the experiences of your fellow IT professionals in adapting and customizing today's systems, applications, and frameworks. Our solution-based books give you the knowledge and power to customize the software and technologies you're using to get the job done. Packt books are more specific and less general than the IT books you have seen in the past. Our unique business model allows us to bring you more focused information, giving you more of what you need to know, and less of what you don't.

Packt is a modern yet unique publishing company that focuses on producing quality, cutting-edge books for communities of developers, administrators, and newbies alike. For more information, please visit our website at www.packtpub.com.

About Packt Open Source

In 2010, Packt launched two new brands, Packt Open Source and Packt Enterprise, in order to continue its focus on specialization. This book is part of the Packt Open Source brand, home to books published on software built around open source licenses, and offering information to anybody from advanced developers to budding web designers. The Open Source brand also runs Packt's Open Source Royalty Scheme, by which Packt gives a royalty to each open source project about whose software a book is sold.

Writing for Packt

We welcome all inquiries from people who are interested in authoring. Book proposals should be sent to author@packtpub.com. If your book idea is still at an early stage and you would like to discuss it first before writing a formal book proposal, then please contact us; one of our commissioning editors will get in touch with you.

We're not just looking for published authors; if you have strong technical skills but no writing experience, our experienced editors can help you develop a writing career, or simply get some additional reward for your expertise.

R for Data Science

ISBN: 978-1-78439-086-0   Paperback: 364 pages

Learn and explore the fundamentals of data science with R

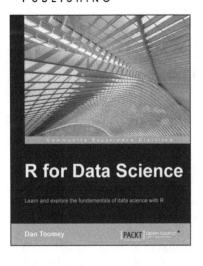

1. Familiarize yourself with R programming packages and learn how to utilize them effectively.

2. Learn how to detect different types of data mining sequences.

3. A step-by-step guide to understanding R scripts and the ramifications of your changes.

Learning Data Mining with R

ISBN: 978-1-78398-210-3   Paperback: 314 pages

Develop key skills and techniques with R to create and customize data mining algorithms

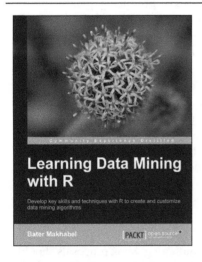

1. Develop a sound strategy for solving predictive modeling problems using the most popular data mining algorithms.

2. Gain understanding of the major methods of predictive modeling.

3. Packed with practical advice and tips to help you get to grips with data mining.

Please check **www.PacktPub.com** for information on our titles

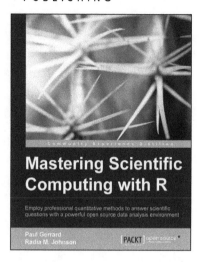

Mastering Scientific Computing with R

ISBN: 978-1-78355-525-3   Paperback: 432 pages

Employ professional quantitative methods to answer scientific questions with a powerful open source data analysis environment

1. Perform publication-quality science using R.

2. Use some of R's most powerful and least known features to solve complex scientific computing problems.

3. Learn how to create visual illustrations of scientific results.

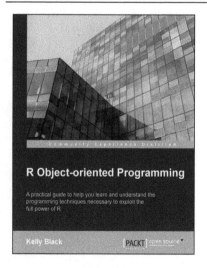

R Object-oriented Programming

ISBN: 978-1-78398-668-2   Paperback: 190 pages

A practical guide to help you learn and understand the programming techniques necessary to exploit the full power of R

1. Learn and understand the programming techniques necessary to solve specific problems and speed up development processes for statistical models and applications.

2. Explore the fundamentals of building objects and how they program individual aspects of larger data designs.

3. Step-by-step guide to understand how OOP can be applied to application and data models within R.

Please check **www.PacktPub.com** for information on our titles

CPSIA information can be obtained
at www.ICGtesting.com
Printed in the USA
FFHW012241190719
53736716-59427FF